SKYLANDERS SWAP FORCE

COLLECTOR'S EDITION GUIDE

TABLE OF CONTENTS

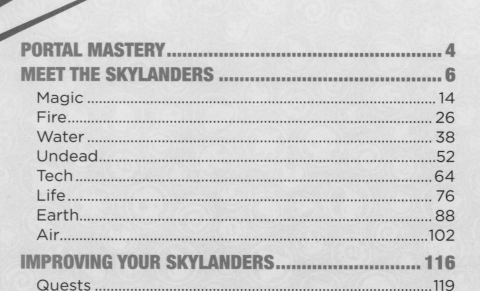

PORTAL MASTERY

Welcome back to Skylands, young Portal Master! In the midst of a vacation, Flynn stumbled upon the latest and most sinister plot Kaos has devised yet.

It is up to you to help him, and his new friend, Tessa, as they try to free her village from a Greeble invasion. What happens afterward, well, that's the adventure ahead, Portal Master. Along the way, you will face many new foes, and meet wonderful new friends, including all-new Skylanders, the SWAP Force. SWAP Force™ characters open up all new challenges, and they're all waiting for you!

WHAT'S NEW IN SKYLANDERS SWAP FORCE™?

If you are a veteran Portal Master, much of what you remember from previous games still holds true, but there are a few new and different things for you to know.

The maximum level is now 20, and while Heroic Challenges have been replaced with a new type of challenge, Arena challenges remain. Two of the biggest changes are SWAP Force Skylanders and Portal Master Rank.

SWAP Force™ Skylanders

The newest type of Skylander is a *SWAP Force* Skylander. These amazing Skylanders can mix and match their torsos and legs, combining abilities and elemental affinities in the process. There are other new Skylanders and new Series 2 and 3 figures as well, but *SWAP Force* Skylanders act just a bit differently.

For the most part, they work just like any other Skylander. They fight, earn XP, and complete quests. It's the top half of each *SWAP Force* character that keeps the money and XP collected, and tracks the completion of quests. The legs have one of eight special abilities that allow them to enter all-new SWAP Zone Challenges.

The top half also has two abilities (activated with the Attack 1 and Attack 3 buttons) while the Attack 2 button ability is tied to the legs. Each half has its own Upgrade Paths.

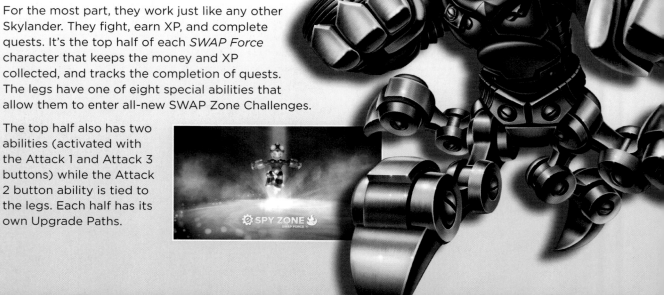

Portal Master Rank

It's no longer just Skylanders who level up! Portal Masters must now earn Stars to increase their rank. For each six Stars you earn, you gain a Portal Master Rank.

There are several ways to earn Stars, and most of them are tied to meeting specific conditions while playing through many of the game's modes.

Earning Stars with Accolades

There are four types of Accolades: Completion, Challenge, Exploration, and Collection. The conditions for completing these Accolades can be found in the Portal Master screen's sub-menus of the same name. New Accolades often become available when you complete ones that are visible, so check back each time you earn an Accolade.

Earn Stars through Special Challenge Modes

There are three types of special challenges: SWAP Zone, Bonus Mission Maps, and Survival Arena. These unique challenges take place on special maps and often include a time limit. Each challenge is worth one, two, or three stars, depending on how well you perform in them.

Earn Stars Three Ways on Story Levels

To begin gaining Portal Master Rank, you need to play through the Story Mode and the two new Adventure Packs. Each Chapter in Story Mode awards up to three Stars based on how well you played through it. After you complete the Story Mode, you also unlock Time Attack Mode and Score Mode. Both Modes award up to three Stars. That means you can earn up to nine Stars from playing the same level in three completely different ways. The best part is that you can earn all these Stars while playing with a friend!

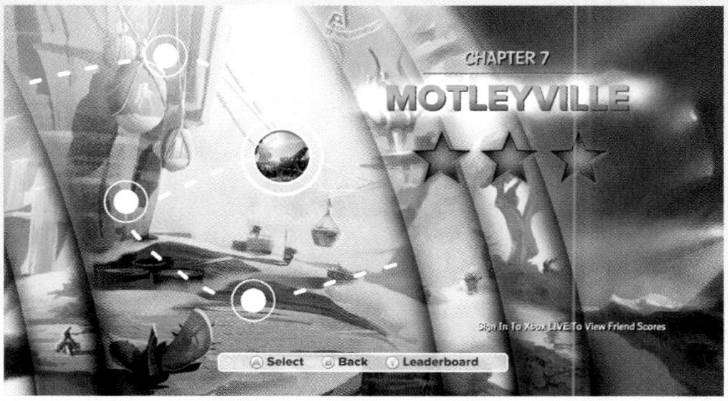

WHAT DO I NEED TO SEE EVERYTHING IN STORY MODE?

In order to access everything found throughout the Story Mode, you need the following:

- One Skylander figure for each of the eight elements.
- One Giant Skylander figure to open special chests found throughout the Story Levels. The Giant Skylander also counts toward covering the eight elements.
- One *Skylanders SWAP Force* figure with each of the eight special abilities: Bounce, Climb, Dig, Rocket, Sneak, Speed, Spin, Teleport. *SWAP Force* Skylanders also count toward covering the eight elements. For example that means Boom Jet counts as both an Air Skylander, and as having the Rocket ability.

You could clear the main story of *Skylanders SWAP Force* with only one Skylander figure, but the more Skylanders you have, the less trouble you run into while playing through the game. Skylanders cannot be revived once they fall in battle, and you must restart the level if you run out of healthy Skylanders. Speaking of Skylanders, turn the page to learn more about them.

MEET THE SKYLANDERS

The following pages cover the newest Skylanders, including their individual stories, stats, powers, and upgrades. Since you can still use the Skylander figures from the earlier games in the series while playing *Skylanders SWAP Force,* they are summarized first. To track your progress, select Collection on the Pause menu and go to the Skylander's tab (look for Spyro's face).

Skylander figures from different games are identified by the color of the plastic on their base. Skylander figures with a green base are from *Skylanders Spyro's Adventure™*. Skylander figures with an orange base are from *Skylanders Giants™*. The newest Skylander figures, those for *Skylanders SWAP Force*, have a blue base.

TYPES OF SKYLANDER FIGURES

SERIES 2: There are two types of Series 2 Skylanders. Orange base Series 2 are new versions of characters for *Skylanders Giants* that first appeared in *Skylanders Spyro's Adventure*. Blue base Series 2 Skylanders are new versions of characters from either of the first two games, created for *Skylanders SWAP Force*. All Series 2 Skylanders have a special "Wow Pow!" power.

SERIES 3: Series 3 Skylanders are new versions of characters that appeared in both of the first two games. All Series 3 Skylanders have a special "Wow Pow!" ability that is different than their Series 2 ability.

LIGHTCORE: LightCore™ Skylanders are special versions of Skylanders whose figures have parts that glow. They cause a damaging shockwave when they are placed on the *Portal of Power™*.

SKYLANDER FIGURES FROM *SKYLANDERS SPYRO'S ADVENTURE*

When these green based Skylanders choose an Upgrade Path, the only way to select the other Upgrade Path is to reset the character in the Manage submenu on the Skylander Stats screen.

Standard Figures

Legendary Figures

Alt Deco

OTHER FIGURES FROM *SKYLANDERS SPYRO'S ADVENTURE*

Adventure Pack Figures

There were four Adventure Packs for *Skylanders Spyro's Adventure*. While playing *Skylanders SWAP Force,* use the Adventure Packs during your regular play to execute a special attack that damages every enemy on the screen.

Adventure Packs also include two Magic Items that aid your Skylander with a special attack or a beneficial effect. The Magic Items have a timer, but it resets whenever you start a new level.

Adventure Pack Figure	Area of Effect Attack
Dragon's Peak	Fireballs
Empire of Ice	Ice Shards
Darklight Crypt	Shadowy Orbs
Pirate Ship	Cannonballs

Anvil Rain

When you put this item on the Portal, anvils fall from the sky, randomly hitting enemies in the area. If an anvil hits your Skylander, it only knocks them back. It does not damage them.

Healing Elixir

This awesome item quickly heals your Skylanders while they wander around. Your Skylanders regain 30 health every second, but Healing Elixir has a short duration.

Ghost Pirate Swords

This Adventure Item spawns in two swords that float around the screen, attacking the Skylander's foes.

Hidden Treasure

When you use Hidden Treasure on a Story Level, a bonus treasure chest is generated. Use the radar at the bottom of the screen to help locate the chest. When playing on the Wii console the Hidden Treasure instead increases the gold you find for a short time.

The following table provides the areas in which the chest will spawn when the Hidden Treasure item is used on the level listed in the first column.

Story Level	Chest 1 Location	Chest 2 Location	Chest 3 Location
Mount Cloudbeak	The Overgrowth	Old Treetop Terrace	Long Worn Hollow
Cascade Glade	Luau Lagoon	Gobblepod Sanctuary	Overlook Heights
Mudwater Hollow	Billy's Bend	Big Gill Water Mill	Muddy Marsh River
Rampant Ruins	Orangutan Tower	Simian Throne Room	Western Watch
Iron Jaw Gulch	The Canteen	Sun Smoked Strand	10,000 Gallon Hat
Motleyville	Arena Overlook	Soggy Fields	Big Bang Bouncers
Twisty Tunnels	Perilous Plateau	Underground Lake	Serene Walkway
Boney Islands	Frozen Fossil Lane	Amber Alley	Glacial Gallery
Winter Keep	The Blizzard Bridges	The Frozen Curtain	Hibernal Harbor
Frostfest Mountains	Typhoon Trail	The Glacier Hills	Perilous Precipice
Fantasm Forest	Troll Toll Bridge	Fantasm Village	Birchberg
Kaos' Fortress	Sheep Tower	Glob Lobber Gangway	Chompy Churners

Sky-Iron Shield

This Adventure Item causes two rotating shields to protect your Skylander for its duration. The Sky-Iron Shield doesn't make your Skylander invulnerable, but it does make them tougher.

Time Twist Hourglass

The Time Twist Hourglass slows down time, putting the game into slow motion for the duration of the spell. The catch is, your Skylander doesn't slow down!

Sparx the Dragonfly

Sparx buzzes around, blasting enemies with his insect breath. He only stays around for about a minute, but can really help in tough fights.

Volcanic Vault

Using Volcanic Vault in *Skylanders SWAP Force* causes fire to rain down from the sky, damaging enemies for a short time.

Winged Boots

With this Adventure Item, your Skylander can run much faster than normal. This item is tremendously helpful during Time Attack.

SKYLANDER FIGURES FROM *SKYLANDERS GIANTS*

When these orange based characters choose an Upgrade Path, the only way to select the other Upgrade Path is to reset the character in the Ownership menu. Series 2 figures are the exception. They can switch between Upgrade Paths while in a Power Pod.

Giant Figures

New Figures

Series 2 Figures

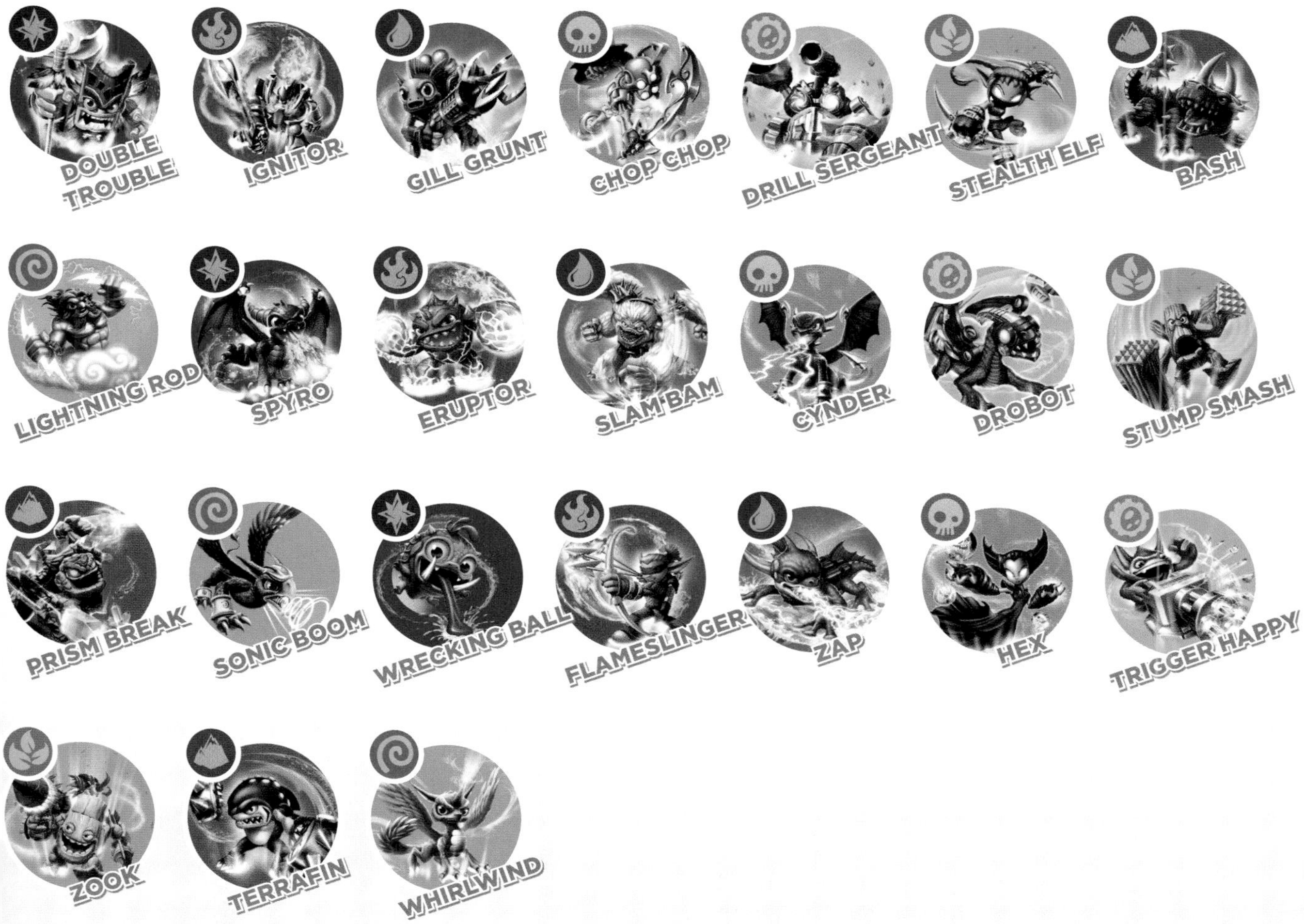

Legendary Figures

Series 2 Legendary Figures

LightCore Figures

Alt Deco

Other Figures From Skylanders Giants

Two special figures were made for *Skylanders Giants*. They both can help clear out enemies and make for smoother travels.

Dragonfire Cannon

The Dragonfire Cannon blasts enemies every few seconds. It also follows Skylanders as they move through levels.

Scorpion Striker

The Scorpion Striker Catapult lobs spiked balls at enemies. If the spiked ball doesn't hit an enemy in the air, it remains on the ground and will explode if an enemy gets close.

Sidekicks

Sidekicks are smaller versions of Skylander figures that follow your full-sized Skylander when they are placed on the *Portal of Power*. They were made available during special promotions after the release of both *Skylanders Spyro's Adventure* and *Skylanders Giants*. There are four sidekicks from both games. These figures are tracked under Other Toys in the Collections/ Skylanders screen.

SKYLANDER FIGURES FOR *SKYLANDERS SWAP FORCE*

When some characters choose an Upgrade Path, the only way to select the other Upgrade Path is to reset the character in the Ownership menu. Series 2 and Series 3 figures can switch between Upgrade Paths while in a Power Pod.

SWAP Force Figures

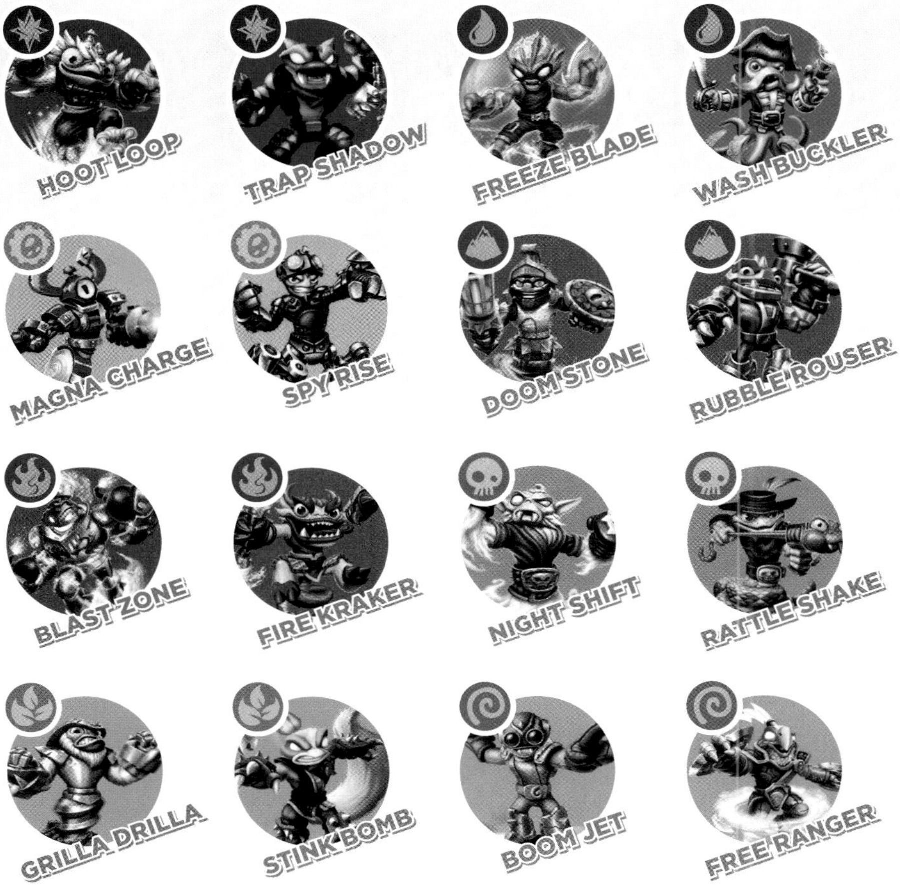

New Figures

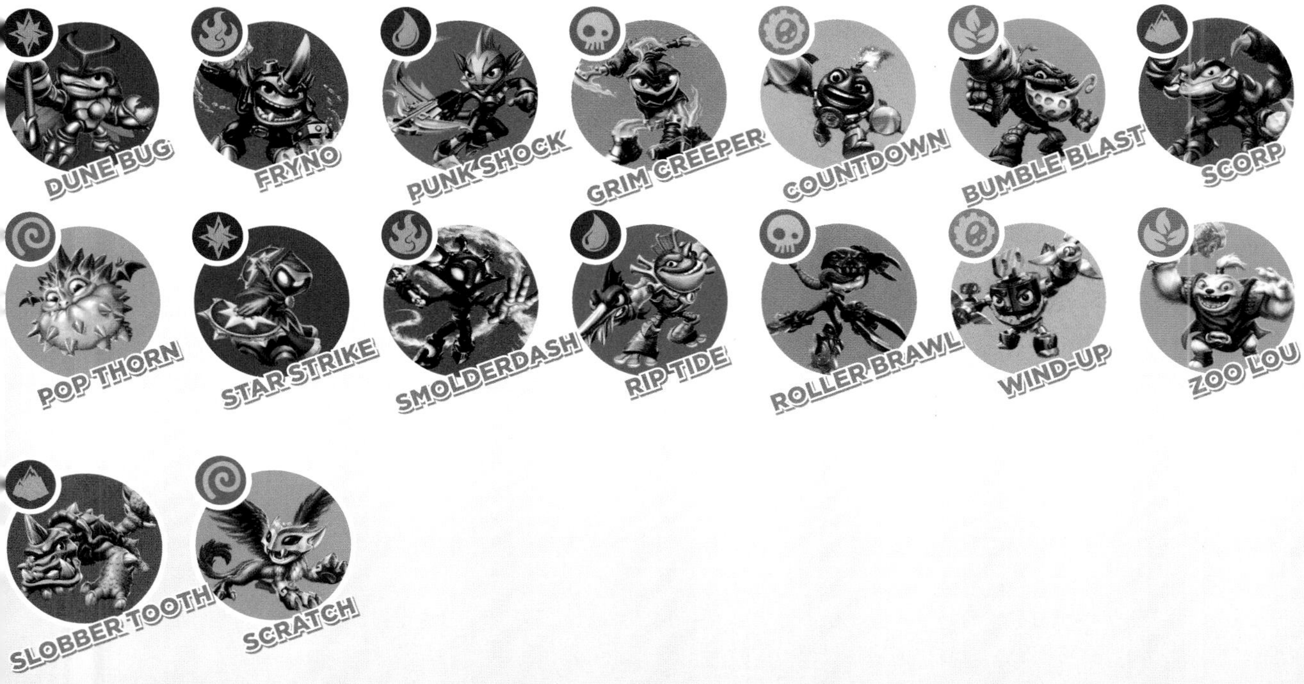

Series 2 Figures

Series 3 Figures

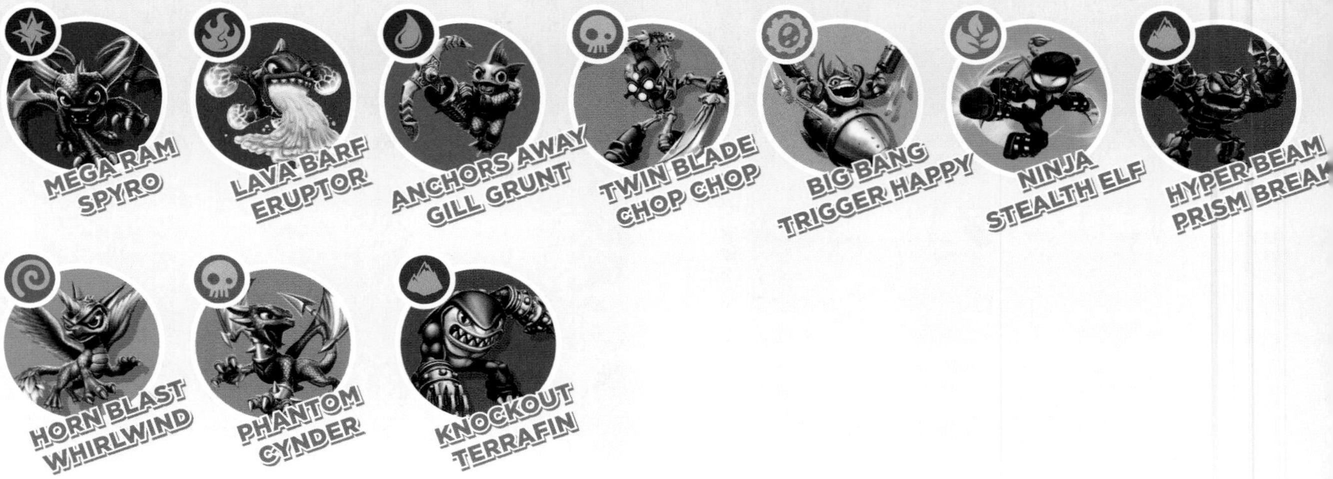

Legendary Figures

LightCore Figures

Alt Deco Figures

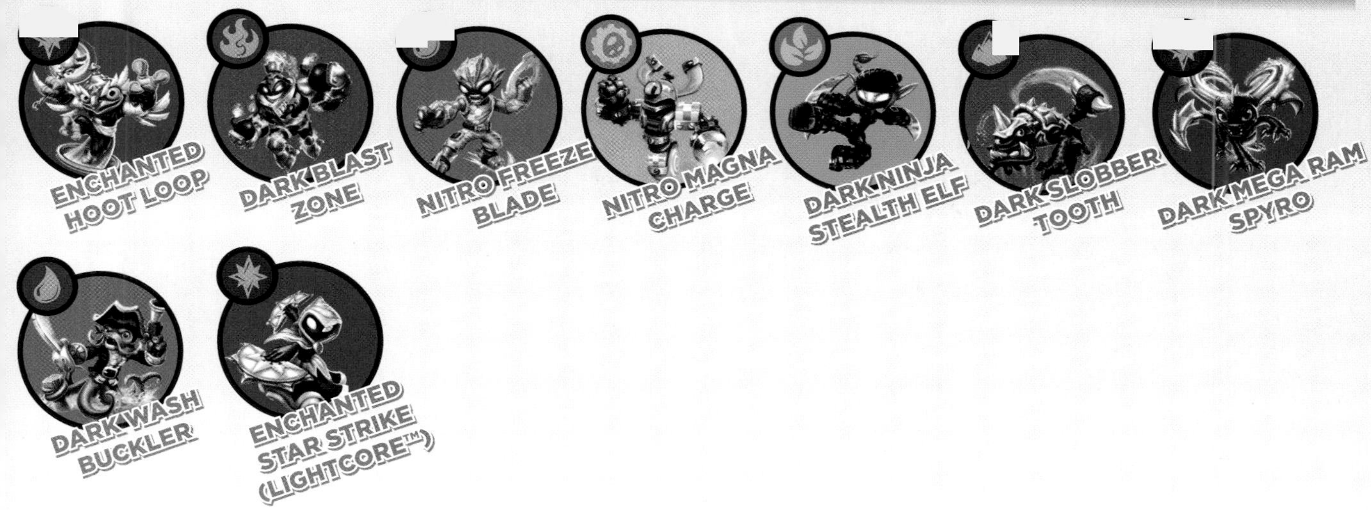

Other Figures From *Skylanders SWAP Force*

Tower of Time

When you place the Tower of Time figure on the *Portal of Power*, it drops gears from the sky, inflicting damage to any enemies on the screen. It also unlocks the Tower of Time Story Level and a new Ring Out Arena, the Tic Toc Terrace. The entrance for the Tower of Time is near the Yard in Woodburrow.

Sheep Wreck Islands

The Sheep Wreck Islands figure opens the Story Level of the same name as well as four Arenas: Vortex Banquet, Cyclops Makeover, Sheep Mage Rage, and Chunky Chompies. The entrance for Sheep Wreck Islands is at one end of The Airdocks.

Arkeyan Crossbow

The Arkeyan Crossbow adds a new Battle Arena called Treacherous Beach and four Survival Arenas: Sand Castle, Beach Breach, Troll Beach Attack, and Chompy Tsunami. It also generates an in-game crossbow with a lob attack. The bolt damages enemies it hits and also creates a watery wave that hits other nearby enemies.

Battle Hammer

A Battle Hammer appears over your Skylander's head. Whenever you press Attack 1, the hammer hits the ground in front of your Skylander (Skylanders still execute their normal attack, though). Nearby enemies take damage and are knocked back.

Fiery Forge

The Fiery Forge adds a new Battle and Ring-Out Arena of the same name. When placed on the *Portal of Power*, a cauldron floats over your Skylander's head. When enemies are near, the cauldron tips over and covers the ground with molten metal, producing an effect similar to Eruptor's attack, Eruption.

Groove Machine

The Groove Machine follows Skylanders and plays music. It also makes enemies dance, preventing them from attacking.

Platinum Sheep

The Platinum Sheep disguises your Skylander as a sheep and restores health over time. Enemies ignore the sheep and allow it to recover health in peace. While you can still move around, you can't perform any other actions (like attack) until the disguise is removed.

Sky Diamond

When the Sky Diamond is active, every defeated enemy drops a diamond worth 20 gold. It's a great way to earn money quickly to help pay for items and Skylander upgrades.

UFO Hat

Placing this Magic Item on the *Portal of Power* unlocks the UFO Hat.

HOOT LOOP

"Let's Ruffle Some Feathers!"

MAXIMUM HEALTH	250
SPEED	43
ARMOR	12
CRITICAL HIT	6
ELEMENTAL POWER	25

Hoot Loop was raised by a guild of magicians in Skylands' most famous traveling circus. At a young age, he perfected illusions and spells that only the very best of their guild could perform, and even mastered the art of teleportation! Soon enough, he became the star of the show, known far and wide as the Amazing Hoot Loop. However, one day an army of Greebles disguised as clowns invaded, determined to destroy the popular circus. It was then that Hoot Loop gave a performance that few would ever forget. Using his incredible powers, he fought off the invaders and saved the circus—to the raucous applause of the many spectators—including Master Eon, who presented Hoot Loop with an opportunity to learn some real magic as a member of the Skylanders.

SWAP FORCE

DéjàBOOM! bounces off its initial target and hits additional targets for less damage. The Dreamweaver Path turns it into a beam that remains active so long as Attack 1 is pressed. The Hypno-Owl Path is two direct upgrades to Hypnotism, an attack that slows enemies (and Hoot) while Attack 3 is pressed.

Loop the Loop begins as a great way to escape enemies but its upgrades, Infinite Loop in particular, turn it into a great offensive weapon. The Telekinesis Path boosts Loop the Loop's damage output. The Escape Artist Path adds a little damage and a wrinkle that leaves enemies guessing where Hoot Loop will appear after teleporting.

Body Soul Gem Ability

WAND OF DREAMS

3500 Gold

PREREQUISITE

Find Hoot Loop's Soul Gem in Woodburrow

Press **Attack 1** to shoot a DéjàBOOM! and two smaller DéjàBOOM! projectiles at once.

Legs Soul Gem Ability

INFINITE LOOP

3500 Gold

PREREQUISITE

Find Hoot Loop's Soul Gem in Woodburrow

Hold **Attack 2** to aim the portal loop, release it under Loop's body to cause a massive attack that damages enemies in a large area.

Special Quest

Wand You Like To Play A Game?

DEFEAT 50 ENEMIES WITH THE FINAL EXPLOSION OF THE FLASHBACK ATTACK.

Completing this quest calls for a touch of patience. After purchasing the Flashback upgrade, allow its explosion to finish off enemies instead of hitting them with other attacks.

HOOT LOOP

BODY

Basic Attacks

DÉJÀBOOM!

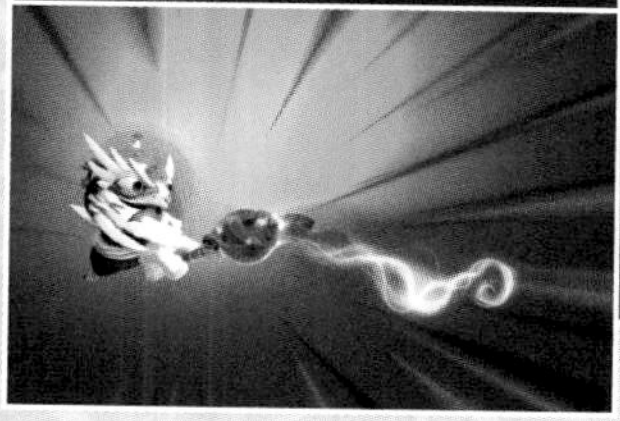

Press **Attack 1** to shoot a magic projectile that hits enemies three times before it disappears.

Upgrades

HYPNOTISM

300 Gold

PREREQUISITE None

Hold **Attack 3** to hypnotize enemies, slowing their movement and attacks.

TRICKED YA!

800 Gold

PREREQUISITE None

Armor increased. Shiny new armor reduces damage.

FLASHBACK

1000 Gold

PREREQUISITE None

Press **Attack 1** to shoot a DéjàBOOM projectile. DéjàBOOM bounces three times and on a third bounce it explodes.

Dream-Weaver Path

DREAM BEAM

1500 Gold

PREREQUISITE
Dream-Weaver Path

Hold **Attack 1** to channel a magical beam of dreams that damages enemies.

BAD DREAMS BEAM

2000 Gold

PREREQUISITE
Purchase Dream Beam ability

Dream Beam does increased damage.

Hypno-Owl Path

MASS HYPNOSIS

1500 Gold

PREREQUISITE
Hypno-Owl Path

Hypnotism becomes more effective, slowing enemies in a larger area.

DEEP ASLEEP

2000 Gold

PREREQUISITE
Purchase Mass Hypnosis ability

Hold **Attack 3** to use a more powerful Mass Hypnosis, dealing increased damage

LEGS

Basic Attacks

LOOP THE LOOP

Press **Attack 2** to teleport forward a short distance and damage nearby enemies.

Upgrades

PORTABLE HOLE

300 Gold

PREREQUISITE None

Hold **Attack 2** to aim the portal loop. Release to teleport to that area and damage all nearby enemies.

TEMPORAL WHACK

800 Gold

PREREQUISITE None

Teleport does increased damage.

TIME SINK

1000 Gold

PREREQUISITE None

Enemies and objects are pulled towards the area where Portable Hole is aimed.

Telekinesis Path

NOW YOU SEE ME

1500 Gold

PREREQUISITE
Telekinesis Path

Hold **Attack 2** to charge Portable Hole, release to do increased damage. Damage is increased the longer it is charged.

COMPLETE CONCENTRATION

2000 Gold

PREREQUISITE
Purchase Now You See Me ability

Now You See Me does increased damage. A very impressive entrance!

Escape Artist Path

NOW YOU DON'T

1500 Gold

PREREQUISITE
Escape Artist Path

Press **Jump** after teleporting to appear back at the previous position.

TELEPORT TURBULENCE

2000 Gold

PREREQUISITE
Purchase Now You Don't ability

All teleport attacks do increased damage.

TRAP SHADOW

"Hide and Sleek!"

MAXIMUM HEALTH	270
SPEED	43
ARMOR	12
CRITICAL HIT	8
ELEMENTAL POWER	25

Once part of an elite tribe of hunters in a remote area of Skylands, Trap Shadow used his cat-like cunning, ingenious traps, and mystical stealth abilities to catch nearly everything that could be caught. As a result, his fame around Skylands grew so much that it attracted the attention of an evil cadre of wizards. They plotted to capture Trap Shadow and use his abilities to ensnare the most uncatchable thing of all—Master Eon himself. But Trap Shadow could sense them coming from miles away. Outsmarted and outmaneuvered, each of the wizards was easily captured by Trap Shadow's bewildering array of traps and snares until they were all locked away for good. Having been saved by the cunning hunter, Master Eon quickly made Trap Shadow a Skylander.

Body Soul Gem Ability

SHADOW STRIKER

3500 Gold

PREREQUISITE
Find Trap Shadow's Soul Gem in Frostfest Mountains

Press **Attack 1** rapidly to do quick claw attacks. Whilte doing claw attacks, hold **Attack 1** to unleash a powerful shadowy dash.

Legs Soul Gem Ability

LIVING SHADOW

3500 Gold

PREREQUISITE
Find Trap Shadow's Soul Gem in Frostfest Mountains

Hold **Attack 2** to prowl and become invisible. Who needs shadows to hide in? Just become one!

SWAP FORCE

Clawing Shadow gains a nice combo addition if you choose the Feral Instincts Path. You must hold Attack 1 after the first hit to initiate the combo. Any swing after that will start up Trap Shadow's Soul Gem ability, Shadow Striker. Catch! is a great upgrade to Snap Trap, and the Trap Trickster Path turns the traps into bombs.

Shadow Kick upgrades into a stealth ability and the Prowler Path plays off that, leaving damaging footprints in Shadow's path. The Shadow Combat Path increases Shadow's direct damage potential. Shadow Kicks hit harder and from a greater distance.

Special Quest

Oh Snap!

DEFEAT 50 ENEMIES WITH YOUR TRAPS.

You can't work on this quest until you purchase Snap Trap, so as soon as it is available, start leavin traps everywhere there are enemies to complete this quest. Catch! makes completing it easier, as does choosing the Trap Trickster Path.

BODY

Basic Attacks

CLAWING SHADOW

Press **Attack 1** to swipe shadowy claws at nearby enemies.

Upgrades

SNAP TRAP

300 Gold

PREREQUISITE None

Press **Attack 3** to throw a magically animated trap which will snap at enemies and damage them.

SHARP MAGIC

800 Gold

PREREQUISITE None

Press **Attack 1** rapidly to use powerful claw attacks that deal increased damage.

CATCH!

1000 Gold

PREREQUISITE Purchase Snap Trap

Hold **Attack 3** to aim Snap Trap, release to throw it.

Feral Instincts Path

ME-OUCH!

1500 Gold

PREREQUISITE
Feral Instincts Path

Hold **Attack 1** to combo into a swipe that knocks enemies into the air.

NOCTURNAL PREDATOR

2000 Gold

PREREQUISITE
Purchase Me-Ouch! ability

Me-Ouch! does increased damage. This kitty has claws... big, pointy claws!

Trap Trickster Path

GLOOM AND BOOM

1500 Gold

PREREQUISITE
Trap Trickster Path

Traps will explode after a short time, damaging all enemies within a large area.

MAKE IT SNAPPY

2000 Gold

PREREQUISITE
Purchase Gloom and Boom ability

All traps are now more powerful and do increased damage.

LEGS

Basic Attacks

SHADOW KICK

Press **Attack 2** to kick a wave of shadows at enemies.

Upgrades

PROWL

300 Gold

PREREQUISITE None

Hold **Attack 2** to prowl for a short time, causing any enemy touched to be damaged.

NINE LIVES

800 Gold

PREREQUISITE None

Health is increased. This cat is never done for.

OUT OF THE SHADOWS

1000 Gold

PREREQUISITE None

Hold **Attack 2** to prowl for a short time, coming out of prowl causes a large explosion that damages nearby enemies.

Shadow Combat Path

DARK MAGIC

1500 Gold

PREREQUISITE
Shadow Combat Path

Press **Attack 2** to kick a wave of shadow that can damage enemies farther away.

BLACK CAT

2000 Gold

PREREQUISITE
Purchase Dark Magic ability

All shadow wave attacks do even more damage.

Prowler Path

SHADE STEPS

1500 Gold

PREREQUISITE
Prowler Path

Hold **Attack 2** to prowl, moving while prowling leaves behind magical pawprints that damage enemies that touch them.

BUMPS IN THE NIGHT

2000 Gold

PREREQUISITE
Purchase Shade Steps ability

Shade Steps do increased damage. Huh? Whose footprints are these?

DUNE BUG

"Can't Beat the Beetle!"

MAXIMUM HEALTH	260
SPEED	35
ARMOR	24
CRITICAL HIT	4
ELEMENTAL POWER	25

Hailing from a race of beetles changed by the powerful secrets hidden in a buried Arkeyan city, Dune Bug was next in line to become the defender of those secrets. As a small pupa, Dune Bug, along with his father, would travel to the ruins where he learned to read the ancient writings using his father's magic staff. On the day Dune Bug was to be given his own magic staff, the city fell under attack by the evil Sand Mages of Doom, who were after the secret Arkeyan tomes. Knowing what he had to do, Dune Bug used his magic to defeat the Mages and bury the city deeper into the ground until it was forever out of their reach. Dune Bug earned his magic staff that day—and a place alongside the Skylanders.

Bursting Magic provides a nice boost to Mystic Missiles, allowing you to to increase the damage output of each missile, but at the cost of reduced movement speed and the attack pausing after a few seconds. Dune Ball is a great defensive weapon. Use it to roll away any enemies that get in too close.

The Scarab Sage Path is the more aggressive way to go. Each upgrade increases Dune Bug's damage output. The Dune Mage Path has defensive abilities. Dune Bomb keeps the space in front of Dune Bug clear while Sparking Wings takes care of the back.

Special Quest

That's How I Roll

ROLL YOUR DUNE BALL A TOTAL OF 5,000 FEET.

This quest only counts the distance Dune Bug rolls his Dune Ball, so you must hold Attack 2 while walking around. There's no other trick to this quest. You could even complete it while walking around Woodburrow.

Basic Attacks

MYSTIC MISSILES

Press **Attack 1** to shoot magical beams of energy from a staff.

DUNE BALL

Hold **Attack 2** to create a large magical ball that can be rolled around and scoop up enemies.

Soul Gem Ability

BUGGY BUDDY

4000 Gold

PREREQUISITE
Find Dune Bug's Soul Gem in Boney Islands!

Press **Attack 2** twice to summon Buggy, a little bug who rides a dune ball and rolls up nearby enemies.

Upgrades

DUNE PARADE

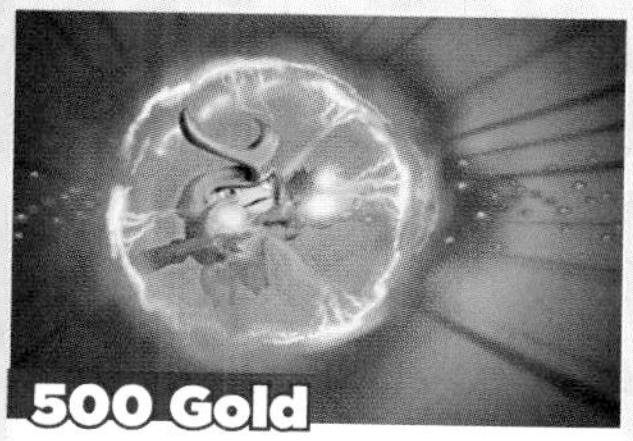

500 Gold

PREREQUISITE None

Hold **Attack 2** to create a Dune Ball. Move the Dune Ball to make it grow, increasing damage, size, and how many enemies can be trapped.

DEBILITATING DUNES

700 Gold

PREREQUISITE None

Hold **Attack 2** to create a Dune Ball. Move the Dune Ball over enemies to trap them. Press **Attack 1** to shoot enemies in the Dune Ball and do increased damage to them.

BURSTING MAGIC

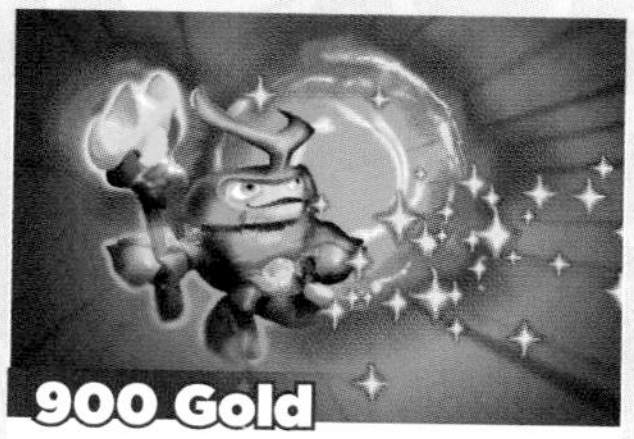

900 Gold

PREREQUISITE None

Hold **Attack 1** to fire rapid streams of powerful magic from a new staff.

BUZZING BEETLE

1200 Gold

PREREQUISITE None

Press **Attack 3** to hover in the air. Speed is increased while hovering!

Scarab Sage Path

STUNNING SPREAD

1700 Gold

PREREQUISITE
Scarab Sage Path

Hold **Attack 1** for a short time to charge the staff, release to shoot three powerful exploding orbs of magic at enemies.

SCARAB POWER

2200 Gold

PREREQUISITE
Scarab Sage Path

Gain a new golden staff that shoots magic projectiles that do increased damage.

MAGIC SCARAB RIDE

3000 Gold

PREREQUISITE
Scarab Sage Path

Jump while hovering to create a large shockwave that damages nearby enemies.

Dune Mage Path

DUNE BOMB

1700 Gold

PREREQUISITE
Dune Mage Path

Hold **Attack 1** for a short time to charge the staff, release to shoot a dune grenade that traps enemies and explodes.

HARDENED SHELL

2200 Gold

PREREQUISITE
Dune Mage Path

Armor is increased. A new hardened shell reduces damage taken.

SPARKING WINGS

3000 Gold

PREREQUISITE
Dune Mage Path

Press **Attack 3** to hover, causing sparks of magic to shoot out from behind.

SUPER GULP POP FIZZ

"Motion of the Potion!"

MAXIMUM HEALTH	270
SPEED	43
ARMOR	18
CRITICAL HIT	6
ELEMENTAL POWER	25

SERIES 2

Nobody is quite sure who Pop Fizz was before he became an alchemist, least of all Pop Fizz himself. After many years of experimenting with magical potions, his appearance has changed quite significantly. In fact, no one even knows his original color. But it's widely known that he is a little crazy, his experiments are reckless, and the accidents they cause are too numerous to measure. Understandably, he has had a difficult time finding lab partners, or anyone that even wants to be near him. In hopes of making himself more appealing to others, he attempted to create the most effective charm potion ever—but that just turned him into a big, wild berserker. Or maybe that's just how he saw the potion working in the first place...

When fully upgraded, Pop Fizz's potions make him a powerful ranged attacker. The yellow potion deals ranged damage. The green potion creates a pool that deals damage to any enemy that touches it. The purple potion summons minions, and gets a big boost with Pop Fizz's new Wow Pow! ability.

The Mad Scientist Path improves potions by combining their effects. The Best of the Beast Path allows Pop Fizz to stay in Beast Form longer and adds potion-based attacks. Yellow is a flame attack, green is a flailing attack that hits multiple times, and purple is a lunging ground pound.

Special Quest

Rampage

DEAL 200 DAMAGE IN A SINGLE RUN IN BEAST FORM.

The only trick to this quest is having enough enemies in the area so you can inflict 200 points of damage before they're all gone. Activate the Best of the Beast Path if your damage output is coming up short.

Basic Attacks

POTION LOB

Press **Attack 1** to launch Pop Fizz's currently equipped potion.

BEAST FORM

Press **Attack 2** to drink a potion and temporarily change into a beasty form.

Soul Gem Ability

SHAKE IT!

4000 Gold

PREREQUISITE
Purchase New Concotions ability

Repeatedly press **Attack 3** to shake the potion bottle until it explodes.

Upgrades

NEW CONCOTION

500 Gold

PREREQUISITE None

Press **Attack 3** to switch to a new potion that can walk on two legs and fight by your side when thrown.

PUDDLE OF PAIN

700 Gold

PREREQUISITE
Purchase New Concotion abitlity

Press **Attack 3** again to switch to a new potion that leaves a damaging puddle of acid when thrown.

RAGING BEAST

900 Gold

PREREQUISITE None

All attacks in Beast Form do additional damage.

DEXTROUS DELIVERY

1200 Gold

PREREQUISITE None

Throw potions and grab new ones much faster.

Mad Scientist Path

MASTER CHEMIST

1700 Gold

PREREQUISITE
Mad Scientist Path

All potions do increased damage and have improved effects.

MIXOLOGIST

2200 Gold

PREREQUISITE
Mad Scientist Path

Mix the effects of different colored potions for brand new effects.

ALL IN

3000 Gold

PREREQUISITE
Mad Scientist Path

Hold **Attack 1** to pull up to three potions out and release to throw them all at once.

Best of the Beast Path

MORE BEAST!

1700 Gold

PREREQUISITE
Best of the Beast Path

Beast Form meter drains slower and recharges faster.

BERSERKER BOOST

3000 Gold

PREREQUISITE
Best of the Beast Path

In Beast Form, damaging enemies recharges the Beast Form meter.

MUTANT BEAST

2200 Gold

PREREQUISITE
Best of the Beast Path

In Beast Form, Press **Attack 3** to perform a special attack based on which potion is active.

Wow Pow!

BEAKER BUDDY

5000 Gold

PREREQUISITE
Purchase New Concotions ability

When throwing Purple Potions, one of the bottles will grow into a giant, special pet.

A "fire-and-forget" ability that you should keep active as often as possible. Unless you're in immediate danger, switch to the purple potion and summon a Beaker Buddy whenever the previous one fades away.

MEGA RAM SPYRO

"All Fired Up!"

MAXIMUM HEALTH	280
SPEED	50
ARMOR	18
CRITICAL HIT	6
ELEMENTAL POWER	25

SERIES 3

Spyro hails from a rare line of magical purple dragons that come from a faraway land few have ever traveled. It's been said that the Scrolls of the Ancients mention Spyro prominently—the old Portal Masters having chronicled his many exciting adventures and heroic deeds. Finally, it was Master Eon himself who reached out and invited him to join the Skylanders. From then on, evil faced a new enemy—and the Skylanders gained a valued ally.

Spyro has abilities that allow him to control the range in fights. Use Charge to move Spyro out of a bad position. Spyro's Earth Pound is a great way to open a fight against bunched up enemies, or as a way to create space around a good spot in a fight.

Selecting which of Spyro's upgrade paths are active boils down to your preferred method of fighting as the dragon. The Sheep Burner Path works best for Spyro players who like to stay away from the crowd. The Blitz Spyro Path is all about getting Spyro's horns dirty.

Special Quest

Full Charge

COLLECT 3 GOLD, EAT 1 FOOD ITEM, AND DEFEAT 2 ENEMIES IN 1 SPRINT CHARGE.

The best place to complete this quest is during an arena challenge where Chompies are the first enemies to appear immediately after you defeat the Food Thief. The Sprint Charge upgrade is a big help as well.

MEGA RAM SPYRO

Basic Attacks

FLAMEBALL

Press **Attack 1** to breathe balls of fire at your enemies.

CHARGE

Press and hold **Attack 2** to lower your horns and charge forward, knocking over anything in your way.

Soul Gem Ability

SPYRO'S EARTH POUND

4000 Gold

PREREQUISITE
Purchase Spyro's Flight ability

This power gives Spyro a new flight attack. Press **Attack 2** while flying to dive bomb.

Upgrades

LONG RANGE RAZE

500 Gold

PREREQUISITE None

Flameball attacks travel farther.

SPYRO'S FLIGHT

700 Gold

PREREQUISITE None

Press **Attack 3** to fly.
Increased speed and resistance while flying.

SPRINT CHARGE

900 Gold

PREREQUISITE None

Can perform Charge attack for increased distance.

TRIPLE FLAMEBALLS

1200 Gold

PREREQUISITE None

Shoot three Flameballs at once.

Sheep Burner Path

FIRE SHIELD

1700 Gold

PREREQUISITE
Sheep Burner Path

A fire shield appears when using the Flameball attack.

EXPLODING FIREBLAST

2200 Gold

PREREQUISITE
Sheep Burner Path

Flameballs do extra damage and the middle one explodes.

THE DAYBRINGER FLAME

3000 Gold

PREREQUISITE
Sheep Burner Path

Hold **Attack 1** to charge up Flameball attack for maximum damage.

Blitz Spyro Path

STUN CHARGE

1700 Gold

PREREQUISITE
Blitz Spyro Path

Enemies hit by Charge Attack become stunned.

COMET DASH

2200 Gold

PREREQUISITE
Blitz Spyro Path

Charge attack does increased damage.

IBEX'S WRATH CHARGE

3000 Gold

PREREQUISITE
Blitz Spyro Path

Charge longer to do extra damage.

Wow Pow!

HEAD START

5000 Gold

PREREQUISITE
None

Summon a magic worm ally at the end of your charge and send it after your enemies.

The magic worm summoned at the end of the charge explodes after making contact with an enemy. You must execute a full charge in order to fire the worm, which may not be easy to pull off in the middle of a fight. It's best to recognize a fight is just ahead and Charge into the area.

STAR STRIKE

"Shoot For the Stars!"

MAXIMUM HEALTH	260
SPEED	43
ARMOR	12
CRITICAL HIT	8
ELEMENTAL POWER	25

Looking for a way to magically banish the Skylanders, Kaos poured through every dusty scroll and ancient tome he could find. Upon stumbling across a rare and extremely powerful spell, he began to recite its words. However, he sneezed midway through the incantation. As a result, instead of sending the Skylanders far away, Star Strike was plucked from her home in the distant cosmos and brought into Skylands. Surprised, Kaos thought he'd won a powerful new ally in the mysterious and reserved Star Strike. But she knew evil when she saw it and promptly unleashed her fierce magical powers on him. Word of her victory over Kaos spread quickly and she was soon asked by Master Eon to join the Skylanders.

LIGHTCORE

Keep Star Strike clear of rough and tumble melee fights and practice using Cosmic Twirl to reflect projectiles, both the initial projectile from Star Gate and defensively to return enemy shots back at them. When you become proficient with Cosmic Twirl, Star Strike has the potential to cruise through any challenge in pristine condition.

Choose the Star Gazer Path to boost Star Strike's area of attack damage via improvements to Starfall, which works better in Arena challenges. If you're working on the Story Mode, opt for the Cosmic Reflector Path as it boosts Star Strike's armor and single target damage.

Special Quest

Deflection Master

DEFELECT THE RETURNING STAR 20 TIMES IN A ROW.

Use Star Gate to fire off a star, then press Attak 2 when the star is within range to deflect it. There's an on-screen visual cue to let you know when to press Attack 2. You can finish this quest anywhere, even Woodburrow.

STAR STRIKE

Basic Attacks

STAR GATE

Press **Attack 1** to summon a powerful star that attacks nearby enemies then returns. Reflect the returning star with **Attack 2** to power it up and do more damage.

COSMIC TWIRL

Press **Attack 2** to perform a magical spin, reflecting any projectiles nearby.

Soul Gem Ability

SHOOTING STARS

4000 Gold

PREREQUISITE
Find Star Strike's Soul Gem in Rampant Ruins

Press **Attack 1** rapidly to shoot many sparkling star projectiles at nearby enemies.

Upgrades

STARFALL

500 Gold

PREREQUISITE None

Press **Attack 3** to cause stars to fall and damage nearby enemies. Press **Attack 2** to deflect the stars at enemies that are farther away.

STAR FILLED SKY

700 Gold

PREREQUISITE
Purchase Starfall ability

Press **Attack 3** to cause even more stars to fall and damage nearby enemies.

YOUR BIGGEST FAN

900 Gold

PREREQUISITE None

Press **Attack 2** to spin and reflect projectiles. Spin radius is now increased, making it more likely to deflect projectiles and power up the star.

STAR POWER

1200 Gold

PREREQUISITE None

Press **Attack 1** rapidly to shoot star shards at enemies that do increased damage.

Star Gazer Path

STAR LIGHT

1700 Gold

PREREQUISITE
Star Gazer Path

Starfall now causes a massive explosive star to fall from the sky. Press **Attack 2** to deflect it at enemies.

STAR STRUCK

2200 Gold

PREREQUISITE
Star Gazer Path

Press **Attack 3** to cause powerful stars that do increased damage to fall and damage nearby enemies.

STAR BRIGHT

3000 Gold

PREREQUISITE
Star Gazer Path

Starfall can be used two times. Set up a star field blockade!

Cosmic Reflector Path

ATOM SPLITTER

1700 Gold

PREREQUISITE
Cosmic Reflector Path

Press **Attack 1** to shoot a star projectile. Press **Attack 2** when it is close to deflect it and shoot two smaller projectiles.

STAR EVASION

2200 Gold

PREREQUISITE
Cosmic Reflector Path

Armor is increased. No one would have thought a dress could be so sturdy.

SUPER STAR

3000 Gold

PREREQUISITE
Cosmic Reflector Path

Press **Attack 1** to shoot a star projectile. Press **Attack 2** when it is close to defelect it. Deflecting it four times makes it grow larger and do more damage.

BLAST ZONE

"Blast and Furious!"

MAXIMUM HEALTH	290
SPEED	43
ARMOR	24
CRITICAL HIT	6
ELEMENTAL POWER	25

As a young furnace knight, Blast Zone was part of the Skylands Bomb Squad, specializing in the safe disarming and removal of troll bombs. But it was not long before the trolls got tired of Blast Zone constantly thwarting their evil plans, so they decided to go after the furnace knight himself. Late one night, an army of trolls snuck into Blast Zone's village and threw 100 bombs down his chimney. Acting quickly, Blast Zone swallowed each bomb and then belched a jet of fire back at the invaders—sending them fleeing with their boots on fire. The tale of the attack eventually reached the ear of Master Eon, who knew the brave furnace knight had all the makings of a Skylander.

Body Soul Gem Ability

BOMB PARTY

3500 Gold

PREREQUISITE
Find Blast Zone's Soul Gem in Fantasm Forest

New armor enhancements allow two Bombs to be thrown at once!

Legs Soul Gem Ability

HOT FEET

3500 Gold

PREREQUISITE
Find Blast Zone's Soul Gem in Fantasm Forest; Purchase Fuel for the Fire ability

A fire trail is left behind while dashing that damages enemies.

SWAP FORCE

Bomb Throw is a quick, lobbed bomb that can bounce one time before exploding. The Ignition Path leads to fiery bombs doing more damage in a larger area. Flame Breath allows for spinning in place while it's active. With the Reaction Satisfaction Path, completing a circle of fire results in an explosion.

Rocket Dash begins as a quick burst but upgrades add damage and greater duration. The Fuel Injected Path ends Rocket Dash with a fiery projectile that damages enemies. The Temperatures Rising Path adds a flame shield at the end of a dash. It doesn't protect Blast Zone, but does deal damage.

Special Quest

If You Can't Stand the Heat

DEFEAT A TOTAL OF 10 ENEMIES FROM YOUR FLAME WALL IN A SINGLE USE OF YOUR FLAME BREATH.

Visit any challenge map where the main enemies are Chompies for quick completion of this quest. You can always depend on them to run directly toward your Skylander, even if it means hurling themselves into fire.

BODY

Basic Attacks

BOMB THROW

Press **Attack 1** to throw a bomb at enemies.

Upgrades

FLAME BREATH

300 Gold

PREREQUISITE None

Hold **Attack 3** while turning to create a wall of fire that damages nearby enemies.

POWER BOMBS

800 Gold

PREREQUISITE None

Press **Attack 1** to throw bombs that do increased damage.

STICKY BOMBS

1000 Gold

PREREQUISITE None

Hold **Attack 1** to charge a Bomb, release to throw a timed sticky bomb.

Ignition Path

FLAMING BOMBS

1500 Gold

PREREQUISITE
Ignition Path

Bombs catch fire when they pass through the fire wall created by Flame Breath, dealing increased damage in an area.

FIRED UP!

2000 Gold

PREREQUISITE
Purchase Flaming Bomb ability

Flaming Bombs do even more damage in a larger area.

Reaction Satisfaction Path

RING OF FIRE

1500 Gold

PREREQUISITE
Reaction Satisfaction Path

Creating a full circle with Flame Breath causes a massive explosion.

RING BLAST

2000 Gold

PREREQUISITE
Purchase Ring of Fire ability

Ring of Fire does increased damage in a larger area.

LEGS

Basic Attacks

ROCKET DASH

Hold **Attack 2** to dash around with rocket boots.

Upgrades

READY FOR BLAST OFF

300 Gold

PREREQUISITE None

Hold **Attack 2** to charge a rocket dash and deal damage to nearby enemies.

ARMOR PLATING

800 Gold

PREREQUISITE None

Armor is increased. Hot off the steel presses!

FUEL FOR THE FIRE

1000 Gold

PREREQUISITE None

Hold **Attack 2** to dash, dashing now lasts for as long as **Attack 2** is held.

Fuel Injected Path

HEAT WAVE

1500 Gold

PREREQUISITE
Fuel Injected Path

A rocket-fueled fireball is shot out at the end of a dash.

TEMPERED FIRE

2000 Gold

PREREQUISITE
Purchase Heave Wave ability

A more powerful Heat Wave is shot out at the end of dashing.

Temperatures Rising Path

FLAMED

1500 Gold

PREREQUISITE
Temperatures Rising Path

A fiery aura appears after dashing, which damages any nearby enemy.

TOO HOT TO HANDLE

2000 Gold

PREREQUISITE
Purchase Flamed ability

An even more powerful fire aura appears at the end of dashing.

FIRE KRAKEN

"Burn To Be Wild!"

MAXIMUM HEALTH	260
SPEED	43
ARMOR	18
CRITICAL HIT	8
ELEMENTAL POWER	25

Raised on a small island surrounded by a vast ocean of fire, Fire Kraken was the swiftest, most agile warrior his tribe had ever seen. When a fleet of Fire Troll ships arrived to steal the legendary Burning Heart, a huge elemental crystal that fueled the fiery seas, Fire Kraken leapt into action. Using a magical staff to control his natural ability to wield fire, he set the mighty ships ablaze, forcing the trolls into a hasty retreat. Having saved the Burning Heart as well as his homeland, Fire Kraken soon joined the Skylanders, where he knew his skills would help those in need.

Body Soul Gem Ability

DANCE OF DRAGONS

3500 Gold

PREREQUISITE
Find Fire Kraken's Soul Gem in Twisty Tunnels

Hold **Attack 3** to start Dragon Parade, release to shoot the sparkling and explosive Dragon costume at enemies.

Legs Soul Gem Ability

THE BIGGER ONE

3500 Gold

PREREQUISITE
Find Fire Kraken's Soul Gem in Twisty Tunnels

The Big One creates a huge colorful explosion that does increased damage in a larger radius.

SWAP FORCE

An upgraded Sparkling Strikes knocks back enemies. The Showcase Path improves the staff and knockback attacks. Dragon Parade damages enemies just by running into them. The Dance of Dragons Path lets you aim and fire one Dragon Parade, then start up another. The Magnficient Parade Path adds fireworks to Dragon Parade.

Start the Show! damages nearby enemies, but the last firework blast is single-target until it's upgraded. The Big One can't be charged (watch for his tail to glow). The Stunning Sparker Path provides a speed boost as the Big One counts down. The Booming Bouncer Path includes a knockback when igniting the Big One.

Special Quest

Don't Rain On My Parade

KNOCK BACK ENEMIES 10 TIMES WITH ONE USE OF YOUR PARADE ABILITY.

Lure a group of at least five enemies tougher than Chompies, but who can't shield themselves, into a tight area. If you hit Dragon Parade just right, it should bounce each enemy twice. The enemies must be able to survive the initial hit to count to the ten necessary to complete the quest.

BODY

Basic Attacks

SPARKLING STRIKES

Press **Attack 1** to swing the sparkler staff, damaging nearby enemies.

Upgrades

DRAGON PARADE

300 Gold

PREREQUISITE None

Hold **Attack 3** to run around in a dragon parade costume, knocking back and damaging enemies in the way.

GLOW STICK

800 Gold

PREREQUISITE None

Press **Attack 1** to swing a new staff that does increased damage.

RISING FOUNTAIN

1000 Gold

PREREQUISITE None

Hold **Attack 1** to charge a staff attack, release to cause a large explosion that knocks up and damages nearby enemies.

The Showcase Path

RISING CHARGE

1500 Gold

PREREQUISITE
The Showcase Path

Rising Fountain causes the next staff attack to cause a large explosion.

FINALE!

2000 Gold

PREREQUISITE
Purchase Rising Charge ability

Rising Fountain does increased damage in a larger area. It's showtime!

Magnificent Parade Path

YEAR OF THE DRAGON

1500 Gold

PREREQUISITE
Magnificent Parade Path

Dragon Parade does increased damage, lasts longer, and reduces damage taken while it is active.

DRAGON CANDLES

2000 Gold

PREREQUISITE
Purchase Year of the Dragon ability

Dragon Parade shoots colorful explosive fireworks at nearby enemies.

LEGS

Basic Attacks

START THE SHOW!

Press **Attack 2** up to three times to perform a firework attack on each press that damages nearby enemies.

Upgrades

SHOW-OFF

300 Gold

PREREQUISITE None

Press **Attack 2** three times to shoot three colorful projectiles at once.

KRAKEN UP

800 Gold

PREREQUISITE None

Press **Jump** to jump, throwing down fireworks and damaging nearby enemies.

THE BIG ONE

1000 Gold

PREREQUISITE None

Hold **Attack 2** for a short time to light a timed fuse that causes a massive firework attack after a short time.

Stunning Sparker Path

UNSTABLE ELEMENT

1500 Gold

PREREQUISITE
Stunning Sparker Path

Speed increases depending on how close The Big One is to exploding. The anticipation!!

SIZZLING SPARKLER

2000 Gold

PREREQUISITE
Stunning Sparker Path

Press **Attack 2** for a spin attack that does increased damage in a larger area.

Booming Bouncer Path

BIGBADABOOM

1500 Gold

PREREQUISITE
Booming Bouncer Path

Press **Attack 2** two times for a bounce attack that does increased damage in a larger area.

STRIKE THE FOES

2000 Gold

PREREQUISITE
Booming Bouncer Path

Hold **Attack 2** for a short time to light the fuse for The Big One and knock away all nearby enemies.

LAVA BARF ERUPTOR

"Born to Burn!"

MAXIMUM HEALTH	290
SPEED	35
ARMOR	18
CRITICAL HIT	6
ELEMENTAL POWER	25

SERIES 3

Eruptor is a force of nature, hailing from a species that lived deep in the underground of a floating volcanic island until a massive eruption launched their entire civilization to the surface. He's a complete hot head—steaming, fuming, and quite literally erupting over almost anything. To help control his temper, he likes to relax in lava pools, particularly because there are no crowds.

Lava Lob is a fast attack, but it lacks range. It strikes enemies who are in higher areas, which is a huge advantage in many situations. Eruption takes time to charge up before it appears, which leaves Eruptor vulnerable to attack. It continues to deal damage to everything it touches, making it terrific against immobile targets.

The Magmantor Path increases the range of Lava Lob and boosts its damage output by 60%. If the Volcanor Path is more your style, get Quick Eruption immediately. The increased damage from the other abilities is great, but faster Eruptions are vital.

Special Quest

Pizza Burp

EAT 10 PIZZAS.

Pizzas appear during story mode, but the fastest way to complete this quest is in an Arena challenge that includes the Food Thief.

Basic Attacks

LAVA LOB

Press **Attack 1** to lob blobs of lava at your enemies.

ERUPTION

Press **Attack 2** to erupt into a pool of lava, damaging enemies all around you.

Soul Gem Ability

MEGA MAGMA BALLS

4000 Gold

PREREQUISITE Purchase Magma Ball ability

Shoot up to three Magma Balls at a time that do extra damage

Upgrades

BIG BLOB LAVA THROW

500 Gold

PREREQUISITE None

Lava Blobs get bigger and do increased damage.

FIERY REMAINS

700 Gold

PREREQUISITE None

Lava Blobs leave behind pools of flame when they hit the ground.

ERUPTION - FLYING TEPHRA

900 Gold

PREREQUISITE None

Lava balls shoot out while performing the Eruption attack.

MAGMA BALL

1200 Gold

PREREQUISITE None

Press **Attack 3** to spit out Magma Balls

Magmantor Path

HEAVY DUTY PLASMA

1700 Gold

PREREQUISITE Magmantor Path

Lava Blobs bounce and travel further.

LAVA BLOB BOMB

2200 Gold

PREREQUISITE Magmantor Path

Lava Blobs explode and damage nearby enemies.

BEAST OF CONFLAGRATION

3000 Gold

PREREQUISITE Purchase Heavy Duty Plasma ability

Lava Blobs do increased damage in the form of a fiery beast.

Volcanor Path

QUICK ERUPTION

1700 Gold

PREREQUISITE Volcanor Path

It takes much less time to perform an Eruption attack.

PYROXYSMAL SUPER ERUPTION

2200 Gold

PREREQUISITE Volcanor Path

Eruption attack does increased damage.

REVENGE OF PROMETHEUS

3000 Gold

PREREQUISITE Purchase Pyroxysmal Super Eruption ability

Eruption causes small volcanoes to form, shooting yet more lava balls.

Wow Pow!

LAVA BARF 2 - BARF HARDER!

5000 Gold

PREREQUISITE Purchase Magma Ball ability

Press **Attack 3** to release Magma Balls, then hold **Attack 3** to eat them and immediately barf them back for extra damage.

Barf Harder is a tricky ability to master. You can't use this ability if any enemy is near you. You need a few seconds for the ability to charge, and the Magma Balls land a short distance away. Any close enemies can stop you and even if they fail, the attack will sail harmlessly over them. On a positive note, the spots where the lava balls land burn for a time and damage enemies that touch them.

FRYNO

"Crash and Burn!"

MAXIMUM HEALTH	300
SPEED	43
ARMOR	6
CRITICAL HIT	4
ELEMENTAL POWER	25

Fryno was once a member of the notorious Blazing Biker Brigade and spent most of his youth riding around Skylands with the rest of his crew. But what Fryno did not realize was that, while he enjoyed a life of freedom and adventure, his crew was responsible for acts of burglary throughout Skylands. When Fryno discovered that he had been riding around with a bunch of villains, he burned with rage and demanded that they make amends for the wrong they had done. This resulted in an epic fight, which Fryno won, and the disbanding of the Blazing Biker Brigade. Fryno was in the midst of returning the valuables his crew had stolen when he met Master Eon, who was impressed with his good character and fighting abilities, and offered him a membership to a new crew—the Skylanders.

You shouldn't have problems in any melee fight as Fryno, but ranged enemies can be challenging. Heated deals damage to enemies near Fryno, and every third swing knocks them back. Heated also increases Fryno's heat level, which improves his damage output. Even Brawl, his other basic attack, becomes more powerful through Heated.

The Brawler Path punishes enemies limited to melee attacks even more. Fryno's Hot Shop Path is a big help when dealing with ranged opponents. The Horn and The Hog is the best way to reach ranged enemies quickly, and what's faster than throwing a motorcycle at them ?

Special Quest

Frequent Frier

DELIVER A TOTAL OF 100 HEAT-IMBUED BLOWS AGAINST ENEMIES.

Use the Heated ability whenever the opportunity arises, whether before a fight starts or during one, and then use Brawl to take out enemies. There's a good chance to complete this quest during the first Story Mode chapter!

Basic Attacks

BRAWL

Press **Attack 1** to punch nearby enemies. Speed and damage of punches is increased depending on heat.

HEATED

Press **Attack 2** repeatedly to smash the ground and increase heat level.

Soul Gem Ability

MADNESS MAXED

4000 Gold

PREREQUISITE
Find Fryno's Soul Gem in Frostfest Mountains

Press **Attack 2** rapidly to make Fryno even more heated. So angry!

Upgrades

THE HORN AND THE HOG

500 Gold

PREREQUISITE None

Press **Attack 3** to dash forward, dealing damage to enemies in the way. When heated, Fryno jumps on a motorcycle to deal damage to nearby enemies.

BUILT TOUGH

700 Gold

PREREQUISITE None

Health is increased. Probably from punching the ground so much...

FIRED UP!

900 Gold

PREREQUISITE None

Press **Attack 2** repeatedly to throw a tantrum and become heated. Tantrums now have increased range and damage.

MOLTEN FURY

1200 Gold

PREREQUISITE None

All attacks do increased damage when heated.

Brawler Path

HOT HANDS

1700 Gold

PREREQUISITE
Brawler Path

Hold **Attack 1** to rapidly punch nearby enemies and release heat.

SPIKED UP

2200 Gold

PREREQUISITE
Purchase Hot Hands ability

New metal gloves causes Hot Hands to do increased damage.

TEMPERATURE TANTRUM

3000 Gold

PREREQUISITE
Brawler Path

Nearby enemies take damage while Fryno is heated.

Fryno's Hot Shop Path

BORN TO RIDE

1700 Gold

PREREQUISITE
Fryno's Hot Shop Path

The Horn and The Hog will always summon a molten motorcycle.

HOT ROD

2200 Gold

PREREQUISITE
Fryno's Hot Shop Path

All attacks with the motorcycle do increased damage.

CRASH AND BURN

3000 Gold

PREREQUISITE
Fryno's Hot Shop Path

Fryno throws the motorcycle at the end of a dash, causing a massive explosion that damages nearby enemies. Who's paying for that...?

FIRE BONE HOT DOG

"See Spot Burn!"

MAXIMUM HEALTH	250
SPEED	43
ARMOR	6
CRITICAL HIT	12
ELEMENTAL POWER	25

Hot Dog was born in the belly of the Popcorn Volcano. While on a nearby mission, a team of Skylanders happened across the stray fire pup when the volcano erupted and Hot Dog came rocketing straight into their camp, accidentally setting Gill Grunt's tent on fire. Using his nose for danger, he helped the Skylanders complete their mission—even pouncing on a lava golem like a blazing comet when it threatened his new friends. After displaying such loyalty and bravery, Hot Dog was brought back to Eon's Citadel where he became a Skylander—and then proceeded to bury Eon's staff.

SERIES 2

Firebark is a ranged attack, but Hot Dog can still use it in multiple combos when upgaded. Wall of Fire is an effective way to control enemy position. Hold Attack 2 and Wall of Fire remains in front of Hot Dog. Release Attack 2 to send the Wall of Fire to clear the path ahead.

The Burning Bow Wow Path adds combo choices to Firebark and some offense to Comet Slam while it's charging. The Pyro Pooch Path makes Wall of Fire more powerful in every way and adds an awesome visual touch with Magmutt Battalion.

Special Quest

Animal Aggravator

EAT 10 HOT DOGS.

Hot Dogs appear throughout the Story Mode, but the fastest way to complete this quest is to attempt challenges that include the Food Thief.

FIRE BONE HOT DOG

Basic Attacks

FIREBARK

Press **Attack 1** to spit fireballs. Press **Attack 1**, **Attack 1**, Hold **Attack 1** for a special combo

WALL OF FIRE

Press **Attack 2** to summon a wall of fire and send it towards enemies.

Soul Gem Ability

DING DONG DITCH

4000 Gold

PREREQUISITE Purchase Comet Slam ability

After a Comet Slam, leave a burning bag that explodes when stepped on.

Upgrades

PYRO PIERCERS

500 Gold

PREREQUISITE None

Fireballs pierce multiple targets and do increased damage.

COMET SLAM

700 Gold

PREREQUISITE None

Press **Attack 3** to flip in the air and slam down on the ground like a comet.

WALL OF MORE FIRE

900 Gold

PREREQUISITE None

Walls of Fire deal increased damage.

SUPER COMET

1200 Gold

PREREQUISITE Purchase Comet

Hold **Attack 3** to charge up the Comet Slam and release to do increased damage.

Burning Bow Wow Path

HOT DOG COMBOS

1700 Gold

PREREQUISITE Burning Bow Wow Path

Press **Attack 1**, **Attack 1**, Hold **Attack 2** for Burnin' Bees. Press **Attack 1**, **Attack 1**, Hold **Attack 3** for Comet Dash.

BARK BOMBS

2200 Gold

PREREQUISITE Burning Bow Wow Path

Fireballs explode on impact and do increased damage.

PYRO PINWHEEL

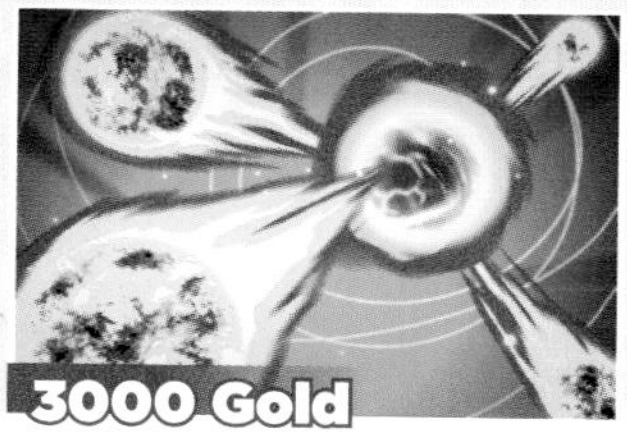

3000 Gold

PREREQUISITE Burning Bow Wow Path

While holding **Attack 3** to charge up the Comet Slam, Hot Dog shoots fireballs from all angles.

Pyro Pooch Path

BLAZING WILDFIRE

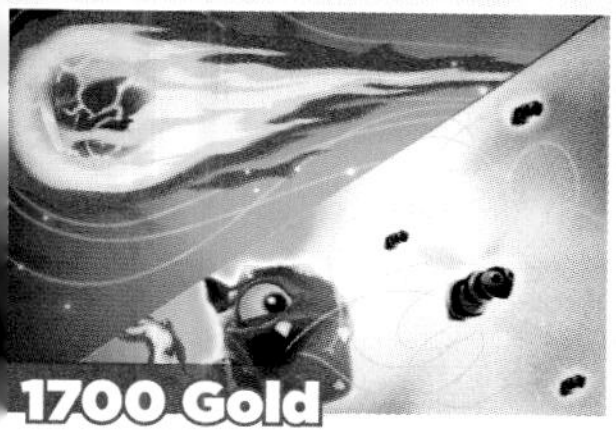

1700 Gold

PREREQUISITE Pyro Pooch Path

Walls of Fire travel faster and do more increased damage.

GREAT WALLS OF FIRE

2200 Gold

PREREQUISITE Pyro Pooch Path

Walls of Fire are bigger and do even MORE increased damage.

MAGMUTT BATTALION

3000 Gold

PREREQUISITE Pyro Pooch Path

Walls of Fire are now made up of fiery dogs that do maximum damage and shoot fireballs whenever Hot Dog fires one.

Wow Pow!

BEES! BEES! BEES!

5000 Gold

PREREQUISITE None

Hold **Attack 1** then release to fire a super powerful blast of bees.

Bees! Bees! Bees! forms a swarm of bees that eventually tracks down and damages an enemy. You don't need to worry about aiming them, just charge them up (Hot Dog can still move, just slowly) and let them fly. The downside to this attack is that you can't use it at the end of a combo. It only works on the first press of Attack 1.

SMOLDERDASH

"A Blaze of Glory!"

MAXIMUM HEALTH	280
SPEED	43
ARMOR	12
CRITICAL HIT	8
ELEMENTAL POWER	25

LIGHTCORE

Smolderdash requires patience and upgrades before you appreciate her potential. Flame Whip is a solid, quick hitting attack, even before upgrades. Solar Orb is a great way to hit enemies at a distance, or knock them into the air to give yourself time to move in closer. The abilities work well together.

If you choose the Sun Forger Path, practice striking Solar Orbs with Flame Whip at different distances and angles. The Sun Forged Path is more effective in situations with weaker enemies that attack in large numbers, such as Arena challenges. Eclipse boosts the damage output of everything Smolderdash does, even jumping!

Special Quest

Event Horizon

KNOCK UP A TOTAL OF 50 ENEMIES WITH YOUR EXPLODING SUN.

Exploding sun means either a second press of Attack 2 when a Solar Orb is on the screen, or striking a Solar Orb with a Flame Whip. Enemies must meet two requirements to count toward this quest. They must survive the explosion (don't expect to pad your numbers with Chompies) and they must be able to go into the air, which rules out enemies like Chompy Pods.

Smolderdash had always wanted to be a royal defender of the Fire Temple—home of the First Flame, a sacred torch that had been ignited by the original Fire Source. Unfortunately, she had been born during an eclipse and was believed by her people to be cursed, which prevented her from such an honor. But when Kaos stole the flame and used it to light the candles on his birthday cake, it was Smolderdash who went after it. Blazing like a comet, she dashed into Kaos' lair, repelled the troll security force with her flaming whip, and retrieved the sacred flame just before Kaos blew out the candles. Smolderdash returned home as a champion of her people and was finally granted the honor of becoming a royal defender. But she graciously declined, having set a new goal for herself—to help fight against Kaos as a member of the Skylanders.

Basic Attacks

FLAME WHIP

Press **Attack 1** rapidly to perform whip combos.

SOLAR ORB

Press **Attack 2** to shoot a fiery orb. Press **Attack 2** again to detonate it.

Soul Gem Ability

SMOLDER DASH

4000 Gold

PREREQUISITE
Find Smolderdash's Soul Gem in Woodburrow; Purchase Eclipse ability

Perform the powerful Smolder Dash when you press **Attack 3** while in Eclipse mode!

Upgrades

ECLIPSE

500 Gold

PREREQUISITE None

Press **Attack 3** to become solar charged for a short time, making all attacks more powerful. Eclipse needs to recharge for a short time after it is used before it can be used again.

SOLAR POWERED

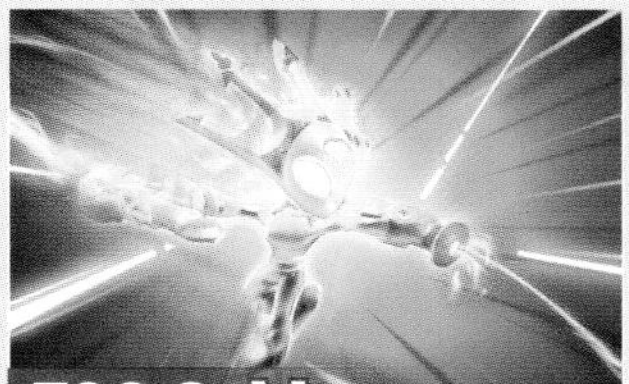

700 Gold

PREREQUISITE None

Speed is increased. Time to blaze through Skylands!

SUNRISE

900 Gold

PREREQUISITE None

Hold **Attack 1** to charge a sun attack, release to jump into the air and slam a huge sun into the ground.

WHIP IT!

1200 Gold

PREREQUISITE None

Press **Attack 1** to attack with more powerful whips that do increased damage. Whip it good!

Sun Forger Path

SUPER GIANT

1700 Gold

PREREQUISITE
Sun Forger Path

Hold **Attack 2** to charge a sun into a super giant sun, release to throw it forward which deals more damage and hits more enemies.

SOLAR FLARE

2200 Gold

PREREQUISITE
Sun Forger Path

Critical Hit is increased. Unleash the power of a solar flare!

SUN SPLITTER

3000 Gold

PREREQUISITE
Sun Forger Path

Press **Attack 2** to shoot a blazing sun at enemies. Press **Attack 1** to strike the sun with a whip attack causing the sun to speed up. Super Giant suns split into two smaller suns when hit.

Sun Forged Path

SOLAR BLAST

1700 Gold

PREREQUISITE
Sun Forged Path

Hold **Attack 1** to charge a sun attack, release to jump into the air and slam a huge sun into the ground, causing five smaller suns to shoot out toward enemies.

SUNNY ARMOR

2200 Gold

PREREQUISITE
Sun Forged Path

Armor is increased. So bright and cheery that enemies' attacks don't do anything to damper the mood!

SUN'S CORE

3000 Gold

PREREQUISITE
Sun Forged Path

Press **Attack 2** to shoot a blazing sun at enemies. Press **Attack 1** to strike the sun with a whip attack and gain a fiery aura that damages nearby enemies.

FREEZE BLADE

"Keeping It Cool!"

MAXIMUM HEALTH	280
SPEED	50
ARMOR	6
CRITICAL HIT	8
ELEMENTAL POWER	25

When he was young, Freeze Blade's family moved from the Frozen Wastelands of Vesh to the Great Lava Lakes. As it turned out, this was a very difficult adjustment for Freeze Blade. Not only was he the sole one of his kind, it was also incredibly hot and there was no ice to skate on whatsoever. But over the years, he learned to fit in with the other fire-like creatures and even discovered he had a magical ability to ice skate on any surface...even bubbling lava. One day, while out setting a new frozen lava speed record, he came across Blast Zone, who had just been ambushed by some nasty Spell Punks. After Freeze Blade stepped in to defend him, Blast Zone was so impressed by his skill in battle that he introduced him to Master Eon, who invited him to join the Skylanders.

Body Soul Gem Ability

WINTER CHAKRAM

3500 Gold

PREREQUISITE
Find Freeze Blade's Soul Gem in Fantasm Forest

Chakram attacks have increased critical hit chance and do extra frost damage.

Legs Soul Gem Ability

ICEBERG ENDURANCE

3500 Gold

PREREQUISITE
Find Freeze Blade's Soul Gem in Fantasm Forest

Dashing does increased damage and does not stop when attacked.

SWAP FORCE

Chakram Throw is a rare ability that works equally well as a ranged attack or as a melee attack. Frigid Whirl is a great upgrade that leaves a chakram whirling around (and damaging) an enemy. The Blizzard Blade Path adds an ice attack to Frigid Whirl. Use Frostcicle to keep enemies briefly on ice. The Ice Sculptor Path turns Frostcicle into an area attack.

Speedy Skates is a damaging dash attack that upgrades to slow enemies who step on its trail. The Trail Freezer Path adds damage to the slowing effect of the trail. The Ice Skater Path lets you turn enemies into weapons.

Special Quest

Chill Out For A Second

FREEZE 100 ENEMIES WITH YOUR FROSTCICLE ATTACK.

Avoid trying for this against weaker enemies that might be defeated by the initial damage of the attack. There should be plenty of enemies who can survive, especially as you play at higher difficulties.

BODY

Basic Attacks

CHAKRAM THROW

Press **Attack 1** to throw an icy chakram.

Upgrades

FROSTCICLE

300 Gold

PREREQUISITE None

Press **Attack 3** to fire a shard of ice that freezes enemies.

ICICLES

800 Gold

PREREQUISITE None

Chakram gains a new layer of ice, making attacks do increased damage.

FRIGID WHIRL

1000 Gold

PREREQUISITE None

Hold **Attack 1** to charge the chakram, then release to throw it.

Blizzard Blade Path

SHAVED ICE

1500 Gold

PREREQUISITE
Blizzard Blade Path

Hold **Attack 1** to charge the chakram, release to throw the chakram and shoot ice in every direction.

WHITEOUT

2000 Gold

PREREQUISITE
Purchase Shaved Ice ability

Ice projectiles from Shaved Ice do increased damage.

Ice Sculptor Path

OH SNOW!

1500 Gold

PREREQUISITE
Ice Sculptor Path

Hold **Attack 3** to charge Frostcicle, release to freeze an entire area.

ICE TO MEET YOU

2000 Gold

PREREQUISITE
Purchase Oh Snow! ability

Frostcicle and Oh Snow! Do increased damage.

LEGS

Basic Attacks

SPEEDY SKATE

Press **Attack 2** to dash forward a short distance and damage enemies in the way.

Upgrades

ICE TRAIL

300 Gold

PREREQUISITE None

Dashing leaves behind a trail of ice that slows enemies.

GLACIAL COAT

800 Gold

PREREQUISITE None

Armor increased. As tough as a glacier!

BLADED BUTTERFLY

1000 Gold

PREREQUISITE None

Hold **Attack 2** to perform a fancy skating trick that damages all enemies nearby.

Trail Freezer Path

FLASH FREEZE

1500 Gold

PREREQUISITE
Trail Freezer Path

Press **Attack 2** to dash, dashing will now leave behind an ice trail that damages enemies.

NICE ICE

2000 Gold

PREREQUISITE
Purchase Flash Freeze ability

Flash Freeze does increased damage. A nasty case of freezer burn!

Ice Skater Path

PENALTY FROST

1500 Gold

PREREQUISITE
Iced Skater Path

Press **Attack 2** to knock back an enemy, wherever the knocked back enemy lands will cause a large freezing explosion.

ICED SKATES

2000 Gold

PREREQUISITE
Purchase Penalty Frost ability

Penalty Frost does increased damage. Don't worry, this is not a typical sports penalty.

WASH BUCKLER

"Eight Legs and No Pegs!"

MAXIMUM HEALTH	270
SPEED	43
ARMOR	24
CRITICAL HIT	8
ELEMENTAL POWER	25

Wash Buckler was an orphan Mermasquid, who grew up on one of the roughest pirate ships in the Skylands. While most pirates were interested in pillaging and plundering, Wash Buckler had other ideas for the future of pirating. Over the years, he earned the respect of his crew and eventually convinced his fellow pirates that they didn't all need to be cantankerous bad guys. Thus, they set forward doing heroic deeds. Of course, this new good guy image did not sit well with other pirating crews, who attempted to sabotage Wash Buckler at every turn. But he was no ordinary pirate, and he defended his ship and his crew against the many attacking hordes. It was then that Master Eon took notice of Wash Buckler and asked him to join the Skylanders.

SWAP FORCE

Sword Slash is a touch slower than many other melee attacks, but hits harder. The Cutlass Captain Path adds a shield to Wash Buckler whenever he hits a bubble-encased enemy with a sword attack. The Bubble Buccaner Path upgrades the initial attack of Bubble Blaster, and the follow up fish attacks.

Somersaulty begins as a combination dash and attack to which Octolash adds occassional tentacle attacks while charging a Somersaulty attack. The Tentacoolest Path changes that to constant tentacle attacks. Ink Jet blinds nearby enemies while using Octolash, and the Ink Artist Path adds an ink attack in Somesaulty's wake.

Body Soul Gem Ability

ON STORMY SEAS

3500 Gold

PREREQUISITE

Find Wash Buckler's Soul Gem in Twisty Tunnels; Purchase Bladesail ability

Hold **Attack 1** to charge Bladesail even further, release to summon a watery pirate ship that rams into enemies.

Legs Soul Gem Ability

TENTACLE CAROUSEL

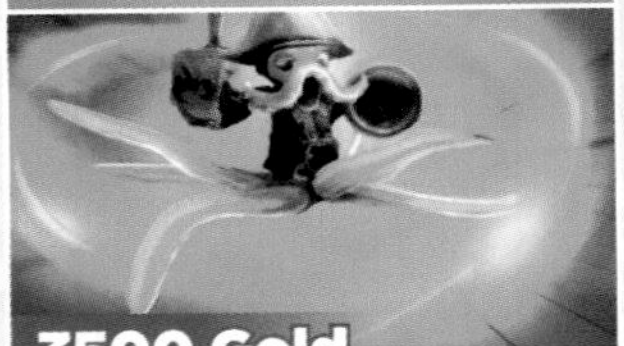

3500 Gold

PREREQUISITE

Find Wash Buckler's Soul Gem in Twisty Tunnels

Press **Attack 2** rapidly to perform a spin attack that damages all nearby enemies.

Special Quest

Sleep With The Fishes

DEFEAT 50 ENEMIES WITH THE FISH IN YOUR BUBBLES.

The first step in completing this quest is purchasing the Dangerous Waters upgrade. A good second step is to choose the Bubble Buccaneer upgrades, which boost the damage done by the piranhas. Finally, pick targets that will survive the intital damage of Bubble Blaster but will fall to the follow-up fish attacks.

BODY

Basic Attacks

SWORD SLASH

Press **Attack 1** to swing a bubbly cutlass at nearby enemies.

Upgrades

BUBBLE BLASTER

300 Gold

PREREQUISITE None

Press **Attack 3** to shoot a bubble that will trap an enemy for a short time.

BLADESAIL

800 Gold

PREREQUISITE None

Sword attacks do increased damage. Hold **Attack 1** to charge the sword, release to perform a dash attack.

DANGEROUS WATERS

1000 Gold

PREREQUISITE
Purchase Bubble Blaster ability

Press **Attack 3** to shoot a piranha filled bubble at an enemy. Warning: these little fish are angry!

Cutlass Captain Path

PARLEY POOPER

1500 Gold

PREREQUISITE
Cutlass Captain Path

Popping bubbles with sword attacks will create a bubble shield that reduces damage and explodes when attacked.

FIRST MATE CUTLASS

2000 Gold

PREREQUISITE
Cutlass Captain Path

Sword attacks do even more damage. The most trusty first mate a pirate could have.

Bubble Buccaneer Path

MAROONED

1500 Gold

PREREQUISITE
Bubble Buccaneer Path

Bubble attacks do increased damage. Hold **Attack 3** to charge the Bubble Blaster, release to shoot two mega bubbles that can trap many enemies.

CAPTAIN OF PIRANHA BAY

2000 Gold

PREREQUISITE
Bubble Buccaneer Path

Piranhas do increased damage. More dangerous than your average piranha!

LEGS

Basic Attacks

SOMERSAULTY

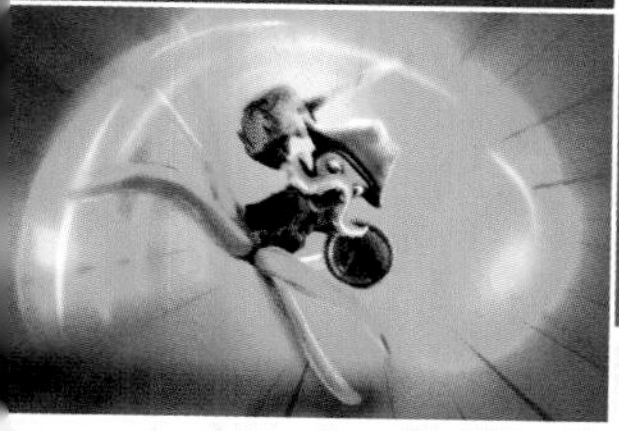

Press Attack 2 to dash forward and roll over enemies with powerful tentacles.

Upgrades

OCTOLASH

300 Gold

PREREQUISITE None

Hold **Attack 2** to slap enemies with two tentacles.

DEEP SKIN

800 Gold

PREREQUISITE None

Health is increased. All of the deep sea treasure hunts have really paid off!

INK JET

1000 Gold

PREREQUISITE
Purchase Octolash ability

Octolash now shoots ink that damages and temporarily causes enemies to have difficulties seeing.

Tentacoolest Path

TENTACLEAVER

1500 Gold

PREREQUISITE
Tentacoolest Path

Hold **Attack 2** to slap enemies repeatedly.

SEA LEGS

2000 Gold

PREREQUISITE
Purchase Tentacleaver ability

Tentacles do increased damage. Whip those enemies into shape!

Ink Artist Path

INK TRAIL

1500 Gold

PREREQUISITE
Ink Artist Path

Press **Attack 2** to leave behind a cloud of ink.

THIS WILL NEVER COME OUT!

2000 Gold

PREREQUISITE
Purchase Ink Trail ability

Ink attacks do increased damage.

BLIZZARD CHILL

"Stay Cool"

MAXIMUM HEALTH	260
SPEED	43
ARMOR	24
CRITICAL HIT	2
ELEMENTAL POWER	25

SERIES 2

Chill was the sworn guardian and personal protector of the Snow Queen. As captain of the queen's guard, her many heroic deeds had earned her the respect of the entire Ice Kingdom. But when the Cyclops army began to expand their empire into the northern realms, the Snow Queen was taken prisoner during her watch, and Chill has never forgiven herself for letting it happen. Ashamed and embarrassed, she left the Ice Kingdom behind and swore never to return until she could reclaim her honor. Now as a member of the Skylanders, she remains courageous and strong, while always on the lookout for her lost queen.

Javelin is a fantastic ranged attack that cuts through enemies. Improving Javelin through the Ice Lancer Path allows Chill to fill the air with icy missiles, especially if you remember to put up Ice Walls before you start throwing them. Ice Wall is a great way to keep enemies away and it can be turned into an offensive weapon with the Glacial Bash upgrade.

If you choose the Frozen Fury Path, Ice Walls improves dramatically. When enemies run into Ice Walls, they explode and form new Ice Blocks. Regardless of the path you choose with Chill, her basic attacks work together beautifully.

Special Quest

Ice Sore

DEFEAT 50 ENEMIES WITH THE CALL THE NARWHAL ATTACK.

Use Call the Narwhal against groups of Chompies whenever possible. If you want to complete this quest quickly, do Arena challenges.

Basic Attacks

ICE JAVELIN

Press **Attack 1** to throw a spinning ice javelin.

ICE WALL

Press **Attack 2** to summon a wall of ice blocks. Can use for protection or to knock back enemies.

Soul Gem Ability

CALL THE NARWHAL!

4000 Gold

PREREQUISITE
None

Hold **Attack 1** to charge and then release to summon a massive narwhal friend!

Upgrades

THE GREAT WALL

500 Gold

PREREQUISITE None

Hold **Attack 2** to extend the length of an ice wall.

GLACIAL BASH

700 Gold

PREREQUISITE None

Press **Attack 3** to bash enemies and ice wall blocks with your shield.

IMPERIAL ARMOR

900 Gold

PREREQUISITE None

New helmet increases Chill's Resistance.

COLD FRONT

1200 Gold

PREREQUISITE
Purchase Glacial Bash abitlity

Hold **Attack 3** to keep the shield raised and block attacks from the front.

Ice Lancer Path

BRRRR BLADE

1700 Gold

PREREQUISITE
Ice Lancer Path

New ice javelin deals increased damage.

SHATTERSPEAR

2200 Gold

PREREQUISITE
Ice Lancer Path

Javelins now split into separate ice spears when passing through an Ice Wall.

TRIPLE JAVELINS

3000 Gold

PREREQUISITE
Ice Lancer Path

Throw three javelins at once.

Frozen Fury Path

ICE BREAKER

1700 Gold

PREREQUISITE
Frozen Fury Path

Ice Wall blocks explode when struck by an ice javelin or by an enemy.

BETTER BASH

2200 Gold

PREREQUISITE
Frozen Fury Path

Glacial Blast hits multiple enemies and Ice Wall blocks in a larger area.

ON THE ROCKS

3000 Gold

PREREQUISITE
Frozen Fury Path

Exploding ice blocks freeze enemies into ice cubes of their own.

Wow Pow!

ORCASTRATION!

5000 Gold

PREREQUISITE
None

Hold **Attack 2** longer and mini orcas appear inside the ice wall, then release to shatter the wall and launch orcas.

Orcastration! does not go off until you release Attack 2. The orcas fly to the side and land at a certain distance away from the wall, but don't seek out nearby enemies. To use this ability effectively, put up a few defensive Ice Walls before you try to charge up an Ice Wall filled with orcas.

ANCHORS AWAY GILL GRUNT

"Fear the Fish!"

MAXIMUM HEALTH	270
SPEED	35
ARMOR	6
CRITICAL HIT	10
ELEMENTAL POWER	25

SERIES 3

Gill Grunt was a brave soul who joined the Gillmen military in search of adventure. While journeying through a misty lagoon in the clouds, he met an enchanting mermaid. He vowed to return to her after his tour. Keeping his promise, he came back to the lagoon years later, only to learn a nasty band of pirates had kidnapped the mermaid. Heartbroken, Gill Grunt began searching all over Skylands. Though he had yet to find her, he joined the Skylanders to help protect others from such evil, while still keeping an ever-watchful eye for the beautiful mermaid and the pirates who took her.

Few Skylanders have abilities where you must press two buttons at the same time to activate them, but Gill Grunt now has two such abilities: his Wow Pow! ability, Anchor Management, and Neptune Gun. Gill Grunt remains the same ranged-focused fighter he has been throughout the Skylanders adventures.

Harpoon Gun is a solid attack, and improving it via the Harpooner Path makes it hit harder and strike more targets. Power Hose and Jetpack are wonderful abilities that become awesome if you choose the Water Weaver Path.

Special Quest
Anchors Away!
DEFEAT 50 ENEMIES WITH THE ANCHOR ATTACK.
Charge up Anchor Cannon when you see an upcoming fight, especially against low health enemies. Fire the Anchor Cannon into the enemies before they can approach your Skylander. Any enemies you can take out of the fight before they get in their first attack is a big help.

Basic Attacks

HARPOON GUN

Press **Attack 1** to shoot high-velocity harpoons at your enemies.

POWER HOSE

Press and hold **Attack 2** to spray water at your enemies to knock them back.

Soul Gem Ability

ANCHOR CANNON

4000 Gold

PREREQUISITE
None

Hold **Attack 1** to charge Anchor Cannon.

Upgrades

BARBED HARPOONS

500 Gold

PREREQUISITE None

Harpoons deal more damage.

HIGH PRESSURE HOSE

700 Gold

PREREQUISITE None

Power Hose attack does extra damage and knocks enemies back further.

HARPOON REPEATER

900 Gold

PREREQUISITE None

Harpoons reload faster.

WATER JETPACK

1200 Gold

PREREQUISITE None

Hold **Attack 3** to fly until the water jetpack runs out. Gain increased speed and resistance while flying.

Harpooner Path

QUADENT HARPOONS

1700 Gold

PREREQUISITE
Harpooner Path

Harpoons deal even MORE increased damage.

PIERCING HARPOONS

2200 Gold

PREREQUISITE
Harpooner Path

Harpoons travel straight through enemies and hit targets behind them.

TRIPLESHOT HARPOON

3000 Gold

PREREQUISITE
Harpooner Path

Shoot three Harpoons at once.

Water Weaver Path

RESERVE WATER TANK

1700 Gold

PREREQUISITE
Water Weaver Path

The Power Hose and Water Jetpack never run out of water.

BOILING WATER HOSE

2200 Gold

PREREQUISITE
Water Weaver Path

Power Hose attack deals even MORE increased damage.

NEPTUNE GUN

3000 Gold

PREREQUISITE
Water Weaver Path

When using the Power Hose, press **Attack 1** to launch exploding sea creatures.

Wow Pow!

ANCHOR MANAGEMENT!

5000 Gold

PREREQUISITE
Purchase Anchor Cannon ability

Charge up the Anchor Cannon and press **Attack 2** to do special damage.

Anchor Management turns the normally straight ahead Anchor Cannon attack into a lob attack and a blender. Where the anchor hits the ground, it sends out a large shockwave, then begins to spin. Any enemy caught by the spinning anchor is dazed for a few seconds after the spin ends. A nice benefit to Anchor Management is that you can use it to reach higher areas and soften up the enemies before taking them on directly.

PUNK SHOCK

"Amp It Up!"

MAXIMUM HEALTH	270
SPEED	43
ARMOR	12
CRITICAL HIT	8
ELEMENTAL POWER	25

Daughter to the most royal family in Wondrous Waters, Punk Shock never really accepted her role as an undersea princess. She preferred a much more exciting life—hunting with her electric crossbow and listening to super-charged music. After journeying to the outer reaches of her kingdom to find adventure, Punk Shock returned home to discover adventure had found her. The kingdom and its people were magically frozen by the Snow Trolls, who were there to steal valuable treasure. Punk Shock used her awesomely charged crossbow to single handedly defeat the Snow Troll army and melt the ice that trapped her kingdom. Gill Grunt heard of the battle and quickly recruited Punk Shock into the Skylanders.

Water and electricity combine to make Punk Shock's attacks shocking for her enemies. Improved Spark Shot inflicts more damage and splits its bolts to hit multiple targets. Splash Bomb doesn't cause much damage by itself, but use Spark Shock on the puddles it leaves behind to damage and stun any enemy in the water.

The Conductor Constructor Path leads to bigger and better Splash Bomb capabilities. Bolting Blob is noteworthy because it doesn't rely on another attack to boost its damage. The Eelectrocutey Path adds some up-close options for this ranged specialist. Re-Volting Shock is great against enemies that get too close.

Special Quest

Hydrostatics

SHOCK ENEMIES WITH ELECTRIFIED WATER ZONES 100 TIMES.

Anytime you're involved in a fight that lasts more than a few seconds, you should throw down a Splash Bomb as often as possible. Use Spark Shot or Spark Splash on the resulting puddle to electrify it. Each enemy caught in the now-electrified puddle counts toward your total.

Basic Attacks

SPARK SHOT

Press **Attack 1** to shoot an electrified bolt. Shoot a Splash Bomb puddle to cause that area to become electrified.

SPLASH BOMB

Press **Attack 2** to throw a larger water balloon that makes a puddle where it lands. Shoot the puddle with Spark Shot to electrify it.

Soul Gem Ability

EELECTROCUTE

4000 Gold

PREREQUISITE
Find Punk Shock's Soul Gem in Kaos' Fortress

Hold **Attack 1** to charge a powerful crossbow attack, release to shoot all enemies around you!

Upgrades

SPARK SPLASH

500 Gold

PREREQUISITE None

Press **Attack 3** to perform a tail attack that shocks nearby enemies. There is a short wait before this ability can be used again.

HIGH BOLTAGE

700 Gold

PREREQUISITE None

Press **Attack 1** to shoot high powered crossbolt attacks that do increased damage.

OHMG

900 Gold

PREREQUISITE None

Press **Attack 1** to shoot electric crossbow bolts that branch out and hit enemies in a larger area.

HYPERCHARGED

1200 Gold

PREREQUISITE None

Increase movement speed. Adding a spark to each step!

Conductor Constructor Path

H2THROW

1700 Gold

PREREQUISITE
Conductor Constructor Path

Press **Attack 2** to throw two additional water balloons. All water balloons last longer.

TROUBLED WATERS

2200 Gold

PREREQUISITE
Conductor Constructor Path

All water balloon attacks do increased damage. Throwing water balloons never hurt so bad!

BOLTING BLOB

3000 Gold

PREREQUISITE
Conductor Constructor Path

Hold **Attack 2** to throw a balloon into the air, release to zap it and electrify all enemies in a very large area.

Eelectrocutey Path

POSITIVELY CHARGED

1700 Gold

PREREQUISITE
Eelectrocutey Path

Gain an electric aura that sometimes shocks and damages nearby enemies.

IT HERTZ

2200 Gold

PREREQUISITE
Eelectrocutey Path

Enemies damaged by electrified water take increased damage. A perfect example of why there is no swimming during a lightning storm.

RE-VOLTING SHOCK

3000 Gold

PREREQUISITE
Eelectrocutey Path

Hold **Attack 3** to tail slap nearby enemies into the air.

RIPTIDE

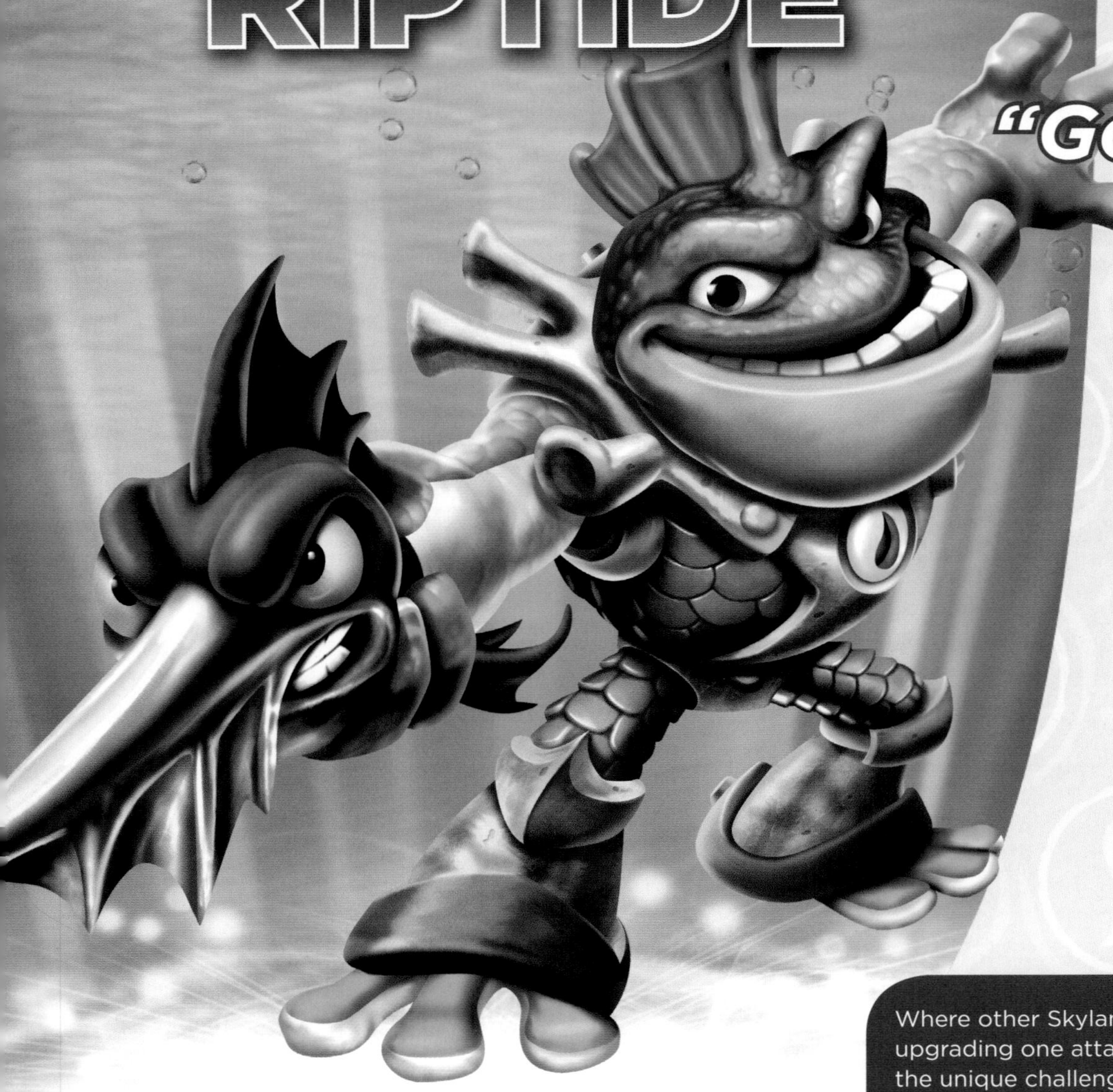

"Go Fish!"

MAXIMUM HEALTH	300
SPEED	43
ARMOR	30
CRITICAL HIT	4
ELEMENTAL POWER	25

Rip Tide was known far and wide as one of the best Aqua-Fighters in Skylands. He mastered a multitude of water techniques and astonished tournament spectators with his ability to adapt his fighting style to any opponent. Amongst his repertoire were Swordfish Fencing, Hammerhead Heaving, and even the rare Blubber Whale Wallop—which he had used on numerous occasions in the legendary Rumble in the Reef. His unrivaled skill as a swordsman soon drew the attention of Master Eon. But when Kaos learned of this, he sent forth a legion of Squidface Brutes to stop Rip Tide before he could join the Skylanders... and everyone knows how that turned out, except for the Squidface Brutes, who after being knocked senseless can't remember a thing.

Where other Skylanders must choose between upgrading one attack over another, Rip Tide faces the unique challenge of deciding which fish to emphasize. Swordfish attacks are lightning quick strikes that work best against weaker enemies which appear in groups. Hammerhead attacks are meaty, deliberate swings that hit much harder and are great against powerful, solo opponents.

The Fishy Fencer and Flounder Pounder Paths emphasize one of the weapons equally. The big difference is the charge attack. Straight as an Angler is a torpedo attack that covers distance quickly. Shark Bite Bait doesn't travel as fast or far, but does more damage.

Special Quest

Whale of a Time

DAMAGE 8 ENEMIES AT ONCE WITH YOUR WHALE ON 'EM ABILITY.

The important word to note for this quest is "damage." You don't need to defeat eight enemies at once, just hit them. Any area filled with Chompies is a good choice since no other enemy swarms quite like they do. Find the right spot and use Whale On 'Em to complete the quest.

Basic Attacks

TETRA ATTACK

Press **Attack 1** to swing the currently held fish at enemies. Swordfish attacks are quick while Shark attacks are slow, but more powerful.

FISH TOSS

Press **Attack 2** to toss the currently held fish at enemies. Fish Toss will also change between Swordfish and Shark.

Soul Gem Ability

REINVENTING THE WHALE

4000 Gold

PREREQUISITE
Find Rip Tide's Soul Gem in Twisty Tunnels; Purchase Whale on 'Em ability

Angry fish explode out of the whale's spout, seeking out and damaging nearby enemies.

Upgrades

WHALE ON 'EM

500 Gold

PREREQUISITE None

Press **Attack 3** to drop a large whale and smack down a large number of enemies.

BIGGER FISH TO FLY

700 Gold

PREREQUISITE None

Press **Attack 2** to throw the held fish, doing increased damage to enemies.

FRESH FISH

900 Gold

PREREQUISITE None

Press **Attack 2** to throw the currently held fish. Press **Attack 1** to attack and critically hit with the new fish.

BLISTERING BLUBBER

1200 Gold

PREREQUISITE
Purchase Whale on 'Em ability

Whale attacks do increased damage. Pocket whales are known for their helpful nature.

Fishy Fencer Path

NIPPING NEEDLE NOSE

1700 Gold

PREREQUISITE
Fishy Fencer Path

Press **Attack 2** to throw the sword fish which does damage over time to enemies that it hits.

PRACTICED PARRY

2200 Gold

PREREQUISITE
Fishy Fencer Path

Swordfish attacks do increased damage. A sword for a nose! Convenient!

STRAIGHT AS AN ANGLER

3000 Gold

PREREQUISITE
Fishy Fencer Path

Hold **Attack 1** to charge a swordfish attack, release to dash through enemies causing them to take damage and be knocked back.

Flounder Pounder Path

SHARK SURPRISE

1700 Gold

PREREQUISITE
Flounder Pounder Path

ress **Attack 2** to throw the shark which ounces off of enemies' heads before landing.

TIME TO HAMMER

2200 Gold

PREREQUISITE
Flounder Pounder Path

Hammerhead shark attacks do increased damage. There is more than one reason why they are called hammerheads.

SHARK BITE BAIT

3000 Gold

PREREQUISITE
Flounder Pounder Path

Hold **Attack 1** to charge a shark attack, release to dash forward biting any enemies in the way.

WHAM-SHELL

"Brace for the Mace!"

MAXIMUM HEALTH	300
SPEED	50
ARMOR	18
CRITICAL HIT	6
ELEMENTAL POWER	25

LIGHTCORE

Wham-Shell was ruler of a kingdom deep in the oceans of Skylands that for a long time lived peacefully. That is, until his underwater utopia was invaded by a legion of oil-drilling trolls that scattered his people to the wind. Armed with a powerful mace that had been handed down from one king to the next for generations, Wham-Shell defeated the greedy trolls and drove them away. Soon after, he joined the Skylanders to help defend against this type of atrocity ever happening again.

"Embrace the mace" should be the motto for Portal Masters using Wham-Shell. An upgraded Malacostracan Mace crushes enemies so well, it makes every other Skylander jealous. Consider Starfish Bullets as something to use while you're moving into the range of your mace attacks. The Commander Crab Path upgrades Starfish Bullets considerably, turning a single shot into three target seeking starfish that also deal damage over time. Choosing the Captain Crustacean Path opens up two new mace combos. Mace Master allows Wham-Shell to walk around and clear out tightly packed enemies. Power Slam is a great way to crush a single enemy.

Special Quest

Irate Invertebrate

DEFEAT 6 ENEMIES WITH ONE POSEIDEN STRIKE.

Since you need to defeat six enemies with one attack, Chompies from any Story Mode Chapter or Arena challenge are your best bet. If your Poseiden Strike isn't hitting hard enough, look into the Captain Crustacean Path to upgrade it.

Basic Attacks

MALACOSTRACAN MACE

Press Attack 1 to swing Wham-Shell's mace at enemies. Press **Attack 1**, **Attack 1**, Hold **Attack 1** for a special combo.

STARFISH BULLETS

Press **Attack 2** to fire starfish bullets from Wham-Shell's mace.

Soul Gem Ability

CARAPACE PLATING

4000 Gold

PREREQUISITE
None

New armor makes Wham-Shell more resistant.

Upgrades

STARFISH GIGANTICUS

500 Gold

PREREQUISITE None

Hold **Attack 2** to charge up your Starfish Bullets attack.

KING'S MACE

700 Gold

PREREQUISITE None

Mace attacks deal increased damage.

STARFISHICUS SUPERIORALIS

900 Gold

PREREQUISITE None

Starfish Bullets deal increased damage.

POSEIDON STRIKE

1200 Gold

PREREQUISITE None

Press **Attack 3** to create an electrified field that damages enemies.

Captain Crustacean Path

CRUSTACEAN COMBOS

1700 Gold

PREREQUISITE
Captain Crustacean Path

Press **Attack 1**, **Attack 1**, Hold **Attack 2** for Mace Master. Press **Attack 1**, **Attack 1**, Hold **Attack 3** for Power Slam.

MEGA TRIDENT

2200 Gold

PREREQUISITE
Captain Crustacean Path

Mace attacks deal even MORE increased damage.

MACE OF THE DEEP

3000 Gold

PREREQUISITE
Captain Crustacean Path

Hold **Attack 3** to create a more powerful Poseidon Strike.

Commander Crab Path

TRIPLICATE STARFISH

1700 Gold

PREREQUISITE
Commander Crab Path

Shoot three Starfish at once.

SEMI-ETERNAL PURSUIT

2200 Gold

PREREQUISITE
Commander Crab Path

Starfish attack homes in on enemies.

NIGHTMARE HUGGERS

3000 Gold

PREREQUISITE
Commander Crab Path

Starfish latch onto enemies, doing continuous damage.

NIGHT SHIFT

"Roll with the Punches!"

MAXIMUM HEALTH	200
SPEED	35
ARMOR	4
CRITICAL HIT	8
ELEMENTAL POWER	25

From high up in the gloomy Batcrypt Mountains, Night Shift was a full-fledged baron and heir to a great fortune. But one day he decided to leave it all behind to pursue his dream as a prizefighter. It wasn't long before Night Shift became the undefeated phantom-weight champion of Skylands, famous for his massive uppercut and for having once bitten an opponent in the ring. Unfortunately, a rule change made teleportation illegal and Night Shift was forced to give up his belt, officially ending his career as a boxer. Crestfallen over being disqualified from a sport he loved so dearly, his spirits picked up when he was sought out by Master Eon, who told him that his skill as a fighter could be put to great use as a member of the Skylanders.

Body Soul Gem Ability

GENTLEMANLY

3500 Gold

PREREQUISITE

Find Night Shift's Soul Gem in Motleyville

All attacks do increased damage at full health. Quite sporting of the enemies to miss so often, yes...quite.

Legs Soul Gem Ability

GRAND ENTRANCE

3500 Gold

PREREQUISITE

Find Night Shift's Soul Gem in Motleyville

Slows down nearby enemies when appearing after a teleport.

SWAP FORCE

Night Shift's reach turns One-Two Punch into a ranged melee attack. The Prize Fighter Path adds damage to, and money from, enemies hit with Don't Move, Just Stick! Vampire's Bite returns a small amount of health and needs a second to recharge. The Proper Vampire Path adds damage over time and extra healing.

Ethereal Shift is a great way to escape a bad location, and the Warping Vortex Path helps in making a clean escape. A Batty Coach might be the best upgrade in the game, and it gets much better with the Underbat Path. Avoiding defeat twice is a great benefit in any situation.

Special Quest

King Of The Ring

HIT 10 ENEMIES AT ONCE WITH YOUR GIANT UPPERCUT PUNCH.

This quest requires the purchase of Night Shift's 1000 Gold upgrade, Don't Move, Just Stick! Next, find an area with 10 enemies that you can force to bunch up close to each other but that won't take out Night Shift before his move finishes charging.

BODY

Basic Attacks

ONE-TWO PUNCH

Press **Attack 1** to punch nearby enemies with enormous boxing gloves.

Upgrades

VAMPIRE'S BITE

300 Gold

PREREQUISITE None

Press **Attack 3** to bite enemies and regain some health.

STING LIKE A BAT

800 Gold

PREREQUISITE None

Punching does increased damage. Give em' the ol' one-two combo!

DON'T MOVE, JUST STICK!

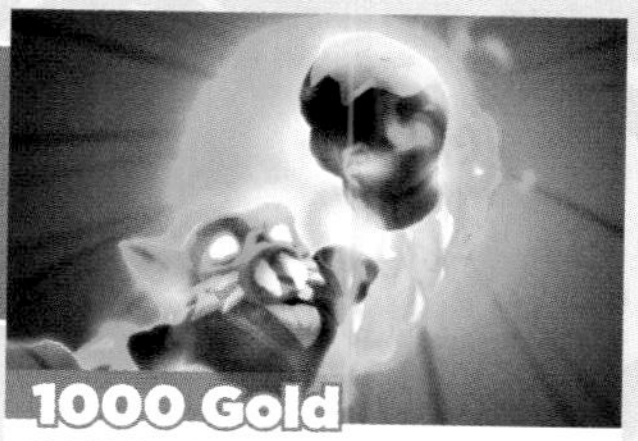

1000 Gold

PREREQUISITE None

Hold **Attack 1** to charge a punch, release to deal a massive uppercut to enemies.

Proper Vampire Path

INFECTIOUS SMILE

1500 Gold

PREREQUISITE
Proper Vampire Path

Vampire's Bite deals damage over time to their targets.

HEALTHY APPETITE

2000 Gold

PREREQUISITE
Proper Vampire Path

Vampire's Bite deals more damage with extra healing. Pack on the pounds!

Champion Fighter Path

PRIZE FIGHTER

1500 Gold

PREREQUISITE
Champion Fighter Path

Hold **Attack 1** to charge a punch, release to do an uppercut that causes enemies that are hit to take damage and drop money.

PAY DAY

2000 Gold

PREREQUISITE
Purchase Prize Fighter ability

Prize Fighter gives more money. Don't spend it all in one place like Moe Money and Moe Problems did.

LEGS

Basic Attacks

ETHEREAL SHIFT

Press **Attack 2** to turn into mist and teleport a short distance forward.

Upgrades

FLOAT LIKE A VAMPIRE

300 Gold

PREREQUISITE None

Press **Attack 2** to teleport and shoot out a projectile that damages nearby enemies.

FOGGY MOVEMENT

800 Gold

PREREQUISITE None

Speed is increased. Become faster than an old fogey!

A BATTY COACH

1000 Gold

PREREQUISITE None

A bat ally prevents being defeated one time. What a great pep talk!

Warping Vortex Path

VORTEX OF DOOM

1500 Gold

PREREQUISITE
Warping Vortex Path

Press **Attack 2** to teleport and create a large vortex that pull in enemies.

CLOSE TO DOOM

2000 Gold

PREREQUISITE
Purchase Vortex of Doom ability

Vortex of Doom now deals damage to enemies. Doooooom!

Underbat Path

ROUND 2

1500 Gold

PREREQUISITE
Underbat Path

A Batty Coach now gives a health boost when returning from defeat. Get back in there!

LUCK OF THE UNDERBAT

2000 Gold

PREREQUISITE
Underbat Path

A Batty Coach can be used twice. Okay, this time it's serious.

RATTLE SHAKE

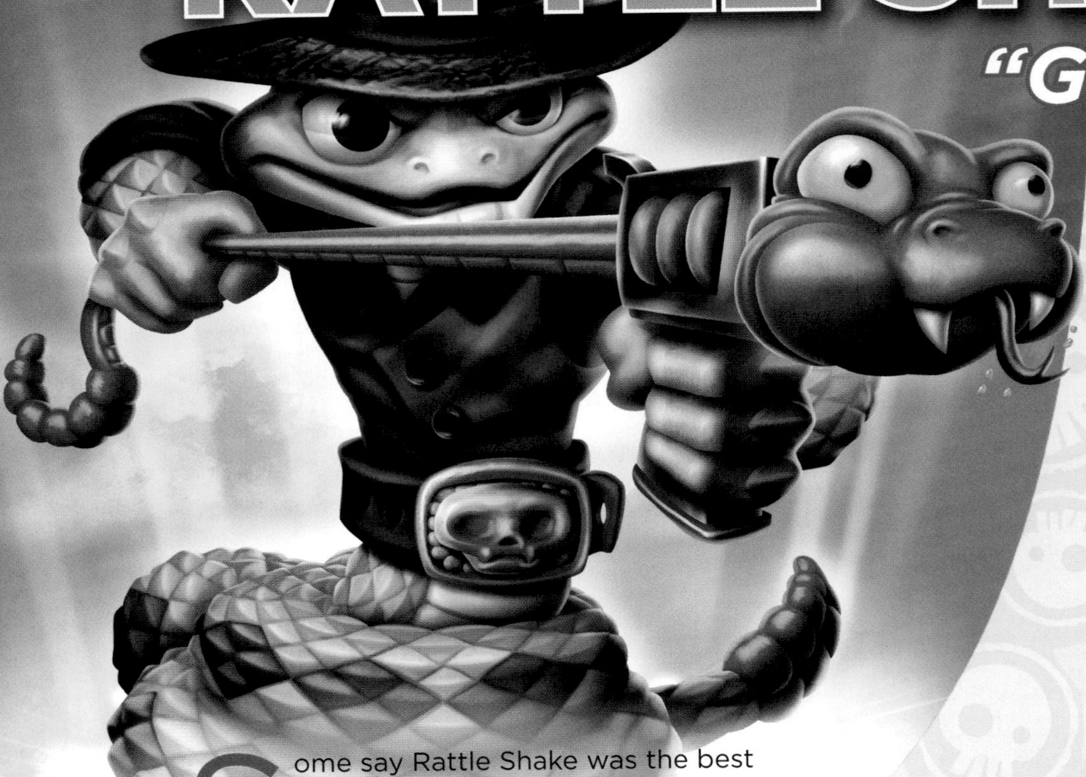

"Go Ahead - Snake My Day!"

MAXIMUM HEALTH	280
SPEED	43
ARMOR	12
CRITICAL HIT	8
ELEMENTAL POWER	25

Some say Rattle Shake was the best tracker in the Cloudbreak Islands. Others say he could strike the center of a Gold coin at a thousand paces. But the legend of Rattle Shake was immortalized when he found himself trapped by the Black Hat Gang, the infamous group of cowboys who literally were large cows...and evil ones at that. They threatened to plunder the local village unless Rattle Shake led them inside the magical volcano Mt. Cloudbreak, where they hoped to discover enchanted treasure. Badly outnumbered, the ever calm Rattle Shake magically summoned every snake in the area and overtook the notorious bovines in an epic fight. The tale of his heroism was heard by Master Eon, who then recruited him to the Skylanders.

SWAP FORCE

Spring Loaded Snake is a big upgrade to Snake's Venom and should be an early upgrade. The Coiled Ammunition Path adds damage over time to enemies hit with Spring Loaded Snakes. Always have Deputy Snake active. It deals extra damage to enemies, and it only gets better with the Deputy's Duty Path.

Tail Sweep is a basic melee attack with two upgrades, though Ssstampede is the upgrade that is affected by the upgrade paths. The Bone Herder Path adds an attack that hits enemies near Rattle Shake. The Grave Springer Path ends with him charging into enemies and inflicting extra damage at the end of the charge.

Body Soul Gem Ability

RAISE THE SNAKES

3500 Gold

PREREQUISITE

Find Rattle Shake's Soul Gem in Cascade Glade

Get a new skin which increases Critical Hit and absorbs damage. Absorbing damage causes the skin to shed then grow back after a short time.

Legs Soul Gem Ability

THE SNAKE-SKINNED KID

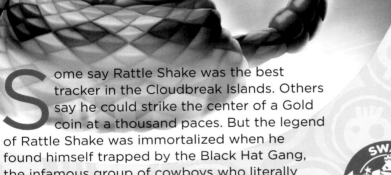

3500 Gold

PREREQUISITE

Find Rattle Shake's Soul Gem in Cascade Glade

Get a new skin which increases speed and absorbs damage. Absorbing damage causes the skin to shed then grow back after a short time.

Special Quest

Bouncing Biter

DAMAGE A TOTAL OF 100 ENEMIES WITH YOUR BOUNCING SNAKE SHOT.

You need to buy the Spring Loaded Snake ability before you can begin working on this quest. After you spend the 1000 gold, charge up the Snake Shot and fire it into groups of enemies whenver possible.

BODY

Basic Attacks

SNAKE'S VENOM

Press **Attack 1** to shoot snake venom at nearby enemies.

Upgrades

DEPUTY SNAKE

300 Gold

PREREQUISITE None

Press **Attack 3** to throw down a snake ally that will attack and slow nearby enemies.

FISTFUL OF SNAKES

800 Gold

PREREQUISITE None

All venom projectiles do increased damage.

SPRING LOADED SNAKE

1000 Gold

PREREQUISITE None

Hold **Attack 1** to charge a Snake Shot, release to shoot a snake that bounces between enemies and collects items along the way.

Deputy's Duty Path

NASTY SSSURPRISE

1500 Gold

PREREQUISITE
Deputy's Duty Path

Deputy Snake causes an acid explosion that damages enemies where it lands.

ARMED TO THE FANGS

2000 Gold

PREREQUISITE
Purchase Nasty Sssurprise ability

Nasty Sssurprise radius and Deputy Snake damage are increased.

Coiled Ammunition Path

SNAKE BITE

1500 Gold

PREREQUISITE
Coiled Ammunition Path

Spring Loaded Snake poisons the first enemy it hits, dealing damage over time.

THIS BITES

2000 Gold

PREREQUISITE
Purchase Snake Bite ability

Enemies poisoned by Spring Loaded Snake take more damage from Snake's Venom.

LEGS

Basic Attacks

TAIL SWEEP

Press **Attack 2** to sweep at nearby enemies with a quick tail strike.

Upgrades

BOUNCE THE BONES

300 Gold

PREREQUISITE None

Press **Attack 2** to shoot one bouncing bone projectile.

ON BRAND

800 Gold

PREREQUISITE None

Hold **Jump** to jump and smash down into the ground, damaging and knocking enemies away.

SSSTAMPEDE

1000 Gold

PREREQUISITE
Purchase Bounce the Bones ability

Press **Attack 2** to shoot three large bone projectiles at once.

Bone Herder Path

GOLIATH BONE SNAKE

1500 Gold

PREREQUISITE
Bone Herder Path

Hold **Attack 2** to charge Ssstampede, release to summon a giant bone snake from the ground.

DANCES WITH SNAKES

2000 Gold

PREREQUISITE
Purchase Goliath Bone Snake ability

Hold **Attack 2** while moving to charge Goliath Bone Snake, release to summon many bone snakes.

Grave Springer Path

SPURRED SPRING

1500 Gold

PREREQUISITE
Grave Springer Path

Hold **Attack 2** to charge Ssstampede, release to spring forward, damaging all enemies in the way.

GRAVEYARD SMASH

2000 Gold

PREREQUISITE
Purchase Spurred Spring ability

Spurred Spring causes tombstones to appear and damage enemies in a large area when landing.

TWIN BLADE CHOP CHOP

"Slice and Dice!"

MAXIMUM HEALTH	300
SPEED	50
ARMOR	24
CRITICAL HIT	2
ELEMENTAL POWER	25

SERIES 3

Chop Chop was once an elite warrior belonging to the ancient race of Arkeyan beings. Like many of the Arkeyans, he was created from a hybrid of elements—in his case, Undead, Magic, and Tech. Chop Chop is a relentless, highly-skilled solider who wields a sword and shield made of an indestructible metal. With the Arkeyans having vanished long ago, Chop Chop wandered Skylands for centuries looking for his creators. Eventually, he was found by Eon and recruited as a Skylander.

Even without a ranged attack, Chop Chop is never at a disadvantage against ranged opponents. Arkeyan Shield, especially after upgrades, keeps him safe while he advances on attackers. His lightning-fast sword strokes finish off the attackers before they can get in too many more shots.

While the Undead Defender Path conveys amazing defensive capabilities, Twin Blade Chop Chop's Wow Pow! ability all but demands the Vampiric Warrior Path. They're both fantastic options and you have the luxury of tailoring your choice to the challenge. Select Vampiric Warrior for speedy destruction of enemies or Undead Defender for more dangerous opponents.

Special Quest

Stalwart Defender

DEAL 10,000 DAMAGE USING BONE BRAMBLER.

Use Bone Brambler when opportunities present themselves. Purchase Cursed Bone Brambler, or use the Arkeyan Leap combo finisher, to complete this quest even faster.

Basic Attacks

ARKEYAN BLADE

Press **Attack 1** to slash away at your enemies with this ancient blade. Press **Attack 1**, **Attack 1**, hold **Attack 1** for a fencing combo.

ARKEYAN SHIELD

Hold **Attack 2** to absorb a limited amount of damage from most attacks, also deflects projectiles.

Soul Gem Ability

CURSED BONE BRAMBLER

4000 Gold

PREREQUISITE
Purchase Bone Brambler ability

Bone brambles deal extra damage.

Upgrades

SPIKED SHIELD BASH

500 Gold

PREREQUISITE None

While holding **Attack 2**, press **Attack 1** to Shield Bash an enemy. Distance increases with absorbed damage.

VAMPIRIC AURA

700 Gold

PREREQUISITE None

The Arkeyan Blade does extra damage and you regain health by defeating enemies.

SHIELD SPARTAN

900 Gold

PREREQUISITE
Purchase Spiked Shield Bash ability

Move faster and block more damage while holding **Attack 2**.

BONE BRAMBLER

1200 Gold

PREREQUISITE None

Press **Attack 3** to attack enemies with bone brambles.

Vampiric Warrior Path

ARKEYAN COMBAT MASTER

1700 Gold

PREREQUISITE
Vampiric Warrior Path

Press **Attack 1**, **Attack 1**, Hold **Attack 2** for Arkeyan Cyclone. Press **Attack 1**, **Attack 1**, Hold **Attack 3** for Arkeyan Leap.

ARKEYAN VORPAL BLADE

2200 Gold

PREREQUISITE
Vampiric Warrior Path

Sword attacks do even MORE increased damage.

DEMON BLADE OF THE UNDERWORLD

3000 Gold

PREREQUISITE
Vampiric Warrior Path

Swords have longer range and do maximum damage.

Undead Defender Path

ARKEYAN SPECTRAL SHIELD

1700 Gold

PREREQUISITE
Undead Defender Path

While holding **Attack 2**, press **Attack 1** to release absorbed damage on your foes.

SHIELD STUN BASH

2200 Gold

PREREQUISITE
Undead Defender Path

Shield Bash attacks stun enemies.

DEMON SHIELD OF THE SHADOWS

3000 Gold

PREREQUISITE
Undead Defender Path

Shield Bash does extra damage. Absorbed damage is automatically released.

Wow Pow!

DICE AND SLICE!

5000 Gold

PREREQUISITE
None

Hold **Attack 1** to charge up Dual Sword Mode, then release to unleash a furious, two-sword attack.

Use Dice and Slice! when you need to deal damage in a hurry. One downside of this ability is a large charge-up time, although he can move around while charging. A meter appears near Chop Chop that fills while Attack 1 is held. As soon as you release Attack 1, Chop Chop rushes ahead with his blades carving up everything in a straight line. It's possible to turn him, but he isn't very responsive.

PHANTOM CYNDER

"Volts and Lightning!"

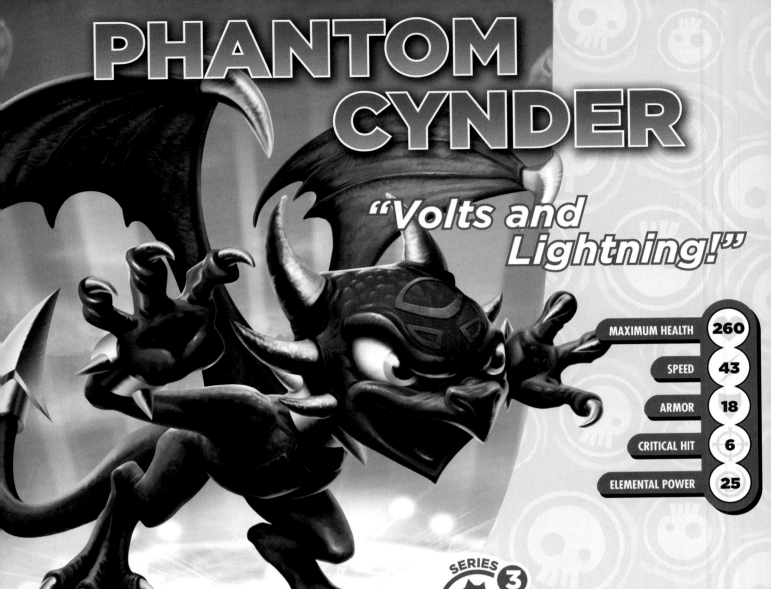

MAXIMUM HEALTH	260
SPEED	43
ARMOR	18
CRITICAL HIT	6
ELEMENTAL POWER	25

SERIES 3

While just an egg, Cynder was stolen by the henchmen of an evil dragon named Malefor and raised to do his bidding. For years, she spread fear throughout the land until she was defeated by Spyro the dragon and freed from the grip of Malefor. But dark powers still flow through her, and despite her desire to make amends for her past, most Skylanders try to keep a safe distance...just in case.

Cynder is a hit and run specialist, with a great ranged attack in Spectral Lightning, and a handy escape ability called Shadow Dash. Spectral Lightning chews through enemy health while they are a safe distance away. Shadow Dash provides a way out of melee combat (not Cynder's strong suit), and leaves behind ghosts who attack nearby enemies.

The Nether Welder Path improves Spectral Lightning and is the way to go if you prefer to handle all the dirty work in combat. The Shadowdancer path boosts Cynder's Shadow Dash and Ghosts, who can take down the small fries while you focus on larger enemies.

Special Quest

On The Haunt

DEFEAT 50 ENEMIES WITH YOUR GHOST ALLY.

The only tricky part to this quest is saving up the Gold to buy Haunted Ally. After that, it is just a matter of flying around with the Ghost in tow to rack up the enemy count.

Basic Attacks

SPECTRAL LIGHTNING

Press and hold **Attack 1** to shock enemies with bolts of lightning.

SHADOW DASH

Press **Attack 2** to dash forward in shadow mode, leaving ghostly allies in Cynder's wake.

Soul Gem Ability

HAUNTED ALLY

4000 Gold

PREREQUISITE
None

A ghost ally travels with you and damages nearby enemies.

Upgrades

CYNDER FLIGHT

500 Gold

PREREQUISITE None

Press **Attack 3** to fly.
Increased speed and resistance while flying.

BLACK LIGHTNING

700 Gold

PREREQUISITE None

Spectral Lightning does increased damage.

DOUBLE SPOOKY!

900 Gold

PREREQUISITE None

Ghosts do increased damage.

SHADOW REACH

1200 Gold

PREREQUISITE None

Shadow Dash Range is increased.

Nether Welder Path

UNSTABLE FORCES

1700 Gold

PREREQUISITE
Nether Welder Path

Hitting a ghost with Spectral Lightning makes it explode, damaging enemies around.

BREATH CONTROL

2200 Gold

PREREQUISITE
Nether Welder Path

Spectral Lightning hold duration is increased

BREATH OF POWER

3000 Gold

PREREQUISITE
Nether Welder Path

Spectral Lightning damages enemies in a larger area.

Shadow Dancer Path

DEATH BOUND

1700 Gold

PREREQUISITE
Shadow Dancer Path

Enemies hit by ghosts move slower.

GHOST HAUNTER

2200 Gold

PREREQUISITE
Shadow Dancer Path

Ghosts last longer, have a greater attack range, and do even more damage.

SHADOW STRIKE

3000 Gold

PREREQUISITE
Shadow Dancer Path

Shadow Dash deals damage to enemies.

Wow Pow!

SKULL-SPLOSION!

5000 Gold

PREREQUISITE
None

While in a Shadow Dash, hold **Attack 2** to morph into a giant skull, which explodes on release.

To make it easier to track Cynder's position, the skull appears just above the ground. The best part about Skull-Splosion! is that it knocks back enemies in addition to dealing damage. That's important for Cynder, who lacks a melee attack.

GRIM CREEPER

"Your Time is Up!"

MAXIMUM HEALTH	250
SPEED	43
ARMOR	6
CRITICAL HIT	8
ELEMENTAL POWER	25

LIGHTCORE

Grim Creeper is terrific against large groups of weaker enemies, but suffers against single enemies with large health bars. Scythe Swing is a decent melee attack but it is a bit slow. The third swing is a spinning scythe attack that hits all nearby enemies. Ghost Form is where Grim Creeper's strengths lie, and it requires practice to master it.

The Spooky Specter Path focuses on Ghost Form and allows the Living Armor to defend itself while Ghost Form is flying free. The Grim Scythe Style Path has two general upgrades and a nice boost to Poltergeist Scythe.

When he was young, Grim Creeper visited the prestigious Grim Acres School for Ghost Wrangling, hoping to attend as a student. But when the Scaremaster interviewed him, he found that Grim didn't have any of the usual training that other students had. Because of this, he was turned away. However, as the young Grim was about to leave, a herd of rampaging ghosts suddenly flooded the school, carrying away the faculty and leaving the students to fend for themselves. Grim Creeper stood his ground, not only defending the other students, but using his amazing reaping talents to fight back the ghosts and contain them until help could arrive. Now a Skylander, Grim is considered one of the best reapers ever to swing a scythe, proving that studies alone are no substitute for bravery, passion, and true heroic spirit.

Special Quest

Aggressive Outfit

HIT 10 ENEMIES IN A ROW WITH YOUR ARMOR WHILE IT TRAVELS BACK TO YOU.

Save this quest until Grim Creeper has advanced a few levels and upgraded Ghost Form. The amount of time required to touch 10 enemies with Ghost Form leaves him open to attacks. To give yourself additional help, set up in a narrow space (down a hall or in a single-room building) so the enemies are forced to bunch up.

Basic Attacks

SCYTHE SWING

Press **Attack 1** to swing a ghostly scythe at nearby enemies.

GHOST FORM

Press **Attack 2** to separate from the armor. Touch up to two enemies while in ghost form to mark them. Press **Attack 2** again to attack them with the living armor.

Soul Gem Ability

HELP FROM BEYOND

4000 Gold

PREREQUISITE
Find Grim Creeper's Soul Gem in Iron Jaw Gulch

A ghost ally appears from defeated enemies that seeks out and attacks other nearby enemies.

Upgrades

POLTERGEIST SCYTHE

500 Gold

PREREQUISITE None

Press **Attack 3** to knock enemies into the air with a spinning spectral scythe.

SPIRIT SCYTHE

700 Gold

PREREQUISITE None

Press **Attack 1** to swing a more powerful scythe that does increased damage.

SPOOK AND DESTROY

900 Gold

PREREQUISITE None

Press **Attack 2** to go into Ghost Form and leave behind Living Armor. Touch up to five enemies while in ghost form to mark them. Press **Attack 2** again to attack them with the living armor.

ARMORED AMORE

1200 Gold

PREREQUISITE None

Living Armor does increased damage when it flies back to Grim Creeper. Those pointy boots hurt!

Grim Scythe Style Path

SPHERE OF FEAR

1700 Gold

PREREQUISITE
Grim Scythe Style Path

Hold **Attack 3** for a short time to spin the scythe in a larger area and repeatedly hit enemies into the air.

GRAVE DANGER

2200 Gold

PREREQUISITE
Grim Scythe Style Path

Critical Hit is increased. Concentrated ghost particles make it easier to do more damage to enemies.

GHASTLY DAMAGE

3000 Gold

PREREQUISITE
Grim Scythe Style Path

All attacks do more damage for a short time after enemies are hit by the Living Armor.

Spooky Specter Path

IT'S ALIVE!

1700 Gold

PREREQUISITE
Spooky Specter Path

Press **Attack 2** to go into Ghost Form and leave behind Living Armor. Living Armor attacks nearby enemies when it is attacked.

HAUNTED HELP

2200 Gold

PREREQUISITE
Spooky Specter Path

Press **Attack 2** to go into Ghost Form and leave behind Living Armor. Enemies between ghost form and the living armor take damage.

SOUL SAMPLER

3000 Gold

PREREQUISITE
Spooky Specter Path

Regain some health for each enemy hit by Spook and Destroy.

ROLLER BRAWL

"Let's Roll!"

MAXIMUM HEALTH	260
SPEED	50
ARMOR	12
CRITICAL HIT	8
ELEMENTAL POWER	25

Roller Brawl grew up with five older vampire brothers, who were all very big and overprotective. Being the smallest of her family, she learned how to use her speed and cunning to become one of the toughest jammers in the Undead Roller Derby League. It was during the championship match when she caught the eye of Kaos, who fell head-over-heels in love with her. But when her overprotective brothers stepped in, Kaos had them captured by Drow and taken prisoner. Roller Brawl swore revenge, but even with her impressive skills, she was no match for an entire Drow army. Having developed a strong distaste for evil, she joined up with the Skylanders to fight against Kaos—while never giving up on her search for her brothers.

What Roller Brawl lacks in defense and ranged abilities is easily made up by Derby Dash. Roller Brawl has multiple attack options while dashing, including a headbutt that, when upgraded, keeps enemies flying helplessly through the air.

The Shadow Skater Path provides a bit more defense to her, but also gives Roller Claws a nice swiping attack that hits more enemies. The Skateblade Siren Path is the more aggressive choice. It increases damage output and provides more Skateblade options. Enemies chasing Roller Blade have as much to fear as the ones she's dashing at to attack.

Special Quest

Sharp Jammer

USE YOUR DEADLY CLOTHESLINE ABILITY TO TAKE OUT 10 ENEMIES AT ONCE.

After you purchase the Deadly Clothesline ability, find a place (an Arena or a Bonus Mission Map) where you can collect 10 Chompies together. Charge up Roller Brawl's Derby Dash and run back through the pile to complete the quest.

Basic Attacks

ROLLER CLAWS

Press **Attack 1** to slash at nearby enemies.

DERBY DASH

Press **Attack 2** to dash and damage nearby enemies when starting the dash. Press **Attack 1** or **Attack 2** to attack while dashing.

Soul Gem Ability

CURSED HELMET

4000 Gold

PREREQUISITE
Find Roller Brawl's Soul Gem in Iron Jaw Gulch

Press **Attack 2** while dashing to head-butt an enemy and create a curse link. Touch enemies with the link to damage them!

Upgrades

SKATEBLADES

500 Gold

PREREQUISITE None

Press **Attack 3** to shoot skate blades that travel along the ground towards enemies.

IMPACT SKATER

700 Gold

PREREQUISITE None

All attacks while dashing do increased damage.

DEADLY CLOTHESLINE

900 Gold

PREREQUISITE None

Hold **Attack 2** to charge a dash, release to dash forward and clothesline any enemies in the way.

AGGRESSION

1200 Gold

PREREQUISITE None

New sharpened blades make claw attacks do increased damage.

Shadow Skater Path

PIROUETTE

1700 Gold

PREREQUISITE
Shadow Skater Path

Hold **Attack 1** during a dash to do a spin attack that damages nearby enemies.

HARDENED HELM

2200 Gold

PREREQUISITE
Shadow Skater Path

A new helmet increases Roller Brawl's armor, reducing damage taken.

BULLRUSH

3000 Gold

PREREQUISITE
Shadow Skater Path

Hold **Attack 2** during a dash to bullrush enemies, damaging and knocking them back.

Skateblade Siren Path

SKATEBLADE TRAP

1700 Gold

PREREQUISITE
Skateblade Siren Path

Press **Attack 3** while dashing to leave behind a trap that damages nearby enemies.

CRITICAL CLAWS

2200 Gold

PREREQUISITE
Skateblade Siren Path

New claws increases Roller Brawl's Critical Hit chance.

SPINNING SAWS

3000 Gold

PREREQUISITE
Skateblade Siren Path

Hold **Attack 3** to create saws that spin around Roller Brawl.

MAGNA CHARGE

"Attract To Attack!"

MAXIMUM HEALTH	280
SPEED	50
ARMOR	18
CRITICAL HIT	6
ELEMENTAL POWER	25

Magna Charge came from the great race of Ultron robots, but was mysteriously created with a giant magnet head. This proved problematic, as his peers were all made of metal and were constantly being pulled towards him. As a result, Magna Charge was exiled to a faraway island, where he eventually learned to control his magnetic powers. After years of training, he returned to his home to demonstrate his abilities, but found everything completely destroyed. In searching for answers, Magna Charge caught the attention of Master Eon, who realized the unique Ultron soldier was a perfect candidate for the Skylanders.

Body Soul Gem Ability

MULTI BARRELLED

3500 Gold

PREREQUISITE

Find Magna Charge's Soul Gem in Mount Cloudbreak

Upgraded Magnet Cannon that shoots three projectiles at once!

Legs Soul Gem Ability

SUPER REPULSOR

3500 Gold

PREREQUISITE

Find Magna Charge's Soul Gem in Mount Cloudbreak

A new wheel makes thrown objects gain increased damage, range and speed.

SWAP FORCE

Magnet Cannon can overheat, but the Magnetic Armaments Path turns that into an advantage, and a fireball blast. Polarized Pickup grabs enemies into a powerful weapon for Magna Charge. With no enemies in range, a metallic object appears over his head. The Magnet Tuner Path adds a knock back and extra damage to Polarized Pickup.

Magneto Ball drags around an enemy caught in its electrical wake and lets you use them as a weapon. The Static Buildup Path focuses damage on enemies caught in Magneto Ball. The Drag Racer Path turns the dragged enemy into a stronger projectile.

Special Quest

Now That's Using Your Head

DEAL 5000 DAMAGE USING YOUR POLARIZED PICKUP.

Damage done to enemies being picked up and the damage done to enemies hit with the slam attack both count toward this total. Choose the Magnet Tuner Path to make this quest go faster.

BODY

Basic Attacks

MAGNET CANNON

Hold **Attack 1** to rapidly fire energy projectiles. Firing for too long will cause the cannon to overheat.

Upgrades

POLARIZED PICKUP

300 Gold

PREREQUISITE None

Press **Attack 3** to pick up enemies. Press **Attack 3** again to slam them. While active, loot will be drawn in from a distance!

PLASMA SHOTS

800 Gold

PREREQUISITE None

Hold **Attack 1** to rapidly shoot a Magnet Cannon that does increased damage. Projectiles heat up after a short time, dealing extra fire damage.

MAGNETIC BUILDUP

1000 Gold

PREREQUISITE
Purchase Polarized Pickup ability

Hold an object with Polarized Pickup for a short time, release it to deal extra damage.

Magnetic Armaments Path

DISCHARGE RECHARGE

1500 Gold

PREREQUISITE
Magnetic Armaments Path

Hold **Attack 1** to overheat the Magnet Cannon, release to shoot a large fireball.

HEAVY BLASTER

2000 Gold

PREREQUISITE
Magnetic Armaments Path

Magnet Cannon does even more damage.

Magnet Tuner Path

BURST PICKUP

1200 Gold

PREREQUISITE
Magnet Tuner Path

Picking up enemies with Polarized Pickup will knock back nearby enemies.

MAGNETIC PERSONALITY

2000 Gold

PREREQUISITE
Magnet Tuner Path

Magnet attacks do increased damage. Two-Ton's Law states: if it has mass, it can be slammed.

LEGS

Basic Attacks

MAGNETO BALL

Press **Attack 2** to drag an enemy around. Press **Attack 2** again to launch them forward. Large enemies cannot be dragged.

Upgrades

EJECT

300 Gold

PREREQUISITE None

Press **Attack 3** while dragging an object or enemy to throw it behind and boost forward.

RAD WHEELS

800 Gold

PREREQUISITE None

Speed is increased. Brand new developments in magnet wheels!

DRAG CAPACITY

1000 Gold

PREREQUISITE None

Two enemies can be dragged at once while dashing.

Static Buildup Path

SHOCK STOP

1500 Gold

PREREQUISITE
Static Buildup Path

Press **Attack 1** while dragging an enemy to drop it in front of you and shock it.

CRASH TEST

2000 Gold

PREREQUISITE
Purchase Shock Stop ability

Shock Stop and Eject do increased damage.

Drag Racer Path

RAPID REPEL

1500 Gold

PREREQUISITE
Drag Racer Path

Press **Attack 1** while dragging an object or enemy to shoot it without stopping.

OPPOSITES REPEL

2000 Gold

PREREQUISITE
Purchase Rapid Repel ability

Rapid Repel does increased damage. Repulsive!

SPY RISE

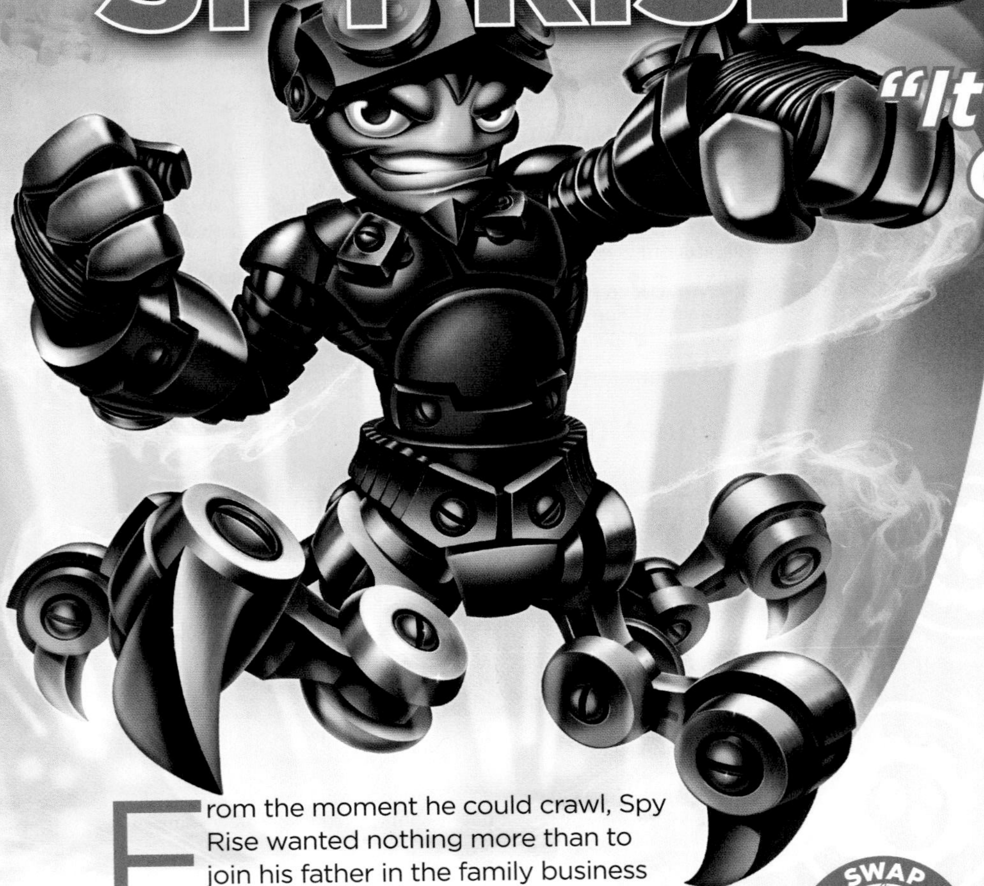

"It's Classified!"

MAXIMUM HEALTH	270
SPEED	43
ARMOR	18
CRITICAL HIT	8
ELEMENTAL POWER	25

From the moment he could crawl, Spy Rise wanted nothing more than to join his father in the family business as a private investigator. But after being hired by a shadowy figure to gather information on the Cloudbreak Islands, his father vanished, leaving Spy Rise alone to search for answers. He scoured the land for clues, using his immense skill in reconnaissance to track down his missing father, but all roads came up empty. Then one day, he received a tip from none other than Master Eon, which led him to a hidden lair near Mt. Cloudbreak, where he not only found his long lost father, but also uncovered an evil plot to take control of the magical volcano during the next eruption ceremony. With his father safe, Spy Rise decided to pursue a new career—as a member of the Skylanders.

SWAP FORCE

Spyder Blaster damages and slows down enemies, a big help in setting up Super Spy Scanner S3, which hits incredibly hard when charged. The Web Spinning Path allows for constant firing of Cocoon Spinner, but leaves Spy Rise stationary. The Shock Spy Path allows movement, but you must charge and aim Electroweb Pulsebomb.

Spyder Climb is a clean escape ability, going into the air where no enemies can follow. The Fire Tech Path adds a flamethrower attack that lasts as long as the button is held. The Electro Tech Path adds a cannon that requires charging each time it's used.

Body Soul Gem Ability

SPY WITH A GOLDEN HAND

3500 Gold

PREREQUISITE

Find Spy Rise's Soul Gem in Boney Islands

Gain a new Golden blaster that shoots five projectiles at once.

Legs Soul Gem Ability

OMEGA SKY LASER

3500 Gold

PREREQUISITE

Find Spy Rise's Soul Gem in Boney Islands

Hold **Attack 1** while in the sky to shoot down a massive laser that stuns enemies.

Special Quest

Finishing Touch

SPYDER STING 25 ENEMIES.

Spyder Sting costs 800 Gold to purchase, and it's a great way to restore health when there aren't any food drops available. Look for an icon to appear near enemies with low health. Move close to them to initiate Spyder Sting (it looks like a short blade attack) to take them out and restore some health to Spy Rise. Do it 24 more times and the quest is complete!

BODY

Basic Attacks

SPYDER BLASTER

Press **Attack 1** to shoot three spyder projectiles that slow any enemy it hits.

Upgrades

SUPER SPY SCANNER S3

300 Gold

PREREQUISITE None

Hold **Attack 3** for a short time to scan a nearby enemy, release to shoot a high-powered laser. Fully scanned enemies take additional damage.

SPYDER STING

800 Gold

PREREQUISITE None

Press **Attack 1** next to an enemy with low health to sting them and steal some health.

FUTURE TECH

1000 Gold

PREREQUISITE
Purchase Super Spy Scanner S3 ability

Super Spy Scanner S3 and Spyder Blaster do increased damage.

Web Spinner Path

COCOON SPINNER

1500 Gold

PREREQUISITE
Web Spinner Path

Hold **Attack 1** to shoot a stream of web projectiles that slow and cocoon enemies.

EXPERIMENTAL WEBS

2000 Gold

PREREQUISITE
Purchase Cocoon Spinner ability

Cocoon Spinner does increased damage. The experiment seems to be going well!

Shock Spy Path

ELECTROWEB PULSE BOMB

1500 Gold

PREREQUISITE
Shock Spy Path

Hold **Attack 1** to charge a web bomb, release to throw it, which damages and slows enemies in a large area.

IMPROVED EPD

2000 Gold

PREREQUISITE
Purchase Electroweb Pulse Bomb ability

Electroweb Pulse Bomb does increased damage and has a larger explosion.

LEGS

Basic Attacks

SPYDER CLIMB

Press **Attack 2** to climb into the air with electro web, dropping back down will damage nearby enemies.

Upgrades

SPYDER MINE

300 Gold

PREREQUISITE None

Press **Attack 2** to climb into the air and drop a spyder mine that will seek out and explode on nearby enemies.

SPYDER MINE 002

800 Gold

PREREQUISITE
Purchase Spyder Mine ability

Press **Attack 2** to climb into the air, dropping two spyder mines at once.

RAPID LASER LEGS V17

1000 Gold

PREREQUISITE None

Press **Attack 2** to climb into the air, Hold **Attack 2** while in the air to drop down and shoot electric bolts at enemies.

Fire Tech Path

FOOT-MOUNTED FLAME

1500 Gold

PREREQUISITE
Fire Tech Path

Hold **Attack 2** to shoot flames from the feet, damaging any enemies that come too close.

BLUE FLAME

2000 Gold

PREREQUISITE
Purchase Foot-Mounted Flame ability

Flamethrower deals increased damage. Experimental feet fuel turns flames blue!

Electro Tech Path

PULSE CANNON

1500 Gold

PREREQUISITE
Electro Tech Path

Hold **Attack 2** to charge a laser blast, release to shoot a massive wave of energy at enemies.

ADVANCED PULSE CANNON

2000 Gold

PREREQUISITE
Purchase Pulse Cannon ability

Increase damage of pulse cannon. At least this one isn't experimental, right?

COUNTDOWN

"I'm the Bomb!"

MAXIMUM HEALTH	290
SPEED	43
ARMOR	12
CRITICAL HIT	8
ELEMENTAL POWER	25

LIGHTCORE

Countdown was discovered by a group of Yetis who were snowboarding one particularly chilly morning when they came across a big bomb encased in ice. After bringing it back to their cabin, they were shocked when it actually came to life. No one, not even Countdown himself, has any memory of where he came from or how he ended up frozen in the mountains. Since Countdown became a Skylander, Master Eon has been graciously trying to help piece together fragments of his past. But this has proven difficult, as Countdown loses some of his memory every time he explodes, which happens a lot. In the meantime, Countdown has enjoyed working with Master Eon and fighting alongside the Skylanders to defend their world against evil—even though he occasionally forgets what he is doing.

There are two steps to follow when you're playing as Countdown. Step one: fill the screen with things that explode. Step two: fill the screen with explosions. Countdown fires rockets that can explode, uses his head as a timebomb, and launches mobile bomb allies that chase down enemies and explode near them. Countdown's Soul Gem ability allows him to even detonate himself!

The Boom Buddies Forever Path improves the bomb allies by allowing more of them, and increasing their damage potential. The Rocketeer Path adds two rockets to Controlled Burst and increases the radius of its explosion.

Special Quest
Out With A Bang
DEFEAT 10 ENEMIES AT ONCE WITH YOUR SELF-DESTRUCT EXPLOSION ABILITY.

Complete this quest against a large group of Chompies (an Arena or Challenge Map works best) where you can gather them in a narrow space (down a hall or in a single-room building) so the enemies are forced to group up and are caught in the explosion.

Basic Attacks

ROCKET BLAST

Press **Attack 1** to fire a rocket

BOMB HEAD

Press **Attack 2** to shoot a Bomb Head that explodes and damages enemies in a large area.

Soul Gem Ability

SELF-DESTRUCT

4000 Gold

PREREQUISITE
Find Countdown's Soul Gem in Cascade Glade

Hold **Attack 2** for a short amount of time to cause a massive amount of damage to every enemy nearby.

Upgrades

CONTROLLED BURST

500 Gold

PREREQUISITE None

Hold **Attack 1** to charge a rocket, release to shoot a large rocket that deals increased damage.

ROARING ROCKETS

700 Gold

PREREQUISITE None

Rockets do increased damage. Kaboom!

EXPLOSIVE FRIENDSHIP

900 Gold

PREREQUISITE None

Press **Attack 3** to summon a bomb ally that explodes near enemies.

HEFTY CONCUSSION

1200 Gold

PREREQUISITE None

Press **Attack 2** to shoot a more powerful Bomb Head that does increased damage. Press **Attack 2** again to detonate the Bomb Head.

Boom Buddies Forever Path

BOOM BUDDIES

1700 Gold

PREREQUISITE
Boom Buddies Forever Path

ress **Attack 3** to summon a bomb ally that xplodes near enemies. Can now have four omb allies at once.

BOMBING BLITZERS

2200 Gold

PREREQUISITE
Boom Buddies Forever Path

Bomb allies do increased damage. Adorable and explosive.

LINGERING SPARKS

3000 Gold

PREREQUISITE
Boom Buddies Forever Path

Bomb allies shoot flames from their fuses that damage nearby enemies.

Rocketeer Path

RIPLE THREAT

1700 Gold

PREREQUISITE
Rocketeer Path

old **Attack 1** to charge a rocket, lease to shoot a large rocket and two maller rockets.

WARHEAD HANDS

2200 Gold

PREREQUISITE
Rocketeer Path

All rocket attacks do even more damage. Danger! Explosive hugs!

MEGA MORTAR

3000 Gold

PREREQUISITE
Rocketeer Path

Controlled Burst does increased damage in a larger area.

HEAVY DUTY SPROCKET

"The Fix is In!"

MAXIMUM HEALTH	240
SPEED	43
ARMOR	30
CRITICAL HIT	2
ELEMENTAL POWER	25

SERIES 2

Sprocket was raised with all the privileges of a rich, proper Goldling, but she cared little for fancy things. Instead, she spent most of her time growing up in her uncle's workshop, learning how to build and fix his many mechanical inventions. But everything changed on the day her uncle mysteriously vanished. When she eventually discovered that Kaos had been behind his disappearance, she constructed a battle suit and went after him, leaving the luxury and comfort of her family's wealth behind. From that moment on, Sprocket was dedicated to fighting the forces of evil, while never losing hope that she would be reunited with her beloved uncle.

Playing as Sprocket demands patience since Turret Gun-o-Matic, one of her primary abilities, requires a bit of set up time. When the ability is completely upgraded, Sprocket can set up one turret and drive around in another one as a tank! The good news is that she can buy time to set up turrets through the use of Wrench Whack, a good melee ability, and Bouncing Betty Mines.

Go with the Operator Path when mobility is needed. It provides more versatility with her Wrench. The Gearhead Path boosts her turret (and tank), which works best when enemies come at her, like during Survival Challenges.

Special Quest

Mined Your Step

DEFEAT 50 ENEMIES USING THE LANDMINE GOLF ATTACK.

After you acquire Landmine Golf and become proficient aiming it, you should complete this quest in no time. To complete it quickly, go to any challenge that uses Chompies as the primary enemy.

Basic Attacks

WRENCH WHACK

Press **Attack 1** to swing the big wrench. Press **Attack 1**, **Attack 1**, Hold **Attack 1** to perform a combo.

TURRET GUN-O-MATIC

Press **Attack 2** to build a turret that shoots enemies. Climb inside by facing the turret and pressing **Attack 2**. Press **Jump** to exit the turret.

Soul Gem Ability

LANDMINE GOLF

4000 Gold

PREREQUISITE
Purchase Bouncing Betty Mines ability

Facing a mine, press **Attack 1** to send it flying towards enemies.

Upgrades

AUTO TURRET V2

500 Gold

PREREQUISITE None

Turret Gun-o-Matic deals increased damage and has more HP.

BOUNCING BETTY MINES

700 Gold

PREREQUISITE None

Press **Attack 3** to toss mines that explode when enemies are near.

2 TIMES THE TURRETS

900 Gold

PREREQUISITE None

Can have two active turrets at once.

TANKS A LOT!

1200 Gold

PREREQUISITE
Purchase Auto Turret V2 ability

When climbing inside a turret, it transforms into a drivable assault tank.

Gearhead Path

MINE DROP

1700 Gold

PREREQUISITE
Gearhead Path

Vhile driving a tank, press **Attack 3** to drop mines out of :he back.

EXPLODING SHELLS

2200 Gold

PREREQUISITE
Gearhead Path

Turret and Tank shells now explode on contact, doing extra damage.

SELF-DESTRUCT SYSTEM

3000 Gold

PREREQUISITE
Gearhead Path

When a Turret or Tank expires, it detonates and damages anything nearby.

Operator Path

SPROCKET COMBOS

1700 Gold

PREREQUISITE
Operator Path

'ress **Attack 1**, **Attack 1**, Hold **ttack 2** for Power Surge. Press **ttack 1**, **Attack 1**, Hold **Attack 3** ›r Mines O' Plenty.

MONKEY WRENCH

2200 Gold

PREREQUISITE
Operator Path

Better wrench does increased damage.

ALL MINES

3000 Gold

PREREQUISITE
Operator Path

Sprocket can now deploy three Bouncing Betty Mines at once.

Wow Pow!

TANKS FOR THE NEW TOY!

5000 Gold

PREREQUISITE
Purchase Tanks a Lot! ability

While driving a tank, hold **Attack 2** to fire a Tesla Cannon. Turrets and Tank do increased damage.

Tanks For the New Toy! is a beam attack you can sweep across the field. It doesn't do much damage to a single target, but is great against large number of enemies. The downside to Tanks for the New Toy is the amount of time needed to get it up and running. Building the tank takes some time, and each Tesla Cannon blast requires charging time before it is discharged.

BIG BANG TRIGGER HAPPY

"No Gold, no Glory!"

MAXIMUM HEALTH	200
SPEED	50
ARMOR	30
CRITICAL HIT	10
ELEMENTAL POWER	25

SERIES 3

Trigger Happy is more than his name—it's his solution to every problem. Nobody knows from where he came. He just showed up one day in a small village, saving it from a group of terrorizing bandits by blasting gold coins everywhere with his custom-crafted shooters. Similar tales were soon heard from other villages, and his legend quickly grew. Now everyone in all of Skylands knows of the crazy goldslinger that will take down any bad guy...usually without bothering to aim.

Both of Trigger Happy's basic attacks are good options. Golden Pistols doesn't do much damage per shot, but has an excellent rate of fire. Trigger Happy also lobs objects at enemies, inflicting good damage when they make contact.

The Golden Frenzy Path powers up Golden Pistols in everyway. The hit harder, can be charged longer, and its bullets bounce off walls!The Golden Money Bags path is the way to go if you prefer dealing with enemies by throwing heavy objects at them. The objects damage multiple enemies and there's a nice game of chance that could result in deploying a mine.

Special Quest

Holding Gold

SAVE UP 50,000 GOLD.

Some quests require some patience. This quest demands a great deal of it! Use everything available (such as Legendary Treasures and the Sky Diamond figure) to help boost the amount of gold you can earn on each level.

Basic Attacks

GOLDEN PISTOLS

Press **Attack 1** to shoot rapid fire coins out of both Golden Pistols.

LOB GOLDEN SAFE

Press **Attack 2** to lob golden safes at your enemies.

Soul Gem Ability

INFINITE AMMO

4000 Gold

PREREQUISITE
Purchase Golden Machine Gun ability

Golden Machine Gun has unlimited Ammo.

Upgrades

GOLDEN SUPER CHARGE

500 Gold

PREREQUISITE None

Hold **Attack 1** to charge up your Golden Pistols, then release to fire a bullet that does extra damage.

POT O'GOLD

700 Gold

PREREQUISITE None

Throw a Pot of Gold, which deals increased damage.

GOLDEN MEGA CHARGE

900 Gold

PREREQUISITE
Purchase Super Charge abitlity

Charge up your Golden Pistols longer to do even MORE damage.

GOLDEN MACHINE GUN

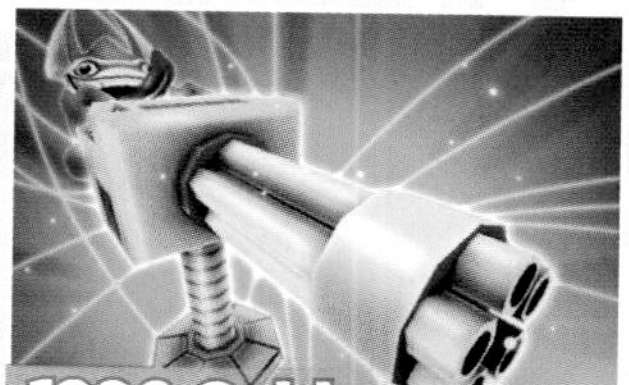

1200 Gold

PREREQUISITE None

Hold **Attack 3** to activate Golden Machine Gun and swivel its aim using the left control stick.

Golden Frenzy Path

HAPPINESS IS A GOLDEN GUN

1700 Gold

PREREQUISITE
Golden Frenzy Path

Golden Pistols deal increased damage.

BOUNCING BULLETS

2200 Gold

PREREQUISITE
Golden Frenzy Path

Golden Pistols' bullets bounce off walls.

GOLDEN YAMATO BLAST

3000 Gold

PREREQUISITE
Purchase Happiness is a Golden Gun

Charge up your Golden Pistols even longer to do maximum damage.

Golden Money Bags Path

JUST THROWING MONEY AWAY

1700 Gold

PREREQUISITE
Golden Money Bags Path

Lob attack has longer range.

COINSPLOSION

2200 Gold

PREREQUISITE
Golden Money Bags Path

Lob attacks explode in a shower of damaging coins.

HEADS OR TAILS

3000 Gold

PREREQUISITE
Golden Money Bags Path

Toss a giant coin that deals extra damage. If it lands on heads, it turns into a mine, damaging enemies that touch it.

Wow Pow!

ROCKET RIDE!

5000 Gold

PREREQUISITE
Purchase Golden Super Charge ability

While holding **Attack 1**, press and hold **Attack 2** to charge up a golden rocket, then release to ride it as a missile.

You can't move while holding Attack 2, only change which way Trigger Happy faces. Rocket Ride! takes a few seconds to charge, and it automatically fires when it's ready. Let go of Attack 2 to jump off, although the resulting explosion does not damage Trigger Happy.

WIND-UP

"All Wound Up!"

MAXIMUM HEALTH	250
SPEED	43
ARMOR	12
CRITICAL HIT	4
ELEMENTAL POWER	25

Built in the enchanted workshop of a toymaker obsessed with time, Wind-Up was created to help keep his massive collection of complicated clocks working perfectly. But when the toymaker popped out of existence in a freak accident caused by putting hot cocoa in a cross-wired Arkeyan oven, Wind-Up found himself surrounded by an invading Cyclops platoon—with an eye towards claiming the toymaker's secrets for themselves. Using split-second timing, clockwork strategy, and his totally wound up energy, Wind-Up bravely sprang into action and handily defeated the Cyclops. He later joined the Skylanders to help swing the pendulum the other way in their fight against anything that threatens Skylands.

Even experienced players may need time to feel comfortable overcranking Wind-Up and using overcranked time effectively. The increased speed and damage dealt while overcranked is offset by the time it takes to build it back up. Wind-Up is capable of demolishing enemies in a hurry, but may end up being easy pickings if the overcrank timer expires at a bad time.

The Toy Box Path is a cautious approach to Wind-Up, with a ranged attack boost, but that's only because the Winder Path includes an ability that requires taking damage. Wind-Up needs to be in the thick of fights to get the most out of it!

Special Quest

All Wound Up

DEAL A TOTAL OF 2500 DAMAGE WHILE OVERCRANKED.

As long as you remember that the Attack 2 button exists, you should complete this quest quickly. Buy a few basic upgrades to make it go even faster.

Basic Attacks

SHORT CIRCUIT

Press **Attack 1** to attack nearby enemies with sparking claws.

WIND UP!

Press **Attack 2** to wind up and damage nearby enemies. Winding up is needed to perform more powerful attacks.

Soul Gem Ability

SPRING-LOADED CRANK

4000 Gold

PREREQUISITE
Find Wind-Up's Soul Gem in Iron Jaw Gulch

Speed is increased. Automatically wind up while running.

Upgrades

OVERCRANK STABILIZER

500 Gold

PREREQUISITE None

Press **Attack 2** to rapidly fill the wind up meter. When full, press **Attack 2** again to overcrank. During overcrank press **Attack 1** to cause a large explosion that damages nearby enemies.

WINDING WEAPON

700 Gold

PREREQUISITE None

Press **Attack 2** to wind up, dealing increased damage and pulling enemies in.

SPRING SHOT

900 Gold

PREREQUISITE None

Press **Attack 3** to shoot a spring shot that launches enemies into the air. Attacking launched enemies will deal automatic critical damage!

POWER PISTONS

1200 Gold

PREREQUISITE None

Press **Attack 1** to deal increased punching damage.

Toy Box Path

CYMBALS

1700 Gold

PREREQUISITE
Toy Box Path

Hold **Attack 1** to charge a cymbal attack, release to attack all enemies in the way with a pair of cymbals.

CRASH CYMBALS

2200 Gold

PREREQUISITE
Purchase Cymbals ability

Cymbal attacks do increased damage. An easy way to crash any party!

TOY GUN

3000 Gold

PREREQUISITE
Toy Box Path

Hold **Attack 3** to shoot rapid fire suction cup projectiles at enemies.

Winder Path

WINDUP PUNCH

1700 Gold

PREREQUISITE
Winder Path

Hold **Attack 1** to charge a boxing glove punch, release to deliver a massive punch to enemies.

AUTO WIND UP

2200 Gold

PREREQUISITE
Winder Path

Taking damage automatically adds to winding up.

POWER CRANK

3000 Gold

PREREQUISITE
Winder Path

Press **Attack 2** rapidly to begin overcranking which now pulls enemies in and deals bonus damage.

GRILLA DRILLA

"If There's a Drill, There's a Way!"

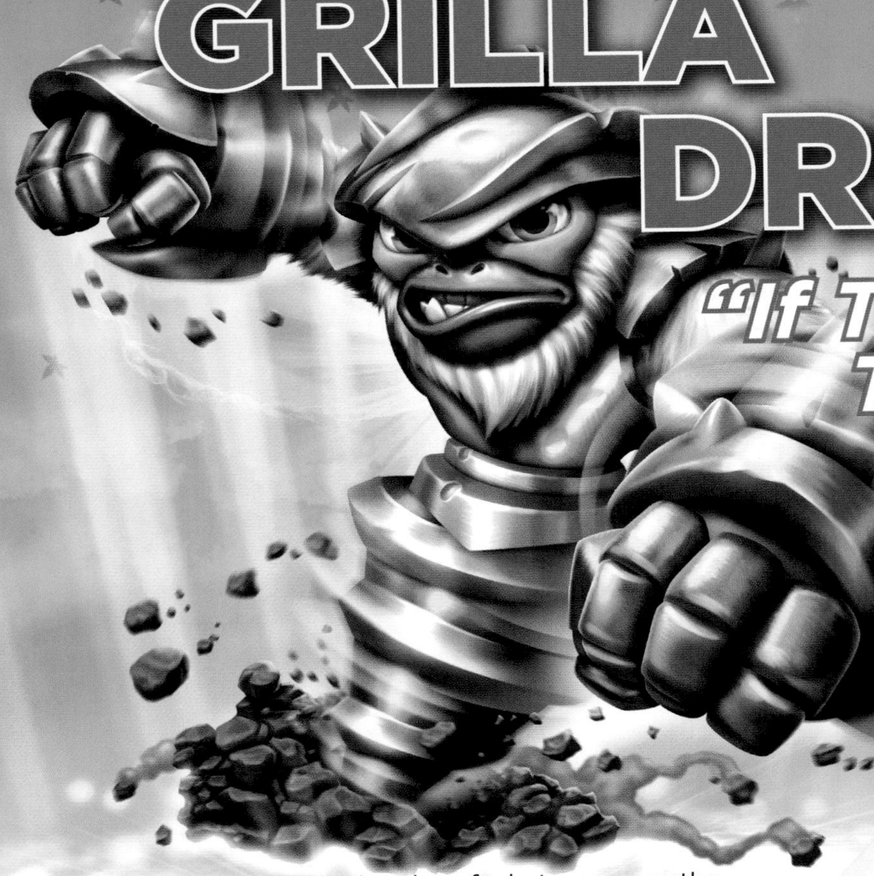

MAXIMUM HEALTH	290
SPEED	43
ARMOR	24
CRITICAL HIT	4
ELEMENTAL POWER	25

In the distant jungles of what was once the sprawling subterranean city of the Drilla Empire, Grilla Drilla served among the guards for the Drilla King. Every seven years, the king would select the bravest and strongest guard to become their leader. It was during the last selection ceremony that a troll mining operation broke through the ground above them and quickly snatched the king, wanting to know the location of the famed Drilla Diamond. Having never ventured above ground, Grilla Drilla risked everything to defeat the trolls and rescue the Drilla King. In return for his bravery, Grilla was selected as the new leader. But he instead decided to join the Skylanders, where he could protect even more residents of Skylands.

Body Soul Gem Ability

RING OF THE GOLDEN MONKEY

3500 Gold

PREREQUISITE
Find Grilla Drilla's Soul Gem in Iron Jaw Gulch; Purchase Silverback ability

Arm Drills become shiny Gold, making punch attacks do extra damage.

Legs Soul Gem Ability

ADAPTIVE NATURE

3500 Gold

PREREQUISITE
Find Grilla Drilla's Soul Gem in Iron Jaw Gulch

All plants gain thorns that damage and push back enemies that step on them.

SWAP FORCE

Punchy Monkey hits multiple enemies in a straight line at the cost of a longer delay between swings. The Drilling Punches Path turns every third consecutive button press into a two-fisted punch. Monkeys summoned with Monkey Call pick their own targets and depart quickly. The Monkey Master Path doubles the number of summoned monkeys.

After purchasing every basic upgrade for Planted Turret, you can plant either a regular turret or a bomb plant depending on the situation. The Coconut Caretaker Path gives Planted Turret explosive shells that damage enemies in an area. The Banana Blaster Path increases the rate of fire for Planted Turrets.

Special Quest

Monkeys Mean Business

DEAL A TOTAL OF 2000 DAMAGE TO ENEMIES WITH SUMMONED MONKEYS.

There's rarely a bad time to summon monkeys to help you take down enemies. Choosing the Monkey Master Path helps, but you'll get this quest quickly enough without it.

BODY

Basic Attacks

PUNCHY MONKEY

Press **Attack 1** to punch at nearby enemies.

Upgrades

MONKEY CALL

PREREQUISITE None

Press **Attack 3** to summon a pair of crazy monkeys!

SILVERBACK

PREREQUISITE None

Press **Attack 1** to unleash punches that deal increased damage.

REACHING MANDRILL

PREREQUISITE None

Press **Attack 1** to punch at a longer range.

Monkey Master Path

TEAM MONKEY

PREREQUISITE
Monkey Master Path

Monkey Call summons four monkeys at once!

KING OF THE JUNGLE

PREREQUISITE
Monkey Master Path

Monkey Call does increased damage. They're going bananas!

Drilling Punches Path

DOUBLE PUNCH

PREREQUISITE
Drilling Punches Path

Press **Attack 1** three times to attack with both drills.

PRIMATE POWER

PREREQUISITE
Purchase Double Punch Ability

Double Punch does increased damage. POW!

LEGS

Basic Attacks

PLANTED TURRET

Press **Attack 2** to plant a coconut turret that attacks nearby enemies.

Upgrades

EXPLOSIVE GROWTH

PREREQUISITE None

Hold **Attack 2** to charge a turret, release to plant a bomb plant that explodes and damages enemies nearby.

SPREADING LIKE WEEDS

PREREQUISITE
Purchase Explosive Growth ability

Explosive Growth bomb plants will explode into three smaller bombs.

NATURE'S BOUNTY

PREREQUISITE None

Press **Attack 2** to plant a coconut turret that shoots at nearby enemies. Press **Attack 2** again to plant another.

Coconut Caretaker Path

THIS IS COCONUTS!

PREREQUISITE
Coconut Caretaker Path

Turret projectiles now explode, causing damage to enemies in a small area.

COCONUT MAYHEM

PREREQUISITE
Coconut Caretaker Path

Coconuts do increased damage. Go nuts for the new and improved Coconut Blaster!

Banana Blaster Path

BANANA SPLIT

PREREQUISITE
Banana Blaster Path

Coconut turret upgrades into a rapid shooting Banana turret.

GO BANANAS!

PREREQUISITE
Purchase Banana Split ability

Bananas do increased damage. Delicious!

STINK BOMB

"Clear the Air!"

MAXIMUM HEALTH	270
SPEED	43
ARMOR	12
CRITICAL HIT	6
ELEMENTAL POWER	25

Stink Bomb studied martial arts under one of the greatest ninja masters in history who believed that surprise was the key to finding your true self. Thus, his master would constantly jump out and frighten him, hoping that it would scare Stink Bomb into finding his innermost strength. On one such occasion, Stink Bomb was so surprised that he instinctively released a cloud of vapor so pungent that it caused his master to disappear and never return. With this newly discovered ability, Stink Bomb developed his own form of martial arts known as Kung Fume, and wandered the land teaching it to all those who wished to learn. It was not long before the news (and smell) of this new form reached Master Eon, who sought out the young ninja at once.

SWAP FORCE

Skunk-Fu Stars begins as a rapid-fire, but weak, ranged attack. The Sweeping Skunk-Fu upgrade is a charged attack that hits much harder. If you choose The Art of Skunk-Fu Path, always keep its shield active. The Art of Acorns Path adds a two-fisted ranged attack to the One-Inch Palm ability.

Skunk Cloud makes Stink Bomb invisible to enemies and upgrades boost its damaging properties. Choosing the Skunk Cloud Controller Path allows Stink Bomb to leave two damaging clouds while going into stealth. The Sneaky Tricks Path upgrades leave damaging items in Bomb's path.

Body Soul Gem Ability

MASTER-STAR TECHNIQUE

3500 Gold

PREREQUISITE

Find Stink Bomb's Soul Gem in Winter Keep

Press **Attack 1** to throw Master Stars that have a higher chance to critically hit!

Legs Soul Gem Ability

STEALTH SKUNK

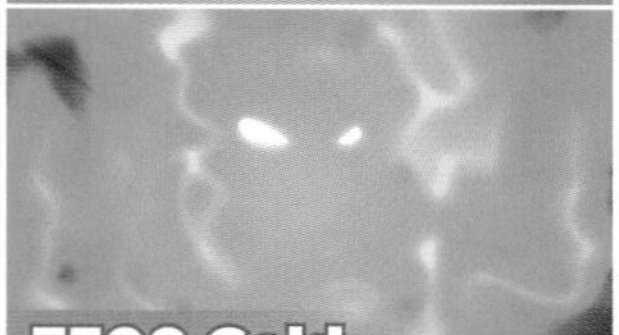

3500 Gold

PREREQUISITE

Find Stink Bomb's Soul Gem in Winter Keep

Remain invisible even after attacking enemies.

Special Quest

What's That Smell?

NAUSEATE ENEMIES 50 TIMES WITH YOUR ONE-INCH PALM.

Target 50 enemies that can withstand the initial blow of One-Inch Palm for this quest. Enemies that are taken out with the initial punch aren't nauseated (they're defeated!) so they won't count.

BODY

Basic Attacks

SKUNK-FU STARS

Press **Attack 1** to throw small stars that can damage enemies at long range.

Upgrades

ONE-INCH PALM

300 Gold

PREREQUISITE None

Press **Attack 3** to deliver a powerful palm attack that knocks away enemies.

NOXIOUS NINJA

800 Gold

PREREQUISITE None

Press **Attack 1** to throw Skunk-Fu Stars that do increased damage.

SWEEPING SKUNK-FU

1000 Gold

PREREQUISITE None

Hold **Attack 1** to charge handfuls of Skunk-Fu Stars, release to damage enemies in all directions.

The Art of Skunk-Fu Path

SKUNK-FU SHIELD

1500 Gold

PREREQUISITE
The Art of Skunk-Fu Path

Sweeping Skunk-Fu creates a whirling shield that damages nearby enemies.

SKUNK-FU MASTER

2000 Gold

PREREQUISITE
The Art of Skunk-Fu Path

Skunk-Fu Shield does increased damage.

The Art of Acorns Path

ACORN ACCURACY

1500 Gold

PREREQUISITE
The Art of Acorns Path

Hold **Attack 3** to charge a powerful poisoned acorn, release to shoot it at enemies.

SKUNK EYE

2000 Gold

PREREQUISITE
Purchase Acorn Accuracy ability

An ancient aiming technique makes acorn attacks do increased damage.

LEGS

Basic Attacks

SKUNK CLOUD

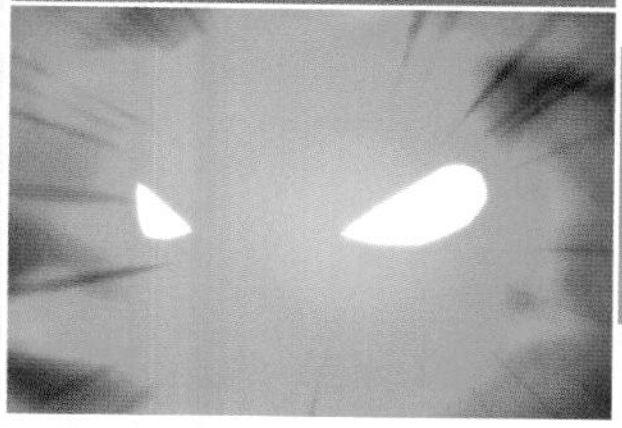

Press **Attack 2** to go invisible and damage enemies with a large obscuring cloud.

Upgrades

HIDDEN TAIL

300 Gold

PREREQUISITE None

Press **Attack 2** while invisible to perform a tail attack that does a large amount of damage to enemies.

SPORTING STRIPES

800 Gold

PREREQUISITE None

Speed is increased. The sport edition is always faster.

SKUNKING AROUND

1000 Gold

PREREQUISITE None

Press **Attack 2** to go invisible and leave a skunk cloud on the ground that damages enemies.

Skunk Cloud Controller Path

ROLLING FOG

1500 Gold

PREREQUISITE
Skunk Cloud Controller Path

Up to two skunk clouds can be active at one time.

CLOUDY CONCOCTION

2000 Gold

PREREQUISITE
Skunk Cloud Controller Path

Skunk cloud does increased damage. What a funky skunk!

Sneaky Tricks Path

SNEAKY TACTICS

1500 Gold

PREREQUISITE
Sneaky Tricks Path

Move forward slowly to cause pointy objects to be left behind that slow and damage enemies.

PAIN IN THE FOOT

2000 Gold

PREREQUISITE
Purchase Sneaky Tactics ability

Sneaky Tactics does increased damage. Tough acting sneaking action!

BUMBLE BLAST

"The Perfect Swarm!"

MAXIMUM HEALTH	320
SPEED	35
ARMOR	24
CRITICAL HIT	4
ELEMENTAL POWER	25

LIGHTCORE

Bumble Blast started life as a humble beehive in the Radiant Mountains, where for ages the bees made the sweetest, most magical honey in all of Skylands. When Kaos heard about this "super honey," he wanted it all for himself and soon launched an attack on the peaceful bees. But when his minions arrived to plunder everything the bees had created, they were met by Bumble Blast. He alone had been home to the bees and considered himself their protector. Using the power of the magic honey, Bumble Blast valiantly battled the evil minions, who felt his powerful sting that day. Afterward, Bumble Blast roamed Skylands as a protector of nature, where he soon joined with the Skylanders.

The honey or the bees? That's the question for Bumble Blast's enemies since they're about to be hit by one or the other, and often both. Bumble Blast is terrific in single target fights, and improves in battles involving larger number of enemies with just a few upgrades.

The Bee Keeper Path improves Bumble Blast's damage output and gives him an option to knock back enemies with a charge up Beezooka shot. The Honey Tree Path is more about control and survival. Bumble Blast gains additional armor, and enemies covered by honey suffer from reduced movement.

Special Quest

Not the Bees!

HIT HONEY-COATED ENEMIES WITH BEES 125 TIMES.

Simply remember to alternate between Bumble Blast's two basic attacks and you should complete this quest quickly. Obtaining Bumble Blast's Soul Gem ability gets you there even faster.

Basic Attacks

BEEZOOKA

Press **Attack 1** to shoot honey homing bees at enemies.

HONEY GLOB

Press **Attack 2** to shoot a big ball of honey that will coat enemies in honey when hit.

Soul Gem Ability

BEE-PACK BACKPACK

4000 Gold

PREREQUISITE
Find Bumble Blast's Soul Gem in Mudwater Hollow

Gain a beehive backpack that automatically launches bees at nearby foes.

Upgrades

HONEY BEECON

500 Gold

PREREQUISITE None

Bees will always target and attack enemies coated in honey.

HUNGRY BEES

700 Gold

PREREQUISITE None

Bees deal increased damage against honeyed targets.

HIVE MIND

900 Gold

PREREQUISITE None

Press **Attack 3** to shoot a beehive into the ground. The hive explodes into honey when an enemy approaches it.

PAINFUL STINGS

1200 Gold

PREREQUISITE None

Bees gain more powerful stingers, increasing their damage!

Bee Keeper Path

BEE ARMADA

1700 Gold

PREREQUISITE
Bee Keeper Path

Hold **Attack 1** to charge the Beezooka, release to shoot three bees at once.

STIRRED UP A NEST

2200 Gold

PREREQUISITE
Bee Keeper Path

A new Beezooka now shoots even more bees that do increased damage!

QUEEN BEE

3000 Gold

PREREQUISITE
Purchase Bee Armada ability

Hold **Attack 1** and charge the Beezooka even longer, release to shoot a Queen Bee that knocks enemies into the air.

Honey Tree Path

HONEY BUZZ BLAST

1700 Gold

PREREQUISITE
Honey Tree Path

Hold **Attack 2** to charge a honey attack, release to shoot a honey glob that contains angry bees.

HEAVY HONEY

2200 Gold

PREREQUISITE
Honey Tree Path

Honey attacks deal increased damage and slow enemies.

HONEYCOMB BARK

3000 Gold

PREREQUISITE
Honey Tree Path

Armor is increased. Bark skin will sometimes drip out honey that coats enemy attackers.

THORN HORN CAMO

"Fruit Punch!"

MAXIMUM HEALTH	300
SPEED	50
ARMOR	24
CRITICAL HIT	6
ELEMENTAL POWER	25

SERIES 2

Hatched at the roots of the Tree of Life, Camo is half dragon and half plant—with effervescent life energy flowing through his scaly leaves. This power allows him to cultivate fruits and vegetables at a highly-accelerated rate, which causes them to explode when they ripen. Camo's unique gift caught the eye of Master Eon, initially because he was hungry and tried to eat a melon that exploded in his face. But upon realizing Camo's true power, Eon convinced him to help the Skylanders protect their world.

Sun Blast begins as a strong ranged attack, and upgrades to a convneniently portable healing ability. Set up Orbiting Sun Shield whenver you have the chance. The globes that heal Camo also hurt the enemies they touch. Firecracker Vines improves quite a bit with upgrades, but remains unpredictable and hard to control. Melon Fountain takes on added importance in ***SWAP Force*** since it ties into Camo's Wow Pow! ability.

The Vine Virtuoso Path makes Firecracker Vines more powerful and numerous, but doesn't provide any additional control. The Melon Master Path is a strong choice, particularly after you purchase the Explosive Harvest ability.

Special Quest

Garden Gorger

EAT 10 WATERMELONS.

Watch for Watermelons throughout the Story Levels. If you aren't using Camo and you see a watermelon drop, switch to him to grab it.

THORN HORN CAMO

Basic Attacks

SUN BLAST

Press **Attack 1** to blast enemies with concentrated life energy.

FIRECRACKER VINES

Press **Attack 2** to conjure up a fast-growing vine of explosive melons.

Soul Gem Ability

ORBITING SUN SHIELD

4000 Gold
PREREQUISITE
None

Hold **Attack 1** to create a Sun Blast Shield. Create three shields to gain a healing effect.

Upgrades

SEARING SUN BLAST

500 Gold
PREREQUISITE None

Sun Blast does increased damage.

MELON FOUNTAIN

700 Gold
PREREQUISITE None

Press **Attack 3** to send melons flying everywhere.

FIRECRACKER FOOD

900 Gold
PREREQUISITE None

Firecracker Vines do increased damage.

VIGOROUS VINES

1200 Gold
PREREQUISITE None

Firecracker Vines move quicker and farther.

Vine Virtuoso Path

MARTIAL BOUNTY

1700 Gold
PREREQUISITE
Vine Virtuoso Path

Firecracker Vines create more explosive melons.

PEPPERS OF POTENCY

2200 Gold
PREREQUISITE
Vine Virtuoso Path

Firecracker Vines do even MORE increased damage.

PROLIFERATION

3000 Gold
PREREQUISITE
Vine Virtuoso Path

Create two Firecracker Vines at once.

Melon Master Path

RING OF MIGHT

1700 Gold
PREREQUISITE
Melon Master Path

The Melon Fountain blasts out more melons.

MELON GMO

2200 Gold
PREREQUISITE
Melon Master Path

The Melon Fountain does increased damage.

MELON FORTRESS

3000 Gold
PREREQUISITE
Melon Master Path

Hold **Attack 3** to hide in the Melon Fountain and release the button to send the melons flying.

Wow Pow!

EXPLOSIVE HARVEST

5000 Gold
PREREQUISITE
None

Any melons can turn into explosive SUPERMELONS and launch at enemies.

If nothing else sways your Upgrade Path choice, then consider how much Explosive Harvest benefits all the upgrades found in the Melon Master Path and then think about how many SUPERMELONS you would be missing out on. Go Melon Master Path!

NINJA STEALTH ELF

"Silent but Deadly!"

MAXIMUM HEALTH	270
SPEED	50
ARMOR	12
CRITICAL HIT	10
ELEMENTAL POWER	25

SERIES 3

As a small child, Stealth Elf awoke one morning inside the hollow of an old tree with no memory of how she got there. She was taken in by an unusually stealthy, ninja-like forest creature in the deep forest. Under his tutelage, she has spent the majority of her life training in the art of stealth fighting. After completing her training, she became a Skylander and set out into the world to uncover the mystery behind her origins.

As sneaky as she is deadly, Stealth Elf is a melee dynamo who can slip out of dangerous situations. She doesn't have a ranged attack, but she is able to reach enemies quickly when it's necessary. Stealth is far more effective against computer enemies than human opponents, but you should use it to buy time and to heal once Sylvan Regeneration is purchased.

The Pook Blade Saint Path adds combos and extra damage to Stealth Elf's bread-and-butter knife attacks. The Forest Ninja Path is a great way to take down enemies while staying relatively safe. Let the scarecrows (and a tiger) do the work.

Special Quest

Stealth Health

GAIN 1000 HP WHILE STEALTHED.

Stealth Elf must gain health for it to count for this quest. Healing done at full health does not count.

Basic Attacks

BLADE SLASH

Press **Attack 1** to slice Stealth Elf's enemies up with a pair of sharp blades. Press **Attack 1**, **Attack 1**, Hold **Attack 1** to perform a special combo.

STEALTHIER DECOY

Press **Attack 2** to have Stealth Elf disappear completely but leave behind a decoy image that enemies are drawn to.

Soul Gem Ability

SYLVAN REGENERATION

4000 Gold

PREREQUISITE
None

Regenerate health over time.

Upgrades

STRAW POOK SCARECROW

500 Gold

PREREQUISITE None

A Scarecrow appears in place of your decoy and distracts enemies.

DRAGONFANG DAGGER

700 Gold

PREREQUISITE None

Blade attacks deal increased damage.

STURDY SCARECROW

900 Gold

PREREQUISITE
Purchase Straw Pook Scarecrow abitlity

Scarecrows last longer and are more resistant

ARBOREAL ACROBATICS

1200 Gold

PREREQUISITE None

Press **Attack 3** to perform a quick acrobatic move. Hold **Attack 3** and flip in any direction using the left control stick.

Pook Blade Saint Path

ELF JITSU

1700 Gold

PREREQUISITE
Pook Blade Saint Path

Press **Attack 1**, **Attack 1**, Hold **Attack 2** for Poison Spores. Press **Attack 1**, **Attack 1**, Hold **Attack 3** for Blade Fury.

ELVEN SUNBLADE

2200 Gold

PREREQUISITE
Pook Blade Saint Path

Blade attacks deal even MORE increased damage.

SHADOWSBANE BLADE DANCE

3000 Gold

PREREQUISITE
Pook Blade Saint Path

Magical Blades fight alongside you.

Forest Ninja Path

SCARE-CRIO TRIO

1700 Gold

PREREQUISITE
Forest Ninja Path

Three Scarecrows are created in place of your decoy.

SCARECROW BOOBY TRAP

2200 Gold

PREREQUISITE
Forest Ninja Path

Scarecrows explode and damage enemies.

SCARECROW SPIN SLICER

3000 Gold

PREREQUISITE
Forest Ninja Path

Scarecrows have axes and do extra damage.

Wow Pow!

SURPRISE, TIGER!

5000 Gold

PREREQUISITE
None

While invisible, press **Attack 3** to summon a powerful tiger ally. Also unlocks Ninja costume!

The summoned tiger attacks in the same direction as Stealth Elf's eyes face. It does a nice bit of damage and knocks down the enemies it hits. The best part about this upgrade is Stealth Elf's awesome new look.

ZOO LOU

"Nature Calls!"

MAXIMUM HEALTH	290
SPEED	43
ARMOR	18
CRITICAL HIT	6
ELEMENTAL POWER	25

Descended from a long line of shamans, Zoo Lou traveled far and wide to the Seven Strange Strongholds—ancient, mysterious sites of great wonder in Skylands—where he studied the wisdom and fighting styles of the Seven Strange Mages. After many years of traveling and studying, Zoo Lou returned to find an army of trolls had invaded his sacred homeland to mine its natural magic resources. Zoo Lou's warrior heart burned with fury. And having now mastered the enchanted art of communicating with nature and summoning animals, he unleashed his great mojo—attacking the trolls and single handedly freeing his lands once again. It was this heroic feat that caught the eye of Double Trouble, who then brought Zoo Lou to Master Eon and the Skylanders.

It would be tough to call Zoo Lou's abilities attacks since he never damages enemies directly. He instead summons jade-powered animals to take care of that for him. Wolf Call is a no-brainer. If you don't see a green wolf, summon one now! Bird Call benefits the most from upgrades, so spend your Gold there first.

The Bucking Boar Path is better against groups of enemies since it includes better armor and an attack that hits multiple targets. The Wild Wolf Path edges it out because Bird Call upgrades also help out against groups and you get extra food as a bonus.

Special Quest

Professional Boar Rider

HIT AN ENEMY WITH THE BOAR DURING 20 FULL-LENGTH BOAR RIDES.

First, you need to buy the Piggyback Ride upgrade. Each time you use the ability, hit an enemy and let the ability run its course without canceling it to get credit toward this quest.

Basic Attacks

BIRD CALL

Press **Attack 1** to summon birds that will attack nearby enemies.

WOLF CALL

Press **Attack 2** to summon a helpful wolf ally.

Soul Gem Ability

BIRDS OF PREY

4000 Gold

PREREQUISITE
Find Zoo Lou's Soul Gem in Mudwater Hollow

Hold **Attack 1** to summon up to five birds, release to have them all swoop in on enemies, doing a devastating amount of damage.

Upgrades

PIGGYBACK RIDE

500 Gold

PREREQUISITE None

Press **Attack 3** to ride around on a wild boar, dealing damage to all nearby enemies. There is a short wait before this ability can be used again.

RAGING BOAR

700 Gold

PREREQUISITE
Purchase Piggyback Ride ability

Boar does increased damage. Riding a raging boar doesn't seem safe...for enemies!

SWOOP RE-LOOP

900 Gold

PREREQUISITE None

Press **Attack 1** to shoot spirit birds that seek out enemies and attack them twice before flying away.

BETTER BEAKS

1200 Gold

PREREQUISITE None

Bird attacks do increased damage. Caw caw caw!

The Bucking Boar Path

ROUGH RIDER

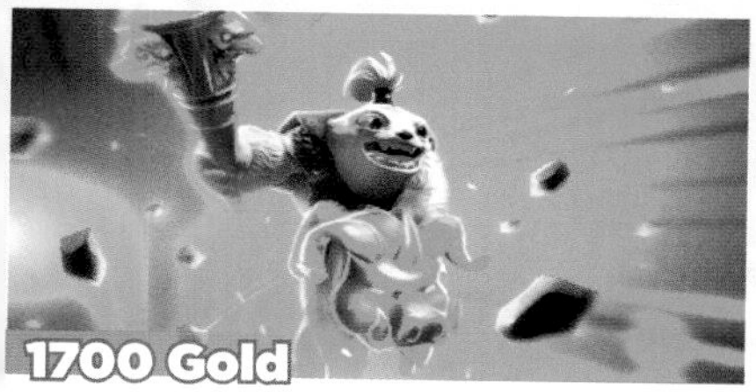

1700 Gold

PREREQUISITE
The Bucking Boar Path

Press **Attack 3** to ride around on a wild boar that kicks up damaging dust and rocks at nearby enemies.

THICKER PIGSKIN

2200 Gold

PREREQUISITE
The Bucking Boar Path

Armor is increased. Thicker skin reduces damage taken from attacks and insults.

HOG WILD

3000 Gold

PREREQUISITE
The Bucking Boar Path

Press **Attack 3** to ride around on a wild boar. After you jump off, the boar continues to trample nearby enemies for a short time.

The Wild Wolf Path

ALPHA WOLF

1700 Gold

PREREQUISITE
The Wild Wolf Path

Press **Attack 2** to summon a more powerful wolf ally that does increased damage and has more health.

HUNGER OF THE WOLF

2200 Gold

PREREQUISITE
The Wild Wolf Path

Each time the wolf attacks it gains increased attack speed.

HUNTER AND GATHERER

3000 Gold

PREREQUISITE
The Wild Wolf Path

The wolf will dig up food when health is low. Such a good little spirit!

DOOM STONE

"Another Smash Hit!"

MAXIMUM HEALTH	280
SPEED	35
ARMOR	30
CRITICAL HIT	6
ELEMENTAL POWER	25

Doom Stone was carved from the strongest and purest stone in Skylands, then magically brought to life by a wizard who was rather lazy and wanted someone strong to carry heavy things and perform other tasks around his castle. Doom Stone happily helped, and in his spare time learned the ancient ways of Stone Fighting should he ever need to protect the wizard, who became like a father to him. Sure enough the need arose when the wizard was kidnapped by his evil twin brother in order to steal his spells for himself. Doom Stone wasted no time in using the skills he learned to save his master. Afterward, the wizard knew Doom Stone had a greater calling and introduced him to Master Eon, who made him a Skylander.

SWAP FORCE

Column Club is a heavy and slow melee attack that can be upgraded into a charged attack. The Column Clubber Path extends the range and damage of these attacks. Living Statue is an amazing defensive ability, blocking attacks and freezing attackers. The Jaded Fighter Path turns the frozen attackers into weapons!

Stoney Spin gains power with each button press (up to a certain point), and upgrades add to its damage and Doom Stone's speed while spinning. The Serious Spinner Path upgrades knock enemies around while spinning. The Carved Belt Path adds jade projectiles with each press of Attack 2 that results in a spin.

Body Soul Gem Ability

STONEY STARE

3500 Gold

PREREQUISITE

Find Doom Stone's Soul Gem in Kaos' Fortress

Hold **Attack 3** to block and cause enchanted snakes to come alive on the shield, damaging enemies while you block.

Legs Soul Gem Ability

SPIN THE TABLES

3500 Gold

PREREQUISITE

Find Doom Stone's Soul Gem in Kaos' Fortress

During the fourth spin, enemies in a large radius are damaged.

Special Quest

Stop Hitting Yourself

DEFEAT 50 CHOMPIES JUST BY BLOCKING.

Chompies aren't known for their self-preservation instincts, so completing this quest is a matter of buying the Living Statue upgrade and waiting for 50 Chompies to throw themselves on Doom Stone's shield.

DOOM STONE

BODY

Basic Attacks

COLUMN CLUB

Press **Attack 1** to swing a heavy column at nearby enemies.

Upgrades

LIVING STATUE

300 Gold

PREREQUISITE None

Hold **Attack 3** to block close attacks. Blocking attacks will cause nearby attackers to turn to jade for a short time.

REJECT AND REFLECT

800 Gold

PREREQUISITE Purchase Living Statue ability

Hold **Attack 3** to block projectile attacks. Blocked projectiles are hit back at enemies, turning them into jade.

COLUMN DUTY

1000 Gold

PREREQUISITE None

Hold **Attack 1** to charge the Column Club, release to cause a large area of damage. Causes more damage the longer **Attack 1** is held.

Column Clubber Path

FALLING TO PIECES

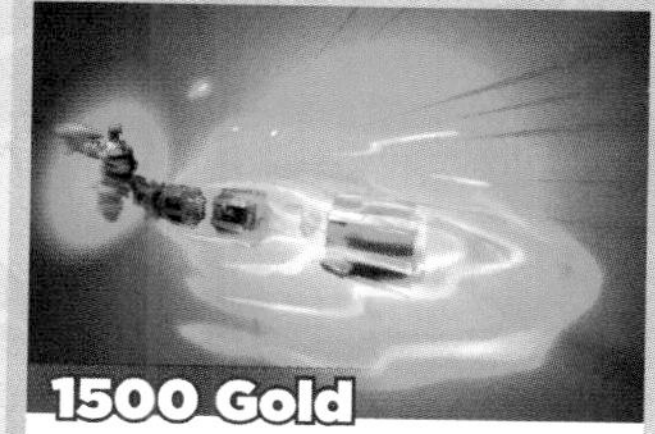

1500 Gold

PREREQUISITE Column Clubber Path

Hold **Attack 1** to charge Column Duty, release to smash the column and break off smaller pieces of it that damage enemies in a larger area.

CLUB DOOM

2000 Gold

PREREQUISITE Column Clubber Path

Column Duty can be charged even longer, dealing more damage in a larger area.

Jaded Fighter Path

CRACKING UP

1500 Gold

PREREQUISITE Jaded Fighter Path

Enemies turned to jade will burst, causing small shards to damage other enemies near them.

MORE DORIC WARFARE

2000 Gold

PREREQUISITE Jaded Fighter Path

Hold **Attack 3** to block attacks and do even more damage to blocked attackers.

LEGS

Basic Attacks

STONEY SPIN

Press **Attack 2** to rapidly attack nearby enemies and charge the stoney belt. The belt increases damage and size the more it is charged.

Upgrades

SPIN RIGHT AROUND

300 Gold

PREREQUISITE None

Hold **Attack 2** to charge a spin, release to bounce between nearby enemies.

REVOLUTIONARY BELT

800 Gold

PREREQUISITE None

Spinning does increased damage.

SPEEDY SPINNER

1000 Gold

PREREQUISITE None

Press **Attack 2** to increase the speed that the belt is spinning. Speed is increased depending on how fast the belt is spinning.

Serious Spinner Path

THE HARDER THEY FALL

1500 Gold

PREREQUISITE Serious Spinner Path

Hold **Attack 2** to charge a spin, release to bounce between enemies and knock the last enemy hit into the air which damages them when they hit the ground.

SPINBALL KING

2000 Gold

PREREQUISITE Serious Spinner Path

Spin Right Around does increased damage. King of the Spinball wizards!

Carved Belt Path

JADED SPIN

1500 Gold

PREREQUISITE Carved Belt Path

Now shoot jade projectiles at enemies when spinning.

BELT PELTERS

2000 Gold

PREREQUISITE Purchase Jaded Spin ability

Press **Attack 2** to spin and shoot powerful jade projectiles at enemies that do increased damage.

RUBBLE ROUSER

"Brace For Impact!"

MAXIMUM HEALTH	280
SPEED	35
ARMOR	24
CRITICAL HIT	6
ELEMENTAL POWER	25

Hailing from a race of creatures who ate rock for a living, Rubble Rouser spent most days digging his way through the vastness of Deep Mountain mouthful by mouthful alongside the rest of his people. But Rubble Rouser found he could eat up far more ground with a swing of his hammer or spin of his drill. However, the leaders of his race wanted no part of changing the way they worked. That is, until the evil Rock Lords trapped them deep within the mountain. It was then that Rubble Rouser showed everyone the power of his ways by defeating the Rock Lords with his mighty hammer and drill. Afterward, the leaders encouraged Rubble Rouser to seek out the Skylanders, who readily welcomed him.

SWAP FORCE

Hammer Swing hits hard, sweeping through nearby enemies, but is slow. The Drill Pitcher Path adds a combo that ends with a thrown hammer. Tools of the Trade is a hopping, overhead attack that crushes anything in front of Rubble Rouser. The Excavator Path upgrades Tools of the Trade to shower the area with bits of rubble that damage nearby enemies.

Deep Dig is an underground quick move with a great upgrade in Minor Miners. The Bolder Boulders Path flings damaging boulders while charging Deep Dig (meaning Rubble Rouser can't be hurt, it's free damage). The Miner Foreman Path doubles the number of Minor Miners and makes them stronger.

Body Soul Gem Ability

OBSIDIAN SKIN

3500 Gold

PREREQUISITE

Find Rubble Rouser's Soul Gem in Winter Keep

Rubble's skin becomes harder than stone, decreasing damage taken.

Legs Soul Gem Ability

POP ROCK

3500 Gold

PREREQUISITE

Find Rubble Rouser's Soul Gem in Winter Keep

Hold **Attack 2** to drill underground, release to toss a huge boulder into the sky which comes down on enemies nearby a short time later.

Special Quest

Oh, What a Drill!

DEAL A TOTAL OF 400 DAMAGE IN ONE DRILLING EARTHQUAKE USING THE DRILL HEAD ATTACK.

Drill Head continues to run as long as Attack 3 is pressed, but Rubble Rouser can't move until it is released. Put Rubble Rouser's back into a corner and let enemies come to attack him, only to crash into his drill.

RUBBLE ROUSER

BODY

Basic Attacks

HAMMER SWING

Press **Attack 1** to swing a massive hammer. Hold to charge up more powerful swings!

Upgrades

TOOLS OF THE TRADE

300 Gold

PREREQUISITE None

Press **Attack 3** to smash nearby enemies with the hammer.

HAPPY HAMMERING

800 Gold

PREREQUISITE None

All hammer attacks do increased damage.

DRILL HEAD

1000 Gold

PREREQUISITE None

Hold **Attack 3** to drill into the ground, causing an earthquake!

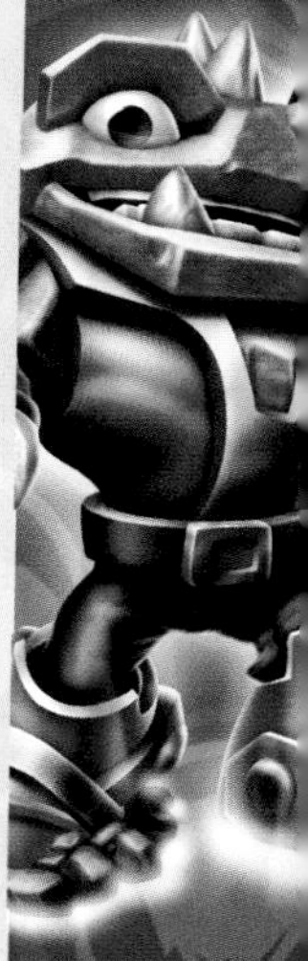

Drill Pitcher Path

NAILED IT!

1500 Gold

PREREQUISITE
Drill Pitcher Path

Press **Attack 1, Attack 1,** and then Hold and release **Attack 1** to throw a charged hammer attack!

SLEDGEHAMMER

2000 Gold

PREREQUISITE
Purchase Nailed It! Ability

Throwing the hammer does increased damage. Don't try this indoors!

Escavator

ROCK SHARDS

1500 Gold

PREREQUISITE
Excavator Path

Press **Attack 3** to send shards of rock flying out of the ground, damaging nearby enemies.

GEM QUALITY

2000 Gold

PREREQUISITE
Purchase Rock Shards ability

Press **Attack 3** to unearth more powerful rock shards that damage nearby enemies.

LEGS

Basic Attacks

DEEP DIG

Press **Attack 2** to quickly dig then come out of the ground, damaging nearby enemies.

Upgrades

MINOR MINERS

300 Gold

PREREQUISITE None

Press **Attack 2** to quickly dig and burst out of the ground a short time later, damaging nearby enemies and summoning small angry miner allies.

EARTHY FORTITUDE

800 Gold

PREREQUISITE None

Health is increased. Tough as stone!

TUNNEL EXPEDITION

1000 Gold

PREREQUISITE None

Hold **Attack 2** to continue drilling while underground, release to surprise enemies from below with a devastating attack.

Bolder Boulders Path

BOULDER TOSS

1500 Gold

PREREQUISITE
Bolder Boulders Path

Hold **Attack 2** to drill underground. While underground, boulders will rapidly shoot out. Aim the boulders towards enemies to damage them.

SO BOLD

2000 Gold

PREREQUISITE
Purchase Boulder Toss ability

Boulders do increased damage. Getting hit with rocks really hurts.

Miner Foreman Path

MINER CRAFT

1500 Gold

PREREQUISITE
Miner Foreman Path

Call up to four miner allies to help you defeat enemies! The cause is righteous.

ON STRIKE

2000 Gold

PREREQUISITE
Miner Foreman Path

Miner allies do increased damage. Oh no, they won't go! Not until experience points show!

FLASHWING

"Blinded by the Light!"

MAXIMUM HEALTH	260
SPEED	43
ARMOR	24
CRITICAL HIT	2
ELEMENTAL POWER	25

LIGHTCORE

Flashwing's true origins are a mystery. But her first appearance came when Bash made a wish that he could fly and looked up to see a shooting star streak across the sky and land in a valley below. In the center of the glowing impact crater was a large, brilliant geode—which suddenly cracked open to reveal Flashwing. Bash may not have soared that day, but his heart sure did, because Flashwing was beautiful...and lethal. As soon as Bash stepped closer, the gem dragon turned towards him. Not knowing if he was friend or foe, she blasted him off of the cliff with a full force laser pulse from her tail! Perhaps Bash flew that day after all.

Name a situation, and Flashwing has an ability to cover it. Enemies trying to move in? Crystal Shards hurts them and pushes them back. Enemies already too close? Shimmering Spin carves a path clear and provides some breathing room. And that's what's available before you choose an Upgrade Path!

The Super Shards Path turns Flashwing into a formidable figher in close quarters. Fully upgraded, Flashwing sticks up to three Crystal Shards into walls, which can attack enemies and heal her. The Super Spinner Path works better for open spaces. Shimmering Spin picks up extra damage, reflects projectiles, and fires lasers.

Special Quest

Let It Shine

DEFEAT 20 ENEMIES WITH ONE CRYSTAL LIGHTHOUSE.

Pick a challenge where the primary enemies are Chompies and set up Crystal Lighthouse in a crowded area.

Basic Attacks

CRYSTAL SHARDS

Press **Attack 1** to fire Crystal Shards.

SHIMMERING SPIN

Press **Attack 2** to spin around and damage anything in Flashwing's path.

Soul Gem Ability

CRYSTAL LIGHTHOUSE

4000 Gold

PREREQUISITE
Purchase Surrounded by Shards ability

Hold **Attack 3** to create a Crystal Lighthouse that fires laser light beams.

Upgrades

SURROUNDED BY SHARDS

500 Gold

PREREQUISITE None

Press **Attack 3** to fire Crystal Shards in all directions but forward.

LUMINOUS LASERS

700 Gold

PREREQUISITE None

Hold **Attack 1** to charge up a powerful laser shot.

LIGHT SPEED SHARDS

900 Gold

PREREQUISITE None

Shoot Crystal Shards much faster and deal extra damage.

ARMORED AURA

1200 Gold

PREREQUISITE None

Condensed light increases your resistance.

Super Shards Path

SHOOTING SHARDS

1700 Gold

PREREQUISITE
Super Shards Path

Crystal Shards stick in walls and shoot their own crystals when **Attack 1** is pressed again.

CRYSTAL CRAZINESS

2200 Gold

PREREQUISITE
Purchase Shooting Shards ability

Up to three crystals stick in walls and shoot their own crystals when **Attack 1** is pressed again.

HEALING CRYSTALS

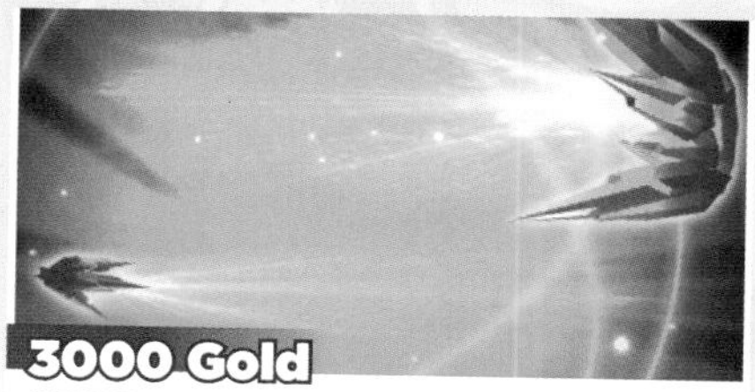

3000 Gold

PREREQUISITE
Purchase Shooting Shards ability

Crystals embedded in a wall heal Flashwing when she is close.

Super Spinner Path

EXTRA RADIANT ROTATION

1700 Gold

PREREQUISITE
Super Spinner Path

Shimmering Spin lasts longer and does increased damage.

REFLECTION DEFLECTION

2200 Gold

PREREQUISITE
Super Spinner Path

Gain extra armor and deflect enemies' shots back at them while spinning.

LIGHTS, CRYSTAL, ACTION!

3000 Gold

PREREQUISITE
Super Spinner Path

While spinning, press **Attack 1** to shoot beams of laser light.

HYPER BEAM PRISM BREAK

"The Beam is Supreme!"

MAXIMUM HEALTH	290
SPEED	35
ARMOR	18
CRITICAL HIT	6
ELEMENTAL POWER	25

Prism Break was once a fearsome rock golem who didn't like to be disturbed. Then, an accidental cave-in left him buried underground. One hundred years later, a mining expedition digging for valuable jewels discovered him by chance with a well-placed blow from a pick axe—something Prism Break doesn't talk about. After 100 years of solitude, he found that the pressure of the earth had transformed him emotionally as well as physically, turning his crude rocky arms into incredible gems with powerful energy. Grateful for being free of his earthly prison, Prism Break decided to put his new abilities to good use and dedicated himself to protecting Skylands.

Old hands with Prism Break are familiar with the angles Energy Beam takes when they hit Crystal Shards, which is a difficult thing to master. If you're new to Prism Break, practice against the Training Dummies in Woodburrow until you get it down. You can still hold or pulse Energy Beam, but there's no way to keep Energy Beam going indefinitely.

The Crystaleer Path improves Crystal Shards and helps keep Prism Break healthy. Choose it when a challenge or level is giving you trouble. Every upgrade on the Prismancer Path improves Energy Beam's damage output, making it ideal for anything with a timer.

Special Quest

Bifurcation Sensation

DEFEAT 100 ENEMIES USING CRYSTAL ERUPTION.

Once you plunk down the 700 Gold to purchase Crystal Eruption, it should become second nature to spawn the ring of crystals when fights get hairy. You should complete this quest in a relatively short time while playing through Story Levels or completing challenges.

Basic Attacks

ENERGY BEAM

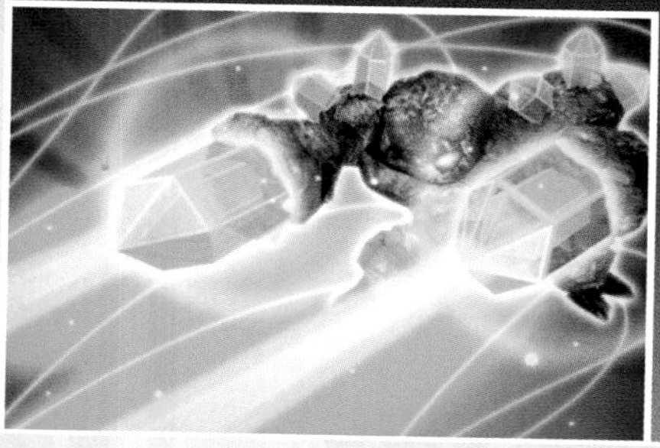

Press and hold **Attack 1** to fire a powerful energy beam.

SUMMON CRYSTAL SHARD

Press **Attack 2** to summon crystal shards to smash enemies and refract your Energy Beam.

Soul Gem Ability

SHARD SOUL PRISON

4000 Gold

PREREQUISITE None

Crystal Shards form when enemies are defeated by your Energy Beam.

Upgrades

SUPER CRYSTAL SHARD

500 Gold

PREREQUISITE None

Summoned Crystal Shards are bigger and do increased damage.

CRYSTAL ERUPTION

700 Gold

PREREQUISITE None

Press **Attack 3** to summon a damaging ring of crystals around you that pushes back enemies.

EMERALD ENERGY BEAM

900 Gold

PREREQUISITE None

Energy Beam does extra damage.

CHAINED REFRACTIONS

1200 Gold

PREREQUISITE None

Split Energy Beams divide again if they pass through a Crystal Shard.

Crystaleer Path

MASSIVE CRYSTAL EXPLOSION

1700 Gold

PREREQUISITE
Crystaleer Path

Crystal Eruption attack does ncreased damage and covers a arger area.

TRIPLE CRYSTAL SHARD

2200 Gold

PREREQUISITE
Crystaleer Path

Summon three Crystal Shards at once.

CRYSTALLINE ARMOR

3000 Gold

PREREQUISITE
Crystaleer Path

A new crystal increases Prism Break's Resistance.

Prismancer Path

GOLDEN DIAMOND ERGY BEAM

1700 Gold

PREREQUISITE
Prismancer Path

nergy Beam attack does even nore increased damage.

TRIPLE REFRACTED BEAM

2200 Gold

PREREQUISITE
Prismancer Path

Energy Beam splits into three beams when refracted through a Crystal Shard.

FOCUSED ENERGY

3000 Gold

PREREQUISITE
Prismancer Path

Energy Beam has increased range.

Wow Pow!

CRYSTAL COMRADE

5000 Gold

PREREQUISITE
Purchase Super Crystal Shard ability

Press **Attack 1** to shoot Crystal Shards and gem shrapnel explode out, damaging enemies and looking cool.

Looking cool refers to both Prism Break's new, red crystal appearance and the new, red look of his Crystal Shards. Either way, Crystal Comrade must also boost Prism Break's ego. Now when he hits Crystal Shards with Energy Beam, gem bits fly off and damage enemies, and he creates a work of art dedicated to himself!

SCORP

"King of the Sting!"

MAXIMUM HEALTH	260
SPEED	35
ARMOR	18
CRITICAL HIT	8
ELEMENTAL POWER	25

Scorp was raised in the Salt Flat Islands, an endless flat plain of rock where every day is very hot. To keep themselves entertained, the residents live for the sport of Sting Ball, an extreme game that only the strongest play to become King of Sting, a title Scorp had won numerous times. During his last championship game, the opposing team cheated by using an enchanted water gem to make it rain. But the spell got out of control and soon a raging thunderstorm flooded the land. Using his powerful claws and incredible agility, Scorp bravely battled the rising waters to retrieve the gem and hurl it far into the clouds, breaking the spell and saving everyone. Seeing how his abilities could be used for more than sport, Scorp soon sought out and joined the Skylanders.

Emerald Crystal and Tail Sting have odd properties that require familiarity to use them effectively. Emerald Crystal is a lob attack that attaches itself to enemies, walls, or floors. After a few seconds, its explodes and deals additional damage. Neither the crystal nor the explosion damages much, but Scorp can fire them off quickly. Tail Sting comes out in a flash and hits multiple enemies, but has a poor recovery time.

The Stinger Path boosts the damage output of Tail Sting, but doesn't help its recovery. The Crystal Venomancer Path increases both the damage done by Emerald Crystals and the area it affects.

Special Quest

Ticking Slime Bomb

DEFEAT 50 ENEMIES FROM THE POISON EXPLOSION OF YOUR MAIN ATTACK.

This is a rare quest where it's easier to finish it before you upgrade your Skylander. It isn't defeating enemies with Emerald Crystal that satisfies this quest's requirements, it's the poison explosion that takes place after the Emerald Crystal attaches itself to something. When an enemy is low on health and has an Emerald Crystal attached to it, move on to another target.

Basic Attacks

EMERALD CRYSTAL

Press **Attack 1** to throw a sticky explosive crystal.

TAIL STING

Press **Attack 2** to sting the ground nearby and poison enemies.

Soul Gem Ability

AVALANCHE DASH

4000 Gold

PREREQUISITE
Find Scorp's Soul Gem in Motleyville; Purchase Boulder Roll ability

Hold **Attack 3** to curl up into a ball and roll around. Dashing now lasts as long as **Attack 3** is held.

Upgrades

BOULDER ROLL

500 Gold

PREREQUISITE None

Hold **Attack 3** to curl up into a ball and roll around, damaging enemies in the way.

CHROME CARAPACE

700 Gold

PREREQUISITE None

Armor is increased. New stone plating causes enemies' attacks to do less damage.

CRYSTAL BALL

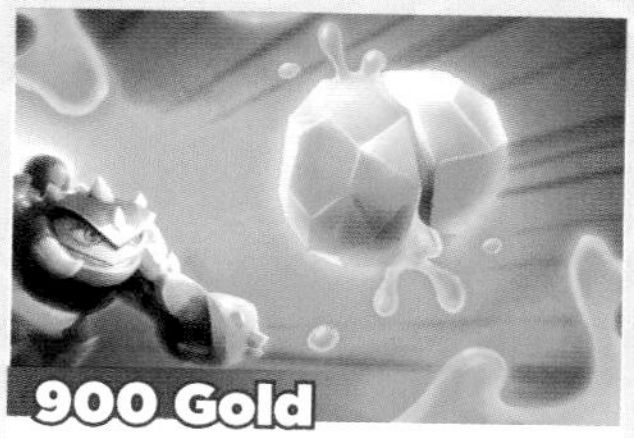

900 Gold

PREREQUISITE None

Hold **Attack 1** to charge a crystal attack, release to smash two crystals together and throw a massive sticky crystal.

EARTHLY POWER

1200 Gold

PREREQUISITE None

Press **Attack 1** to throw a sticky explosive that now does increased damage to an enemy.

Stinger Path

FUMING FISSURE

1700 Gold

PREREQUISITE
Stinger Path

Press **Attack 2** to strike the ground with a poison tail and cause a large shockwave that shoots out towards enemies.

SCORPION STRIKE

2200 Gold

PREREQUISITE
Stinger Path

Poison from tail strikes does increased damage.

POTENT POISONS

3000 Gold

PREREQUISITE
Stinger Path

Press **Attack 2** to strike with a poison tail, that now damages enemies over a longer amount of time.

Crystal Venomancer Path

CRACKED CRYSTALS

1700 Gold

PREREQUISITE
Crystal Venomancer Path

ress **Attack 1** to throw a powerful sticky xplosive crystal that now does damage to nemies in a larger area.

CRYSTAL SHARDS

2200 Gold

PREREQUISITE
Crystal Venomancer Path

Emerald Crystal attacks now do even more damage. So pretty, yet so painful!

VENOMOUS CRYSTALS

3000 Gold

PREREQUISITE
Crystal Venomancer Path

When Crystal Ball explodes, it splits into two smaller crystals. Each new crystal does very powerful poison damage over time when it explodes.

SLOBBER TOOTH

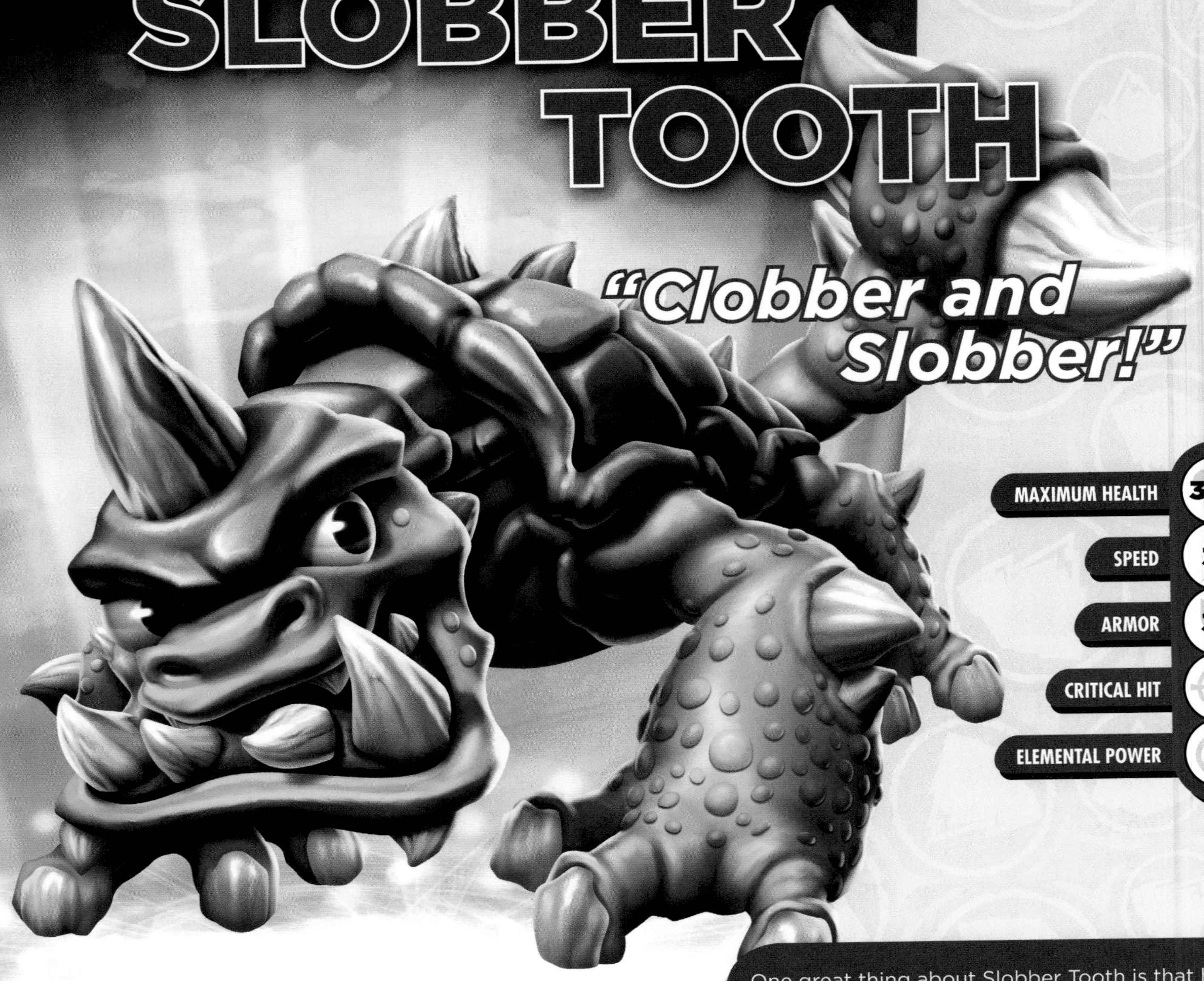

"Clobber and Slobber!"

MAXIMUM HEALTH	300
SPEED	35
ARMOR	30
CRITICAL HIT	2
ELEMENTAL POWER	25

Having been asleep for thousands of years, Slobber Tooth was awakened by the fiery eruption of two volcanic islands crashing together. Immediately sought out by Kaos to become one of his minions, Slobber Tooth was promised great power. But the gruff and headstrong fighter chose to follow his own path instead. For this, Kaos attacked his ancient petrified homeland. As the only one who could protect his hibernating race, Slobber Tooth fought tooth and tail against Kaos and his minions, ultimately driving them away. For his heroism, Master Eon asked Slobber Tooth to join the Skylanders, where he could continue defending Skylands against the evil Kaos.

One great thing about Slobber Tooth is that he's rarely without food. Where other Skylanders must wait for food to appear, Slobber Tooth swallows nearby enemies and restores a bit of his own health after a few seconds. With his health full, use swallowed enemies as projectiles to damage enemies just outside of the range of Slobber Tooth's other basic attack, Horn Swipe.

The Food Fighter Path boosts both the healing from Chomp, and the damage done by Chuck. The Seismic Tail Path turns Slobber Tooth into a nightmare to face in close quarters. Shockwave becomes much better in every way.

Special Quest

Hungry Like a Hippo

SWALLOW 25 ENEMIES.

You must use Chomp & Chuck on 25 different enemies that can be swallowed and they must stay in Slobber Tooth's mouth until he swallows them to restore his health. Look for a heart on the screen to let you know when it's safe to swallow another enemy.

Basic Attacks

HORN SWIPE

Press **Attack 1** to perform a head swipe that damages nearby enemies.

CHOMP & CHUCK

Press **Attack 2** to grab enemies with a slobbery mouth attack. Press **Attack 2** again to spit them out.

Soul Gem Ability

IRON JAW

4000 Gold

PREREQUISITE
Find Slobber Tooth's Soul Gem in Cascade Glade

Gain an iron jaw, causing all head attacks to deal increased damage.

Upgrades

UNSTOPPABLE FORCE

500 Gold

PREREQUISITE None

Hold **Attack 1** to charge forward a short distance with a powerful headbutt attack.

TOUGH HIDE

700 Gold

PREREQUISITE None

Gain bonus armor. Skin as tough as nails and rocks mixed together.

SHOCKWAVE

900 Gold

PREREQUISITE None

Press **Attack 3** to do a tail slam on the ground, damaging all enemies nearby.

LOOGEY

1200 Gold

PREREQUISITE None

Press **Attack 2** after holding an enemy with a Chomp attack to spit them out and deal increased damage.

Food Fighter Path

SNOT ROCKET

1700 Gold

PREREQUISITE
Food Fighter Path

Enemies hit with a spit attack will be covered in goo and take damage over time.

OM NOM NOM

2200 Gold

PREREQUISITE
Food Fighter Path

Press **Attack 2** to eat enemies, enemies being eaten will give more health back over a short time.

FEAST

3000 Gold

PREREQUISITE
Food Fighter Path

Hold **Attack 2** to pull enemies into a chomping mouth attack.

Seismic Tail Path

FLING

1700 Gold

PREREQUISITE
Seismic Tail Path

Press **Attack 3** to do a tail slam on the ground, press **Attack 3** again to fling all nearby enemies into the air.

WEIGHT GAIN

2200 Gold

PREREQUISITE
Seismic Tail Path

Gain a new spikey tail, causing Shockwave attacks to do increased damage.

EARTH SHAKER

3000 Gold

PREREQUISITE
Seismic Tail Path

Hold **Attack 3** to continue tail slamming the ground, causing waves of rocks to spread out and damage enemies in the way.

KNOCKOUT TERRAFIN

"It's Feeding Time!"

MAXIMUM HEALTH	310
SPEED	35
ARMOR	18
CRITICAL HIT	6
ELEMENTAL POWER	25

SERIES 3

Terrafin hails from The Dirt Seas, where it was common to swim, bathe, and even snorkel beneath the ground. But a powerful explosion in the sky created a blast wave that turned the ocean of sand into a vast sheet of glass, putting an end to Terrafin's duty as the local lifeguard. Not one to stay idle, the brawny dirt shark found himself training in the art of boxing, and not long after he was local champ. Fighters came from all around to challenge him, but it was a chance meeting with a great Portal Master that led him to give up his title for a greater purpose.

Even before upgrades, Earth Swim is a valuable ability that allows Terrafin to pass enemies and hazards without getting hurt. Punch is exactly what it sounds like: Terrafin's fists slamming into faces and objects, breaking both. It's not fancy, but it is effective.

The Sandhog Path gives some offensive punch to Earth Swim, which helps out his Wow Pow! ability at the same time. However, Earth Swim is generally used to bring enemies in range of Punch, which is where the Brawler Path comes in. Terrafin hits harder and gets more combo options. Both make for a happy Terrafin.

Special Quest

Land Lubber

EAT 20 FOOD ITEMS WHILE BURROWING.

This quest requires the Surface Feeder upgrade. Just remember to use Earth Swim when you see a food item and you should complete this quickly. If you want to get it done even faster, go to any challenge with the Food Thief.

Basic Attacks

PUNCH

Press **Attack 1** to punch the enemy. Press **Attack 1**, **Attack 1**, Hold **Attack 1** to perform a combo.

EARTH SWIM

Press **Attack 2** to burrow and while underground, press **Attack 1** to perform a Belly Flop.

Soul Gem Ability

SURFACE FEEDER

4000 Gold

PREREQUISITE
None

Collect power-ups while burrowed.

Upgrades

BRASS KNUCKLES

500 Gold

PREREQUISITE None

Punch attacks do increased damage.

MEGA BELLY FLOP

700 Gold

PREREQUISITE None

Belly Flop does increased damage and affects a larger area.

FEEDING FRENZY

900 Gold

PREREQUISITE None

Press **Attack 3** to spawn mini-sharks that burrow and latch onto enemies.

MULTI TARGET PUNCHES

1200 Gold

PREREQUISITE None

Punch attack hits multiple enemies.

Sandhog Path

MASTER EARTH SWIMMER

1700 Gold

PREREQUISITE
Sandhog Path

Increased speed while burrowing.

HOMING FRENZY

2200 Gold

PREREQUISITE
Sandhog Path

Mini-sharks home in on enemies and do extra damage.

RAZORFIN

3000 Gold

PREREQUISITE
Sandhog Path

While burrowed, your dorsal fin does damage to enemies.

Brawler Path

PUGILIST

1700 Gold

PREREQUISITE
Brawler Path

Press **Attack 1**, **Attack 1**, Hold **Attack 2** for Body Slam. Press **Attack 1**, **Attack 1**, Hold **Attack 3** for Uppercut.

SPIKED KNUCKLES

2200 Gold

PREREQUISITE
Brawler Path

All punch attacks do even MORE damage.

FRENZY SHIELD

3000 Gold

PREREQUISITE
Brawler Path

You launch mini-sharks at enemies who damage you.

Wow Pow!

HAVE YOU MET MY KIDS?

5000 Gold

PREREQUISITE
Purchase Feeding Frenzy ability

While burrowed, press **Attack 3** to launch at enemies and hit them with a claw swipe move as well as with mini-shark allies.

The best part about Have You Met My Kids? is that it doesn't end Earth Swim immediately. In fact, when you get the timing down, it's possible to use this attack and follow it up immediately with a Belly Flop. That leads to a world of pain for any enemies who get hit with both attacks.

BOOM JET

"Bombs Away!"

MAXIMUM HEALTH	260
SPEED	43
ARMOR	24
CRITICAL HIT	6
ELEMENTAL POWER	25

No matter what Boom Jet did, he always had to be the best. He could be seen day and night above his home in the Billowy Cloudplains gunning his engines and performing daredevil maneuvers as he trained to become the best sky surfer in all of Skylands. Unfortunately, Boom Jet never had a chance to compete for the championship because a day came that changed his life forever. The Darkness had come. And with his town on the verge of being completely consumed by the ominous evil force, Boom Jet took action. Using his incredible flying skills, he raced from house to house, rescuing all of the citizens and carrying them to safety...just before The Darkness destroyed his homeland. It was then he realized the protection of Skylands was more important than personal glory, so he sought out Master Eon to offer his services to the Skylanders.

Body Soul Gem Ability

SUPPLY DROP

3500 Gold

PREREQUISITE

Find Boom Jet's Soul Gem in Motleyville; Purchase Air Strike ability

Air Strike has a chance to drop health supplies if health is low.

Legs Soul Gem Ability

MACH 2

3500 Gold

PREREQUISITE

Find Boom Jet's Soul Gem in Motleyville

Mach 1's speed is increased and a large blast damages enemies at the beginning of the dash.

SWAP FORCE

Football Bomb becomes a much better ability when you buy the Go Long! upgrade. The Storm Bomber Path adds stationary, damaging clouds of smoke to the aftermath of a Go Long! explosion. Air Strike blasts the ground in a straight path, and the Squad Leader Path adds bombs for extra damage.

Wind Turbine needs upgrades before it does more than annoy enemies. Mach 1, for example, turns Boom Jet into a Chompy destroyer. The Sky Writer Path adds a damaging smoke trail in his wake, aiding Jet's mobility. The Ace Gunner Path is more direct damage. Two missiles are fired, and seek out targets.

Special Quest

Tactical Strikes

DEFEAT 747 ENEMIES WITH YOUR AIR STRIKE ABILITY.

Use Air Strike often in Chompy-filled areas, and to finish off low health enemies everywhere and you'll hit this quirky number in a hurry.

BODY

Basic Attacks

FOOTBALL BOMB

Press **Atttack 1** to throw a football sized bomb.

Upgrades

AIR STRIKE

PREREQUISITE None

Press **Attack 3** to call for help from the skies. An airstrike shoots projectiles at enemies on the ground.

TIGHT SPIRAL

PREREQUISITE None

Press **Attack 1** to throw a football bomb that does increased damage.

GO LONG!

PREREQUISITE None

Hold **Attack 1** to charge a football bomb, release to throw a Super Bomb.

Storm Bomber Path

STORM BOMB

PREREQUISITE
Storm Bomber Path

Hold **Attack 1** to charge a football bomb, release to create storm clouds where the bomb lands that shock nearby enemies.

UNFRIENDLY SKIES

PREREQUISITE
Purchase Storm Bomb ability

Storm Bomb does increased damage. Shocking!

Squad Leader Path

BOMBERS

PREREQUISITE
Squad Leader Path

Air Strike now drops bombs that do damage in a large area.

TIGHT FORMATION

PREREQUISITE
Squad Leader Path

Press **Attack 3** to call in an Air Strike that does increased damage.

LEGS

Basic Attacks

WIND TURBINE

Hold **Attack 2** to shoot wind at nearby enemies, pushing them backwards.

Upgrades

MACH 1

PREREQUISITE None

Press **Attack 2** two times to dash forward. Hold **Attack 2** to continue dashing quickly.

ACE PILOT

PREREQUISITE None

Speed is increased. Tuned up with brand new turbo!

TURBULENCE

PREREQUISITE None

Hold **Attack 2** to shoot three homing propellers at enemies.

Sky Writer Path

SKY WRITING

PREREQUISITE
Sky Writer Path

A smoke trail is left behind while dashing that stuns and damages enemies.

THICK SMOKE

PREREQUISITE
Purchase Sky Writing ability

Sky Writing does increased damage and stays around longer.

Ace Gunner Path

GUN SHIP

PREREQUISITE
Ace Gunner Path

Press **Attack 2** to shoot missiles from a powerful new mounted turret.

ROCKET FUEL

PREREQUISITE
Purchase Gun Ship ability

New turret designs make Gun Ship do increased damage.

FREE RANGER

"Whip Up a Storm!"

MAXIMUM HEALTH	280
SPEED	43
ARMOR	18
CRITICAL HIT	8
ELEMENTAL POWER	25

Free Ranger was hatched during a storm when a thunderous bolt of lightning struck his egg. From that very moment, his destiny was clear—he would become the greatest storm chaser ever known! He spent his entire life pursuing hurricanes, spinning inside tornados, and riding lightning. But a day came when he encountered a storm unlike any other. It was unnatural and ominous, billowing with evil, and leaving only desolation in its wake. Free Ranger was standing at its edge, moments from boldly leaping into it, when he was stopped by none other than Master Eon. The wise Portal Master told him that it was The Darkness that raged before them, and if he were up to the challenge, he could join the Skylanders to help defend against it in the Cloudbreak Islands.

Body Soul Gem Ability

STORMING STORMBLADES

3500 Gold

PREREQUISITE

Find Free Ranger's Soul Gem in Mudwater Hollow

Press **Attack 1** to attack with more powerful Stormblades that deal extra lightning damage.

Legs Soul Gem Ability

CHARGED WINDS

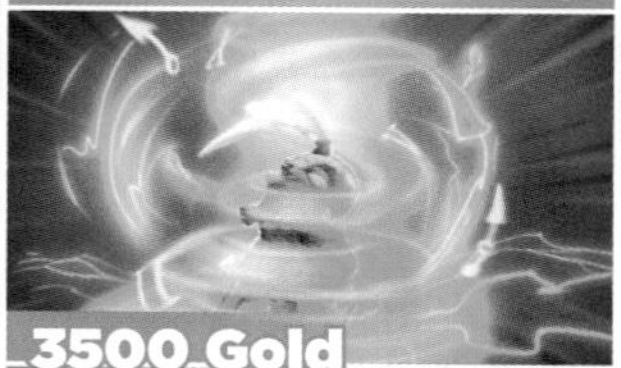

3500 Gold

PREREQUISITE

Find Free Ranger's Soul Gem in Mudwater Hollow

Hold **Attack 2** to become a tornado filled with lightning, dealing damage to all enemies in the way.

SWAP FORCE

Stormblade Slash is a series of melee attacks that is enhanced nicely by Gale Slash. The Wind Slasher Path adds a charged up opening attack to Stormblade Slash. Eyes of the Storm is a low powered eye beam that jumps between enemies. The Storm Focus Path turns it into a powerful, charged single shot.

Ride the Wind is an amazing ability to use against shielded enemies. They are whirled around and their shields drop. The Lightning Linguist Path adds an attack that hits enemies near Free Ranger when a tornado begins. The Tornado Thrower Path attack appears at the end and hits multiple enemies in a line.

Special Quest

Ruffled Feathers

HIT ENEMIES 25 TIMES WITHOUT STOPPING YOUR MELEE ATTACKS.

Find an area filled with enemies and keep hitting Attack 1 while avoiding the enemy attacks that can interrupt Free Ranger's swings. If you don't hit any enemies while swinging, that won't hurt anything, just keep pressing Attack 1 and hitting enemies.

BODY

Basic Attacks

STORMBLADE SLASH

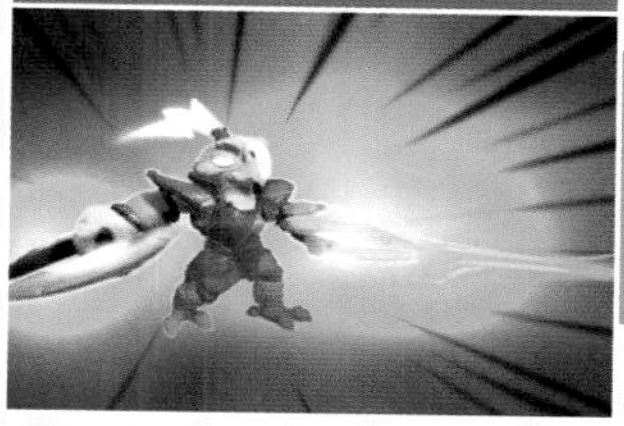

Press **Attack 1** to slash at enemies with powerful Stormblades.

Upgrades

EYES OF THE STORM

300 Gold

PREREQUISITE None

Press **Attack 3** to shoot a bolt of lightning from the eyes, stunning the first enemy and chaining to others.

CHARGED BLADES

800 Gold

PREREQUISITE None

Press **Attack 1** to slash with more powerful Stormblades that do increased damage.

GALE SLASH

1000 Gold

PREREQUISITE None

Press **Attack 1** three times to send a wave of powerful air at enemies.

Wind Slasher Path

SLICING STORM

1500 Gold

PREREQUISITE
Wind Slasher Path

Hold **Attack 1** to charge the Stormblades, release for a devastating combo attack.

FEATHERED FURY

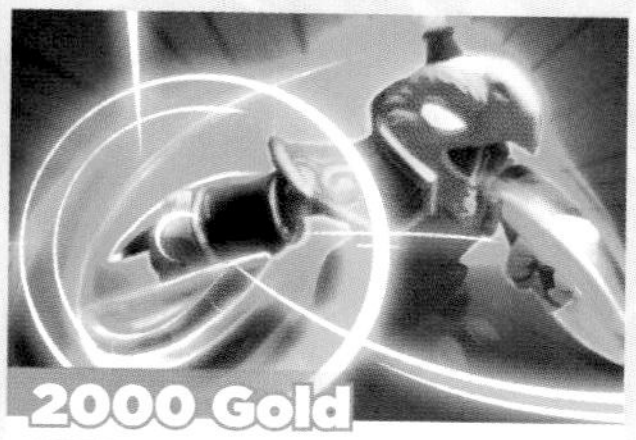

2000 Gold

PREREQUISITE
Purchase Slicing Storm ability

Slicing Storm does increased damage. Unleash the full fury of the bird!

Storm Focus Path

LIGHTNING STRIKES THRICE

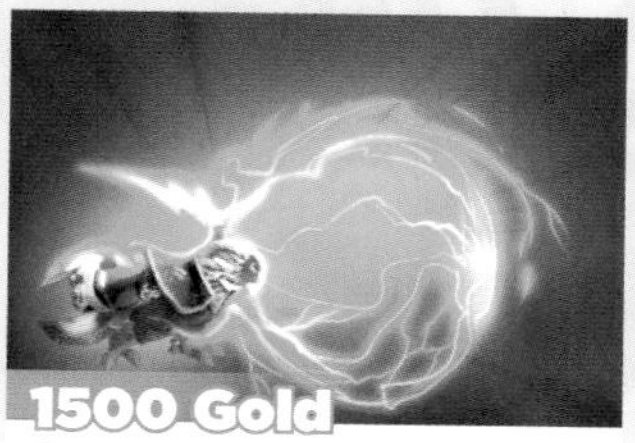

1500 Gold

PREREQUISITE
Storm Focus Path

Hold **Attack 3** to charge Eye of the Storm, release to shoot a larger bolt of lightning.

CHARGED GIGAWATT BOLT

2000 Gold

PREREQUISITE
Purchase Lightning Strikes Thrice ability

Lightning Strikes Thrice does increased damage. More powerful than lightning.

LEGS

Basic Attacks

RIDE THE WIND

Hold **Attack 2** to become a tornado and damage nearby enemies.

Upgrades

APPROACHING STORM

300 Gold

PREREQUISITE None

Hold **Attack 2** to become a tornado, speed is increasd while the tornado is active.

WIND POWERED

800 Gold

PREREQUISITE None

Becoming a tornado will last longer.

TORNADO VACUUM BOOST

1000 Gold

PREREQUISITE None

Tornadoes now pull in enemies from further away.

Lightning Linguist Path

LIGHTNING NOVA

1500 Gold

PREREQUISITE
Lightning Linguist Path

Blast all nearby enemies with a powerful lightning bolt when becoming a tornado.

NOVA FLASH

2000 Gold

PREREQUISITE
Purchase Lightning Nova ability

Lightning Nova does increased damage.

Tornado Thrower Path

WILD TORNADO

1500 Gold

PREREQUISITE
Tornado Thrower Path

When becoming a tornado ends, a powerful tornado is shot out, damaging all enemies in the way.

TWISTED TWISTER

2000 Gold

PREREQUISITE
Purchase Wild Tornado ability

More powerful tornadoes are shot forward that do increased damage to enemies.

TURBO JET-VAC

"Hawk and Awe!"

MAXIMUM HEALTH	240
SPEED	50
ARMOR	30
CRITICAL HIT	4
ELEMENTAL POWER	25

SERIES 2

Jet-Vac was the greatest, most daring flying ace in all of Windham. He was given his magical wings when he was young, as was the tradition for all Sky Barons. But when his homeland was raided, he chose to sacrifice his wings to a young mother so she could fly her children to safety. This act of nobility caught the attention of Master Eon, who sought out the young Sky Baron and presented him with a gift—a powerful vacuum device that would allow him to soar through the skies once again. Jet-Vac accepted the gift with gratitude, and now daringly fights evil alongside the other Skylanders.

Vac-Blaster blasts air out at enemies, dealing respectable damage with nice range. A flip of the switch (well, pressing the other Attack Button) results in Suction Gun sucking in enemies and dealing damage to them. Jet-Vac also uses an air-powered backpack to fly, though he can't stay aloft for long. Using Suction Gun replenishes the air that powers his backpack a bit quicker.

The Bird Blaster Path is designed to handle groups of enemies, allowing Vac-Blaster shots to damage more enemies. The Vac-Packeteer Path focuses on his Jet Pack, giving it more airtime and a new attack.

Special Quest

Bird Cleaner

TRAVEL 5000 FEET WHILE FLYING.

Flying is second nature to an eagle! To complete this quest faster, activate the Vac-Packeteer Path and purchase the ability Tank Reserves.

Basic Attacks

VAC-BLASTER

Press **Attack 1** to shoot enemies with a powerful blast of air.

SUCTION GUN

Hold **Attack 2** to suck enemies into the spinning fan blades.

Soul Gem Ability

EAGLE-AIR BATTLE GEAR

4000 Gold

PREREQUISITE
None

Jet-Vac gets enhanced resistances and a pretty sweet visor.

Upgrades

FEISTIER FAN

500 Gold

PREREQUISITE None

Bigger spinning fan blades on the Suction Gun do increased damage to enemies.

JET-VAC JET PACK

700 Gold

PREREQUISITE None

Press **Attack 3** to take flight. Press **Attack 1** while flying to shoot blasts of air.

VAC BLASTER 9000

900 Gold

PREREQUISITE None

Vac-Blaster does increased damage.

TURBINE SUCTION FAN

1200 Gold

PREREQUISITE
Purchase Feistier Fan ability

Suction Gun attacks do even MORE increased damage.

Bird Blaster Path

PIERCING WINDS

1700 Gold

PREREQUISITE
Bird Blaster Path

Vac-Blaster does even more increased damage and pierces multiple enemies.

VAC MASTER-BLASTER 20X

2200 Gold

PREREQUISITE
Bird Blaster Path

Vac-Blaster does maximum damage.

SUPER SUCTION AIR BLASTER

3000 Gold

PREREQUISITE
Bird Blaster Path

Suck up enemies with the Suction Gun to give the Vac-Blaster super shots.

Vac-Packeteer Path

TANK RESERVES

1700 Gold

PREREQUISITE
Vac-Packeteer Path

Can remain in flight longer and recharge faster.

THE MULCHER

2200 Gold

PREREQUISITE
Vac-Packeteer Path

Suction Gun attacks do maximum damage.

FLYING CORKSCREW

3000 Gold

PREREQUISITE
Vac-Packeteer Path

While flying, press **Attack 2** to blast forward and perform a powerful corkscrew attack.

Wow Pow!

SHOOT THE BREEZE!

5000 Gold

PREREQUISITE
None

Hold **Attack 1** to charge up the Vac Blaster, then release to release a gigantic tornado.

The fact that Shoot the Breeze! doesn't slow Jet-Vac while it's charging up makes it one of the more practical charged up attacks around. The tornado hits enemies in a straight line, so you can damage multiple enemies with one shot if you line them up correctly.

POP THORN

"Straight to the Point!"

MAXIMUM HEALTH	280
SPEED	43
ARMOR	24
CRITICAL HIT	6
ELEMENTAL POWER	25

Pop Thorn hails from a race of creatures known as Pufferthorns. Often considered one of the cutest creatures in all of Skylands, they are generally quite timid and puff out sharp spines when scared. It is this ability that long ago led to the unfortunate legacy of being used as combs by giant trolls everywhere, as the sharp spines are perfect for brushing out tangles from their long, matted hair. But not long ago, one Pufferthorn took a stand. Tired of his race being used for nothing more than good grooming, Pop Thorn used his naturally thorny abilities to stand up and fight back against the giant trolls. Soon after, Master Eon made Pop Thorn a Skylander. And to this day, no trolls dare to comb their hair.

To play Pop Thorn to his full potential, you need to learn how to control him in both his puffed state, and his popped state. Pop Thorn floats while puffed, and his primary attack fills the air with tiny spikes that seek out nearby enemies. While popped, Pop Thorn scurries around on the ground and uses a breath attack.

The Tough and Puffed Path ignores the popped state and makes Pop Thorn tougher while floating. The Controlled Breather Path boosts some of Pop Thorn's attacks, allowing them to damage more enemies in a single move.

Special Quest

Take A Deep Breath

HIT ENEMIES WITH A SINGLE STREAM OF BREATH 100 TIMES IN A ROW.

Holding Attack 2 while Pop Thorn is popped results in a continual gust of wind. You must hit enemies 100 times in a row with this gust to complete the quest. If Pop Thorn is hit, the streak ends. Go for this quest where there are no ranged enemies!

POP THORN

Basic Attacks

PUFF

Press **Attack 1** to Puff and damage nearby enemies. While puffed, rapidly press **Attack 1** to shoot out homing spikes at nearby enemies.

POP

Press **Attack 2** to Pop and shoot a large wind blast. While popped, hold **Attack 2** to shoot gusts of wind at enemies.

Soul Gem Ability

TO PUFF OR NOT TO PUFF

4000 Gold

PREREQUISITE
Find Pop Thorn's Soul Gem in Mount Cloudbreak

While popped, speed is increased. While puffed, armor is increased, which reduces damage taken.

Upgrades

FRESH BREATH

500 Gold

PREREQUISITE None

Press **Attack 2** to Pop. After popping, hold **Attack 2** to shoot more powerful air projectiles for a short time.

PUFFBALL POUND

700 Gold

PREREQUISITE None

Press **Attack 1** to Puff. Press **Attack 3** while puffed to slam into the ground, damaging all nearby enemies.

POLISHED SPIKES

900 Gold

PREREQUISITE None

Press **Attack 1** to Puff. After puffing, press **Attack 1** rapidly to shoot more powerful spike projectiles for a short time.

WIND TRAP

1200 Gold

PREREQUISITE None

While popped, press **Attack 3** to leave behind a spiny mine. The mine puffs and explodes when enemies approach, launching them into the air.

Tough and Puffed Path

ROLLERPUFF

1700 Gold

PREREQUISITE
Tough and Puffed Path

While puffed, hold **Attack 3** to roll forward, damaging all enemies in the way.

BOUNCEBACK

2200 Gold

PREREQUISITE
Tough and Puffed Path

Puffing deals increased damage and reflects nearby projectiles.

PRICKLY BODY

3000 Gold

PREREQUISITE
Tough and Puffed Path

While puffed, taking damage releases a spike projectile that damages an attacker.

Controlled Breather Path

AERO TRAMPOLINE

1700 Gold

PREREQUISITE
Controlled Breather Path

While puffed, hold **Attack 3** to charge a powerful slam attack, release to bounce multiple times, damaging all enemies in the way.

DEEP BREATH

2200 Gold

PREREQUISITE
Controlled Breather Path

While puffed, press **Attack 2** to shoot three air blasts instead of one.

SCATTERED WINDS

3000 Gold

PREREQUISITE
Controlled Breather Path

While popped, air beams now shoot multiple projectiles that spread.

SCRATCH

"The Luck of the Claw!"

MAXIMUM HEALTH	260
SPEED	50
ARMOR	6
CRITICAL HIT	8
ELEMENTAL POWER	25

High in the peaks of the Cats Eye Mountain sits a towering city of crystal and Gold that can only be reached by creatures of the Air Element. It was here that Scratch spent her youth soaring playfully in the clouds or exploring the endless number of crystal mines. One day, an army of Pirate Greebles arrived in a fleet of airships, looking to steal ancient magic crystals buried deep in the mountain. Donning specially made armor, Scratch led an epic battle against the pirates, using her incredible fighting skills to defend the crystals and save the city. Tales of her heroism soon made their way to Jet-Vac, who traveled to Cats Eye Mountain and recruited Scratch to join the Skylanders.

She may look and sound like a playful kitten, but Scratch is a fierce Skylander. Cat Scratch is a series of rapid paw swipes that doesn't have many upgrades, but all increase her damage output. Playful Pounce is a great way to reach a spot quickly. It includes a target laser that shows you exactly where Scratch will land.

The Ruby Path is straightforward: Scratch's attacks deal more damage to more enemies. The Sapphire Path becomes more valuable against tougher enemies that don't fall quickly. After all, how much does it matter if something is slowed if it goes down in two swipes?

Special Quest

Purrfect Pounce

DEFEAT 50 ENEMIES BY POUNCING ON THEM.

Chompies are the ideal target for this quest, but you must be careful about aiming your laser. Don't hit the Chompy with the laser, just get it close enough for Scratch's Playful Pounce to do the job.

Basic Attacks

CAT SCRATCH

Press **Attack 1** to scratch at nearby enemies.

PLAYFUL POUNCE

Hold **Attack 2** to shoot a movable laser onto the ground, release to pounce where the laser was pointing.

Soul Gem Ability

GEM AFFINITY

4000 Gold

PREREQUISITE
Find Scratch's Soul Gem in Fantasm Forest

Gain health from collecting gems, coins and money.

Upgrades

WING SPARK

500 Gold

PREREQUISITE None

Press **Attack 3** to dodge an attack and knock away all enemies in an area around you.

SILVER CLAWS

700 Gold

PREREQUISITE None

Gain new silver claws that deal increased damage!

WHIRLWING

900 Gold

PREREQUISITE
Purchase Wing Spark ability

Hold **Attack 3** to pull enemies into a massive whirlwind and do damage to all of them caught inside.

SILVER MASK

1200 Gold

PREREQUISITE None

Gain a new silver mask! Hold **Attack 2** to shoot a powerful new laser at the ground, release to do a devastating pounce attack that does increased damage.

Ruby Path

SHARPENED RUBIES

1700 Gold

PREREQUISITE
Ruby Path

Sharpened rubies grant increased chance to critically hit!

RUBY RAGE

2200 Gold

PREREQUISITE
Ruby Path

Claw damage is increased. Hold **Attack 1** to charge a claw attack, release to slash through nearby enemies.

RUBY MASK

3000 Gold

PREREQUISITE
Ruby Path

Hold **Attack 2** to shoot a laser at the ground that damages enemies in a larger area.

Sapphire Path

SPEEDY SAPPHIRE

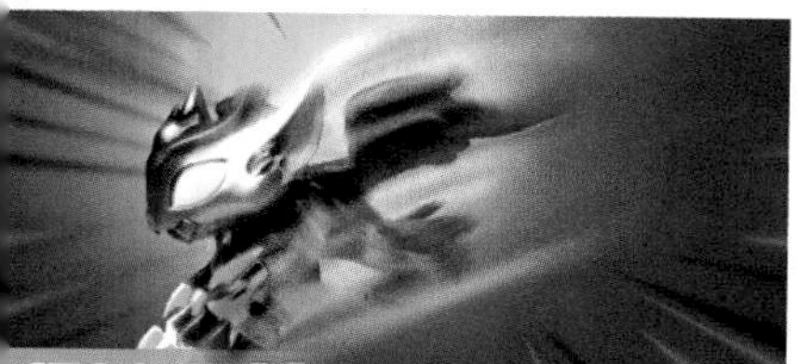

1700 Gold

PREREQUISITE
Sapphire Path

Speed is increased. Sapphires infused with the speed of wind!

SAPPHIRE SLASH

2200 Gold

PREREQUISITE
Sapphire Path

Claw damage is increased. Hold **Attack 1** to charge a wing attack, release to shoot a vortex that pulls enemies into it.

SAPPHIRE MASK

3000 Gold

PREREQUISITE
Sapphire Path

Hold **Attack 2** to shoot a laser at the ground that damages and slows enemies.

WARNADO

"For the Wind!"

MAXIMUM HEALTH	310
SPEED	35
ARMOR	30
CRITICAL HIT	2
ELEMENTAL POWER	25

LIGHTCORE

Warnado was hatched in the fury of a rare and powerful Enchanted Twister. Although initially frightened and quite dizzy, over the passing years he grew to enjoy his whirling surroundings and learned many abilities and secrets of the Air Element. This led to Warnado becoming a powerful force and the only known turtle of his kind. Now, the only time he gets dizzy is when standing still.

With Spin Attack, Warnado flings his body around the area quickly, damaging multiple enemies while staying relatively safe inside his shell. Summon Tornado begins as a simple whirlwind that can trap a single enemy, but upgrades turn it into a force of nature that runs down enemies.

The Eye of the Storm path improves Spin Attack but also provides some difficult-to-use upgrades to his flight ability. The Wind Master Path turns Summon Tornado into an ability that brings forth a whirlwind that chases down enemies on its own while a second whirlwind is under your control.

Special Quest

Chompy Catcher

CATCH 100 CHOMPIES IN YOUR TORNADOES.

To find a good spot to work on this quest, pick a challenge with Chompy in the title; you can't go wrong. If you're impatient, choose the Wind Master Path and its upgrades for Summon Tornado. You'll be done in no time!

Basic Attacks

SPIN ATTACK

Press **Attack 1** to spin Warnado's shell at enemies.

SUMMON TORNADO

Press **Attack 2** to execute a high velocity spin that generates a tornado to pick up enemies.

Soul Gem Ability

THICK SHELLED

4000 Gold

PREREQUISITE
None

This ability gives Warnado a thicker shell, reducing damage he takes from enemies.

Upgrades

SHARP SHELL

500 Gold

PREREQUISITE None

Spin Attack deals more damage.

EXTEND TORNADO

700 Gold

PREREQUISITE None

Hold **Attack 2** to extend the range of the attack.

HIGH WINDS

900 Gold

PREREQUISITE None

Tornadoes can damage multiple enemies.

WHIRLWIND FLIGHT

1200 Gold

PREREQUISITE None

Press **Attack 3** to Fly. Warnado gains increased speed and resistance while flying.

Eye of the Storm Path

LOW FRICTION SHELL

1700 Gold

PREREQUISITE
Eye of the Storm Path

Spin attack strikes father and faster.

FLYING MINI TURTLES

2200 Gold

PREREQUISITE
Eye of the Storm Path

Mini-Warnados fly with you. Press **Attack 1** to launch them at your enemies.

TURTLE SLAM

3000 Gold

PREREQUISITE
Eye of the Storm Path

While flying, hold **Attack 1** to slam down on your enemies.

Wind Master Path

GUIDED TWISTER

1700 Gold

PREREQUISITE
Wind Master Path

Hold **Attack 2** to manually control the direction of your tornado attack using the left control stick

SUMMON CYCLONE

2200 Gold

PREREQUISITE
Wind Master Path

Tornadoes are super-sized and deal more damage.

WIND ELEMENTAL

3000 Gold

PREREQUISITE
Purchase Summon Cyclone ability

Tornadoes will attack enemies on their own.

HORN BLAST WHIRLWIND

"Twists of Fury!"

MAXIMUM HEALTH	270
SPEED	50
ARMOR	18
CRITICAL HIT	10
ELEMENTAL POWER	25

SERIES 3

Whirlwind is an air dragon with unicorn ancestry—two species that could not be more opposite in nature—which made her never quite fit in with either group. Other dragons were envious of her beauty, while unicorns shunned her for her ability to fly. But Whirlwind found peace within the dark and stormy clouds, where she learned to harness the tempest power within her. Despite her turbulent youth, she was the first to defend both dragons and unicorns when the trolls began hunting them, unleashing her ferocity in a brilliant and powerful rainbow that could be seen throughout many regions of Skylands. From that day forward, evil-doers would quake when dark clouds brewed, and run from the rainbow that followed the storm.

Rainbow of Doom hits harder than most other ranged attacks, but it has a slow rate of fire and is difficult to aim. What's great about Rainbow of Doom is that upgrading Tempest Cloud, Whirlwind's other basic attack, benefits Rainbow of Doom as well. Rainbow of Healing increases Whirlwind's value when two Skylanders are working together, but doesn't benefit Whirlwind directly.

The Ultimate Rainbower Path allows Whirlwind to fire two rainbows at once and even create a rainbow singularity. The Tempest Dragon Path allows Whirlwind to create a nice defensive ring of clouds to protect her position when necessary.

Special Quest

What Does It Mean?

DEAL 10,000 DAMAGE WITH RAINBOWS.

Unless your Attack 1 button malfunctions right after you place Whirlwind on the Portal of Power, you should earn this quest quickly. Rainbow of Doom should be your primary source of damage, so hitting 10,000 damage shouldn't take long.

Basic Attacks

RAINBOW OF DOOM

Press **Attack 1** to fire an arced blast of rainbow energy.

TEMPEST CLOUD

Press **Attack 2** to send forth clouds that electrocute enemies. Hold **Attack 2** to make Tempest Clouds travel farther.

Soul Gem Ability

RAINBOW OF HEALING

4000 Gold

PREREQUISITE
None

Rainbows heal your allies!

Upgrades

RAINBOW CHAIN

500 Gold

PREREQUISITE None

Rainbows do extra damage. Hit a Tempest Cloud with a Rainbow of Doom and a second rainbow chains off of it.

TRIPLE TEMPEST

700 Gold

PREREQUISITE None

Have three Tempest Clouds active at once. Tempest Clouds do extra damage.

DRAGON FLIGHT

900 Gold

PREREQUISITE None

Press **Attack 3** to fly. Whirlwind gains increased speed and resistance while flying.

DUEL RAINBOWS

1200 Gold

PREREQUISITE
Purchase Rainbow Chain ability

Hit a Tempest Cloud with a Rainbow of Doom and two rainbows will chain off of it.

Ultimate Rainbower Path

DOUBLE DOSE OF DOOM

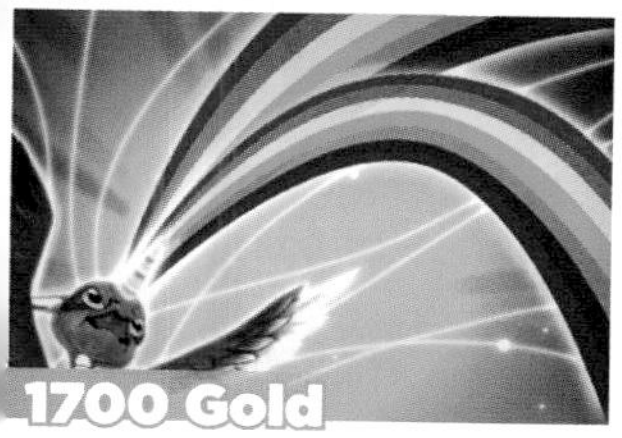

1700 Gold

PREREQUISITE
Ultimate Rainbow Path

Shoot two Rainbows of Doom at once.

ATOMIC RAINBOW

2200 Gold

PREREQUISITE
Ultimate Rainbow Path

Rainbow of Doom attack does increased damage.

RAINBOW SINGULARITY

3000 Gold

PREREQUISITE
Ultimate Rainbow Path

Hold **Attack 1** to charge up a super powerful Rainbow of Doom black hole.

Tempest Dragon Path

TRIPLE RAINBOW, T'S FULL ON

1700 Gold

PREREQUISITE
Tempest Dragon Path

it a Tempest Cloud with a ainbow of Doom and three ainbows will chain off of it.

TEMPEST TANTRUM

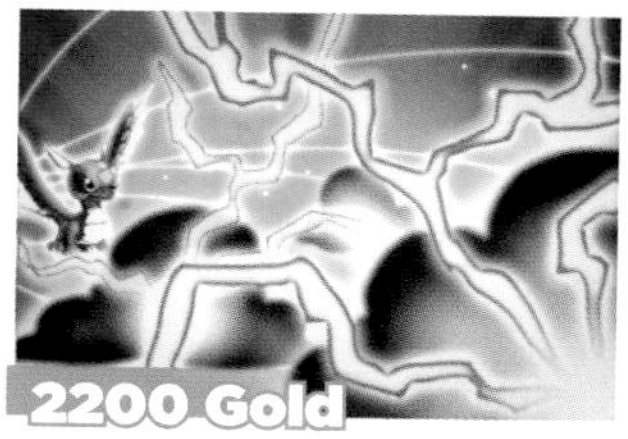

2200 Gold

PREREQUISITE
Tempest Dragon Path

Bigger Tempest Cloud does increased damage with increased range.

TEMPEST MATRIX

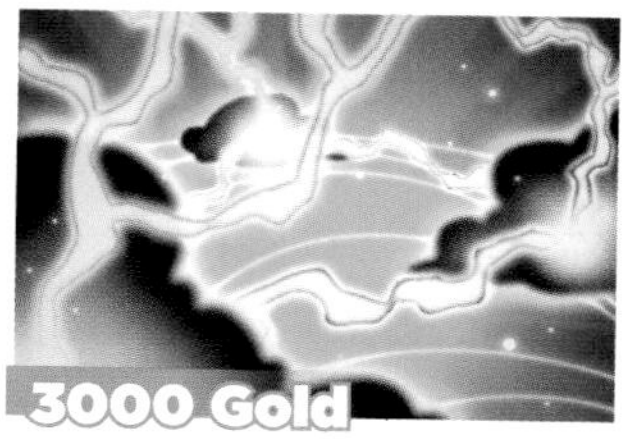

3000 Gold

PREREQUISITE
Tempest Dragon Path

Electricity forms between Tempest Clouds that hurts enemies.

Wow Pow!

RAINBOW RUSH!

5000 Gold

PREREQUISITE
Purchase Dragon Flight ability

Hold **Attack 3** to take flight and release powerful rainbow shockwaves with each wing flap.

Rainbow Rush! is a visually impressive ability that suffers from a lack of mobility. Whirlwind hovers in place and blasts the area directly in front of her with rainbow blasts. You can spin her in place, but she can't move from the spot where she began to use the ability.

IMPROVING YOUR SKYLANDERS

As a Portal Master, one of your primary tasks is improving your Skylanders so they can stand up to their enemies throughout the Skylands. This chapter covers the many facets and methods of improving and customizing your Skylanders.

LEVELING

Whenever you defeat an enemy, they leave behind tiny XP orbs. When your Skylanders absorb these orbs, they gain experience and get closer to leveling up. You can see how close your Skylander is to leveling up by examining the XP Bar just below their health. All Skylanders can reach level 20.

STATS

Each Skylander has five Stats: Max Health, Speed, Armor, Critical Hit, and Elemental Power. Max Health is the only stat that increases when your Skylander gains a level. Elemental Power increases when you add Skylanders of the same Elemental type to your collection.

Max Health

This is your Skylander's most important statistic. Whenever their health reaches zero, they are knocked out and you must place another Skylander on the portal.

Speed

This is how fast your Skylander can move around.

Armor

Whenever a Skylander is hit by an enemy attack, it has a chance to be completely deflected by their armor. This stat reflects that chance. For every six points of armor your Skylander has, they have a 1% chance of deflecting an enemy attack. So, a Skylander with 90 Armor has a 15% chance to deflect an attack.

Critical Hit

This stat determines the chance a Skylander will score a Critical Hit or "crit." A crit scores 150% of regular attack damage. For every five points in Critical Hit, the chance to score a crit increases by 1%. So a Skylander with 50 Critical Hit has a 10% chance of scoring a crit.

Elemental Power

Throughout the Skylands, certain zones have favored elements. If you are using a Skylander of that element in one of these zones, they get bonus damage based on how high their Elemental Power is. Each point adds 1% to the bonus damage, so a Skylander with 100 Elemental Power will get 100% bonus damage in their favored zone.

POWERS & UPGRADES

Each non-*SWAP Force* Skylander starts out with two Powers. For more details on what powers your individual Skylanders start out with, check out The Skylanders chapter. *SWAP Force* Skylanders begin with one power for their body, and another power for their legs. In addition to these starting powers, each regular Skylander and *SWAP Force* body can also purchase an additional power in the Power Pod, but it costs gold.

The remaining Power Upgrades are all purchased from Power Pods. There is one Power Pod in Woodburrow, and others are found at Checkpoints in most Story Levels.

Upgrade Paths

Skylanders must also choose a Path. This Path represents the Skylander choosing to develop one power or ability over another. Most Skylanders must permanently commit to one path once they have unlocked their first four power upgrades. *SWAP Force* Skylanders have Upgrade Path choices for both their body and their legs.

The exceptions to this rule are the Series 2 and Series 3 figures. After committing to a path, these Skylanders may switch paths while inside a Power Pod.

Soul Gem Ability

All characters introduced in *Skylanders SWAP Force* must find their Soul Gem before they can purchase their Soul Gem Ability. The walkthrough contains more information on where to find each Soul Gem, or check out The Skylanders section of the guide. Skylanders from the previous games may purchase their Soul Gem Power without the need to find a Soul Gem.

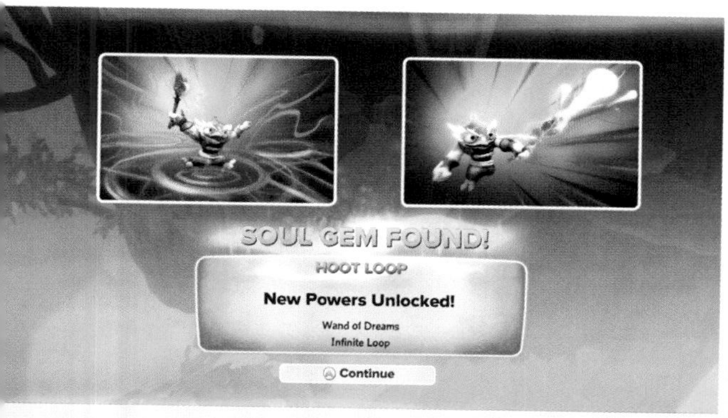

Wow-Pow! Powers

Series 2 and Series 3 figures have new Wow-Pow! powers that are expensive, but significantly improve an existing power. For more details on Series 2 and 3 Wow Pow! powers, check out The Skylanders chapter.

HATS

Each Skylander can wear one magic hat which provides bonuses to stats. Hats are available for purchase from Tuk's Emporium, and found throughout Story Mode Levels. Use Hats to supplement your Skylander's weaker Stats. For instance, if your Skylander has low armor, look for a hat that provides additional armor! You can change your Skylander's Hat at any time via the Skylanders menu. Once you find a Hat, you can put it on as many Skylanders as you like. See our Collectibles chapter for more information on individual Hats.

LEGENDARY TREASURES

After Tibbet unlocks Legendary Treasure Pedestals, you have a new way to boost your Skylanders. Placing a Legendary Treasure on one of these Pedestals conveys a bonus that applies to every aspect of the game. The best part about Legendary Treasures is that you can tailor the ones in use to your needs. If you have a new Skylander and want to hit level 20 as quickly as possible, opt for Tik Tok Neck Clock or Urban Art which boost your XP. If you're short on gold because of all the Hats you need to buy, put The Brass Tap and Bubble Chest on the Pedestals to increase the gold you find.

Some of the bonuses are oddly specific, but they could be a tremendous help for you when you're shooting to complete certain Challenges, whether it's in the Arena, Time Attack, or just finishing off Kaos for the first time.

CHARMS

Except for a few Tuk sells, you must earn Charms by completing Bonus Mission Maps and Arena challenges. Each Charm is active as soon as you acquire it. All the effects are cumulative and the bonuses from Charms are active at all times.

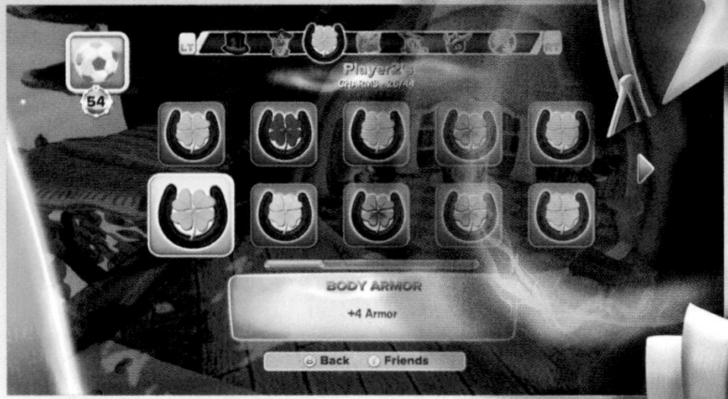

QUESTS

All Skylanders have nine Quests to complete. You can check your Skylander's progress on any of these quests at any time by entering the Skylander menu and selecting Quests. Completing these quests improves their rank. Also when a Skylander receives a Quest medal, they receive +25 of Max. Health Bonus. So completing all the Quests earns a Skylander +75 of their Max. Health. Improving a Skylander's rank gives them a medal next to their name and also works toward Portal Master Accolades.

Bronze Toy Quest Medal	Complete 3 Quests
Silver Toy Quest Medal	Complete 7 Quests
Gold Toy Quest Medal	Complete 10 Quests

Every Skylander shares six quests, and each Skylander of the same Element shares another two. Elementalist appears as an Elemental quest, but the condition for completing it is the same for every character. Each Skylander has a unique quest as well. For more information about unique quests, check out the individual Skylanders sections found earlier in this guide.

General Quests

Badguy Basher	Defeat 1000 enemies.
Fruit Frontiersman	Eat 15 fruits in Story Levels or Arenas.
Flawless Challenger	Complete a non-Story Mode level with full health.
True Gladiator	Win 10 PVP matches.
Totally Maxed Out	Reach level 20 and purchase all Upgrades for this Skylander.

General Elemental Quest

Elementalist	Cause 7500 elemental bonus damage.

Magic

Puzzle Power	Push a Lazer Puzzle Beam to defeat an enemy.
Mage Rivalry	Defeat a total of 25 Ranged Cyclops.

Fire

Mega Melter	Defeat a total of 25 Ice Golems.
Bombardier	Defeat a total of 30 enemies with bombs.

Water

Extinguisher	Defeat a total of 25 Fire Golems.
A-Fish-Ionado	Catch 25 fish with the fishing rod.

Undead

Witherer	Defeat a total of 25 Life Spellpunks.
Back from the Brink	Defeat a boss while at critically low health.

Tech

Out-Teched	Defeat Glumshanks in Jungle Rumble without switching Skylanders.
Problem Solver	Complete a total of 25 lockpicking puzzles with this Skylander.

Life

Defender of Life	Defeat a total of 25 Undead Spellpunks.
Fully Stocked	Defeat a total of 250 enemies while at full health.

Earth

Savior of the Land	Free the Terrasquid in the Twisty Tunnels without switching Skylanders.
Unearthed	Use shovels to dig a total of 25 holes.

Air

Geronimo!	Travel over 250 feet in one fall.
Skylooter	Collect a total of 500 gold in midair.

MINIONS OF KAOS

CHOMPIES

Chompy

Appears in:
MOUNT CLOUDBREAK, CASCADE GLADE, MUDWATER HOLLOW, IRON JAW GULCH

A familiar foe to veteran Portal Masters, Chompies are tiny, vicious creatures that attack in large numbers. Even if they are alone, they run directly at your Skylander and attack with a lunging bite. Chomp!

Chompy Powerhouse

Appears in:
MOTLEYVILLE, TWISTY TUNNELS

These Chompies put on dark masks and wear dark gloves to show just how powerful they are. They might be tough for a Chompy, but they're still just a Chompy. Just take them out before they can attack. Your only concern is their numbers.

Chompy Blitzbloom

Appears in:
WINTER KEEP, FROSTFEST MOUNTAINS

These red and yellow Chompies wear shoes in icy areas to help with their traction on slippery surfaces. Unfortunately, for them, it doesn't improve their ability in combat.

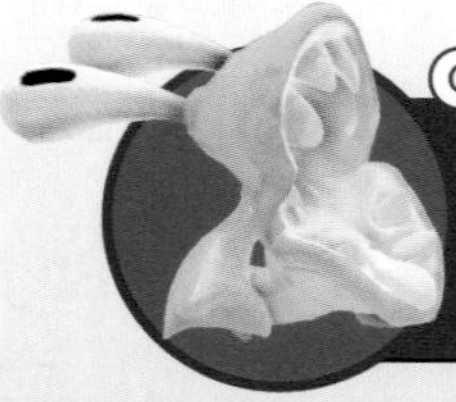

Chompy Pastepetal

Appears in:
KAOS' FORTRESS

The first attack on these bright yellow creatures splits them into two halves. The two halves continue to attack until you take them out.

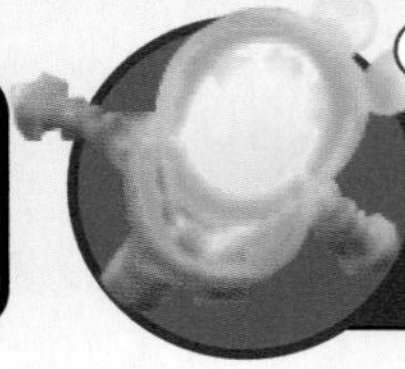

Chompy Rustbud

Appears in:
RAMPANT RUINS, CLOUDBREAK CORE

Chompies often take on the characteristics of the area where they spawn. These slightly more powerful cousins of Chompies are only a tad more difficult to handle than regular Chompies.

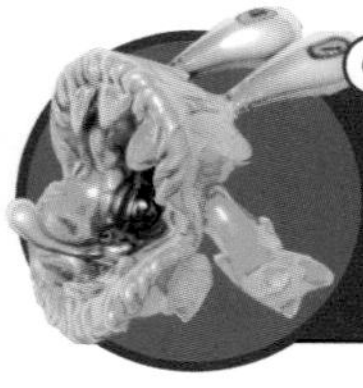

Chompy Frostflower

Appears in:
BONEY ISLANDS

Chompy Frostflowers are Chompies encased in ice. The ice makes them a bit tougher, but not much more of a challenge in a fight. These Chompies freeze a Skylander if they bite them.

Chompy Boomblossom

Appears in:
FANTASM FOREST

Chompy Boomblossoms take the self-destructive streak shared by Chompies to the next level. When they draw close enough to a Skylander, they glow orange and detonate, inflicting a considerable amount of damage to anything too close. Take them out before they're able to explode or your Skylander will pay the price.

Chompy Pod

Appears in:
ANYWHERE CHOMPIES DO!

Chompy Pods take on the colors of the Chompies they produce. They do not attack on their own, they produce Chompies and let the tiny terrors do all the work.

GREEBLES

Greeble

Appears in:
MOUNT CLOUDBREAK

Greebles are Kaos' newest allies, though they seem inexperienced at the evil game at first. They carry spiked clubs, which likely outweigh them, into battle. The clubs are so large, the Greebles swing slowly, and take some time to pull the club out of the ground.

Evilized Greeble

Appears in:
CASCADE GLADE, MOTHERLY MAYHEM

After their exposure to crystallized darkness, Greebles trade in their too-heavy clubs for machetes. However, not much has really changed when you encounter these purple creatures. They still telegraph their attacks with a big wind up, and the time they need to recover from the attacks leaves them vulnerable to your counterattacks.

Greeble Ironclad

Appears in:
CASCADE GLADE

These bruisers are the first shielded enemy you face. Until they attack, their body is protected from harm. When they draw close, they draw back a fist and swing it. If you manage to avoid the attack, Greeble Ironclads are left off-balance and open. Strike while they are recovering their balance and score as much damage as you can before they are shielded again.

Pirate Slamspin

Appears in:
IRON JAW GULCH, MOTHERLY MAYHEM

Pirate Slamspins are similar to Arkeyan Rip-Rotors, but they stay on the ground at all times. They're invulnerable while spinning, so stay at a safe distance until the spinning stops. Attack them while they're dizzy to take them out safely. Greeble Slamspins, which appear during Motherly Mayhem, are the same creature, but aren't dressed as pirates.

Grumblebum Thrasher

Appears in:
MUDWATER HOLLOW, CLOUDBREAK CORE

These mutated creatures lack a ranged attack, but they're strong enough to use their club effectively. They're slow swingers, so you can attack before they swing or after a miss, which leaves them briefly off balance.

Greeble Screwball

Appears in:
MOUNT CLOUDBREAK

Greeble Screwballs carry a tube that lobs a glowing rock into the air. They're slow to fire and even slower at reloading their tube, which is when they are most vulnerable to attack.

Greeble Blunderbuss

Appears in:
CASCADE GLADE, MOTHERLY MAYHEM

They may have a more menacing look, but Greeble Blunderbusses are simply evilized Greeble Screwballs. They are tougher and more powerful, but still use an easy-to-avoid attack. Attack them while they're reloading their weapon, and they fall quickly.

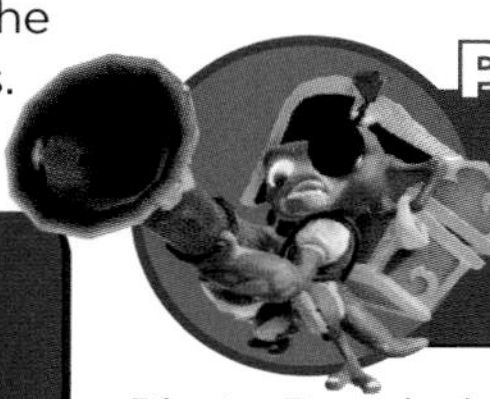

Pirate Powderkeg

Appears in:
IRON JAW GULCH

Pirate Powderkegs are similar to Greeble Blunderbusses. They carry a large cannon, which can be fired one time before it needs reloading. Avoid the cannonball, then attack the vulnerable Powderkeg before he can reload.

Greeble Heaver

Appears in:
MOTLEYVILLE, MOTHERLY MAYHEM

Greeble Heavers lob three shells into the air before reloading. Avoid the red circles on the ground, then attack the Greeble Heaver while it reloads.

Grumblebum Rocketshooter

Appears in:
MUDWATER HOLLOW

Grumblebum Rocketshooters hide inside wooden turrets and use red-and-white rockets in two ways. First, they light a fuse and fire them in a straight line. They take a moment to reload, which is your chance to attack. After destroying Grumblebum Rocketshooters, their last rocket flies into the air and explodes on impact with the ground or a Skylander.

ARKEYANS

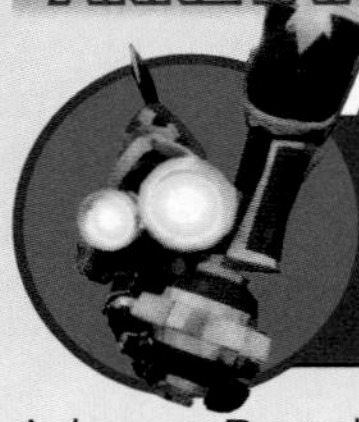

Arkeyan Barrelbot

Appears in:
RAMPANT RUINS, CLOUDBREAK CORE

Arkeyan Barrelbots use a double-barrel energy blaster that can tear through a health bar quickly. Listen for the build up of energy, then dodge the blast and retaliate while the Barrelbot reloads.

Arkeyan Rip-Rotor

Appears in:
RAMPANT RUINS, MOTLEYVILLE

Arkeyan Rip-Rotors are invulnerable while spinning, so stay clear when they're airborne. They are dazed shortly after touching down on the ground, and that's your opening to attack. If you can't finish them off quickly enough, move away before they start spinning again.

Arkeyan Slamshock

Appears in:
RAMPANT RUINS, MOTLEYVILLE

These large enemies are invulnerable until they pound the ground and send out a golden energy blast. The blasts travel directly ahead of the Slamshock, so step to the side and attack while its hands are still on the ground.

Arkeyan Knuckleduster

Appears in:
JUNGLE RUMBLE, MOTLEYVILLE, CLOUDBREAK CORE

Arkeyan Knuckledusters are small in size, but as tenacious as Chompies. Watch out for the cannon on their right hand which shoots multiple energy blasts. Dodge the shots to avoid taking unnecessary damage

CYCLOPES

Coldspear Cyclops

Appears in:
BONEY ISLANDS, WINTER KEEP, FROSTFEST MOUNTAINS, CLOUDBREAK CORE, SHEEP WRECK ISLANDS

A Coldspear Cyclops rushes forward and performs a rapid-thrust attack. They don't move while they are attacking, so all you need to do is avoid the spear point (or the sword in warmer climes), then hit them with your own attack from anywhere else except directly in front of them.

Cyclops Gazermage

Appears in:
BONEY ISLANDS, FROSTFEST MOUNTAINS, CLOUDBREAK CORE

Cyclops Gazermages focus a powerful beam through a magnifying glass. They also mark their targets first, and a noise builds up to let you know when they are about to fire. They're fragile foes, so avoid their beams and they should drop quickly.

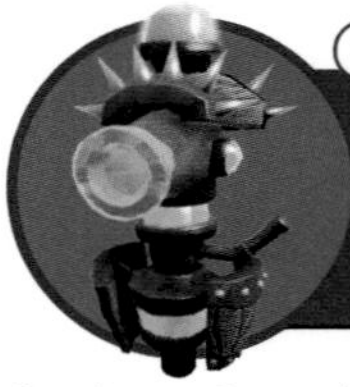

Cyclops Snowblaster

Appears in:
BONEY ISLANDS

Cyclops Snowblasters are automated defense turrets. Watch for a power build-up at the tip of its barrel to know when one will fire again. Avoid its shots, then hit it with your own attacks.

Cyclops Sleetthrower

Appears in:
WINTER KEEP, SHEEP WRECK ISLANDS

Cyclops Sleetthrowers are parka-wearing troublemakers wh scoop up a shovelful of snow and lob it. A red circle indicate their target location, and their reload time is considerable. Avoid the snowball and get on them before they can reload and fire again. On Sheep Wreck Islands, these foes leave behind their parkas and lob jellyfish instead of snows.

Twistpick Cyclops

Appears in:
WINTER KEEP

A Twistpick Cyclops is invulnerable while spinning, but they telegraph their movements. Watch for a red arrow on the ground at their feet as they start spinning. Move your Skylander out of the path indicated by the red arrow, then attack the dizzy Cyclops after its spin ends. Twistpick Cyclops will sometimes change directions after a short spinning dash.

Cyclops Brawlbuckler

Appears in:
FROSTFEST MOUNTAINS, CLOUDBREAK CORE, SHEEP WRECK ISLANDS

Cyclops Brawlbucklers are shielded before they strike. They telegraph their attack by swinging their mace over their head, where it crackles with energy, before slamming it into the ground. Striking them when they are extended and vulnerable knocks them back and they drop their mace and shield.

K-BOTS

K-Bot Gloopgunner

Appears in:
KAOS' FORTRESS

K-Bot Gloopgunners are automated defense systems that fling gloop from the top of their heads. Avoid the green glob and attack the machine before it can reload and fire.

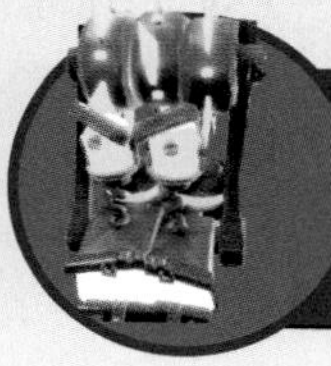

K-Bot Splodeshard

Appears in:
KAOS' FORTRESS

K-Bot Splodeshards use a wicked front wheel to pull themselves forward and grind up anything in front of them. Dodge the attack and blast them while they recover.

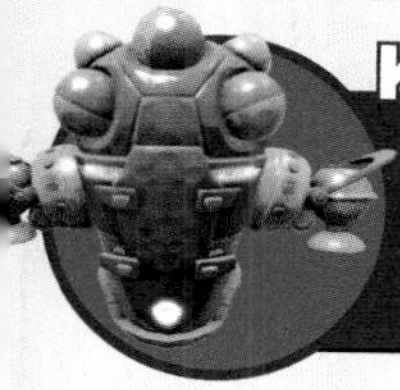

K-Bot Mineminer

Appears in:
KAOS' FORTRESS

K-Bot Mineminers fire three explosive spheres at a time from their heads. Watch for the electrical charge build up around the sockets where these mines appear for an idea of when they will be fired. K-Bot Mineminers have two more annoying tricks up their sleeves. First, they extend an electrical charge in two directions from their base and spin it around in a painful circle. Jump over the electricity when it's near. Their final ability is the most annoying. They teleport! Just when you think you have them right where you want them, they'll vanish and appear nearby.

TROLLS

Cadet Crasher

Appears in:
TWISTY TUNNELS, FANTASM FOREST, CLOUDBREAK CORE, TOWER OF TIME

Cadet Crushers are the first troll enemy you meet in the Cloudbreak Islands. These hammer-swinging trolls have only melee attacks, but do hit hard. They take a big wind up before swinging their hammer overhead. When the hammer is stuck on the ground, it's your opening to attack.

Boom Boss

Appears in:
TWISTY TUNNELS, CLOUDBREAK CORE, TOWER OF TIME

Boom Bosses lob explosive barrels that bounce a few times before exploding. They need a moment to reload, which is the best time to take them out.

Loose Cannon

Appears in:
BONEY ISLANDS, TOWER OF TIME

Loose Cannon are large trolls that employ missiles and shields in combat. They fire off three missiles before applying shields while reloading. There's a small window to strike them immediately after firing missiles and before their shields go up.

Cadet Crasher (Undead)

Appears in:
FANTASM FOREST, SUMMONED BY UNDEAD SPELL PUNKS

These skeletal trolls act just like the fleshy trolls they resemble. They swing a big hammer to attack and are vulnerable while they try to pull the hammer back over their heads.

Missile Mauler

Appears in:
FANTASM FOREST, CLOUDBREAK CORE

Missile Maulers are ranged trolls that fire a single missile with some tracking capability. Their missile launcher requires a long time to reload before they can fire again. Attack them between their missile launches and they should go down quickly.

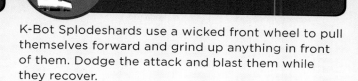

THE EVILIZED

Evilized Bog Hog

Appears in:
MUDWATER HOLLOW, MOTHERLY MAYHEM

Bog Hogs charge in a straight line until they crash into a solid object. Avoid the charge and the Bog Hog will be stunned while recovering its wits after a collision. Pour on the damage while it's vulnerable, but be ready to move out of its way when it clears its head.

Evilized Kangarat

Appears in:
IRON JAW GULCH, MOTHERLY MAYHEM

Evilized Kangarats attack by jumping into the air and landing on the spot indicated by a large, violet circle on the ground. Avoid the landing spot, then knock the crystallized darkness out of it while it's recovering.

Evilized Chillydog

Appears in:
FROSTFEST MOUNTAIN, MOTHERLY MAYHEM

Evilized Chillydogs dig up an evilized crystal from the ground and heave it into the air. Look for the large, violet circle on the ground to see where the crystal will land. The Evilized Chillydogs then hop away and repeat the process.

Evilized Sugarbat

Appears in:
RAMPANT RUINS, MOTHERLY MAYHEM

These unfortunate creatures charge in a straight line to deal damage. When they crash into a wall, they are momentarily stunned and vulnerable to attacks.

Evilized Snowroller

Appears in:
WINTER KEEP, MOTHERLY MAYHEM

Evilized Snowrollers attack in two stages. First, they curl up and build up momentum before rolling directly ahead. While they are curled up and rolling, their thick hides protect them from most damage. At the end of the roll, they launch crystallized darkness shards into the air, which come down at the spot marked in red on the ground. They are momentarily vulnerable while on their backs after the shard attack, but spin in place before righting themselves.

Evilized Screecher

Appears in:
FANTASM FOREST, MOTHERLY MAYHEM

After a shrill cry, Evilized Screechers fly just above the ground with a line of evilized fire stretching out from their wings. When the Screechers draw close, jump over them (or the evilized fire) to avoid taking damage. When the Screecher runs into a wall, it becomes stunned. Attack it before it can climb back into the air.

GEARGOLEMS

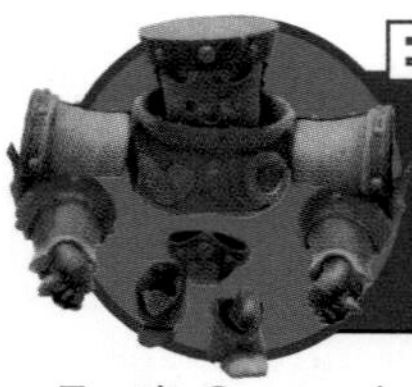

Earth Geargolem

Appears in:
MOTLEYVILLE

Earth Geargolems smash their fists into the ground to create a shockwave of destruction. Jump over the shockwave and attack the massive creature while its fists are stuck in the ground.

Air Geargolem

Appears in:
TWISTY TUNNELS, BONEY ISLANDS, CLOUDBREAK CORE

Air Geargolems spin in the air, then come crashing down with a powerful two-hand slam. They use powerful air currents to hold their targets in place, so stay on the move to avoid their devastating attack.

Fire Geargolem

Appears in:
IRON JAW GULCH, MOTLEYVILLE, TWISTY TUNNELS, BONEY ISLANDS, CLOUDBREAK CORE

Fire Geargolems turn in place to track your Skylander's position, then stop and bathe the area directly in front of their hands with fire. Avoid the fire blast and attack the Fire Geargolem from anywhere not directly in front of it while it's standing still.

Tech Geargolem

Appears in:
FANTASM FOREST, CLOUDBREAK CORE

Tech Geargolems fill the area with gears fired at high velocity. Watch for the Tech Geargolem to shrink (its upper body covers its legs) to know when it is preparing to fire. It pivots at the waist, so you must stay mobile while attacking it.

Clock Geargolem

Appears in:
TOWER OF TIME

Clock Geargolems spin constantly, with their arms outstretched. Avoid them until you are able to freeze time (fortunately, these enemies appear only in areas with time stopping mechanisms!). With time frozen, hit them hard and fast, but be ready to move away when time resumes its normal flow.

Vortex Geargolem

Appears in:
SHEEP WRECK ISLANDS

Vortex Geargolems employ a variety of tricks. First, they spawn enemies from the vortex in their chest that gives them their name. Second, they shoot out golden vortices that pull whatever they touch, directly in front of the Vortex Geargolem. Finally, they have a ground slam attack that sends a shockwave over a small area.

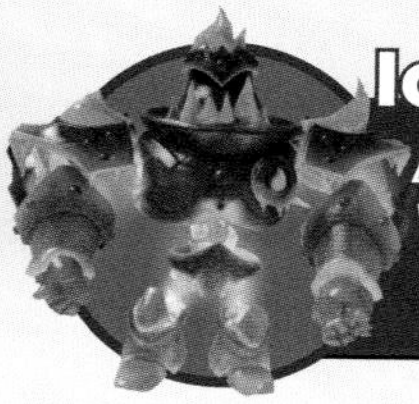

Ice Geargolem

Appears in:
WINTER KEEP, CLOUDBREAK CORE

Ice Geargolems fire ice shards from their fists after charging up the attack. Once energy appears on its fists, the Ice Geargolem won't change its position. The ice shards fire out in a spread pattern, so the safest spot to be is directly behind it. Attack the Ice Geargolem immediately after it fires, but get away before it fires again.

SPELL PUNKS

Life Spell Punk

Appears in:
MUDWATER HOLLOW, MOTHERLY MAYHEM

This can't be stressed enough: If a Life Spell Punk is alive and in a fight, you need to take it down before you mess with any other enemy. They ignore your Skylander, and instead direct their abilities at their allies. They restore health to every enemy within the range of their spells. Until your Skylanders are powered up, it is difficult to deal damage faster than Life Spell Punks can heal it.

Time Spell Punk

Appears in:
TOWER OF TIME

Time Spell Punks have the ability to negate the effects of the time-stopping mechanisms in the tower of time. They also project fireballs for a long-range attack, and ignite a wall of flames directly in front of themselves to ward off melee attacks.

Air Spell Punk

Appears in:
TWISTY TUNNELS, BONEY ISLANDS

These white-clad wizards boost the speed of every nearby enemy. Target the Air Spell Punk first, but making them your top target is not as vital as it is when there are Life Spell Punks in a fight.

Undead Spell Punk

Appears in:
FANTASM FOREST

Undead Spell Punk, makes its debut before your Skylander can touch the hydrant. Undead Spell Punks summon skeletal Cadet Crushers that act much like their fleshy selves. Undead Spell Punks don't attack directly, they let their minions do the dirty work.

Magic Spell Punk

Appears in:
KAOS' FORTRESS

Magic Spell Punks don't attack Skylanders directly but instead aid the other enemy units in the area by turning them invisible. There isn't much to follow when trying to figure out where enemies are (no shadow, no rippling effect, or anything like that). The best thing to do is focus on the Spell Punk. When it is defeated, its spells stop working.

Baron Von Shellshock & Evilized Whiskers

APPEARS IN: CHAPTER 7: MOTLEYVILLE, PAGE 172

Kaos' Mom & Bubba Greebs

APPEARS IN: CHAPTER 16: MOTHERLY MAYHEM, PAGE 236

Mr. Chompy

APPEARS IN: CHAPTER 15: KAOS' FORTRESS, PAGE 226

Cluck

APPEARS IN: THE TOWER OF TIME ADVENTURE PACK, PAGE 250

Super Evil Kaos

APPEARS IN: CHAPTER 17: CLOUDBREAK CORE, PAGE 172

Evil Glumshanks

APPEARS IN: CHAPTER 5: JUNGLE RUMBLE, PAGE 162

Mesmeralda

APPEARS IN: CHAPTER 13: MESMERALDA'S SHOW, PAGE 216

Fire Viper

APPEARS IN: CHAPTER 8: TWISTY TUNNELS, PAGE 182; CHAPTER 9: SERPENT'S PEAK, PAGE 190

Sheep Mage

APPEARS IN: THE SHEEP WRECK ISLANDS ADVENTURE PACK, PAGE 240

MOUNT CLOUDBREAK

OBJECTIVES

Story Goals

- ◯ Get to Woodburrow

Dares

- 5 Flynn's Missing Stuff
- 50 Enemy Goal
- 0 No Skylanders Defeated

New Enemies

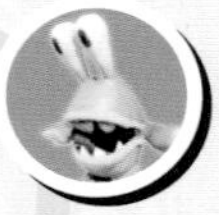
Chompy

Greeble

Greeble Screwball

Chompy Pod

Collections

- 13 Areas Discovered
- 3 Treasure Chests
- 1 Giant Treasure Chest
- 2 Soul Gems
- 1 Legendary Treasure
- 3 Hats
- 1 Bonus Mission Map
- 1 Winged Sapphire
- 1 Story Scroll

A NEW ADVENTURE BEGINS

Where there's Flynn, there's adventure! The intrepid pilot's vacation is cut short when an unknown villager lands on his ship looking for help from the Skylanders. Before she can provide more details, mysterious ships chase Flynn into a volcano, and your next adventure as a Portal Master kicks off! After you choose your Skylander, clear the debris from the deck of Flynn's boat.

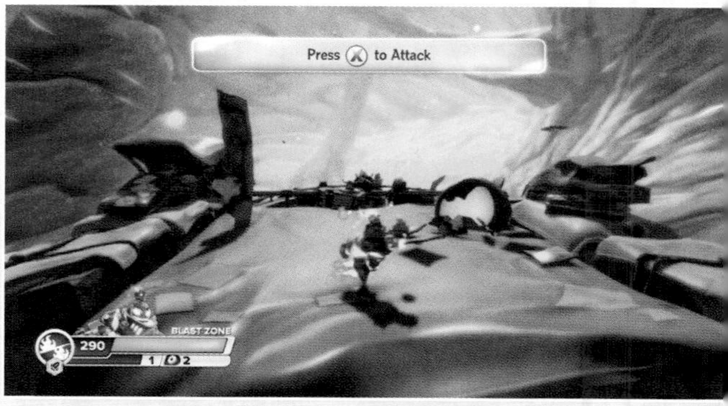

After you complete that task, the pursuit ships overtake Flynn and two waves of enemies land on the deck. The first wave consists of the familiar Chompies, while the second wave is made up of previously unknown enemies called Greebles. Neither enemy is a threat, so take your time while battling them to become more familiar with the game's controls.

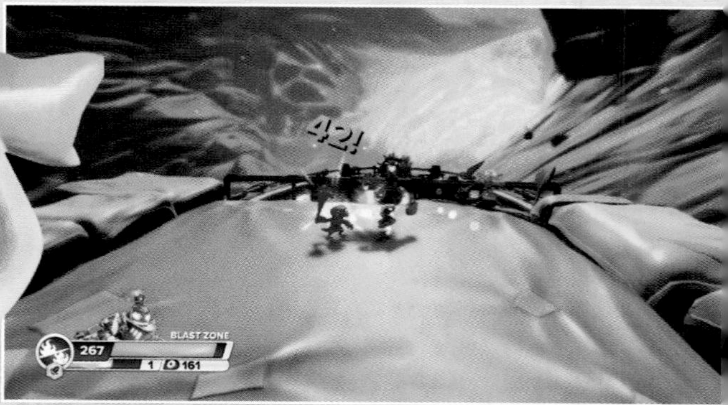

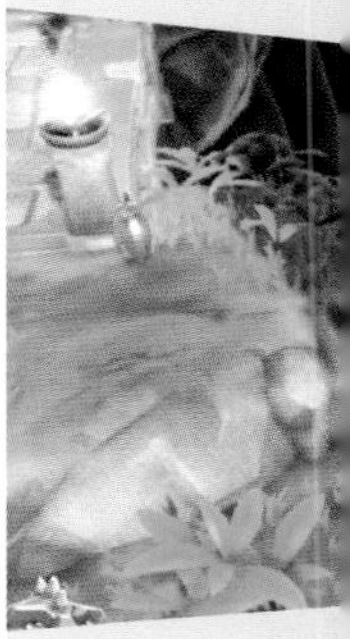

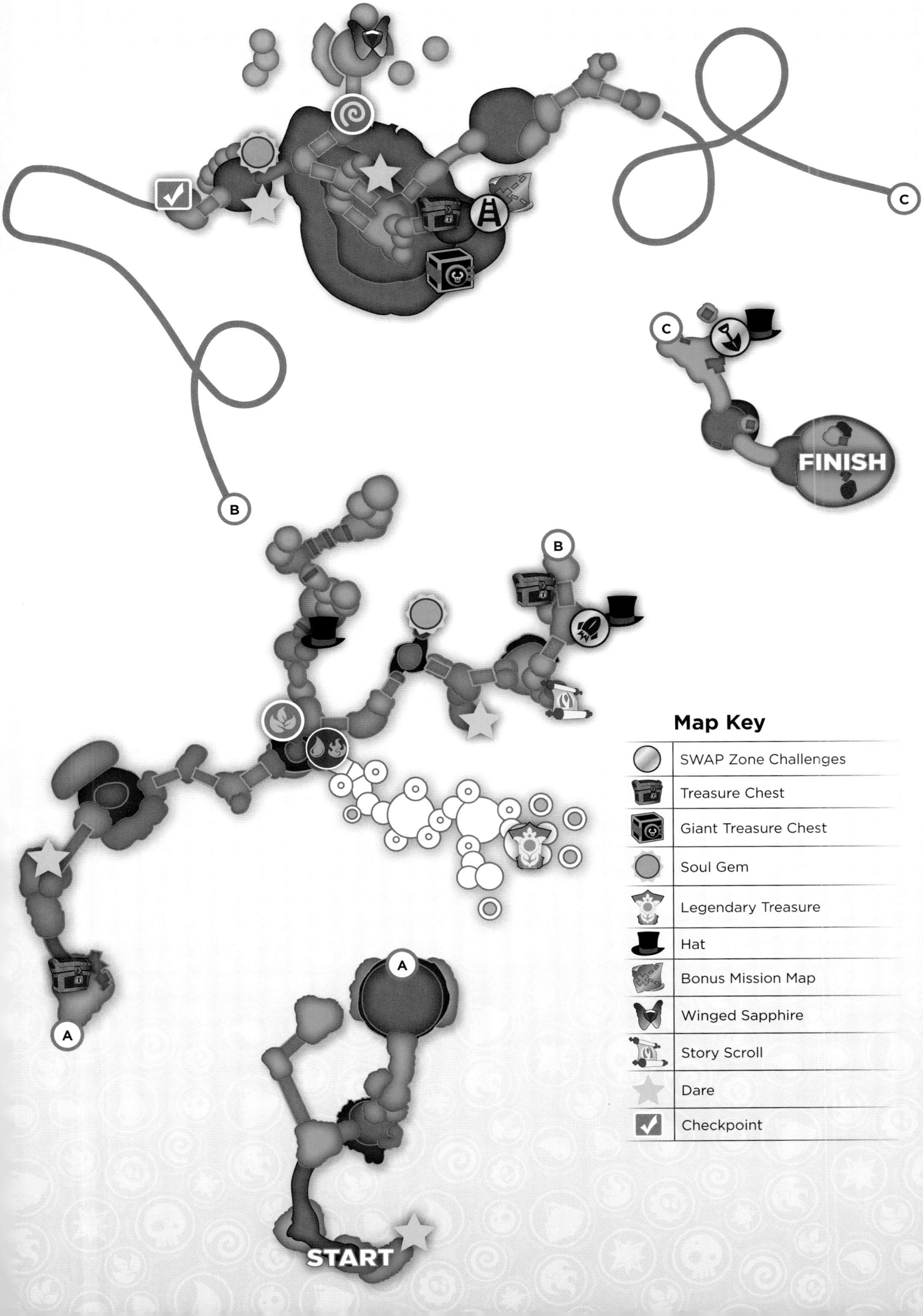

Map Key

(icon)	SWAP Zone Challenges
(icon)	Treasure Chest
(icon)	Giant Treasure Chest
(icon)	Soul Gem
(icon)	Legendary Treasure
(icon)	Hat
(icon)	Bonus Mission Map
(icon)	Winged Sapphire
(icon)	Story Scroll
(icon)	Dare
(icon)	Checkpoint

FIRE IS STRONGER IN THIS AREA

THE OVERGROWTH, TRAPPING PIT, & TANGLED THICKET

After Flynn's spectular landing, you must find the way to Tessa's village, Woodburrow. While Tessa and Flynn wait up ahead, turn around and collect the first item of **Flynn's Missing Stuff**, a **Water Buoy,** just behind the starting point. After speaking with Tessa and Flynn, start up the path and collect the piles of gold. Hop up the ledges, destroy the bamboo gate, and speak with Barkin.

The ground gives way (don't worry about falling, there aren't any hazards on the way down) and a Battle Gate blocks the path out of the Trapping Pit. Take out the Chompies to unlock the Battle Gate and clear the way to the Tangled Thicket.

Mount Cloudbreak's first **Treasure Chest** is marked with an arrow just off the main path. Crack it open to claim the gold inside, then speak with Tessa to free the creatures caged by the Greebles. There are more cages ahead, but these are guarded by a Greeble Screwball. Avoid its lob attack and take it out. Go around the left side of the cages to recover the second item of **Flynn's Missing Stuff**, a **Life Preserver**.

Use the cages to return to the main path. A group of Woodburrow villagers are caged high above the ground. Use the switch to lower the villagers to the ground. This sets them free and creates steps to continue along the path to Woodburrow. Unfortunately, a Locked Gate soon blocks the path ahead. The good news is that the Key needed to open the Locked Gate is not too far from it.

There are two elemental gates on the other side of the Locked Gate. One gate is the same as the gates encountered in previous Skylander adventures, requiring a Skylander of the matching element to open it. The other is a new type of gate, known as a Dual Element Gate. It requires two different elements to be present in order for it to be unlocked. The gate opens when both elements are present, whether you choose to use two different Skylanders, or a single *SWAP Force* Skylander with the required elements.

CANOPY HOT SPRINGS

Canopy Hot Springs is free of enemies but loaded with Bounce Pads. The only hazards in the area are water jets that push around Skylanders, but don't damage them. Carefully explore the area and collect all the gold you can. The present at the back of the area turns into the Legendary Treasure, **Mostly Magic Mirror,** when you open it. Use the portal just beyond it to quickly return to the gated area's entrance.

PRICKLY PASTURES

Little Bro Pete lost three sheep and found them caged by Greebles in Prickly Pastures. To make matters worse, the Greebles set up spike traps to keep out intruders. To avoid taking damage from the traps, watch for the black holes turning to white. The color change means the spikes are about to emerge, so keep clear!

To free the sheep, destroy their cages. The Greebles are led by Lt. Woalf who appears to be in charge of the area, but he's not much more of a threat than the Greeble Screwballs under his command. After you free three sheep, Little Bro Pete hands over the **Stovepipe Hat** as a reward.

EARTH IS STRONGER IN THIS AREA

OLD TREETOP TERRACE

Cross the bridge beyond the elemental gates area and use the empty cages as steps. The next empty cage has a blue arrow on top of it. Arrows on top of items indicate the direction or directions you can move it. Push the first cage into the gap and cross over the newly-formed bridge. There are two more cages to push ahead. Push the first toward the Soul Gem floating on a stump until the cage drops down. Hop up to the stump and claim Pop Thorn's **Soul Gem (To Puff or Not to Puff)**.

Return to the main path and use the other cage to reach a stone bridge. Cross the bridge and bear slightly right where you can pick up more of **Flynn's Missing Stuff**, **Fuzzy Dice**. The main path leads across a stone bridge guarded by Chompies and Greeble Blunderbusses. Clear out the enemies, collect **Story Scroll: Magical Pyrotechnics,** and switch to a SWAP Skylander with the Rocket Power to tackle your first SWAP Zone challenge.

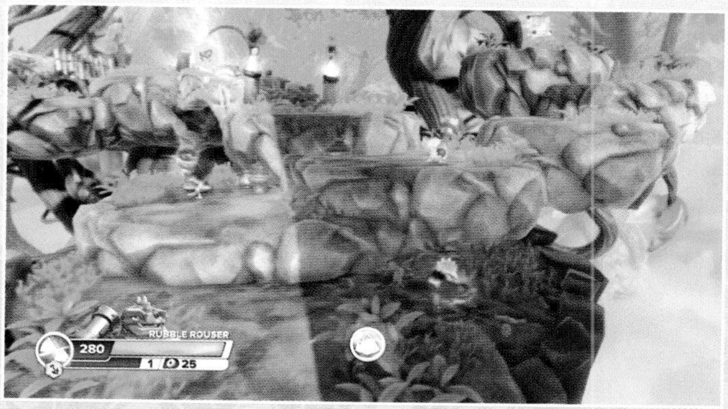

SWAP Zone
Forest Flyby

ROCKET TO THE FINISH!
Turn to page 272 for tips on how to clear this SWAP Zone Challenge. Your reward for completing this challege is the **Greeble Hat**.

Don't cross the next stone bridge before you empty the **Treasure Chest** on a nearby, lower ledge. On the other side of the bridge, Tessa pops up, riding Whiskers, to explain how to use the vines to travel to the next area quickly. Step on the glowing platform and follow the on-screen prompts to begin a wild ride through the trees. There are neither hazards nor enemies on the vines, so concentrate on timing your jumps to collect the coins floating above the path.

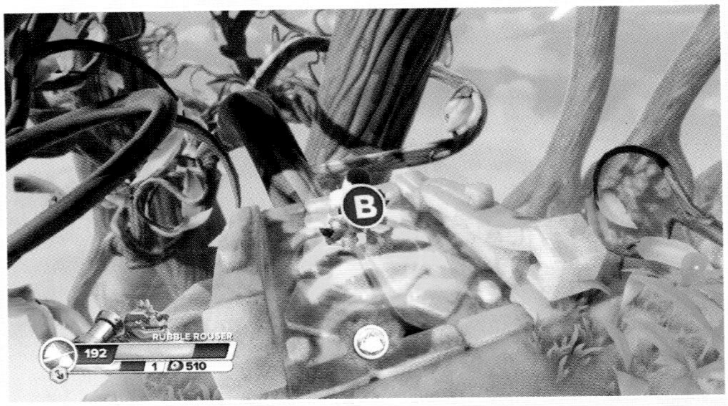

Your vine ride ends at an earthen ledge that doubles as a Checkpoint. Walk up the short bridge and destroy the Chompy Pod (and its Chompies) infesting the enormous treestump. Don't move ahead just yet! Drop off the stump's left side and descend the stone steps. The glowing cave entrance at the bottom of the steps leads to Honey Trove.

EARTH IS STRONGER IN THIS AREA

HONEY TROVE, LONG WORN HOLLOW, CANOPY CAVE & GOLD HEWN BASIN

There are two important items inside the cave, and you must move the cages around to get them. Push the first cage over the edge, then move the second into the new gap. Push the cage in the middle of the stone bridge until it's out of the way, then claim Magna Charge's **Soul Gem (Multi Barrelled / Super Repulsor).** Push the cage back across the bridge, then toward the back of Honey Trove until it drops into a gap between ledges. There's more of **Flynn's Missing Stuff**, another **Buoy** on the other side of the gap, and you can reach it now that the empty cage is properly placed.

Return to the spot where you smashed the Chompy Pod and follow the line of coins to a wooden gate. Knock down the gate and step into the elemental gate on the other side.

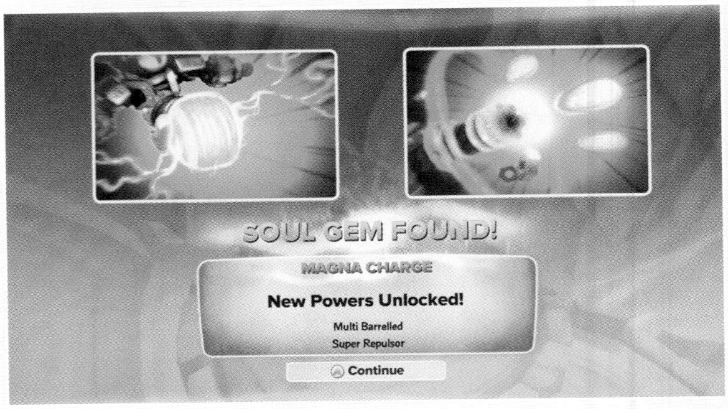

BULWARK OVERLOOK

Before speaking with Wixxon at the back of the elemental zone, scour the area for gold coins and piles of gold. Wixxon asks you to demonstrate the Cannon's power by shooting down 50 Bombers. Hold down the indicated button to fire off rapid shots at the Bombers and the missiles they fire at the turret (the missiles damage the turret if they aren't destroyed). The turret locks onto targets when the crosshairs pass over them, so don't linger on a target once it has been marked by the turret and you've fired at it. Keep moving and firing until you down 50 Bombers. There are larger Bombers that require multiple shots to destroy, so don't move off these larger targets too quickly! After sending 50 Bombers crashing to the ground, Wixxon presents you with a **Winged Sapphire**.

Return to the Long Worn Hollow and cross the first of a pair of stone bridges. There's another glowing, yellow cave entrance at the end of a path that branches to the right of the main path. The area on the other side of the entrance is known as Canopy Cave and it has a special type of Treasure Chest, one that requires a Giant to open. Before you can even reach the **Giant Treasure Chest**, however, you must contend with Greeble Blunderbusses. There's a second **Treasure Chest** in the cave, found at its highest point, but it's a standard chest, which can be opened by any Skylander.

Return to the main path and cross the second stone bridge. Push the cages off either side of the bridge, then follow them off the right side. Push the cage toward the last of **Flynn's Missing Stuff**, another **Life Preserver** and use the cage as a bridge to claim it. Flynn will be happy to get back all of his missing stuff. Boom!

After sliding it forward a few times, the other cage continues the main path to Woodburrow. Before you continue that way, take a minute to try out the nearby Climb SWAP Zone challenge.

SWAP Zone
Tree Top Jaunt

CLIMB TO THE TOP!

Turn to page 269 for tips on how to clear this SWAP Zone Challenge. Your reward for completing this challege is the **Bonus Mission Map, Fruit Fight**.

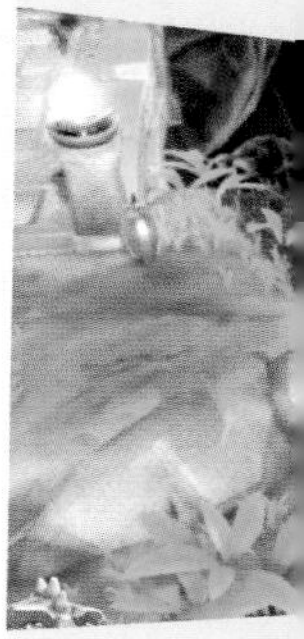

The path beyond the SWAP Zone challenge doesn't remain clear for long. Free the trapped villagers and hop up to where a Locked Gate blocks the way. The key for the Locked Gate was thrown down a hole that leads to Gold Hewn Basin. Eliminate the Greeble Blunderbusses inside the cave, pick up the piles of gold laying around the area, and take the key back to the gate to unlock it.

WATER IS STRONGER IN THIS AREA

KNOTTED HEIGHTS & WOODBURROW LANDING

The area immediately beyond the locked gate is guarded by more Greeble Blunderbusses. After you clear them out, use the glowing platform to start another trip along tree branches and vines. Mount Cloudbreak's final SWAP Zone challenge is near the area where the vine ride ends.

SWAP Zone
Spiky Pit

DIG UP THE BLUE CRYSTALS!
Turn to page 271 for tips on how to clear this SWAP Zone Challenge. Your reward for completing this challege is the **Life Preserver Hat**.

Now you're ready to free the citizens of Woodburrow! There are Chompy Pods and Greebles guarding the village's gates. Watch the ground carefully while there are still active Greeble Screwballs. There may be so many enemies on the screen that you miss the tell-tale red targeting circles they use to aim. Stay on the move and be ready to switch to a fresher Skylander should the enemy numbers prove too much for you. Once you've dealt with all the enemies, the gates to Woodburrow fly open and ecstatic villagers pour out to express their appreciation. Good job, Portal Master!

Your First Trip To Woodburrow

After completing most Story Mode chapters, you return to Woodburrow as it slowly recovers from the Greeble attack. You first meet Rufus, the town crier. He stands in the center of town and directs you to the village's other citizens. Rufus first directs you to meet with Tuk and Gorm, but before you visit them, follow Rufus's eyes up the wooden ramp that leads to Woodburrow Gates. Open the box found at the gates to get the **Puma Hat**.

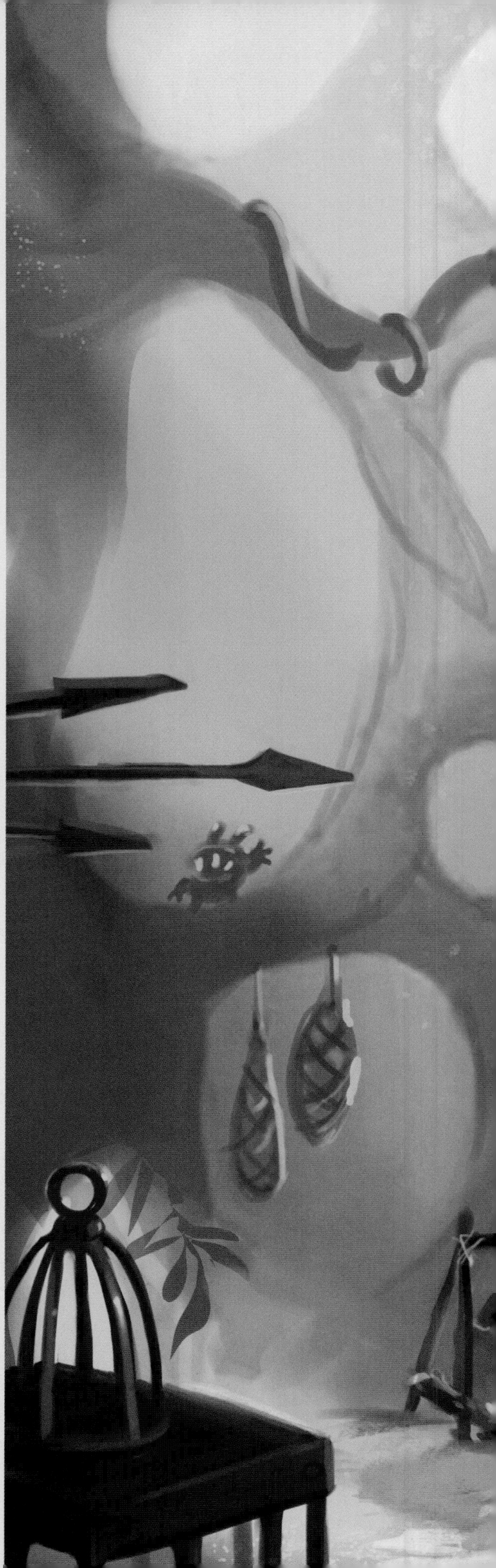

Return to Rufus's location, then go up the stairs he pointed out earlier to meet the HipBros, Gorm and Tuk. Gorm is in charge of the town's Power Pod, which allows Skylanders to purchase additional abilities. At least, it would if Gorm hadn't broken it! Follow the prompts to repair the Power Pod, then spend some of the gold you earned while freeing Woodburrow from the Greebles.

When you're done, Tuk points out the training dummies and their numerous uses. What he doesn't tell you is that the training dummies are stuffed with gold coins! Pound on each of the dummies until it stops giving up coins, then move on to the next and repeat the process. There's one last trick to check out before you leave the training dummy area. Take a stroll through the flowers on Skylanders of different elements and watch what happens! When you're done tip-toeing through the tulips, use the Epic Jump Pad near the brothers to fly over to the Airdocks and check in with Flynn.

CASCADE GLADE

OBJECTIVES

Story Goals

- ○ Rescue the Chieftess

Dares

- 5 Seed Packets
- 50 Enemy Goal
- 0 No Skylanders Defeated

New Enemies

Evilized Greeble

Greeble Blunderbuss

Greeble Ironclad

Collections

- 13 Areas Discovered
- 4 Treasure Chests
- 1 Giant Treasure Chest
- 3 Soul Gems
- 1 Legendary Treasure
- 3 Hats
- 1 Bonus Mission Map
- 1 Winged Sapphire
- 1 Story Scroll

AIR IS STRONGER IN THIS AREA

LUAU LAGOON

A few steps into Cascade Glade, you are introduced to Gobble Pods. This native plant species has developed a taste for the enemies you face throughout the Cloudbreak Isles. When one of these voracious plants consumes an enemy, it regurgitates an item worth some gold and XP bubbles.

They are also connected to Seeker Scopes you find from time to time. Approach these binocular objects whenever you see them and use them to reveal valuable objects (the objects look just like the binoculars you use to find them) you must collect later. To reveal the treasure, listen for the audio cue that speeds up as you are moving in the correct direction. Left and right on the control stick move your field of vision in those directions. Pushing up zooms in, while pushing down zooms out.

After uncovering the treasure, follow the wooden bridge and drop off the end near the pair of sliding blocks. Push one block in front of the bridge you just walked over, and the other block to the left bridge. Jump between the blocks over to the bridge and follow it to Cascade Glade's first **Treasure Chest**.

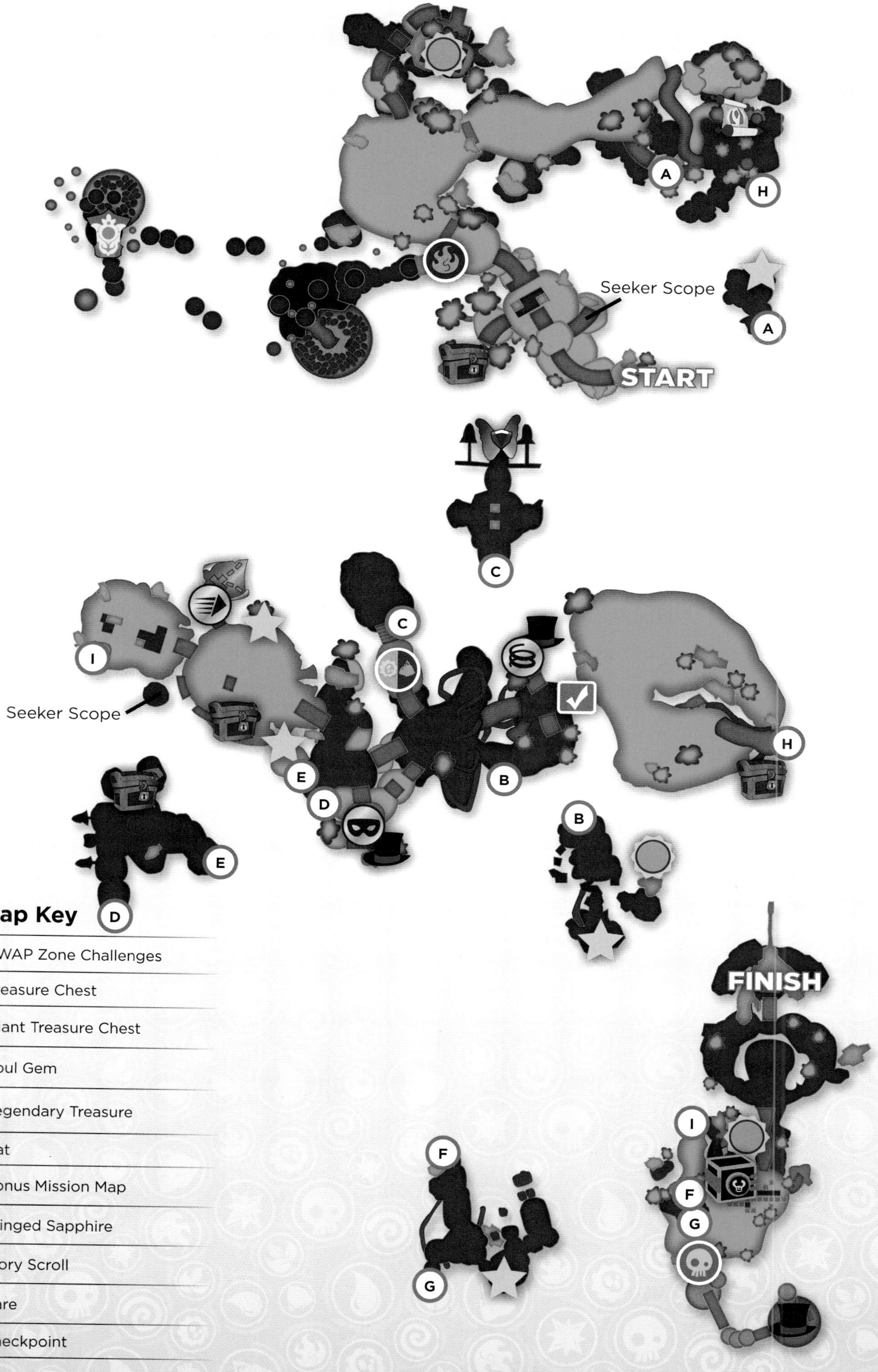

Map Key

	SWAP Zone Challenges
	Treasure Chest
	Giant Treasure Chest
	Soul Gem
	Legendary Treasure
	Hat
	Bonus Mission Map
	Winged Sapphire
	Story Scroll
	Dare
	Checkpoint

Return to the sliding blocks and push the block that was closer to the left bridge so that it lines up with the first block to create a straight path to the higher wooden platform. A chime plays when you have the blocks in the proper alignment. The other end of the bridge is blocked by a new type of puzzle, a Spark Lock.

Your other reward for getting past the Spark Lock is an introduction to Evilized Greebles and a Fire elemental gate. Take out the pair of upgraded Greebles, then step up to the elemental gate.

SPARK LOCK

Mix and Meet

To open a Spark Lock, you must join Shock and Bolt together. You earn extra rewards if you guide Shock to the blue lightning bolt and Bolt to the green lightning bolt found inside the puzzle before joining them together.

If Spark or Bolt hop on top of the buttons on the floor, they toggle the area where the color matches that button. In Mix and Meet, depressing a button raises or lowers the platforms of the same color. In later puzzles, there are other challenges to overcome, but for Mix and Match, just move both Shock and Bolt toward the center. When they combine, the lock vanishes and showers your Skylander with gold.

SCORCHED EARTH

Scorched Earth is filled with moving platforms you must jump across to reach the big reward at the back of the area: the Legendary Treasure, **Cascade Bust**. There aren't any enemies in the area, but the volcano tops damage any Skylander caught in their blasts. Yes, even Fire Skylanders!

The initial platforms droop under the weight of a Skylander on them, but they won't drop away entirely. If you miss a jump here, use the volcano tops to hop back up to the platforms. Don't linger on the volcano tops or your Skylander may end up being singed! The free-floating platforms are always on the move, but easily support the weight of a Skylander. Cross the platforms and collect the coins along the way to the wrapped gift in the back. Use the highlighted platform behind the gift to return to the area's entrance.

Back in Luau Lagoon, follow the uphill path and speak with the gillman standing with Flynn and Tessa. There's a stack of destructible boxes hiding a sidepath just a few steps away from them. Smash the boxes and hop up to the ledge with a Gobble Pod. Follow the broken wooden scaffold that wraps around the large stone statue to the top. Grab Countdown's **Soul Gem (Self-Destruct)** then return to where you spoke with the gillman.

Break down the wooden gate blocking the path. The area just beyond it is protected by a Battle Gate. You must take down a few waves of Greeble Blunderbusses (evilzed Greeble Screwballs) and a handful of Chompies to clear the Battle Gate and open the way to Totem Trail.

AIR IS STRONGER IN THIS AREA

TOTEM TRAIL & DUSTY CAVERN

Take the right fork of the path beyond the Battle Gate and claim the Seeker Scope treasure you uncovered earlier. Cross the wooden bridge and enter the glowing blue cave entrance, which leads to Dusty Cavern. Grab the **Seed Packet** from the back of the cavern, then return to Totem Trail.

The left fork ends at a sliding stone puzzle, which leads to an Epic Jump Pad and Cascade Glade's **Story Scroll**. Push one of the stones into the gap against the back wall between the ledge with the Epic Jump Pad and the Story Scroll. Push the other stone to the right and use it to jump up to the ledge with the Epic Jump Pad. As soon as your Skylander's feet touch down on the ledge, a Greeble Blunderbuss appears on the stump in the back.

Eliminate the intruder quickly. Jump over to the ledge with the **Story Scroll, Greeble Lands**, then back to the Epic Jump Pad. The Epic Jump Pad is a direct shot (no coin collecting while vine sliding here) to Gobblepod Sanctuary.

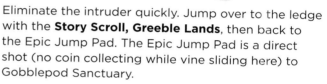

LIFE IS STRONGER IN THIS AREA

GOBBLEPOD SANCTUARY & TOURIST TRAP

Just beyond the landing spot, a gillman named Pollywog implores you to stop the Greebles from harming the Gobble Pod in the next area. Move ahead slowly and hop up to the left side ledge. There's a small gap in the grass just beyond a statue that marks the spot to jump up. Open the **Treasure Chest** on the ledge, then drop back down and take on the Greebles and Chompies. If any of the enemies followed you to the ledge, you'll be safe from them until you drop down. They can't jump up to the ledge! Two Greeble Blunderbusses join the fight, so free the Gobble Pods from the cages to nudge the odds to your favor.

Cascade Glade's Checkpoint is up next and there are three paths to take after you improve your Skylanders at the Power Pod. The short right path ends at a Bounce SWAP Zone Challenge. The left path ends at a glowing blue cave mouth, which is the entrance to Tourist Trap.

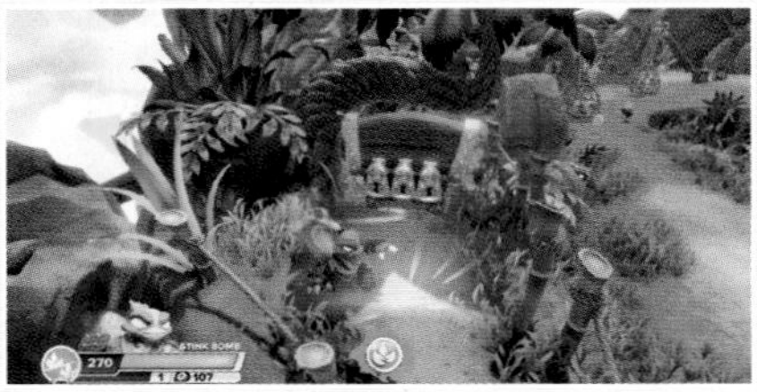

SWAP Zone
Sunny Heights

POP THE KAOS BALLOONS!
Turn to page 268 for tips on how to clear this SWAP Zone Challenge. Your reward for completing this challege is **The Outsider** hat.

The trail of coins to the left ends at a **Seed Packet** at the back of the area. Once you have that, pick up the coins to the right and drop off the right side to land on a small stone platform. There is a series of unconnected stone platforms you must cross to reach an exit point at the back of the cave. Only the first platform moves; the remaining platforms do not budge when anything lands on them. Outside the cave, a handful of jumps between wooden platforms is all that stands between you and Slobber Tooth's **Soul Gem (Iron Jaw)**. Retrace your path back through Tourist Trap to Gobblepod Sanctuary.

The final stretch of Gobblepod Sanctuary is guarded by a new enemy—a Greeble Ironclad! These bruisers are shielded until they attack, so you must dodge their attacks and strike while they are recovering their balance. Elminate the Greeble Ironclad and the small group of Greeble reinforcements before you take on the Tech/Earth elemental gate to the right, or the Sneak SWAP Zone to the left. The blue cave entrance near the SWAP Zone Challenge leads to Honeybadger Hollow.

If you're playing on the Wii console, the Sneak Swap Zone is to the right of the Push Blocks Puzzle in the Bamboo Bridge area.

BOULDER GULLY

In order to claim the **Winged Sapphire** from behind the locked door, you must repair the door opening mechanism with the missing gears found on the two platforms on either side of the cave.

To reach the gears, move one of the stones to the center spot in the row closest to the ledge at the bottom of the screen (where you entered the room). Move the other stone into the middle row and push it all the way to the left or right to reach one of the gears. Push the stone in the middle row to the opposite side and grab the other gear. Take both gears to the opening mechanism, then use the switch to open the door and reveal your reward.

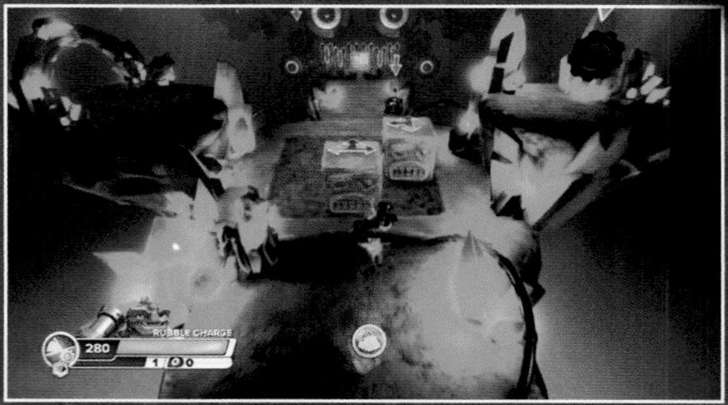

SWAP Zone

Area Fifty Tree

SNEAK IN AND DESTROY THE FORTRESS! DON'T GET CAUGHT BY SPOTLIGHTS.

Turn to page 274 for tips on how to clear this SWAP Zone Challenge. Your reward for completing this challege is the **Rain Hat**.

LIFE IS STRONGER IN THIS AREA

HONEYBADGER HOLLOW & OVERLOOK HEIGHTS

Follow the coins up the left side of the Hollow to reach a **Treasure Chest**. Continue across the stone platforms and exit the cave. When you're back in Gobblepod Sanctuary, drop down the ledge opposite The Spark Lock (there's a gap in the fence there) and grab the **Seed Packet**. You need to pass through Honeybadger Hollow again to reach the Spark Lock.

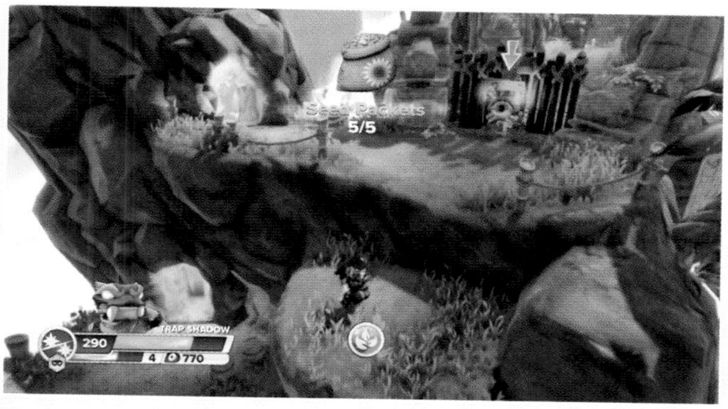

SPARK LOCK

Going Up

Send Shock across the gap on the purple slider, then hop on the blue button. Switch to Bolt, ride the blue slider across the gap, and step on the orange button to lower the orange squares. Move Bolt on top of the left orange platform, then return Shock back across the gap on the purple slider. Move Shock down to the blue slider (don't accidently push Shock into Bolt when they are next to each other!) and send him across to claim the blue lightning bolt. Grab the green lightning bolt with Bolt, then bring the two together to complete the Spark Lock.

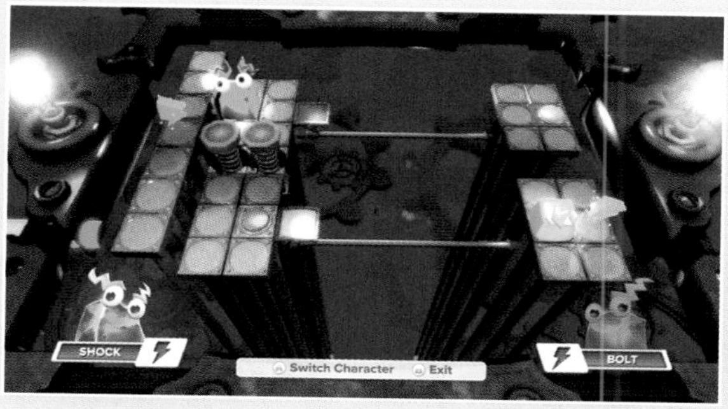

Go through the gate to reach Overlook Heights. Watch out for the Greeble Blunderbuss holding the high ground on the left. Run past him, then follow the dirt path to the left to take him out. Use the nearby Seeker Scope to uncover a treasure. There's also a **Treasure Chest** on a tree stump under some palm trees in the area as well. The opposite side of the area has a Speed SWAP Zone Challenge for you to complete and a **Seed Packet** for you to collect.

SWAP Zone

Woodlands Speedstacle

RACE TO THE FINISH!

Turn to page 275 for tips on how to clear this SWAP Zone Challenge. Your reward for completing this challege is the **Plants Vs. Cakes Bonus Mission Map.**

The center path leads to another gillman, named Barbfin, who provides an update on the Greebles' activities. Push the stone block just past Barbfin into the low spot, then jump up to the higher ground. Push both stone blocks off the same spot of the higher ledge to stack them on top of each other. Jump to the ledge with the Epic Jump Pad and use it to travel to the Bamboo Bridge.

MAGIC IS STRONGER IN THIS AREA

BAMBOO BRIDGE & SPELUNK SHALLOW

Free the Gobble Pod from its cage before tackling the Greeble and pair of Greeble Ironclads. After clearing the path, enter the glowing cave entrance of Spelunk Shallow.

Cross the first leg of floating stone platforms, and be ready to face a group of Chompies supported by a Greeble Blunderbuss standing on higher ground. Ignore the line of coins near the Greeble Blunderbuss's position and look to the left for sliding platforms. A mix of Greebles and Greeble Blunderbusses wait in ambush on a larger stone landing. Take them down and resume hopping between floating platforms until you reach a **Seed Packet** guarded by a pair of Greebles. There are stones moving in almost every direction, so don't get frustrated should you fall a few times due to a missed jump.

Retrace your steps back to the area where you first encountered the Chompies in Spelunk Shallow. Follow the trail of coins to the exit, which leads back outside to Bamboo Bridge and an Undead elemental gate.

SPOOKY SIDETRACK

Skully lost his lucky top hat to a Greeble and would like it back. Walk to the back of the area where the offending Greeble has set up an ambush with four of his fellow miscreants. You must clear two waves of Greebles and Greeble Blunderbusses before the top hat-wearing ringleader enters the fight. He has more health than other Greebles, but uses only melee attacks.

After dealing with his threat and claiming Skully's top hat, jump up to the landing on the left and use the Seeker Scope to reveal a treasure. Return the hat to Skelly, who happily presents you with the **Glittering Tiara**.

Return to Bamboo Bridge and continue down the main path. Take out a few Greebles on the way to a large sliding stone puzzle. Push the stones to clear a path to the right. The Seeker Scope treasure hovers over the ground near a Gobble Pod across a short wooden bridge.

Return to the sliding stone puzzle and push the blocks to clear the way to a **Giant Treasure Chest** on the left. Continue to the left and grab Rattle Shake's **Soul Gem (Raise the Snakes/The Snake-Skinned Kid)**. Return to the gate and get ready for a Spark Lock.

SPARK LOCK: Shocking Jailbreak

Move Bolt to the red and orange sliders and step on the orange button. Switch to Shock and move him on top of the lowered orange column. Change to Bolt and step on the orange button again. Move Bolt toward the lowered orange column. Move Shock to the purple button. Guide Shock to the blue lightning bolt near the orange button. Change to Bolt and move him across both sliding platforms, over the purple columns and on top of the lowered orange column and step on the orange button. Move Bolt to the green lightning bolt, then move him straight down to where the red slider comes to rest when Shock rides it back across from the smaller platforms.

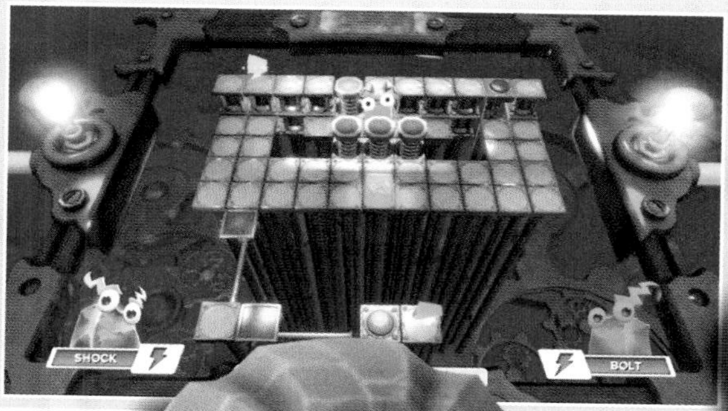

MAGIC IS STRONGER IN THIS AREA

OVERFLOW GROTTO

There's one last Battle Gate to pass before you reach the Chieftess. You must clear two waves of evilized Greebles sandwiched around a handful of Chompies to destroy the Battle Gate. There are two caged Gobble Pods in the area that are helpful allies in the battle. Before you meet the Chieftess, grab the Seeker Scope treasure to the left of the gate. Speak with the Chieftess to return to Woodburrow.

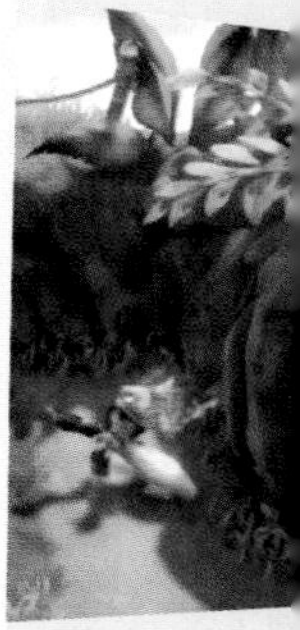

Back in Woodburrow

The Chieftess enters a meeting with the other elders, which leaves you with enough time to help the other Hip Bro, Tuk, open his Emporium. He asks for you to complete three tasks to rebuild his store and make it ready for customers. After you help him put up shelves, rebuild the roof, and make a sign, he hands over a **Winged Sapphire**. He's also open for business, though most of his merchandise won't be ready until you complete more of the adventure.

When you're done shopping, Tuk sends you to meet with the Chieftess in the Great Hollow. Inside the Great Hollow, two of the other elders you set free have a surprise for you. One set up an Elemental Treasure Chest and the other has a place for you to practice Spark Lock puzzles. Check back often for rewards from these two chests.

Speak with the Chieftess in the back of the Great Hollow for an update on Kaos' plans. She sends you to speak with Tessa at the Airdocks to help protect the Ancient Elementals.

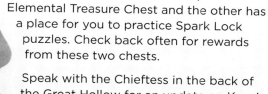

MUDWATER HOLLOW

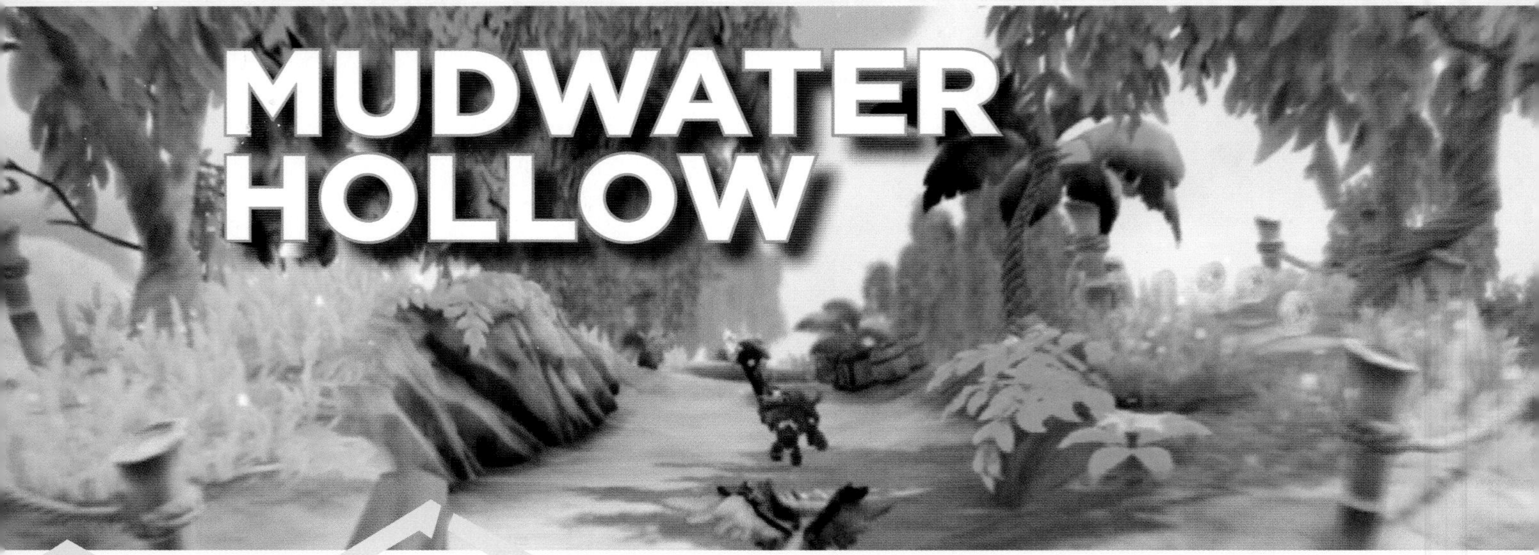

OBJECTIVES

Story Goals

- ◯ Get to the Ancient Flashfin
- ◯ Catch 3 Piranhas
- ◯ Catch the Gear Fish
- ◯ Save the Village
- ◯ De-Evilize the Bog Hog
- ◯ Destroy the Crystals

Dares

- 6 Floaty Life Preserver
- 50 Enemy Goal
- 0 No Skylanders Defeated

New Enemies

Grumblebum Thrasher

Life Spell Punk

Grumblebum Rockshooter

Evilized Bog Hog

Collections

- 26 Areas Discovered
- 6 Treasure Chests
- 1 Giant Treasure Chest
- 3 Soul Gems
- 2 Legendary Treasures
- 2 Hats
- 1 Bonus Mission Map
- 1 Winged Sapphire
- 1 Story Scroll

AIR IS STRONGER IN THIS AREA

WOODBRIDGE WAY, FROGHOLLOW FISHIN' POND & SNAGGLESCALE'S BUNGALOW

Woodbridge Way begins at the foot of a wooden bridge, but the action doesn't pick up until your Skylander crosses it. A mutated new enemy, called a Grumblebum Thrasher, patiently waits on the other side. These creatures lack ranged attacks, but their club hits hard. They're slow swingers, so you can attack before they swing or after a miss, which leaves them briefly off balance. After you deal with that first enemy, grab the **Floaty Life Preserver** from the ridge just to the left of where the bridge ends.

Watch out for a Chompy ambush where the next bridge ends. They pop out of a stack of barrels near a branch in the path. There's a **Story Scroll, Magic Recycling**, guarded by two Grumblebum Thrashers down the short branch of the path.

The wooden path swings around a big bend, then ends abruptly at Froghollow Fishin' Pond. Look for a **Treasure Chest** on a dock a short jump from the shore on the far right. The far left side of the hollow has a Rocket SWAP Zone Challenge.

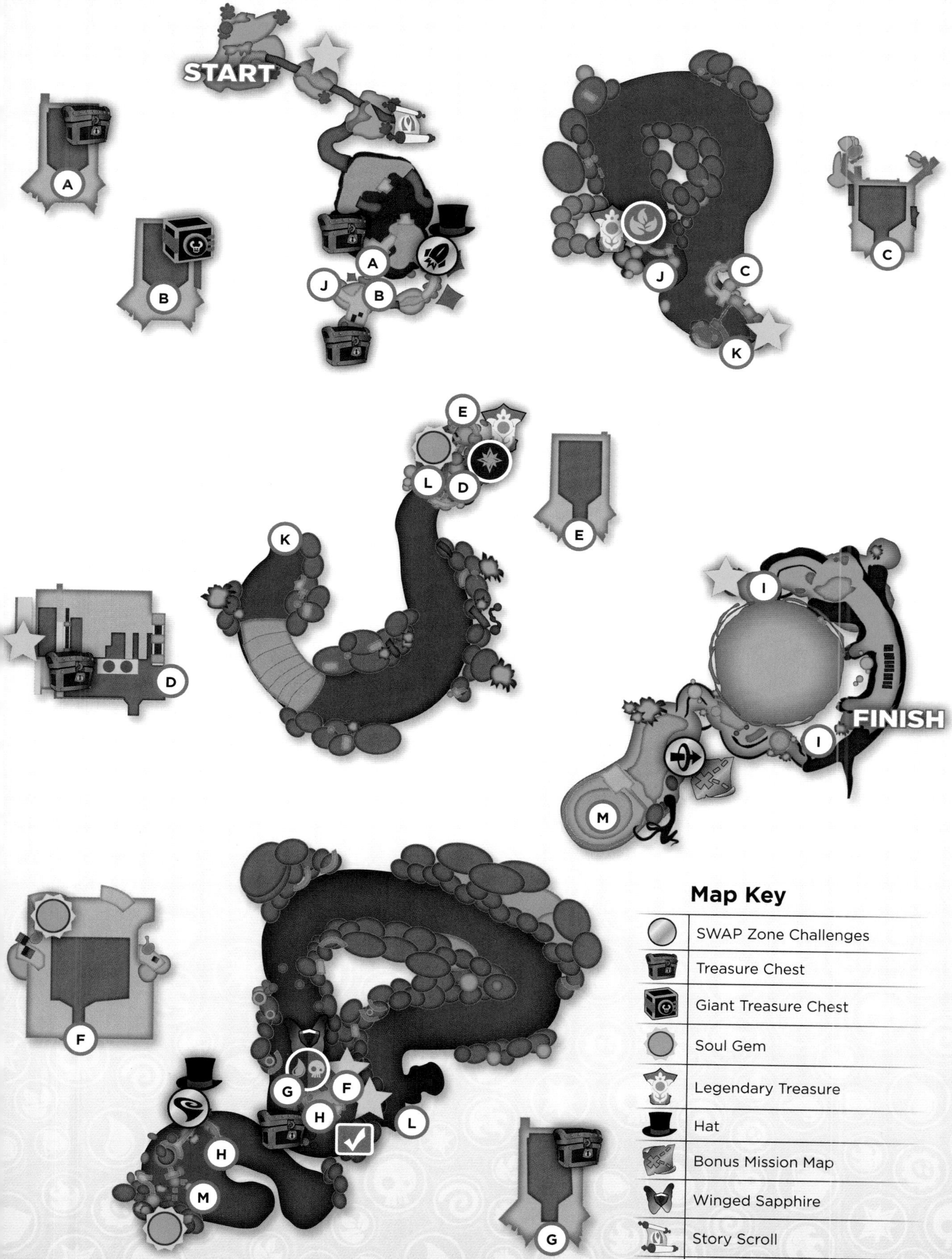

START

A

B

J A B

J C

C

K

E

L D

E

K

I

FINISH

D

I

M

F

G F

H L

H ✔

M

G

Map Key

⬤	SWAP Zone Challenges
📦	Treasure Chest
📦	Giant Treasure Chest
⬤	Soul Gem
✦	Legendary Treasure
🎩	Hat
🗺	Bonus Mission Map
🦋	Winged Sapphire
📜	Story Scroll
★	Dare
✔	Checkpoint

When you're ready to continue on to help Ancient Flashfin, speak with the gillman, Snagglescale, standing under a bucket lamp. He has been trying to build tube bridges, but blue piranha keep popping the tubes. Use the nearby fishing pole to catch the fish. After all three piranha are out of the way, Snagglescale completes the bridge.

SNAGGLESCALE
Them pesky piranha keep sinkin' their teeth in these tube bridges and poppin' 'em. Wou

SWAP Zone
Tree Scraping

ROCKET TO THE FINISH!

Turn to page 272 for tips on how to clear this SWAP Zone Challenge. Your reward for completing this challege is **Boater Hat**.

The path ahead splits into two directions. The Battle Gate on the left is guarded by Grumblebum Thrashers and a new enemy, a Life Spell Punk. Whenever you see these green-clad annoyances in a fight, they should be your first target. They don't attack directly, but they continually heal the other enemies in the area. Until your Skylanders are powered up, it is difficult to deal damage faster than Life Spell Punks can heal it.

The small house on the right is Snagglescale's Bungalow. Use the fishing pole just outside the entrance to catch a single fish (if an eel touches the fish while it is on your line, the fish escapes) and earn a gem as a reward. The bungalow itself is empty, save for a Spark Locked **Treasure Chest**. The wooden bridge near the bungalow leads to Billy's Bend.

SPARK LOCK
My Biggest Fan

Send Shock sliding down the icy squares. He bounces off two angled fences and ends up on the orange button. Switch to Bolt and step on the green button to start the fan. This time when you send Shock down the icy squares, he's blown to the green lightning bolt. Jump on the purple button, then switch to Bolt and move him up to the top platform via the sliding pad. Move him left a few spaces, so he's between the two spots where the ice path touches the regular path.

Move Shock up to the top area via the second sliding pad, then send him up and around the ice path. While he's sliding, switch to Bolt and pick up the green lightning bolt. When Shock stops sliding around, pick up the blue lightning bolt. Return them both to the top platform and bring them together to open the lock.

AIR IS STRONGER IN THIS AREA

BILLY'S BEND, BILLY'S BEND STOREHOUSE, SNAGGLESCALE SWAMP & QUIET TIME SHALLOWS

Three Grumblebum Thrashers guard the middle of the bridge, but the locked gate beyond them is likely a greater challenge.

The lock's key isn't far, but it's on the other side of a chasm. You must slide two of the three huts into the chasm in order to reach the key. Start by pushing the hut in the center out to the side so that you can push the one closest to the chasm into it. Use either of the two remaining huts to complete the bridge over the chasm. Push the third over them and on top of the boarded-over hole. Open the **Treasure Chest** on the higher platform, then grab the key and open the Locked Gate. The nearby bungalow, Billy's Bend Storehouse, contains a **Giant Treasure Chest** but is otherwise empty.

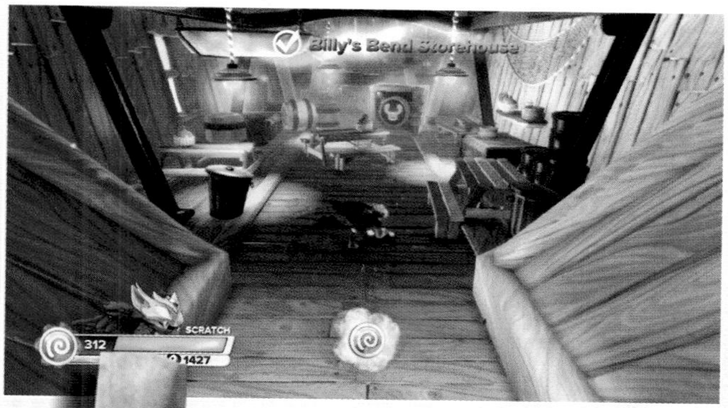

The path beyond the Locked Gate goes to Snagglescale Swamp where a few known enemies are joined by a new one, a Grumblebum Rockshooter. These clever foes hide inside wooden turrets and use red-and-white rockets in two ways while trying to stop you. First, they light a fuse and fire the rockets in a straight line. They take a moment to reload, which gives you a chance to attack.

Don't think these enemies are done attacking because you are soaking up the XP bubbles. After you destroy a Grumblebum Rocketshooter, its last rocket flies into the air and explodes on impact with the ground or a Skylander! Stay clear of the red circle on the ground after you dispatch these crafty enemies. There are two rewards for clearing out these enemies: a Life Gate and an exciting tubing trip through mine-infested waters.

CRYSTAL POND

Crystal Pond is Gilly Greg's secret fishing spot and he promises an amazing treasure if you can catch a few fish. Fishing here works the same as it has in previous holes, but there are three whirlpools and four eels you must avoid while reeling in your four catches. Watch the eels to learn their movement patterns before you start reeling in the fish. Since the eel in the center does not swim around one of the whirlpools, it moves back and forth quickly. After you pull in the four fish, Gilly Greg hands over the **Luminous Lure** Legendary Treasure.

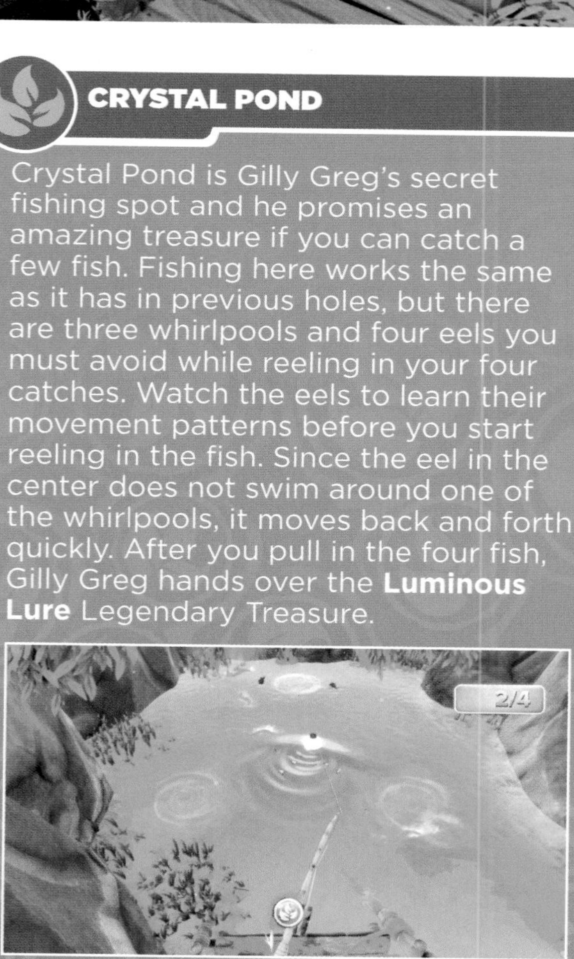

Speak with the loquacious Snagglescale to start a trip down the deceptively named Quiet Time Shallows. While Snagglescale provides the forward motion (and the talking) you must guide the ship down the river. To steer in a direction, move your Skylander to that side of the raft. The further left or right the Skylander goes, the harder the raft moves to the left or right.

Watch for the buoys with green-glowing arrows for cues on safe paths. There are mines scattered throughout the water, and coins floating above it. Crashing into the buoys destroys them, but doesn't hurt. Crashing into mines destroys them, but really does some damage! The trip comes to an abrupt end at Lazy Lock Isles, where a stone structure blocks the way.

FIRE IS STRONGER IN THIS AREA

LAZY LOCK ISLES, LAZY LOCK ISLES GATEHOUSE & LAZY LOCK

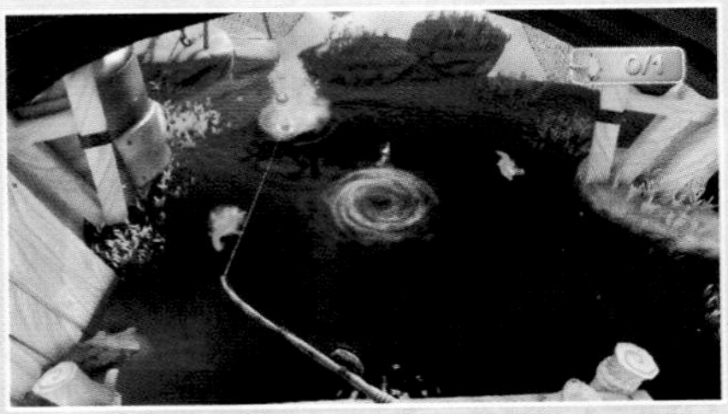

Snagglescale sends you to find the gear necessary to get the gate working again. Watch out for off-screen attacks here! Grumblebum Rockshooters are all over the place, so listen as well as look for them. Destroy the pile of crates and tubes under the gear mechanism in the wall. Run down the path, take out the two Grumblebum Rockshooters, and pick up the **Floaty Life Preserver** behind them.

Return to where the raft is docked, then go up the Grumblebum Rockshooter-filled wooden path. The Lazy Lock Isles Gatehouse is on the top level of the path, and it's where Salvage Steve explains what happened to the gear. Time for fishing!

With the gearfish in hand, return to the dock (a token force of Chompies pops up along the way) and follow the onscreen prompts to open the gate. Jump back on the raft and prepare yourself to steer the raft through a second round of mine-filled whitewater.

FIRE IS STRONGER IN THIS AREA

BOOM BOOM WATER WAY & BROKEN BOG BAY

This stretch of water has more mines and more coins, but ends the same way as before—the water is blocked by a gate that is missing a gear. There's a moss-covered stone arch just on the other side of a fight against a host of enemies (including a Life Spell Punk, so you know what to target first!) but stop by the nearby Magic Gate if you're not in a hurry to complete the level.

MYSTERIOUS MAGICAL MAZE

The Mysterious Magical Maze is a throwback sidescrolling area where you must jump over gaps in the floor and battle enemies in order to reach your ultimate goal, the **Bubble Chest** Legendary Treasure. Use the portal just beyond the treasure for a shortcut back to the entrance of the gate.

If you're playing on the Wii console, the Bubble Chest is in a gift box to the right of the second river lock, in Broken Bog Bay.

FIRE IS STRONGER IN THIS AREA

BIG GILL WATER MILL & DON'S BAITSHOP

Smash through the barrels and tires near the moss-covered stone archway to open up the path to Don's BaitShop. A quick fight slows your progress, but it's not a bad thing. Look for the row of narrow huts on a raised platform not far from where the fighting took place. Ignore most of the huts and move the one furthest back to get to Zou Lou's **Soul Gem (Birds of Prey)**.

Continue to the small bungalow beyond where you found the Soul Gem. The interior of Don's BaitShop is filled with flopping fish. Destroying the fish is tricky since they never stop moving, but your patience is rewarded with a few piles of gold. Collect your money and head back downhill to the stone archway you passed earlier.

The archway is the entrance to Big Gill Water Mill and the gear you need is inside. Push the stone block against the wall to open the way to the upper level. Before you move on, smash the wooden items in the corner of the main level to expose a **Treasure Chest**.

Jump up the platforms against the wall and push the two sliding blocks on the higher ledges in the directions indicated by their arrows. The first block allows access to the short ledge. The second block starts the large gear moving, which allows you to reach the small tube rafts bobbing in the small pool of water. On the other side of the pool, ride one of the large gear's teeth up to the next level.

Go up the short flight of stairs and push the two sliding blocks into the middle of the room so you can use them to get over the line of blocks in front of the larger set of stairs. How you align them isn't important, but pushing them both against the wall makes for the easiest jumps.

The gear you need is just beyond the line of blocks, and the exit is just behind the gear. Before you leave the mill, jump through the gap in the wall to the left of the doorway. Grab the **Floaty Life Preserver**, then use the exit to return outside and replace the gear on the gate opening mechanism. Open the gate and ride the rapids once more!

FIRE IS STRONGER IN THIS AREA

BROKEN BOG BAY LOCK & RUMBLIN' RAPIDS

As with the two previous times you've been asked to steer Snagglespear's raft, avoid the mines while trying to collect as many of the gold coins as you can. The twist to this trip is the huge waterfall in the middle of it. The raft moves more quickly from this point forward, and there are mines everywhere. Safe navigation of the rapids ends at a Checkpoint and Muddy Marsh Village.

TECH IS STRONGER IN THIS AREA

MUDDY MARSH VILLAGE, SALTYTOOTH'S SCRAP SHOP, JUG JAMBOREE INN & MUDDY MARSH SECRET

Use the Power Pod and spend all the gold you collected while navigating the waterway. If you're just a bit short of an upgrade, there's a **Treasure Chest** behind a bungalow not far from the Power Pod. Stay close to the water and go to the right side of the village for a **Floaty Life Preserver**. If you were too close to the village and started the fight with the Grumblebum army inside, the life preserver will still be there after you deal with the enemies.

When the last of the Grumblebum forces falls, the Magic Circle in the middle of the village is available to use. The villagers ask you to look around before you leave, and there are a few things you should collect before moving on.

Jump on the sick boar near the back of the village several times to get a **Floaty Life Preserver.**

The building between the Magic Circle and the elemental gate is Saltytooth's Scrap Shop. It has a Spark Locked **Treasure Chest**. The building across from the scrap shop is the Jug Jamboree Inn. Destroying the objects on the upper floor opens the path to Muddy Marsh Secret, the hiding place of Free Ranger's **Soul Gem (Storming Stormblades/Charged Winds).** After you've collected all the villager's gifts, use the Magic Circle to zip up to Chompy Chew Shortcut.

If you're playing on the Wii console, the Floaty Life Preserver is on the right at the beginning of Muddy Marsh Village.

SPARK LOCK: Free Me!

Send Shock up the ice path to trip the orange button a few times. Move Bolt over the lowered columns each time Shock hits the button. Have Bolt return the favor for Shock, sliding up to the orange button each time Shock needs to move over the orange columns. Join Shock and Bolt together after each has collected their lightning bolt.

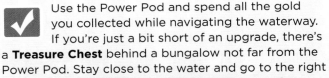

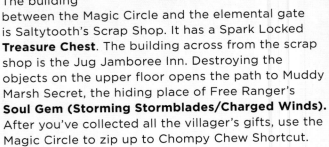

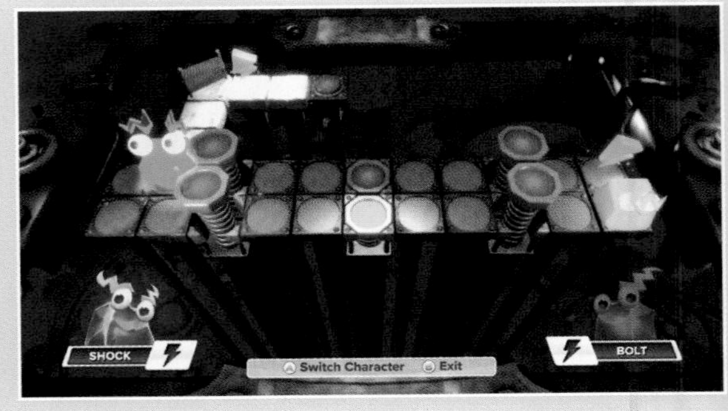

PRECIOUS PONDS

The reward from Precious Ponds is hidden behind a trick Battle Gate. The trick is that after you defeat a wave of enemies, the gate does not automatically open. Instead, three switches emerge from the water. One of the switches opens the gate. The other two summon more monsters. Monsters that, annoyingly, do not drop loot or XP. When you hit the proper switch to open the gate, your reward is a **Winged Sapphire.**

MAGIC IS STRONGER IN THIS AREA

CHOMPY CHEW SHORTCUT

The winding wooden path leads to a SWAP Zone and a Battle Gate blocked by Evilzed Bog Hogs. Pick up all the treasures in the area before dropping down into the battle arena, because there's no way back up once you hop down.

SWAP Zone

Marbled Gardens

DESTROY THE KAOS STATUE!

Turn to page 277 for tips on how to clear this SWAP Zone Challenge. Your reward for completing this challege is **Stone Hat**.

The Bog Hog charges in a straight line until it crashes into the arena's walls. Avoid the charge and the Bog Hog is stunned while recovering its wits after colliding with the wall. Pour on the damage while it's vulnerable, but be ready to move out of its way when it clears its head. Repeat these actions until the hog is freed and the Battle Gate opens.

Go through the opened Battle Gate and veer right over floating rafts, staggered wooden platforms, and Greeble forces until you run into Bumble Blast's **Soul Gem (Bee-pack Backpack)**. Drop off the side of the ledge where you picked up the Soul Gem for a shortcut back to the main path. Follow the path away from where you picked up the Soul Gem to reach Muddy Marsh River.

TECH IS STRONGER IN THIS AREA

MUDDY MARSH RIVER

A tough fight against Grumblebum Rockshooters and two pairs of tube bridges are all that stand between you and the Magic Circle needed to reach Ancient Tree Terrace, where the Ancient Flashfin is under attack.

WATER IS STRONGER IN THIS AREA

ANCIENT TREE TERRACE

As soon as your Skylander touches down at Ancient Tree Terrace, a few more Evilized Bog Hogs attack and you must defeat them to open the Battle Gate. A Teleport SWAP Zone and a narrow path are on the other side of the Battle Gate.

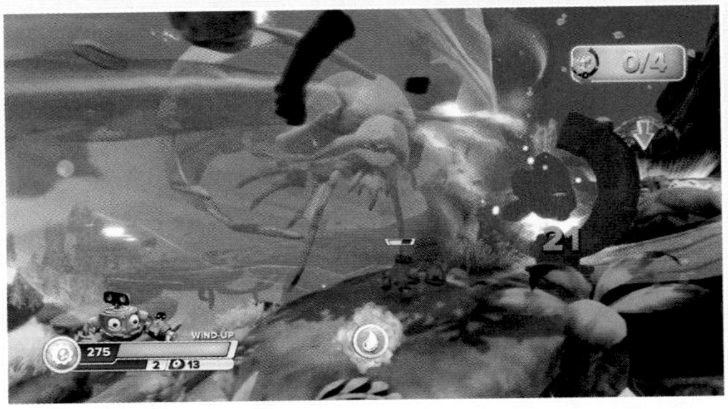

SWAP Zone

Going Whoosh

COLLECT THE MAGIC RUNES TO SEAL THE DIMENSIONAL RIFT!

Turn to page 278 for tips on how to clear this SWAP Zone Challenge. Your reward for completing this challege is the **Master Chef Bonus Mission Map**.

After a jubilant group of gillmen emerge to express their gratitude, Flynn relays your final objective. You must destroy the four crystals being used against the Ancient Flashfin to thwart Kaos's plans. The first crystal is not guarded, so hammer it with attacks to destroy it. Use the Magic Circle to fly to the next crystal.

The remaining crystals are all heavily guarded, so you must clear out Grumblebums and Chompies before you can take down the crystals. Grab the **Floaty Life Preserver** located just behind the touchdown spot of the Magic Circle before you leave the area to destroy the last three crystals. After the last crystal is destroyed, the Ancient Flashfin travels to Woodburrow.

Back at Woodburrow

The Chieftess is waiting near The Airdocks. She needs help with completing a summoning spell. The spell connects Master Eon with the residents of Woodburrow, and he offers what help he can to aid in the struggle against Kaos. He unlocks your ability to rank up as a Portal Master, and tallies everything you've accomplished up to this point. For now, the most important thing your Portal Master rank does is unlock new items at Tuk's Emporium. Stop by his shop and see what he has to sell and what ranks you need to reach to unlock additional inventory.

The Chieftess opened up a new area of Woodburrow when she summoned Master Eon. The orange ledges on the tree now act as stairs to the top of the giant tree. Stop halfway up the tree and claim Hoot Loop's **Soul Gem (Wand of Dreams/Infinite Loop)** before continuing to the top. There's a **Winged Sapphire**, boxes of fireworks, and an Epic Launch Pad at the top. Try various fire-based attacks on the fireworks until you set them off. Using the Epic Launch Pad sends your Skylander to a hidden area filled with coins and the gift-wrapped **Turkey Hat**. When you're ready to continue your adventure, speak with Tessa and Snagglescale at The Airdocks.

RAMPANT RUINS

OBJECTIVES

Story Goals

- ◯ Un-Evilize the Sugarbats
- ◯ Activate the Stone Monkey
- ◯ Get to the Stone Monkey

Dares

- 5 Grave Monkey Totems
- 50 Enemy Goal
- 0 No Skylanders Defeated

New Enemies

Chompy Rustbud

Arkeyan Barrelbot

Evilized Sugarbat

Arkeyan Rip-Rotor

Arkeyan Slamshock

Evil Glumshanks

Collections

- 12 Areas Discovered
- 5 Treasure Chests
- 1 Giant Treasure Chest
- 2 Soul Gems
- 2 Legendary Treasures
- 2 Hats
- 1 Bonus Mission Map
- 1 Winged Sapphire
- 1 Story Scroll

AIR IS STRONGER IN THIS AREA

IRON TOMB TRAIL

Follow the path from the starting point until you meet up with Woody, an archaeologist studying petrified darkness. After speaking with him, step up to the Seeker Scope to uncover a treasure to collect later. Continue down the path and meet the first of many new enemies in Rampant Ruins, Chompy Rustbuds. These slightly more powerful cousins of Chompies are only a tad more difficult to handle than regular Chompies. You should have no problem taking them out and grabbing the **Grave Monkey Totem** from the stump behind their spawn point.

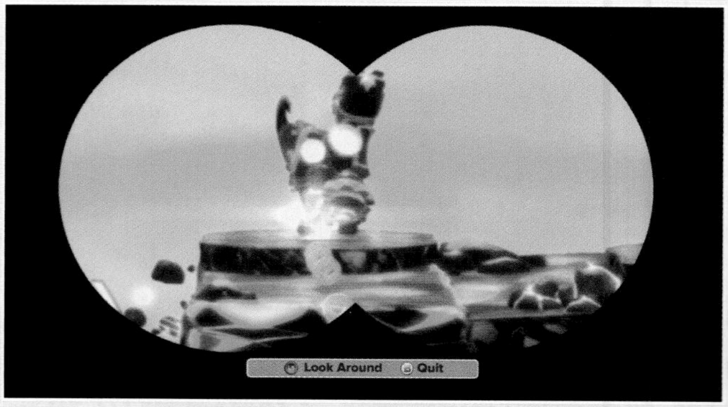

Carefully time the two spear traps on the downhill slope of the path. The next new enemy, the Arkeyan Barrelbot, is a real threat. Their double-barrel energy blasters can tear through a life bar quickly. Listen for the build up of energy, dodge the blast, and retaliate while the Barrelbot reloads. With the Barrelbots nullified, check out the nearby dual element gate. The bridge to the next area falls under your Skylanders as they run over it, so don't move ahead without getting everything in the initial area.

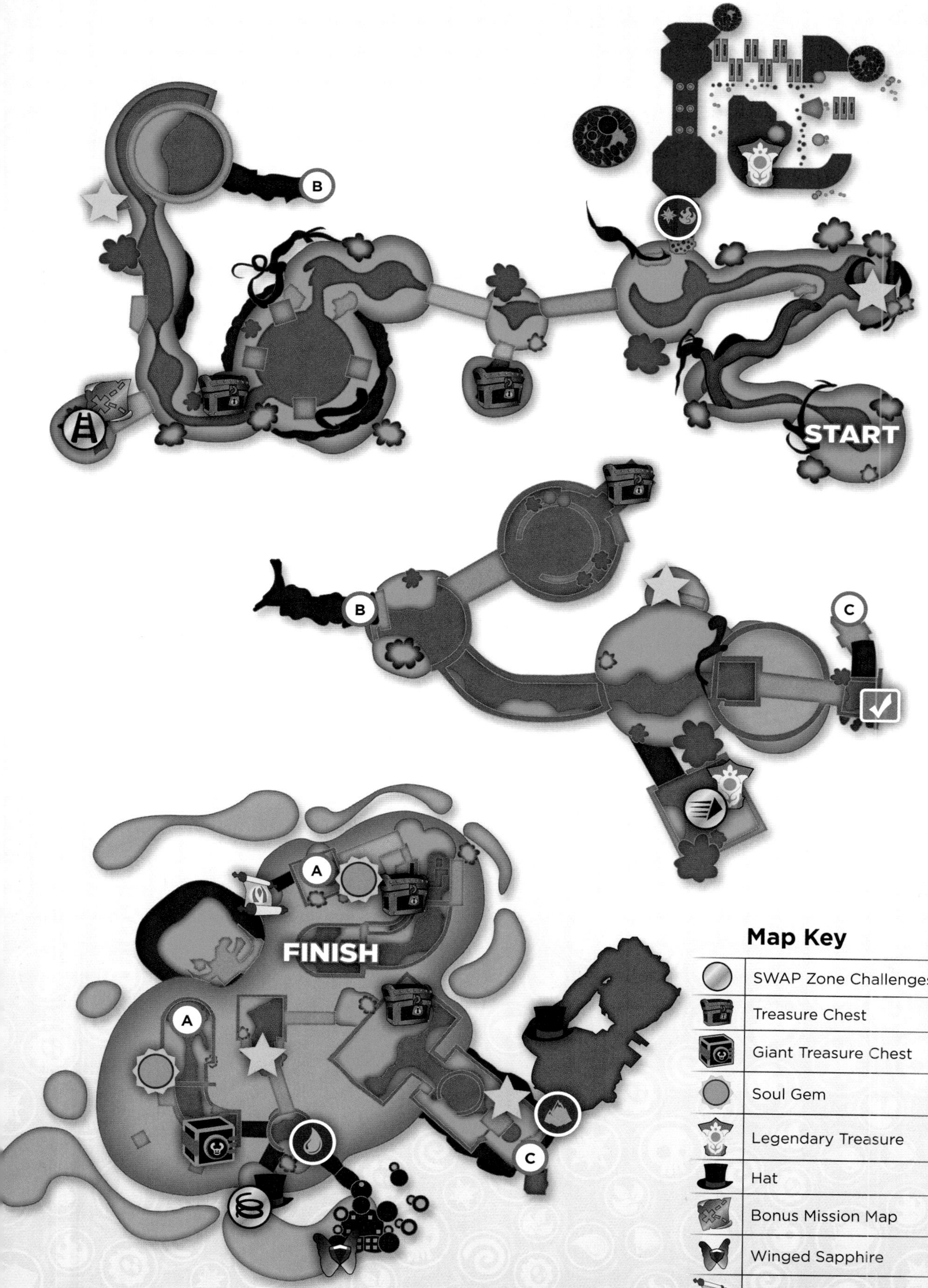

Map Key

- SWAP Zone Challenges
- Treasure Chest
- Giant Treasure Chest
- Soul Gem
- Legendary Treasure
- Hat
- Bonus Mission Map
- Winged Sapphire
- Story Scroll
- Dare
- Checkpoint

MYSTIC FLAME ROTUNDA

The goal is to reach to oversized Arkeyan Barrelbot in the center of the zone, but it's not an easy trip. You must avoid fire spouts, contend with sliding platforms, and avoid the Barrelbot's energy blasts, sometimes all at the same time.

When you reach the center, take down the Barrelbot as quickly as possible. His health pool and damage output are as oversized as his frame! Once he's dealt with, claim your reward, **The Monkey's Paw** Legendary Treasure. Use the portal in the center area to return to the gate.

SPARK LOCK
Slide and Shuffle

Shock is trapped behind the green columns until Bolt takes a ride on all three of the sliding platforms. The purple button resets the locations of the sliding platforms, while the green button lowers the green columns. Switch to Shock and hit the orange button to lower the orange column. Move him next to the first sliding platform. Grab the green lightning bolt with Bolt, then send Shock around the room. Before he hits the green button, move Bolt to the space next to the orange button. Move Shock on top of the orange platform and raise it with Bolt. Grab the blue lightning bolt, then backtrack to the green button. Join Shock and Bolt together to unlock the Treasure Chest.

LIFE IS STRONGER IN THIS AREA

GIBBON ANTECHAMBER

Take the left branch of the path for a Spark Locked **Treasure Chest**. The main branch leads to a Battle Gate guarded by three Evilzed Sugarbats. These unfortunate creatures charge in a straight line to deal damage. When they crash into a wall, they are momentarily stunned and vulnerable to attacks.

If you're playing on the Wii console, this Spark Lock is not in your game.

Speak with Willowbark on the other side of the Battle Gate to learn more about what has been done to the normally docile Sugarbats. Drop down into the nearby arena floor for another go at a Battle Gate. This time, the Evilized Sugarbats are aided by Chompy Rustbuds.

ORANGUTAN TOWER

As soon as you enter the Orangutan Tower area, look to the right for a gap in the iron fence. Open the **Treasure Chest** in the clearing and return to the path. The next thing you encounter in Orangutan Tower is a SWAP Zone Challenge.

SWAP Zone
Robot Ramparts

CLIMB TO THE TOP!
Turn to page 269 for tips on how to clear this SWAP Zone Challenge. Your reward for completing this challege is the **Fishy Fishing Bonus Mission Map**.

To get over the gap in the path beyond the SWAP Zone, push one of the sliding blocks to the side (there's a spot for it there) and use the other two to create a bridge. Avoid taking damage from the spear trap on the other side. Speak with Forest to learn about the gate puzzles. To open the doors with the purple and yellow gems set in a monkey design, you must use the trigger of the same color to stop the moving arm so gems of the same color align with the stationary gem on the frame.

Your progress is slowed by another new enemy guarding a Battle Gate. Arkeyan Rip-Rotors are invulnerable while spinning, so stay clear when they're airborne. They are dazed shortly after touching down on the ground, and that's your opening to attack. Watch them closely even when they're down. If you can't finish them off quickly enough, move away before they start spinning again.

There are a few waves of Rip-Rotors to face, and a few Barrlebots join the fun as well. After you open the Battle Gate, look for a piece of the wall on the right where the fence ends. Run along the wall until you pick up the **Grave Monkey Totem** there. Go through the Battle Gate and down the large pipe to reach the Simian Temple.

FIRE IS STRONGER IN THIS AREA

SIMIAN TEMPLE & SIMIAN THRONE ROOM

Avoid the main path for now, and opt for the short sidepath to the left. The path ends in a circular platform that is blocked off as a group of Sugarbats undergoes the evilization procedure. Free the Sugarbats and eliminate the horde of Chompy Rustbuds to open the Battle Gate opposite the entrance. Open the **Treasure Chest** and claim its contents.

Return to the main path, which ends at another of the new gate puzzles. Before you can attempt to line up the gems, two Arkeyan Slamshocks get in your way. These large enemies are invulnerable until they pound the ground and send out a golden energy blast. The blasts travel directly ahead of the Slamshock, so step to the side and attack while its hands are still on the ground.

After you take care of the Slamshocks, look for a short path to the right, one that leads to a SWAP Zone Challenge. Walk down the sarcophagus lid on the left of the gate puzzle (near where the fence ends). Grab the **Grave Monkey Totem**, then return to the gate puzzle and solve it by aligning the yellow gem on the moving arm with the fixed one in the frame.

SWAP Zone
Frenetic Fog

RACE TO THE FINISH!
Turn to page 275 for tips on how to clear this SWAP Zone Challenge. Your reward for completing this challege is the **Major Award Monkey Legendary Treasure**.

Don't move in front of the door while it's opening. An Arkeyan Slamshock is on the other side. It's all alone, so the fight should be quick. The bridge beyond the Slamshock drops into the green water below as your Skylander walks over it. You don't need to hurry across it, however. Each segment drops down only after your Skylander moves to the next piece.

Continue down the path past the Power Pod and drop into the courtyard. There's an Earth Gate in the courtyard where the path ends. Just beyond the Earth Gate, use the jutting pieces of stone in the wall to hop up to the **Grave Monkey Totem** on top of a pedestal.

GIBBON'S GARDEN

Gibbon's Garden is filled with spear traps complicating the solutions to both sliding stone puzzles and gate puzzles. Be patient while solving each puzzle. Watch the spear traps carefully since they're the only things in the area that deal damage. The puzzles are fairly simple, but the spear traps could drain your Skylander's health before you know it. After you unwrap the **Boonie Hat**, drop down the side of the ledge for a quick return to the Simian Throne Room.

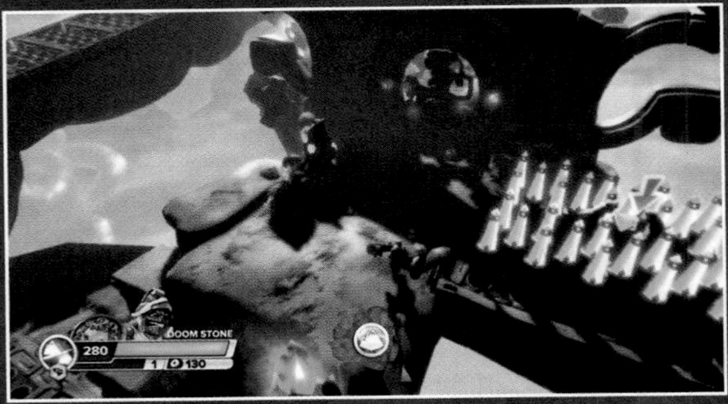

The next gate puzzle switches are blocked by Battle Gates. You must defeat the waves of Arkeyan units (they all put in an apperance during this fight) to gain access to the switches. You must align both switches before the gate opens. The area beyond the opened gate is known as Guardian's Lookout.

EARTH IS STRONGER IN THIS AREA

GUARDIAN'S LOOKOUT & WESTERN WATCH

The first area beyond the gate appears to have two paths, but they both lead to the same spot. You can walk down either way, or make a complete circuit to collect all the coins. There's a **Treasure Chest** inside the gated off area surrounded by the spear traps.

Evil Glumshanks makes his debut here, although his only involvement at this point is to fire rockets from a distance away. Avoid the red circles when they appear on the ground to stay safe. Cross the stone bridge, which falls apart as your Skylander moves over it.

Deal with the Chompy Rustbud ambush quickly, then get to work on the sliding stone puzzle. To open the path, push either of the outside stones off to the side of the bridge. To get the **Grave Monkey Totem**, push the stone it floats over on top of the stone you just pushed over the edge. Hurry across the bridge made up of spear traps. The spears alternate from one side to the other, so you may need to zig zag to avoid taking damage.

The area beyond the bridge is loaded! A Water Gate and a SWAP Zone Challenge are both short distances off the main path. The main path has its share of collectibles as well.

HIDDEN TEMPLE

Use the switches in the pools to raise and lower platforms, which help you reach the top pool where you meet Stone Block. Stone Block asks for helping hands (since he doesn't have any hands) with his itchiness. Push him in the right direction a few times and he reavals a bounce pad, which allows you to reach the gift-wrapped **Winged Sapphire** above him.

STONE BLOCK
Hey you wanna give me a hand? Cuz I don't have any and my back is all itchy. Push me up

SWAP Zone

Lonely Springs

POP THE KAOS BALLOONS!

Turn to page 268 for tips on how to clear this SWAP Zone Challenge. Your reward for completing this challege is the **Sawblade Hat**.

There's a **Giant Treasure Chest** near the wooden bridge where the Western Watch begins. Jump up and over the wall made up of stone blocks to begin a fight against Evilized Sugarbats and Arkeyan Barrelbots. To reach the Barrelbot on the high ground (on the same ledge as the purple gem switch), slide the block along its track and down into the square hole. After opening the door, go left along a side path (it's the shoes of a giant Arkeyan construct) and use the bounce pad to get Roller Brawl's **Soul Gem (Cursed Helmet)**.

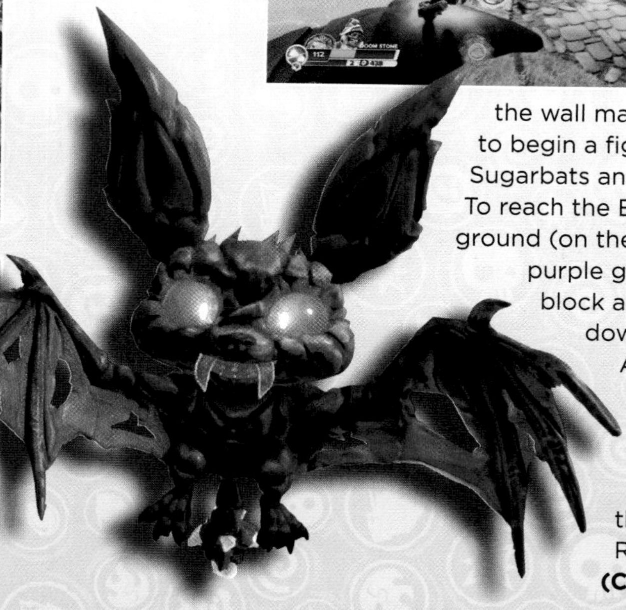

At the other end of the area, Willowbark explains how to reactivate the Stone Monkey. The mechanism works the same as the gate puzzles, but your target is now the gap between the monkey statue's hands. Hit the switch so that the beam passes through the gap and reaches the statue on the central pedestal, then use the Magic Circle to jump to the next area.

UNDEAD IS STRONGER IN THIS AREA

MONKEY MONK'S PATH & EASTERN WATCH

Arkeyan forces are waiting at the landing spot, but they underestimated how much damage a Skylander does after traveling so far! A few enemies survive and attack immediately, but shouldn't pose much of a threat. The path ahead is composed almost entirely of spear traps, and a Soul Gem is on top of a large stone, just out of reach.

Before you tackle the spear traps, turn around and cross the short, wooden bridge. Grab the **Story Scroll** floating above a round, grassy islet.

The spear traps in the path here work the same way as the ones you encountered earlier, but there are many more of them! The holes glow brighter and brighter as the spearheads get closer to the surface. Use the convenient gaps in the stones to avoid taking damage when the spears emerge, and pick up some food and extra loot.

After moving past the final spear trap, use the smaller stone blocks to hop up to the moss-covered stone block. Quickly jump to the spear trap-topped stone block, then over to Star Strike's **Soul Gem (Shooting Stars)**. Return to the end of the spear trap path by whichever means is best for you (hopping over gaps or running on the ground while avoiding spears).

To open the gate puzzle around the next corner, you need to slide the stone block on the ground forward and to the left. Use the block to jump up to the ledge and take out the Arkeyan Barrelbot. His friend on the other side keeps firing as well, so stay sharp. With the first Barrelbot out of the picture, push the two blocks off the ledge. The second block needs to slide all the way over to the stone spot below the other ledge. Jump up and deal with the second Barrelbot, then turn your attention to the gate puzzle.

Align the purple gem properly, then hurry across to the ledge with the yellow switch. If you're overcome with eagerness and leave for the yellow side before the purple one is properly aligned, don't worry about it. The order in which you align the gems isn't important. When both are in the right place, the gate drops away and you're off to the Eastern Watch.

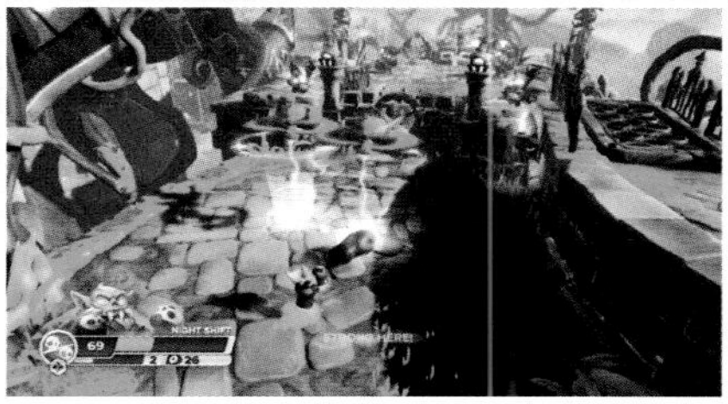

Collect the coins on the path and note the location of the Treasure Chest on the right side. You can't get it yet, but you'll be back soon for it.

When the Battle Gate comes into view, Evil Glumshanks wakes up and fires a volley of rockets, but stops when the Arkeyan Barrelbots and Rotor-bots join the fight. Take them out to open the Battle Gate, but don't move ahead to engage the Arkeyan Slamshocks until after you jump up to the right side wall, move past the spear trap, and finally open the **Treasure Chest** you saw earlier.

The Slamshocks are supported by Arkeyan Barrelblots and more rockets fired by Evil Glumshanks. A second wave of enemies pops up after the first is defeated. This wave is Arkeyan Rotor-bots and Chompy Rustbuds. With that group out of the way, the Battle Gates blocking the yellow and purple gem switches are cleared away. Evil Glumshanks keeps lobbing rockets into the area, changing the tricky task of aligning the monkey statues properly into a dangerous one!

There's no time to relax after activating the Stone Monkey; now you must face Evil Glumshanks in battle!

JUNGLE RUMBLE

OBJECTIVES

Story Goals

- ◯ Defeat Evil Glumshanks
- ◯ No Skylanders Defeated
- ◯ No Damage Taken

New Enemies

Arkeyan Knuckleduster

DEFEAT EVIL GLUMSHANKS - STAGE 1

There are two hazards to avoid during every stage of the battle against Evil Glumshanks and his improvised Arkeyan tank. The first hazard is Evil Glumshanks. Except for one exception covered in the next paragraph, stay away from it. The other hazard is the spear-lined walls of the arena. Do not touch them at any point!

During the first stage of the fight, Glumshanks puts his headlights on your Skylander and they slowly change color from yellow to red. When the headlights turn red, the tank charges in a straight line across the arena floor. You must not only avoid the charge attack, but you need to bait Glumshanks into driving his tank into one of the panels of spikes. When you are successful, Glumshank's tank loses its Arkeyan armor and is vulnerable to attack. Continue to attack, even while the tank re-armors itself. When the tank is fully re-armored, it sends out a non-damaging pulse to push away nearby objects, including pesky Skylanders!

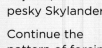

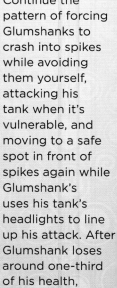

Continue the pattern of forcing Glumshanks to crash into spikes while avoiding them yourself, attacking his tank when it's vulnerable, and moving to a safe spot in front of spikes again while Glumshank's uses his tank's headlights to line up his attack. After Glumshank loses around one-third of his health, he changes things slightly.

DEFEAT EVIL GLUMSHANKS - STAGE 2

Glumshanks realizes the spikes are hurting him, so he removes half of them from the walls. The second thing that he does is to launch rockets (watch for the tell-tale red circles on the ground for their target location) before using his headlights to acquire his target.

Your tasks are essentially unchanged during this stage. Avoid incoming rockets, then stand in front of a panel of spears until the tank's headlights turn red. Avoid the charge and lay into the unarmored tank until its armor reforms around it. When Glumshanks is down to one-third health remaining, he calls for reinforcements.

DEFEAT EVIL GLUMSHANKS - STAGE 3

Glumshanks spawns Arkeyan Knuckledusters for help. These pint-sized terrors are as tenacious as Chompies, but carry a big mace for clubbing Skylanders. To make matters worse, Evil Glumshanks continues to use rockets.

You must now take down the Arkeyan Knuckledusters, avoid the rockets falling from above, and still move in front of the sole set of spikes before the tank's headlights go red. Just to keep things lively, each time you successfully lure Glumshanks into the spikes, he changes which wall is active!

Back In Woodburrow

Rufus informs you that Snagglescale has set up a hut near The Airdocks, and has a way to help you improve your skills in battle. Speak with Snagglescale to learn more about Arenas, and even try out the first one! When you are ready to continue the adventure, speak with Tessa about Iron Jaw Gulch.

When you deplete Glumshank's health entirely, his coating of darkness is removed and he realizes he's just no Kaos.

IRON JAW GULCH

OBJECTIVES

Story Goals

- ◯ Destroy the Airships

Dares

- **5** Marshal Wheellock Plushies
- **50** Enemy Goal
- **0** No Skylanders Defeated

New Enemies

Pirate Powderkeg

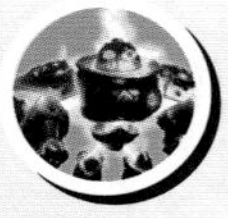

Fire Geargolem

Pirate Slamspin

Evilized Kangarat

Collections

- **15** Areas Discovered
- **2** Treasure Chests
- **1** Giant Treasure Chest
- **3** Soul Gems
- **2** Legendary Treasures
- **2** Hats
- **1** Bonus Mission Map
- **1** Winged Sapphire
- **1** Story Scroll

MAGIC IS STRONGER IN THIS AREA

IRON JAW GULCH

When you take control of your Skylander, turn around and grab the **Marshal Wheellock Plushie** directly behind the starting point. It's underneath a water tower, so you need to engage in a little destruction before you can get it. Head back to the Iron Jaw Gulch sign to speak with the real Marshal Wheellock to learn more about what Kaos and his minions are doing.

If you're playing on the Wii console, there is no water tower to destroy to pick up the Marshal Wheellock Plushie.

Move up the path until you meet your first Pirate Powderkeg, a new enemy who is similar to a Greeble Blunderbuss. These eye-patched plunderers carry a large cannon, which can be fired one time before it needs reloading. Avoid the cannonball, then attack the vulnerable Powderkeg before he can reload.

Pull the nearby lever to extend a bridge. The next landing is infested with pirate-themed Chompies supported by a Pirate Powderkeg. Clear out the scalawags, then use the Bounce Pad to claim a second **Marshal Wheellock Plushie**.

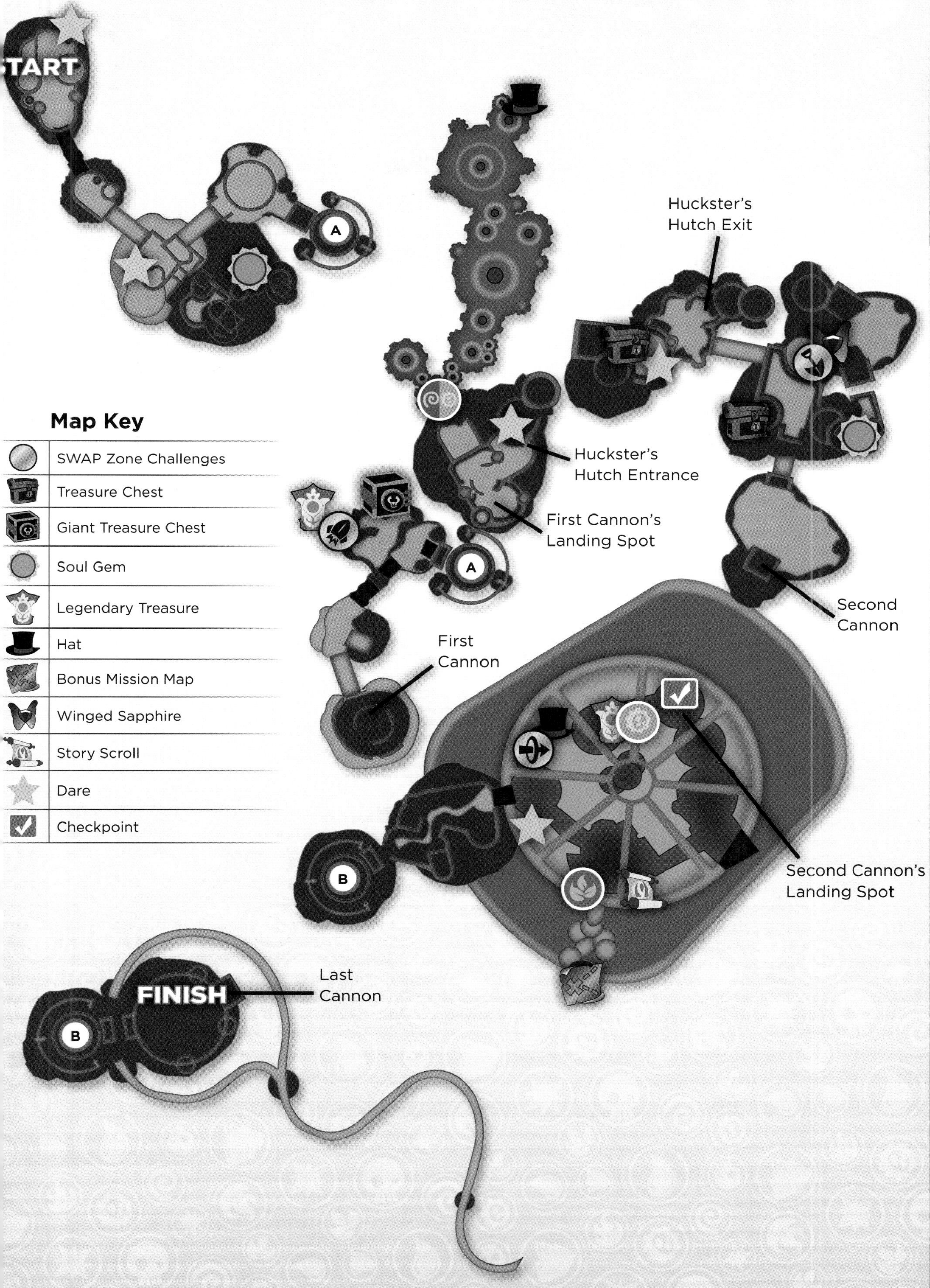
START
A
Huckster's
Hutch Exit
Map Key
SWAP Zone Challenges
Treasure Chest
Giant Treasure Chest
Soul Gem
Legendary Treasure
Hat
Bonus Mission Map
Winged Sapphire
Story Scroll
Dare
Checkpoint
Huckster's
Hutch Entrance
First Cannon's
Landing Spot
A
Second
Cannon
First
Cannon
Second Cannon's
Landing Spot
B
Last
Cannon
FINISH
B

Ignore the lever for now. Drop down to the sandy area near the Bounce Pad and use the round rooftops to jump over to Wind-Up's **Soul Gem (Spring-Loaded Crank)**. Return to the lever and extend the bridge to the next area.

A new, hot enemy appears on the other side of the bridge. Fire Geargolems bathe the area directly in front of their hands with fire. Avoid the fire blast and attack the Fire Geargolem from anywhere not directly in front of it while it's standing still.

When the Fire Geargolem falls, a wave of Chompies appears from under the sand. When all the enemies are eliminated, follow the short path that ends at a circular platform filled with wooden barrels. Ride it up to the next area, Cactus Pass.

CACTUS PASS, THE CANTEEN & IMPENETRABLE FORT

The initial part of Cactus Pass is clear of enemies, but does have both a **Giant Treasure Chest** and a SWAP Zone. The wooden bridge near the SWAP Zone is filled with mines, so be careful as you cross it.

SWAP Zone
Storm of Sands

ROCKET TO THE FINISH!

Turn to page 272 for tips on how to clear this SWAP Zone Challenge. Your reward for completing this challenge is the Legendary Treasure, **Jolly Greeble**.

Speak with Terrel, the kangarat near a broken switch. Go into The Canteen (through the nearby door) where Rio explains how the Ho-Down Squares work. Bounce on all four pads without hitting the ground to open the back door and get to the missing handle.

Head back out to Terrel, replace the handle, and use the switch to extend the bridge. There's another new enemy waiting to face you on the other side.

Pirate Slamspins are similar to Arkeyan Rotor-bots, but they stay on the ground at all times. They're invulnerable while they're spinning, so stay at a safe distance until the spinning stops. Attack them while they're dizzy to take them out safely.

The Battle Gate here blocks one of the cannons Marshal Wheellock mentioned earlier. You must take out a few waves of enemies, which are mostly the new pirate enemies from Iron Jaw Gulch and a Fire Geargolem. When the last enemy falls, load your Skylander into the cannon and take out the first Airship.

Use the Bounce Pads scattered around the area where your Skylander lands to grab some gold and reach the roof of the building. There's a **Marshal Wheellock Plushie** up there, and it's not coming down on its own! Check out the Air/Tech gate before entering the building that had the plushie on top of it.

SKY GEAR GULCH

Use the levers as you encounter them to shift the gears around, opening up new paths and Bounce Pads. Use the Bounce Pads to collect the gold floating above them.

Mines are the only hazards you face at first, but there are four Pirate Powderkegs you must defeat to clear the Battle Gate from the area's penultimate lever. Open the package to get the **Gaucho Hat**. Pull the last lever for a shortcut back to the gate.

FIRE IS STRONGER IN THIS AREA

HUCKSTER'S HUTCH, SUN SMOKED STRAND & CUDDY'S COTTAGE

The building next to the dual elemental gate is Huckster's Hutch. Bounce on the five Ho-Down Squares without touching the floor (hitting the same one more than once is fine) to open the large doors at the end of the room. Go through the door to enter Sun Smoked Strand.

Kangarats just can't keep track of handles! Squink needs help finding one, and you can't get to the next cannon without it. Use the Bounce Pad to reach the roof of the nearby building. Avoid the mines and destroy the water tower to uncover a **Treasure Chest**.

Drop back down to the ground and enter the nearby building, Cuddy's Cottage. A Chompy Pod and a Pirate Powderkeg guard the handle. Clear out the enemies, but don't leave the cottage until you bounce on each of the beds until it breaks. One of the beds yields a **Marshal Wheellock Plushie**.

If you're playing on the Wii console, the Marshal Wheellock Plushie is behind the beds.

Return to Squink and extend the bridge. The next area has two building entrances, a Dig SWAP Zone, a Soul Gem atop a building, and a bridge-extending switch missing its handle.

Ignore the buildings for now. Drop down into an alley near the SWAP Zone. Avoid the mines and take out the Pirate Powderkegs guarding the path to a Bounce Pad. Bounce up to the roof and pick up Grim Creeper's **Soul Gem (Help from Beyond)**. Hop down from the roof and return to the handle-less switch.

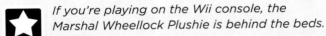

SWAP Zone

Submerged Sands

FIND YOUR WAY THROUGH THE DARK! DIG UP THE BLUE CRYSTALS BEFORE TIME RUNS OUT!

Turn to page 271 for tips on how to clear this SWAP Zone Challenge. Your reward for completing this challenge is a **Winged Sapphire**.

If you're playing on the Wii console, the Winged Sapphire is the reward for completing the Dig Swap Zone in the Impenetrable Fort area, before the Tech and Air elemental zone.

FIRE IS STRONGER IN THIS AREA

IRON JAW INN & QUAINT COTTAGE

The building next to the switch is the Iron Jaw Inn. The handle you need is inside, but it's locked behind a Battle Gate. Take down the Chompy Pod and Pirate Powderkegs to open the gate. Grab the key and take a victory lap around the room by bouncing on the beds until they fall apart. Replace the handle but don't cross the bridge just yet.

The other building in the area is the Quaint Cottage. It has beds to destroy and a Spark Locked **Treasure Chest**.

SPARK LOCK

Let's Take This to the Next Level!

Send Shock to the green button and then the blue button. Move Bolt to the green column just below the green lightning bolt. Hit the green button again so Bolt can grab the lightning bolt. Switch to Bolt and move to the sliding panel next to the blue button, but don't jump on it yet! Shock needs to be on the lowered blue platform before Bolt hits the button. Grab the blue lightning bolt and move Shock and Bolt together to open the lock.

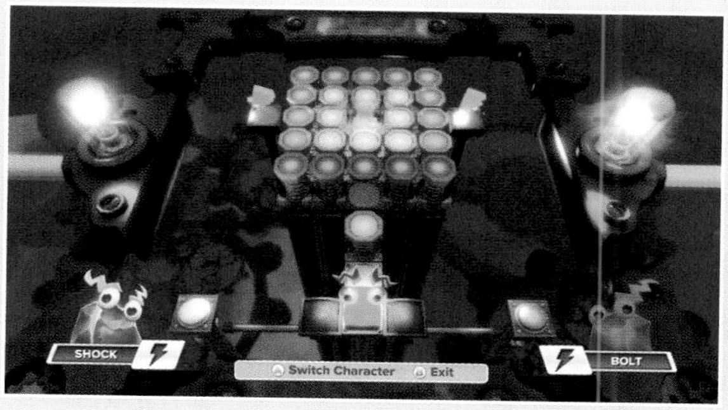

If you're playing on the Wii console, this Spark Lock does not appear in your game.

The next cannon is across the bridge, but the Greebles get there first and turn the kangarats against you! Avoid the Evilized Kangarat's landing spot after it goes airborne (look for the large, violet circle on the ground) and knock the crystallized darkness out of it while it's recovering.

A few Evilized Kangarats augment the waves of Pirate forces guarding the cannon. The Airship flying nearby is also a threat, as it lobs cannonballs into the area. Avoid the red circles on the ground. Load your Skylander into the cannon when it's ready and take down the second Airship.

UNDEAD IS STRONGER IN THIS AREA

10,000 GALLON HAT

✓ The cannon fires your Skylander into a building near a Power Pod and an elemental gate. The nearby bridge is infested with mines, so exercise caution when you cross it.

PUMP STATION

There are no enemies to fight in the Pump Station, but there are plenty of moving parts that increase the difficulty of jumping safely across gaps. Your reward for reaching the end is the **Tik-Tok Neck Clock** Legendary Treasure. Pull the lever near the treasure for a quick trip back to the gate.

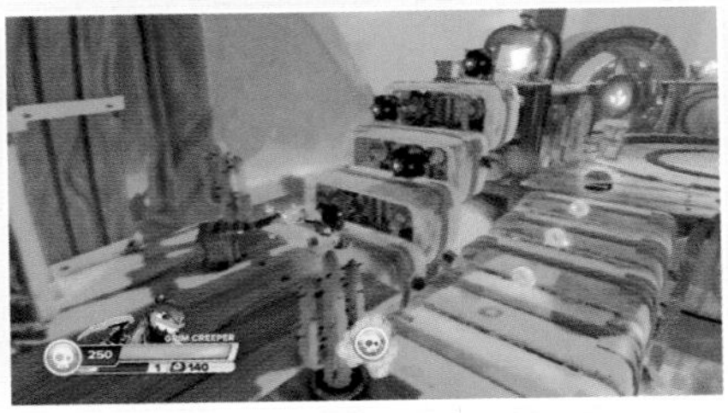

The switch on the other side of the bridge is missing its handle. Since a missing handle is involved, there must be Kangarats nearby. Enter the nearby building (it's the Kangarat Groove Hut, go figure!) and bounce on the seven Ho-Down Squares before touching the floor to open the door and get the handle you need.

Extend the bridge, then backtrack when a second bridge appears. Get the **Story Scroll** from behind the mines, then drop down to the first bridge. The circular platform has both a Battle Gate and a Life Gate.

GROOVING GARDENS

Use the huge mushroom in the entry area to reach a much more difficult musical challenge than the Kangarats have offered. There are seven Ho-Down Squares to bounce off of in order to open the gate on the other side of the area. The real challenge here is that three of the platforms flip over slowly and the rocky underside doesn't bounce your Skylander back into the air.

The good news is that you can use the same pad more than once. Time your jumps to hit the flipping platforms when the musical note is showing, then land on one of the four stable platforms. Your reward for completing this challenge is the **Egg Royale Bonus Mission Map**. Use the giant mushroom to return to the gate.

The enemies guarding the Battle Gate fight dirty. The Pirate Powderkegs stay on top of the high platform until you defeat the Evilized Kangarats (who are only on the ground long enough to recover from their jumping attacks) and the Fire Geargolem that appears after you free the first Kangarat.

UNDEAD IS STRONGER IN THIS AREA

OKEY DOKEY CORRAL & LAST TRAIN WEST

The area beyond the Battle Gate doesn't have any enemies, but does have mines and a Teleport SWAP Zone. Use the Bounce Pad near the SWAP Zone to reach the final **Marshal Wheellock Plushie**. Destroy the water tower past the mine-filled bridge to reveal a **Treasure Chest**. The action really heats up here as Pirate forces swarm the area and the Airship fires into the fight. Destroy the Chompy Pod tucked against a building to reveal a Bounce Pad. Use it to reach the roof, destroy the water tower and grab Grilla Drilla's **Soul Gem (Rings of the Golden Monkey/Adaptive Nature)**. Take the round platform at the end of the path up to the final area of Iron Jaw Gulch, Last Train West.

If you're playing on the Wii console, there is no water tower to destroy in order to reach the Treasure Chest.

SWAP Zone

Hourglass Blink

COLLECT THE MAGIC RUNES TO SEAL THE DIMENSIONAL RIFT!

Turn to page 278 for tips on how to clear this SWAP Zone Challenge. Your reward for completing this challenge is the **Zombeanie** hat.

As if Pirate Powderkegs weren't enough, you need to keep clear of the mines, watch out for Evilized Kangarats flying in from above, and a horde of Chompies scurrying around on the ground. Just when you think the fight is over, Pirate Slamspins and a Fire Geargolem join the fun, and the Airship peppers the area with cannon fire.

When you survive that wave of attackers and open the Battle Gate, load your Skylander into the cannon on the ground and destroy the last Airship.

Back in Woodburrow

Rufus directs you to speak with Tibbet in the Trophy Room, who explains what the pedestals found around Woodburrow are for. He also hands over the **Navigator Compass** Legendary Treasure. For a complete listing of pedestal locations, check out the Woodburrow section of the guide. When you're ready to continue the adventure, speak to Tessa at The Airdocks.

MOTLEYVI[redacted]LE

OBJECTIVES

Story Goals

- ◯ Stop Baron von Shellshock
- ◯ De-Evilize Whiskers

Dares

- 5 Toy Trains
- 50 Enemy Goal
- 0 No Skylanders Defeated

Collections

- 24 Areas Discovered
- 5 Treasure Chests
- 1 Giant Treasure Chest
- 3 Soul Gems
- 2 Legendary Treasures
- 2 Hats
- 1 Bonus Mission Map
- 1 Winged Sapphire
- 1 Story Scroll

New Enemies

Chompy Powerhouse

Greeble Heaver

Earth Geargolem

FIGHT EVILIZED WHISKERS

The action begins before you reach Motleyville! Baron von Shellshock and his band of Greebles evilize the normally placid Whiskers, and he attacks immediately.

Watch the ground for a glowing circle (it looks the same as the ones used by Evilized Kangarats) when Evilzed Whiskers is in the air. When Whiskers slams into the ground, a shockwave spreads out along the ground. Jump over the shockwave, then attack Whiskers while his head is stuck in the ground. When Whiskers is down to three-quarters health, he jumps and lands three times before his head becomes stuck in the ground and you can attack. At 50% health, Whiskers flies off, and you're free to enter Motleyville.

UNDEAD IS STRONGER IN THIS AREA

ARENA OVERLOOK, ARENA BOMB CAR & ABANDONED MINE TRACK

Follow the path from the spot with the Whiskers fight to a lever. Pull the lever to extend a bridge to the next area where a more powerful Chompy, the Chompy Powerhouse, pops up and attacks. Grab the nearby **Treasure Chest** after dealing with the Chompies.

MOTLEYVILLE

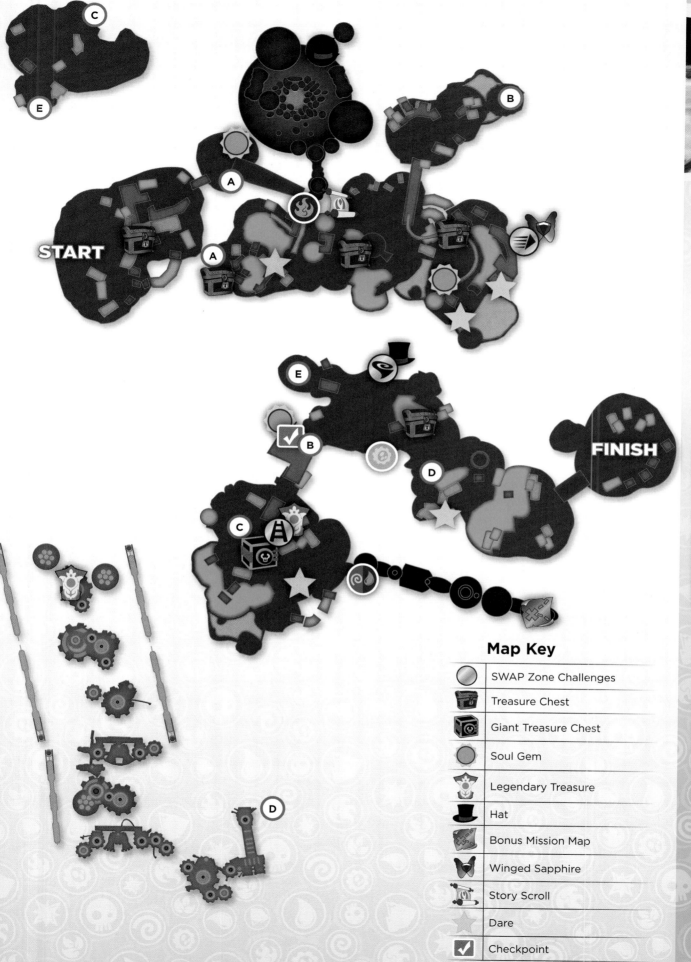

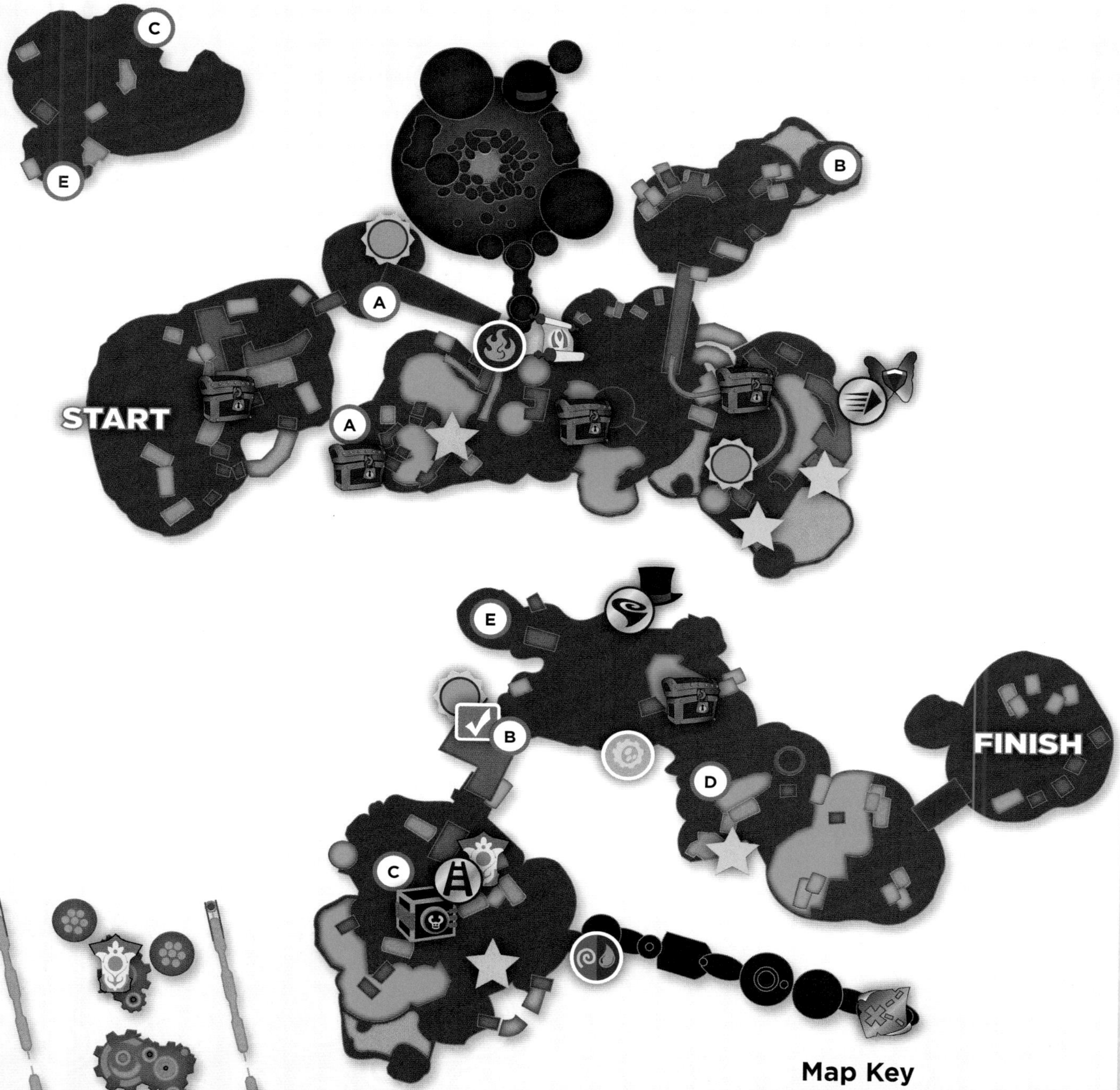

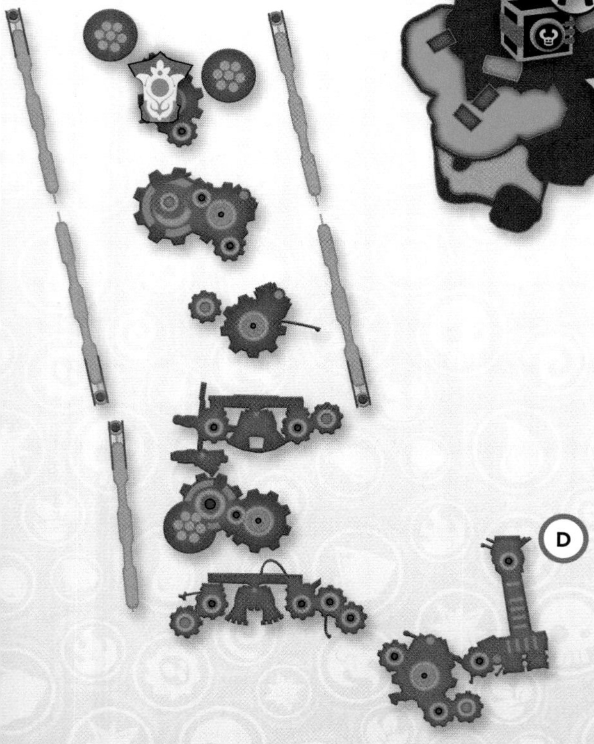

Map Key

- SWAP Zone Challenges
- Treasure Chest
- Giant Treasure Chest
- Soul Gem
- Legendary Treasure
- Hat
- Bonus Mission Map
- Winged Sapphire
- Story Scroll
- Dare
- Checkpoint

The wooden walkway leads you to a new type of locked gate, one that requires dynamite to open, and an encounter with a new enemy, Greeble Heaver. Greeble Heavers lob three shells into the air before reloading. Avoid the red circles on the ground, then attack the Greeble Heaver while it reloads.

Take out the enemies guarding the gate. The dynamite you need to clear the door is inside the Arena Bomb Car. Its entrance glows yellow and has an image of a lit dynamite bundle over it.

The dynamite is timed, so hurry back to the gate and toss the dynamite at it to clear the path. After Baron von Shellshock's taunting, take out his Chompy and Greeble minions. Don't use the launcher until after you grab Boom Jet's **Soul Gem (Supply Drop/Mach 2)** from on top of the stacked boxes. The first jump from the short platform near the launcher to the lowest box is tricky. You need to jump as close to the edge of the platform as possible to clear the gap.

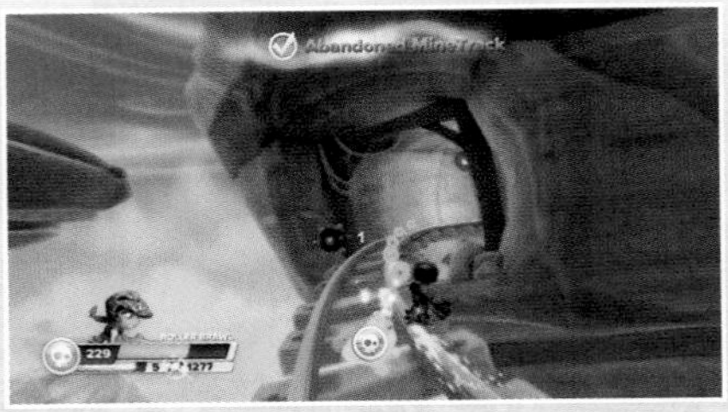

The launcher sends your Skylander on a rail-guided trip along the Abandoned Mine Track. The rails are covered with coins and you can tap left and right to switch tracks. Some coins are higher over the track than others. Hit Jump to grab those coins. There are hazards along the way as well. Mines and wooden structures inflict harm on any Skylander that crashes into them. Avoid the hazards by either switching rails or jumping over them.

UNDEAD IS STRONGER IN THIS AREA

SOGGY FIELDS & BOMB BAY

The goo covering areas of the Soggy Fields is so toxic, it damages anything that comes into contact with it. Falling in won't knock out your Skylanders immediately, but touching the goo does ticks off damage every few seconds.

Hop across the tire bridge to the right for a pile of gold. Cross the next set of tires and destroy a few boxes and barrels to uncover a **Treasure Chest**. Push the mine cart along the track to reach a raised area with a few enemies and an elemental gate.

LAVA FIELDS

Lone Shark encountered some problems while cleaning, and left his lucky hat behind. There aren't any enemies in the area, but the volcano in the middle of the zone continually spews dangerous boulders that explode when they hit the ground. Jump between the platforms, avoid the exploding boulders, and claim the **Roundlet** hat at the top.

Push the cart on the upper level off the edge. Use the cart to jump up to the higher area. Avoid the swinging pulley hooks. The first **Toy Train** is to the right of the first pulley hook, but you need to use the metal boxes beyond the hook to reach it.

Continue past the next two pulley hooks and drop down into another goo-covered area. There are two gates here, one is a Battle Gate with a **Treasure Chest** behind it, and the other requires dynamite to open.

You can either push the cart down the track, or use the floating tubes and a sandy path to reach the upper area with the gates. Use the small wooden platform below the Dynamite Gate to jump over to the wobbly round top of a stone formation, then make another jump to reach Night Shift's **Soul Gem (Gentlemanly/Grand Entrance)**.

There's another **Treasure Chest** on the roof of the building with the dynamite needed to open the gate. The area is crawling with Arkeyan units and Greebles, but at least the dynamite is not guarded. Destroy the gate and speak with Clunker after Baron von Shellshock departs.

MAGIC IS STRONGER IN THIS AREA

LESTER'S LANE, SHADY SHOPPE & LESTER'S STORAGE SHED

Follow Clunker after speaking with him. Pull the switch to extend a bridge to reach an area with a SWAP Zone and a pair of Dynamite Gates. The Shady Shoppe has the dynamite needed to open the gates, but you must defeat the Chompy and Arkeyan enemies to get to it. There's one big Arkeyan waiting behind the Battle Gate, so don't relax after taking out the initial wave.

There is a **Toy Train** behind the Dynamite Gate closer to the SWAP Zone block. Blow up the Dynamite Gate closer to Shady Shoppe to reach Gibbs. Gibbs just happens to have the cannon you need to reach the village.

SWAP Zone
Drag Stripped

RACE TO THE FINISH!
Turn to page 275 for tips on how to clear this SWAP Zone Challenge. Your reward for completing this challenge is a **Winged Sapphire**.

Before you put the cannon to use, destroy everything in the courtyard below the cannon. There's an Arkeyan Rotor-bot inside the large box, so be ready for a quick fight. The doorway at the bottom of the ramp leads to Lester's Storage Shed, Destroy everything inside to reveal a second Arkeyan Rotor-bot and a **Toy Train**.

Blast the gate with the cannon. Push the cannon along the track and continue to blast the gates. Watch out for the Chompy Powerhouses hidden along the track while you're moving the cannon. When the cannon hits a dead end, pull the nearby lever to raise it up. The lever extends a bridge for your Skylander at the same time.

Blast the thick wall blocking the bridge. Take down the Arkeyans that rush out from behind the destroyed barricade. Push the cannon back toward the platform you used to raise it up and fire it again. A series of overturned train cars leads to an area with Motleyville's **Story Scroll, Motleyville Junk**. Return to the cleared bridge (ignore the stairs leading downward; you followed Clunker that way earlier). Ghost Town is on the other side.

MAGIC IS STRONGER IN THIS AREA

GHOST TOWN & VIEW POINT RUN

Ghost Town begins with an earth-shattering bang. A Battle Gate blocks the first area, and one of its guardians is the powerful Earth Geargolem. Earth Geargolems smash their fists into the ground to create a shockwave of pain. Jump over the shockwave and attack the massive creature while its fists are stuck in the ground.

After you eliminate the lone Earth Geargolem, a wave of Arkeyan units, Chompy Powerhouses, and Pirate Powderkegs emerges from the sand to support the second Earth Geargolem you must face in order to open the Battle Gate.

Use the launch pad near where Baron von Shellshock taunted you again to begin another trip along the rails of View Point Run. Avoid the mines and wooden structures while collecting as many coins as possible. Some of the mines jump track, and Greeble Heavers add some shells to the mix as well. The rail ends at a Checkpoint, so take the opportunity to purchase upgrades at the Power Pod.

LIFE IS STRONGER IN THIS AREA

STACK O' TRAINS & THE SECRET WAY

Evilized Whiskers lobs energy blasts into the air and destroys most of the area. Avoid the glowing circles on the ground and jump over the gaps he created. Jump up on the right side to reach a wooden pathway that leads away from Whiskers. Scorp's **Soul Gem (Avalanche Dash)** is there.

When your Skylander reaches Evilzed Whiskers, he flies off. Walk down the path until you find a gate and a mining cart next to each other. Push the mining cart along the rails to open the gate to The Secret Way.

Grab the **Giant Treasure Chest**, then use the track switch. You need to hit the switch to align the tracks properly first, otherwise the cart bounces back to its starting point. The small platform near the track is the start of a path that leads to a small, underground area called Beneath the Sand. You can also reach it by missing the floating tires and falling into the whirlpool on the other side of the gate you just opened.

Beyond the pool with the floating tires is an area littered with wrecked trains and surprise enemy encounters, although Evilized Whiskers is strictly an observer here. Pull the lever to extend an unfinished bridge. Follow the path past the swinging pulley hooks to reach a dual elemental gate.

MAGIC IS STRONGER IN THIS AREA

BENEATH THE SAND

Regardless of how you reached this area, check its full length for piles of gold and a handful of enemies. It's a small area, so it won't take long for you to explore it all.

KESTREL BATH

The first water jet is unguarded, but it sends your Skylander to a watery platform filled with Arkeyan Knuckledusters. The next two platforms are guarded by Greeble Heavers and Strongarm Chompies. Each level has a spinning water sprayer, but it only pushes things around. It doesn't do any damage.

Defeat all the enemies and your reward is the **Sleepy Turtles Bonus Mission Map**. Run over the glowing spot in the pool beyond the reward for a fast return trip to the Secret Way.

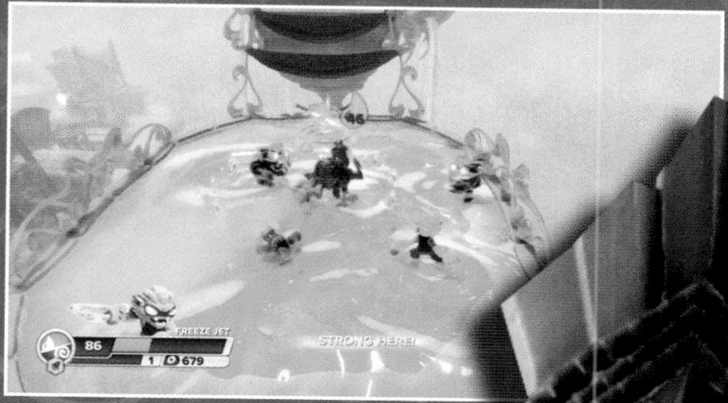

Back in the Secret Way, clear the enemies guarding the rails near the next cart. When they're out of the way, push the cart before touching the track switch. There's a **Toy Train** on a ledge that's too high to reach with an unaided jump.

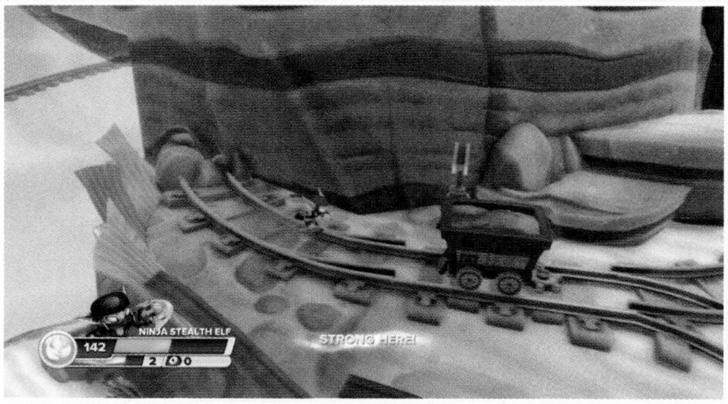

If you're playing on the Wii console, this toy Train is on a platform which can be reached by jumping on a tipped over minning cart before the goo pit in the Fixin' Station area.

Push the cart back up to its starting point, then hit the switch and push the cart again. Use the stone formation next to the track you can use to jump on top of the cart (it's possible to jump on it from the ground, but it's easier from the stones). There's a pile of gold near the gate that can be reached only in this way.

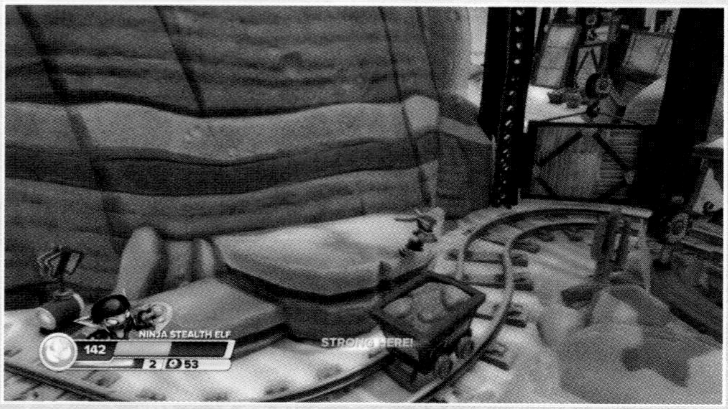

LIFE IS STRONGER IN THIS AREA

STACK O'TRAINS & RED CRAB FIREWORKS

There are two things waiting for you at the entrance to this area. The first is a SWAP Zone, and the other is a local named Birdwatcher, who lets you know Evilized Whiskers is just ahead.

SWAP Zone: Junkside Climb

CLIMB TO THE TOP!

Turn to page 269 for tips on how to clear this SWAP Zone Challenge. Your reward for completing this Challenge is the **Bling Grille** Legendary Treasure.

This fight against Whiskers begins with him bombarding the ground from a perch that's too high for your Skylander to reach. Avoid the target spots on the ground, then avoid three ground slam attacks. After the third ground slam, Whiskers is vulnerable to attack.

The good news for you is that Whiskers begins the fight at around half health. At one-third health, Whiskers mixes things up after you get in your attacks. Instead of returning to his perch immediately, Whiskers fires out an energy beam. Get behind him to avoid being hit by this attack, because it hits hard. Whiskers mixes up his attacks at this point, so be prepared to avoid any of his abilities and strike when he's vulnerable.

Before you ride down the rails, step inside the nearby doorway. Red Crab Fireworks is filled with money and you've certainly earned it after de-evilizing Whiskers!

EARTH IS STRONGER IN THIS AREA

LAST TRAIN STOP, FIXIN' STATION & BIG BANG BOUNCERS

The trip down the rails should be a familiar one by now. There's a mine shooter near the end, but nothing else new to worry about. Unfortunately, Baron von Shellshock's Arkeyan forces are waiting in ambush as soon as the ride ends.

The area beyond the Battle Gate is the Fixin' Station. There are two gates nearby. One is a SWAP Zone Challenge, and the other is a Tech Gate.

HAMMERHEAD HARDWARE

Hammerhead Harry has created a teleporting system and needs your help testing it out. Whenever the teleporting ball is thrown and lands safely, your Skylander is teleported to that location instantly (usually—this is a test after all!). There are teleporter ball generators in various places, but getting from one platform to another is not always as simple as throwing the ball.

There are large gears to ride, and enemies are scattered throughout the area. The reward for successfully testing the teleporting system is the **Crooked Currency** Legendary Treasure.

If you're playing on the Wii console, Crooked Currency is in a gift box at the end of a path to the right after the last railway in the Fixin' Station area.

SWAP Zone
Twisted Towers

DESTROY THE KAOS STATUE!
Turn to page 277 for tips on how to clear this SWAP Zone Challenge. Your reward for completing this challenge is the **Capuchon** hat.

There's a large goo whirlpool beyond the two gates. Follow the path on the Cliffside that leads to a cave mouth. Falling into the whirlpool or the cave mouth both ead to the same place: Under the Whirl. There's a **Toy Train** on a platform on the left side of the whirlpool. Greeble Heavers are also in the area, so expect a fight to reach it.

There are two carts beyond the whirlpool, but you need to clear out the enemies in the lower area before you can safely use them (the Greeble Heaver up top is out of range until you move the first cart). Push the first cart down the track, take out the Greeble Heaver and grab the dynamite from inside Big Bang Bouncers.

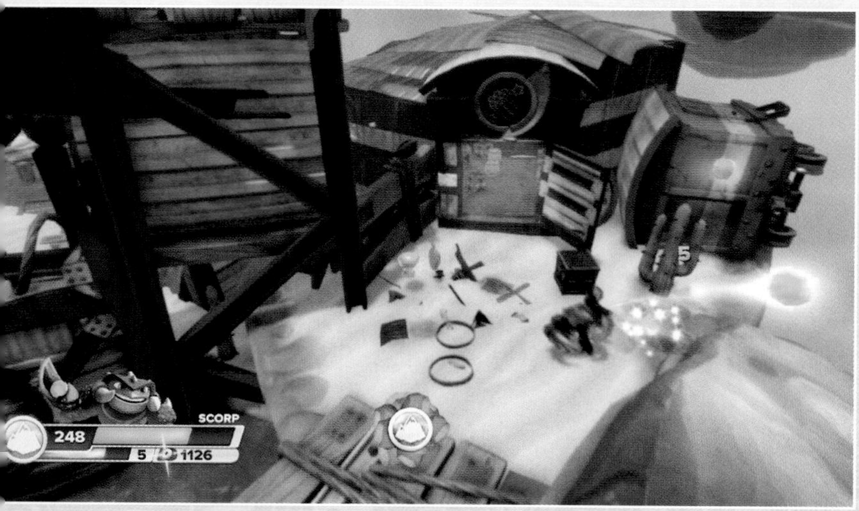

The dynamite clears the first gate, but not the second. Hit the track switcher and push the second cart down the track to move the second gate of the way. The newly opened path leads to Shark Town.

LIFE IS STRONGER IN THIS AREA

UNDER THE WHIRL

This area is just as small as Beneath the Sand and contains about as many enemies. The big difference is the **Treasure Chest** located at the end of the tunnel.

EARTH IS STRONGER IN THIS AREA

SHARK TOWN & MOTLEYVILLE MALL

Shark Town is not a large area. It serves as a line of defense for Baron von Shellshock's hinted-at surprise in Motleyville. You must defeat the waves of Greeble and Arkeyan enemies, as well as an Earth Geargolem. When the Battle Gate clears, move ahead to face Baron von Shellshock in Motleyville Mall.

Baron von Shellshock's surprise is an armored vehicle. It is immune to regular attacks most of the time. During the first stage of the battle, the Baron launches various enemies to keep you occupied. He also throws bundles of dynamite at the end of a string of cannonballs. Avoid the cannonballs, grab the dynamite, and throw it at the Baron before the timer hits zero.

When the dynamite impacts the Baron's vehicle, the vehicle loses a chunk of health, its defenses vanish, and it becomes vulnerable temporarily. Hit it with your best attacks as quickly as possible, but watch out for the enemies the Baron launched earlier. He may be down, but they can keep attacking.

Take out the minions while you're waiting for the next bundle of dynamite, but don't worry about finishing them off if there's dynamite ready for use. This is especially true at the end of the fight. As soon as Baron von Shellshock's health is gone, every enemy assisting him is destroyed instantly.

Back in Woodburrow

Wheellock has taken up residence in Woodburrow, and opens up a new area and a Fishing mini-game, located in The Hollow. The Hollow also has a **Story Scroll**, and a large vault locked by various elemental gates. Open all the gates for a nice haul of gold and Smolderdash's **Soul Gem (Smolder Dash)**.

When you're ready to continue on to the Twisty Tunnels, talk to Sharpfin at The Airdocks.

TWISTY TUNNELS

OBJECTIVES

Story Goals

- 3 Destroy the Evilizer Crystals
- ◯ Get to the Ancient Terrasquid

Dares

- 5 Rubber Duckies
- 50 Enemy Goal
- 0 No Skylanders Defeated

Collections

- 16 Areas Discovered
- 5 Treasure Chests
- 1 Giant Treasure Chest
- 3 Soul Gems
- 2 Legendary Treasures
- 2 Hats
- 1 Bonus Mission Map
- 1 Winged Sapphire
- 1 Story Scroll

New Enemies

Cadet Crusher

Boom Boss

Air Spell Punk

Air Geargolem

Fire Viper

TECH IS STRONGER IN THIS AREA

MYTHIC MESA & PERILOUS PLATEAU

The action picks up not far from the bickering duo of Flynn and Sharpfin. A new enemy, the Cadet Crusher, is the first troll enemy you've met in the Cloudbreak Islands, but it won't be the last. These hammer-swinging trolls have only melee attacks, but hit hard.

Not far from where you fought the trolls, more familiar enemies, a Fire Geargolem and Strongarm Chompies, pop up and attack alongside another group of Cadet Crushers. There's a **Treasure Chest** behind a pile of destructible objects not far from where Sharpfin waits near a lever. Get the chest before you speak with him!

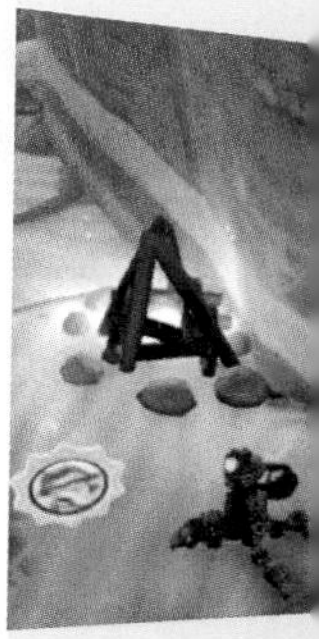

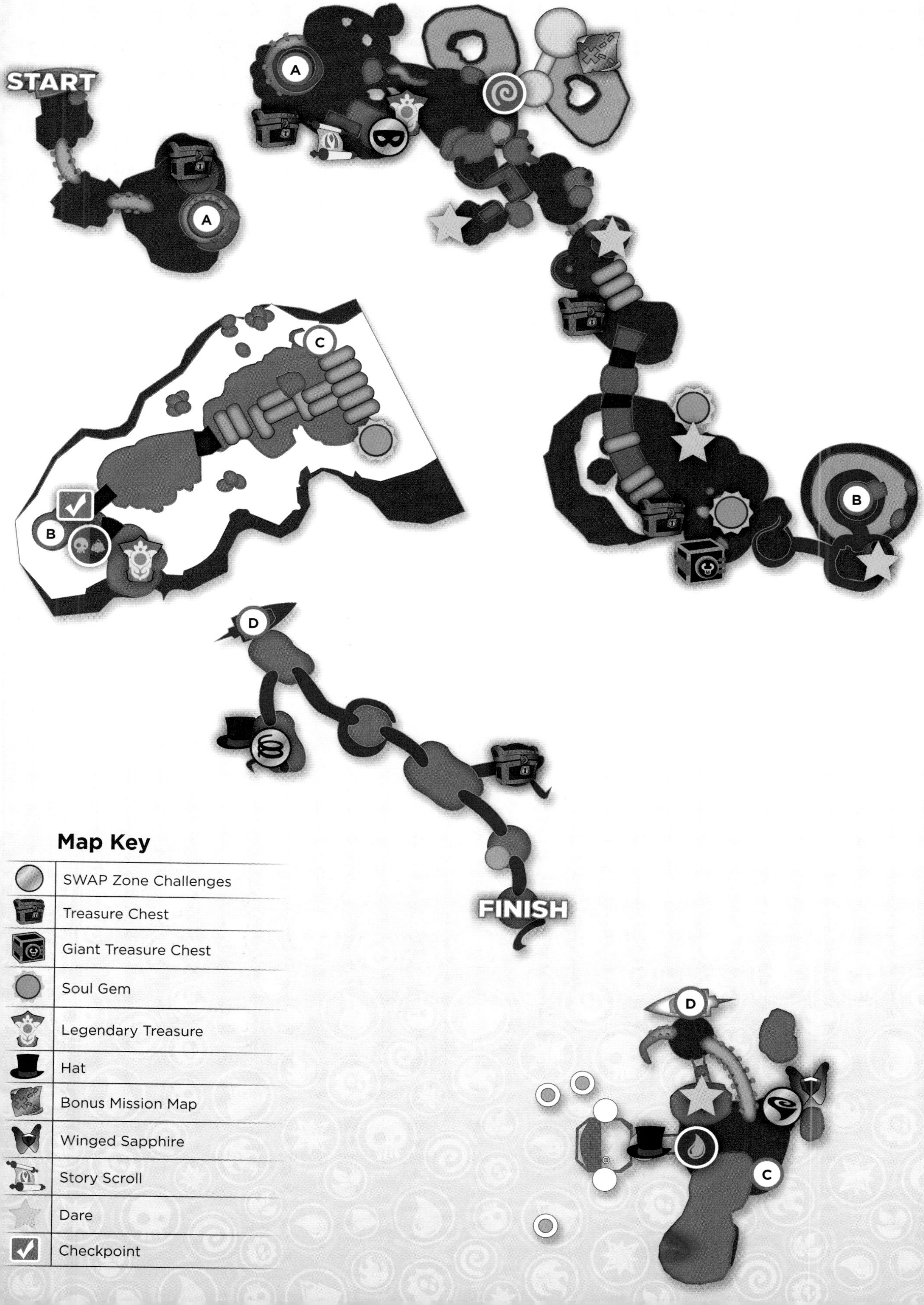

TWISTY TUNNELS

Map Key

- SWAP Zone Challenges
- Treasure Chest
- Giant Treasure Chest
- Soul Gem
- Legendary Treasure
- Hat
- Bonus Mission Map
- Winged Sapphire
- Story Scroll
- Dare
- Checkpoint

Speak with Sharpfin, who abruptly sends your Skylander to Perilous Plateau. Try to make the best of the trip and grab as many coins as possible. If you miss out on them, don't worry. There's a **Treasure Chest** behind a pile of wooden boxes off the right side of where your Skylander lands.

When you see Sharpfin again, he's standing near a SWAP Zone. There's also a **Story Scroll** a short walk up the stone ramp next to the SWAP Zone.

SWAP Zone
Sunken Sand Base

SNEAK IN AND DESTROY THE FORTRESS! DON'T GET CAUGHT BY SPOTLIGHTS.

Turn to page 274 for tips on how to clear this SWAP Zone Challenge. Your reward for completing this challenge is the **Moltenskin Scale** Legendary Treasure

The gate near Sharpfin is locked and the key is buried somewhere in the sand. Pick up the shovel, follow the dotted lines, and dig on the "X" to uncover a treasure, an enemy, and eventually the key.

There's a warm greeting for you on the other side of the locked gate. A new enemy, the Boom Boss, debuts near an Air Gate. These trolls lob explosive barrels that bounce a few times before exploding. They need a moment to reload, which is the best time to take them out. Blast through the wall of cages behind one of the initial Boom Bosses and follow the stone pathway over a short hop. Grab the **Rubber Ducky** and go back the way you came.

HIGH IN THE SKY

Take a ride on Razortooth's hot air balloon. It flies through coin-filled, fiery mine-infested airspace. Coins appear in huge groups, but you must be agile to collect even half of them and still avoid all the mines. If you complete the trip, the **Magic Cells Bonus Mission Map** is your reward.

If you're playing on the Wii console, the Magic Cells Bonus Mission Map comes from a gift box to the left of the Serene Walkway area. Your reward here is the Peacock Hat.

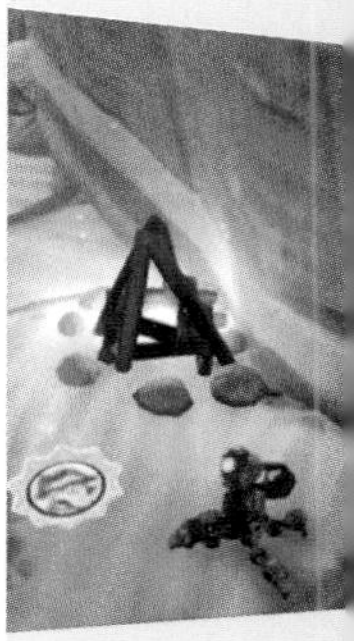

Hop on the rising and falling platform topped with rotating coins. The Battle Gate up ahead is guarded by Cadet Crushers and a Fire Geargolem, followed by a pair of Boom Bosses.

Cross the short tentacle bridge near the Evilizer Crystal but drop off the side of the ledge before you approach the crystal. Use the shovel stuck in the sand to dig in the area until you unearth a **Treasure Chest**. Use the Bounce Pad to get back up to the higher ledge and continue to the Evilizer Crystal.

TECH IS STRONGER IN THIS AREA

CRYSTAL CRASHING

After observing a shrinking troll, Sharpfin suggests following his lead. There's really just one type of hazard in the area, but it's put to use often. The electrified spinning arms must be either avoided or hopped over. They deliver a jolt that drains away a bit of health with each touch.

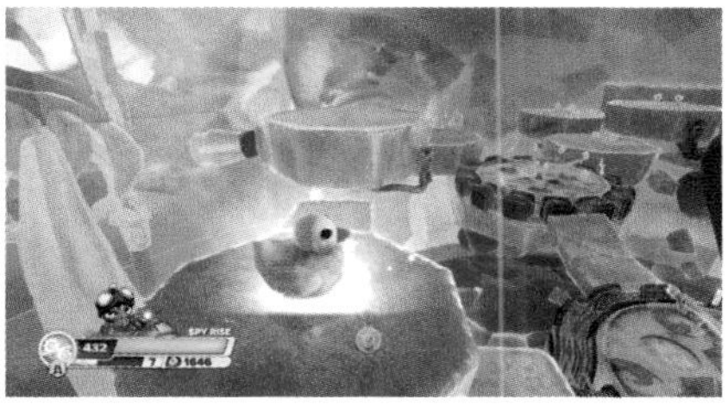

There's one detour to make on the way to incapacitate the Evilizer Crystal: a **Rubber Ducky**. Watch the left side of the area for its location. You can't get it as soon as it's visible. You need to advance past a few more gates before the path to it is available. There are two screws holding wires at the top of the Evilizer Crystals. Unscrew them both to deactivate the crystal. Don't worry about finding a way down, your Skylander takes care of that with a growth spurt.

TECH IS STRONGER IN THIS AREA

GUARDIAN GANGWAY, SANDY CAVERN & SANDSTONE SECRET

Carefully cross the green, segmented bridge. It's spinning, so a few quick jumps will make crossing it a bit easier. Destroy the stack of wooden boxes behind the troll guards. You may as well take out the trolls since they're right there.

The Fire Viper makes its debut here, but only to make your bridge crossing more exciting. Avoid the red circles when they appear. It's good practice for later.

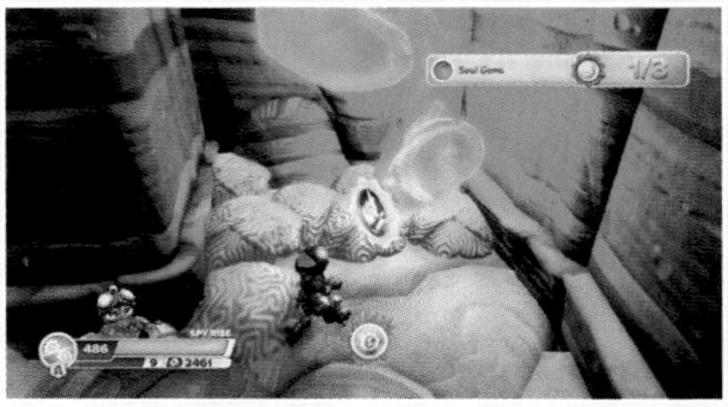

Let one of the rolling green sections of the bridge drag your Skylander off to the side. There's a cave on the lower ledge, called Sandy Cavern, with a Battle Gate-locked **Treasure Chest**. All you need to do is clear out two large waves of trolls, a Fire Geargolem and a horde of Strongarm Chompies. No problem!

Return to the bridge for a preview of the next Evilizer Crystal and a quick appearance from the Ancient Terrasquid. When you see three quicksand pits in a patch of sand, fall down each one for a nice haul of coins, a **Giant Treasure Chest**, and Rip Tide's **Soul Gem (Reinventing the Whale)**. Use the giant mushroom to return to the surface. Walk through the yellow doorway to get to the Arid Cave.

FIRE IS STRONGER IN THIS AREA

ARID CAVE

A new area means a new enemy guarding a Battle Gate. In this case, it's the Air Spell Punk. These white-clad wizards boost the speed of every nearby enemy. Target the Air Spell Punk first, but making them your top target is not as vital as it is when there are Life Spell Punks in a fight.

With the Battle Gate out of the way, use the Bounce Pad near the exit to reach the higher ledge. Don't leave the area until you grab the **Rubber Ducky** a short walk from the exit. It's behind a few destructible items, but it's a quick pick up.

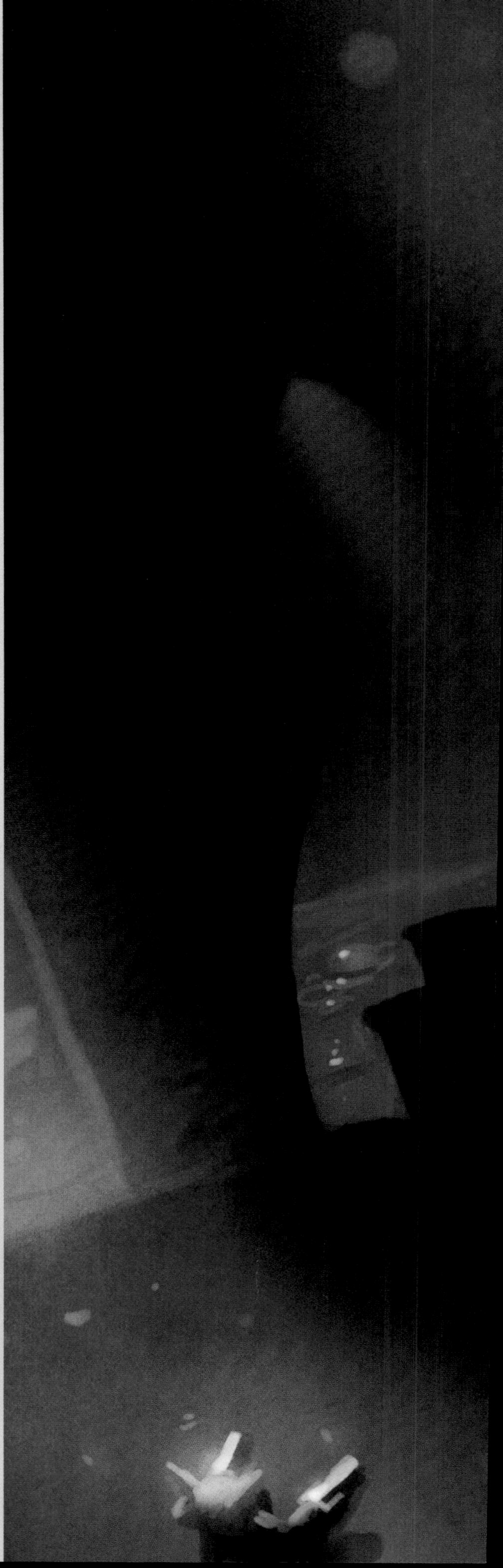

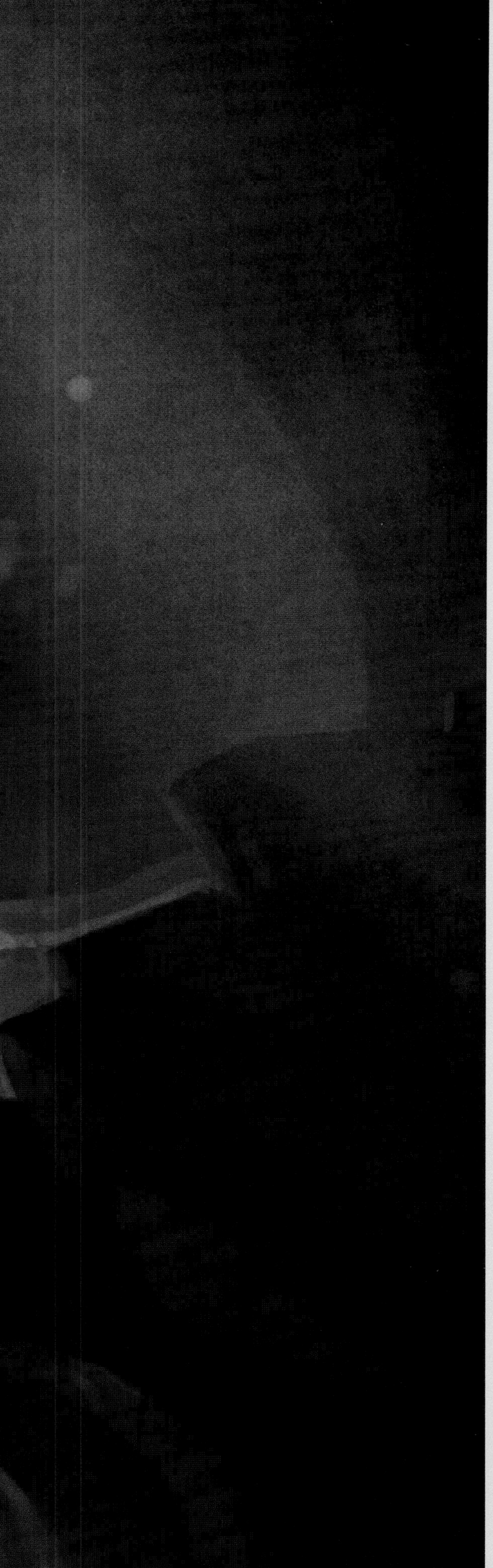

FIRE IS STRONGER IN THIS AREA

HAZARDOUS HIGHWAY & ENERGETIC EVILIZER

While you start back on the Guardian Gangway, the Fire Viper adds a few fiery mines to turn the place into a Hazardous Highway! Just before you reach the mines, turn down the side path to the left. Follow it to pick up Wash Buckler's **Soul Gem (On Stormy Seas/ Tentacle Carousel)**.

The mine-filled path ends at the next Evilizer Crystal. Shrink down to enter the crystal. There are no enemies to worry about inside, just the electrified swinging arms. There's a **Rubber Ducky** inside the crystal, and you must grab it before destroying it. It's on a ledge just beyond the screws you must remove. Outside the now-destroyed crystal, speak with Sharpfin, but be ready for another taste of his idea of rapid transit. For this trip, you must avoid fiery mines while trying to collect coins.

FIRE IS STRONGER IN THIS AREA

UNDERGROUND LAKE

✔ Use the Power Pod at the bottom of the drop to improve your Skylanders, and take a trip through the nearby elemental gate. There are new enemies to face ahead, but they'll still be there when you get back from the trip inside the gate.

UNDEAD UPRISING

Mako has opened a few holes to the Underlands and asks for your help in sealing them with dynamite. To complicate matters, skeletal trolls rush out of the holes while you're trying to seal them. Most of the holes are close enough that any Skylander can handle the task. However, there are a few that may call for someone with an ability that allows them bursts of speed. After you seal all the holes, Mako hands over the **Crystal Fire Hearth** Legendary Treasure.

Cross the short bridge to meet that new enemy, the Air Geargolem. Air Geargolems spin in the air, then come crashing down with a powerful two-hand slam. They use powerful air currents to hold their targets in place, so stay on the move to avoid their devastating attack.

Continue past the area where you defeated the Air Geargolem, Jump up the stairs cut in the stone and cross the wooden bridge. When you encounter more spinning green bridge segments, get ready for another dance with multiple fiery mines. Weave through the mines while trying to cross the spinning segments (an occasional jump helps). Use the Bounce Pad next to the exit to get up to the longest stretch of spinning bridge segments yet. The fiery mines here aren't floating in a pattern, they're being fired from somewhere below and exploding on impact. If you manage to make it across, your reward is Fire Kraken's **Soul Gem (Bottle Rocket Powered/Dance of Dragons)**. Exit the area through the glowing yellow door.

FIRE IS STRONGER IN THIS AREA

SERENE WALKWAY

The paths ahead are mercifully free of mines. There's a SWAP Zone Challenge not too far from the doorway, a trail of coins leading to a Water Gate tucked around a corner, and a tentacle bridge leading ahead.

SWAP Zone
Warped Sands

DESTROY THE KAOS STATUE!

Turn to page 277 for tips on how to clear this SWAP Zone Challenge. Your reward for completing this challenge is a **Winged Sapphire**.

BOUNCE FOUNTAIN

Rockgill's mates are trapped on top of water globs. In order to bring them down safely, someone must bounce on the moving Water Bounce Pad to lower the pillars of water. Since Rockgill is more of a swimmer than a bouncer, he asks you.

Each successful bounce lowers the pillars, but each missed bounce sends them back up. Rockgill also neglected to mention the fiery mines that appear from time to time. You must avoid those as well! When both of Rockgill's friends are freed, you are rewarded with the **Peacock Hat.**

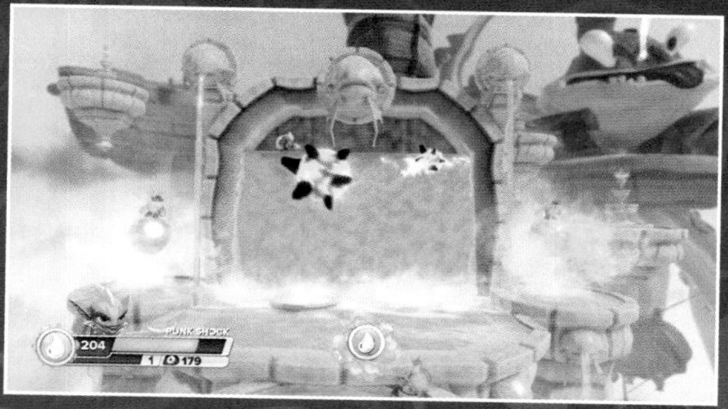

At the top of the tentacle bridge, go left for a **Rubber Ducky**. Join Sharpfin on his boat. He asks you to act as the gunner and clear the way through the Greeble fleet. The more ships you shoot down in each wave, the better the bonuses you can earn.

With the Greeble ships out of the way, Sharpfin lands at the Floating Foray, one of the last stops on the way to end Kaos's threat to the Ancient Terrasquid.

MAGIC IS STRONGER IN THIS AREA

FLOATING FORAY & CATALYTIC CRYSTAL

The left branch of the path leads to the final Evilizer Crystal, and the right to a SWAP Zone Challenge. Both paths are covered in fiery mines, so proceed with caution.

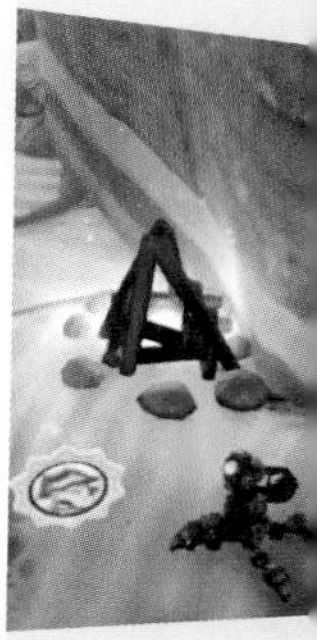

SWAP Zone
Parched Heights

POP THE KAOS BALLOONS!

Turn to page 268 for tips on how to clear this SWAP Zone Challenge. Your reward for completing this challenge is the **Tricorn Hat.**

There are a few landings with enemy encounters on the left branch. The first landing has an Air Spell Punk, Strongarm Chompies, and a few trolls. The second has an Air Geargolem and an Air Spell Punk (the path that runs off to the side here has a **Treasure Chest**). The final landing has a single Boom Boss. The Fire Viper aids their cause by lobbing fiery mines into the mix.

Sharpfin waits near the final Evilizer Crystal. Like the previous crystals, there are no enemies inside Catalytic Crystal. You must avoid the electrified swinging arms and unscrew the wires at the top.

When the chapter ends and your stars are rewarded, don't relax! You aren't headed back to Woodburrow yet. It's time to deal with the Fire Viper.

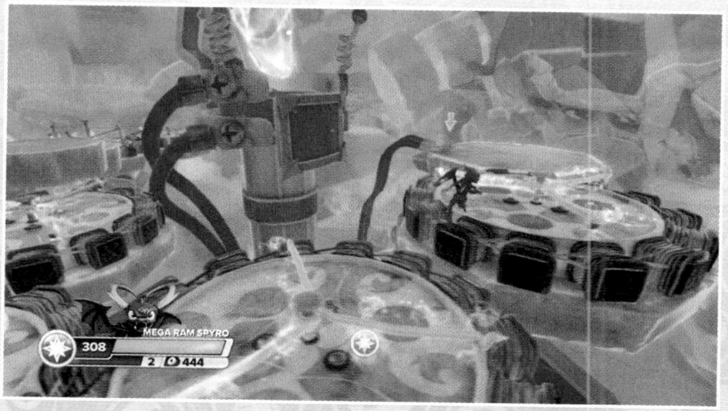

SERPENT'S PEAK

OBJECTIVES

Story Goals

- ◯ Defeat Fire Viper
- ◯ No Skylanders Defeated
- ◯ No Damage Taken

DEFEAT THE FIRE VIPER - STAGE 1

Sharpfin set up two giant crossbows that fire cables at the Fire Viper. You know they are loaded and ready to use when red suction cups are visible at the front of each weapon. To fire a crossbow, you just need to be close enough to get a button prompt to appear over it. Sharpfin will also helpfully leave food items between the crossbows at certain points, so if your Skylander needs a recharge, keep an eye open.

The Fire Viper coughs up fiery mines into the air. A red target circle appears on the ground where one will hit. During the first stage, all you need to do is avoid the circles and fire off both crossbows to bring the Fire Viper's head down to the ground. Don't move too close until after the head touches down. There's a minor shockwave that pushes away anything too close.

The first time you bring down the Fire Viper's head, Sharpfin pops up and points out the crystallized darkness on top of it. Run up to the crystals and deal as much damage as you can. After inflicting a certain amount of damage, the Fire Viper shakes off the suction cups and sends your Skylander to the back of the area, near a pool of damaging goo.

The next thing the Fire Viper does is spray the entire area with fiery breath. Fortunately, two tentacles appear and offer a place to hide from the sweeping breath attack. Repeat the process of using both crossbows and damaging the crystals on top of Fire Viper's head again.

This time after the Fire Viper shakes free, he covers the area in fiery mines that you must avoid. They are not like the ones that explode on contact with the ground. These mines do not go away, even after they crash into your Skylander. Your Skylander takes damage, but the mine sticks around!

Take down the Fire Viper with the crossbows again, and avoid the fiery mines while hiding behind the tentacles during Fire Viper's fiery breath attack. A third successful attack on the crystals atop the Fire Viper's skull initiates the second stage of the battle.

DEFEAT THE FIRE VIPER - STAGE 2

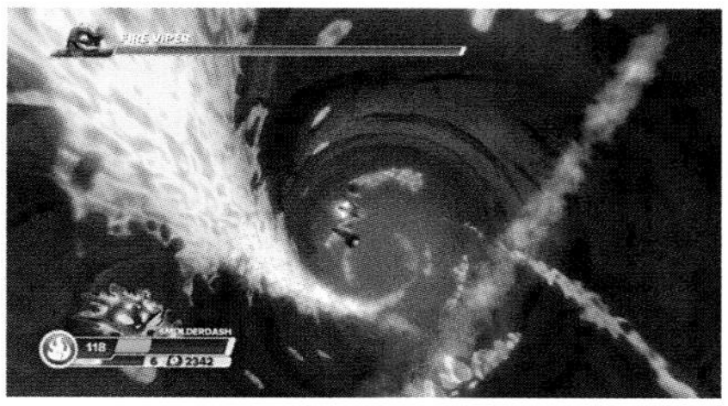

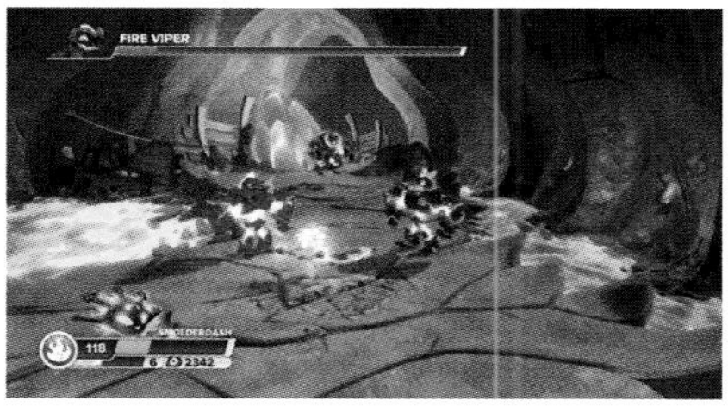

This stage begins when Fire Viper swallows your Skylander whole! During the trip down the beast's gullet, avoid the violet jets of flame that appear a few times. You'll need every bit of health for the upcoming battle against three Fire Geargolems. You catch a bit of a break as the third Fire Geargolem begins the battle a short distance away, but two at once is bad enough!

Stay on the move as much as possible. Standing still to attack invites one of the other golems to bathe your Skylander in flames, which usually results in the need to change Skylanders on your Portal of Power.

When all three Fire Geargolems are down, the hardest part of the battle is over. All that's left to do is destroy the crystal formation at the back of the chamber. When that's done, you return to Woodburrow, joined by a grateful Ancient Terrasquid.

Back in Woodburrow

Rufus sends you to speak with Tessa, who has set up a turret mini-game above the Trophy Room with Wheellock's help. The turret mini-game is a way to practice your shooting skills. You have a chance to earn gold, especially when you get a perfect wave bonus. The mini-game ends as soon as you hit one mine. When you're done trying out the turret, speak with Sharpfin at The Airdocks.

BONEY ISLANDS

OBJECTIVES

Story Goals

- ◯ Find Fossil Fuel
- ◯ Find More Fossil Fuel
- ◯ Help the Caravan Escape
- ◯ Return to the Caravan

Dares

- 4 Museum Souvenirs
- 50 Enemy Goal
- 0 No Skylanders Defeated

Collections

- 16 Areas Discovered
- 5 Treasure Chests
- 1 Giant Treasure Chest
- 2 Soul Gems
- 2 Legendary Treasures
- 2 Hats
- 1 Bonus Mission Map
- 1 Winged Sapphire
- 1 Story Scroll

New Enemies

Coldspear Cyclops

Cyclops Gazermage

Cyclops Snowblaster

Chompy Frostflower

Loose Cannon

...AND INTO THE FIRE

Boney Islands gets off to a hot start as you must take down not one, but two Fire Geargolems as soon as you get control of your Skylander! Don't worry about Flynn and your new blue-skinned friend. They'll patiently wait to speak with you until after you take out the Geargolems and grab the piles of gold from the wooden docks. Isn't Flynn always so helpful?

FROZEN FOSSIL LANE

Hurry ahead of the Caravan and take on the first of many new enemies, the Coldspear Cyclops. These one-eyed menaces rush forward and perform a rapid-thrust attack. They don't move while they are attacking, so all you need to do is avoid the spear point, then hit them with your own attack from anywhere else except directly in front of them.

Push the orange sliding block into the hole. There is a ramp on the left side of the wooden platform. Go up that ramp and jump over the gaps in the platform to grab a **Treasure Chest**.

BONEY ISLANDS

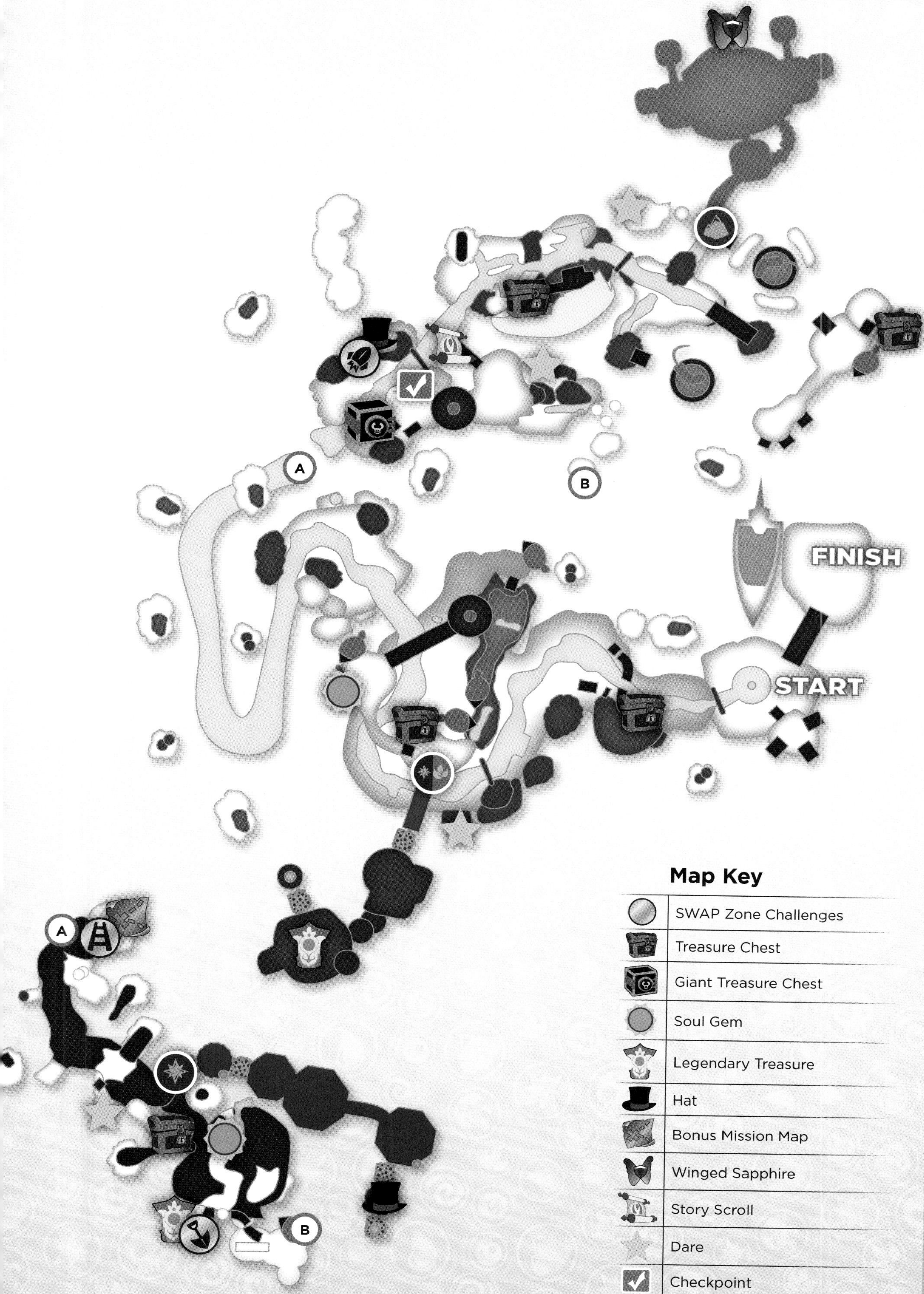

Map Key

- SWAP Zone Challenges
- Treasure Chest
- Giant Treasure Chest
- Soul Gem
- Legendary Treasure
- Hat
- Bonus Mission Map
- Winged Sapphire
- Story Scroll
- Dare
- Checkpoint

A new wave of enemies blocks the path ahead, but continues on after you take down the group of trolls and a Fire Geargolem. Push the orange blocks beyond the enemy encounter into the holes in the road to allow the caravan to pass, though it can't go past the locked gate just past the orange stones. At least, not before it blasts down the doors.

Before going through the opened door, follow the wooden path to the left of the locked gate to a **Museum Souvenir**. The road ahead has holes again that you must fill with the orange blocks blocking the road.

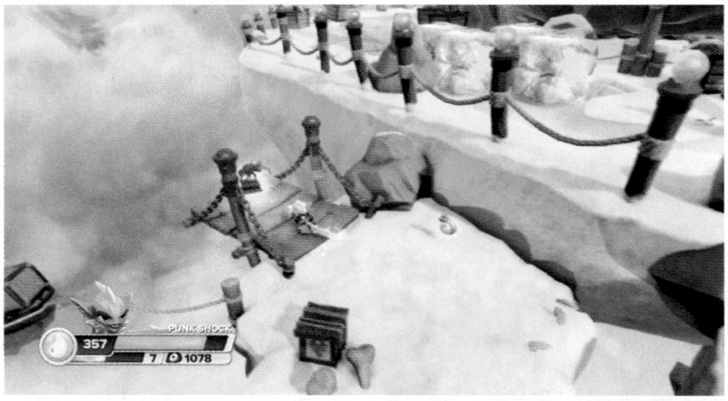

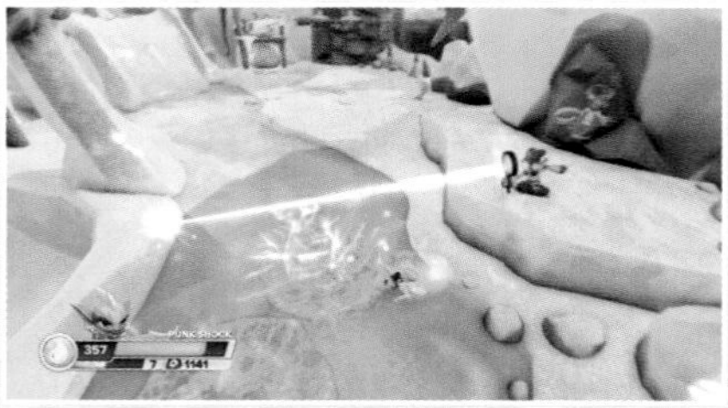

After the caravan blasts open the next set of doors, you must take on another new enemy type, the Cyclops Gazermage. They focus a powerful beam through a magnifying glass. They also use a low power, non-damaging, beam to mark their targets first, and a noise builds up to let you know when they are about to fire. They're fragile foes, so avoid their beams and they should drop quickly.

There are more enemies just ahead, and the caravan comes to a halt until you defeat them all. When the caravan still doesn't move after all the enemies are cleared, you get a bit of bad news.

WATER IS STRONGER IN THIS AREA

GIFT BOAT ROW & RELIC ROOM

Use the newly uncovered Bounce Pad to jump up to the wooden platform. Jump to the spinning snowy platforms to the left of the path, then on up to the larger platform where Spy Rise's **Soul Gem (Spy with a Golden Hand/Omega Sky Laser)** waits to be claimed.

Bounce back to the main path. The next new enemy, Cyclops Snowblaster, is an automated defense turret. Watch for a power build-up at the tip of its barrel to know when it will fire again. Avoid its shots, then hit it with your own attacks.

Walk up the ramp. The gate on the next rise is locked. To unlock the gate, slide the crystal in the direction indicated by the arrow on top of it. When it's in place, its light melts the lock mechanism on the gate, and it opens.

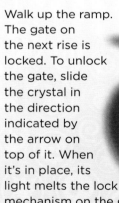

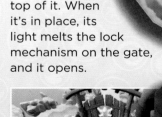

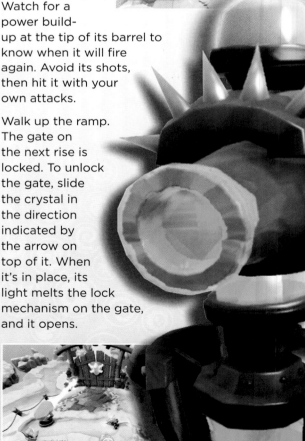

Take out the small group of enemies on the other side of the door, and slide the orange block into the hole. The air pressure builds up under the block when a Skylander steps on it, sending it higher in the air.

Use the orange block to reach the next ledge, which has a dual elemental gate, a new type of Chompy, and a Chompy Pod in a new color scheme. Chompy Frostflowers are Chompies encased in ice. The ice makes them a bit tougher, but not much more of a challenge in a fight.

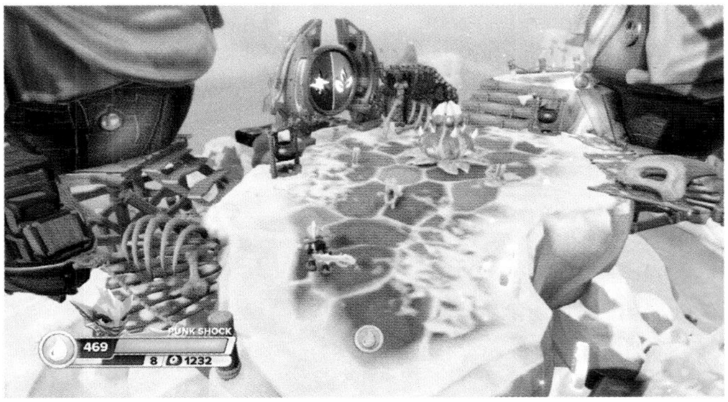

FROSTY ENCHANTMENT

There are a few sliding block puzzles and a quick enemy encounter inside this area. The orange blocks rise into the air when a Skylander lands on it, which allows you to reach higher areas. The fight takes place in a bad starting position. Cyclops Gazermages and Cyclops Snowblasters guard the area, and some are stationed on a ridge too high to reach with a jump. Move one of the orange blocks over to the gray frame on the ground to reach them. After clearing out all the trolls, claim the **Geode Glider** Legendary Treasure and return to Gift Boat Row.

Go through the doorway across from the elemental gate entrance to reach the Relic Room. Smash the objects and collect all the coins. To get the **Treasure Chest** here, you must clear its Spark Lock.

SPARK LOCK

Synchronized Sliding

Timing the fans is the key to solving this lock. They are completely automated. The only buttons in the room control the orange and purple columns behind Shock's and Bolt's starting positions. Start sliding Shock and Bolt (one at a time) about halfway through their respective fan's "on" cycle to reach the buttons at the back. With the platforms lowered, move either Shock or Bolt back across to their starting point. From there, go to the now-lowered columns on the opposite side (Shock to the orange, or Bolt to the purple) to one of the columns under the conveyor belt. Slide the other guy back to his starting point, then down one spot so he's on a lowered column. Put your first guy on the conveyor belt, and he should end up at your other guy's starting point. Move your second guy over to the opposite starting point. Both Shock and Bolt should be in position to grab their respective lightning bolts if you time the fans properly. Grab the lightning bolts and bring them together to complete the puzzle.

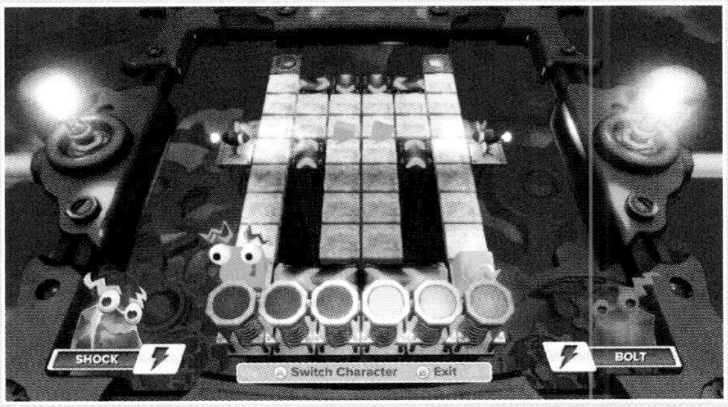

If you're playing on the Wii console, this Treasure Chest is not in your game.

You still need to find the fossil fuel for the caravan. Run up the path until you hit a locked gate and a more yellow entryway. The door leads to McElfy's Diode Shoppe.

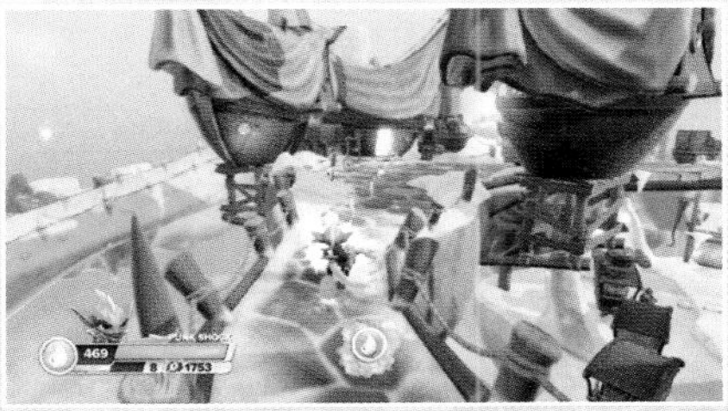

WATER IS STRONGER IN THIS AREA

MCELFY'S DIODE SHOPPE, CURATOR'S OFFICE & DUSTY ARCHIVE

Complete the laser puzzle inside McElfy's Diode Shop by sliding the crystal on the left once toward the entrance, then push it one space closer to the emitter crystal. Turn the valve near the emitter crystal until the beam shines into the second crystal and opens the door.

Grab the key behind the gate and be ready for a quick fight outside the Shoppe. Unlock the gate and go into the building directly ahead. A slightly larger group of enemies tries to keep you from getting the fuel you need, and you must defeat them all to open the Battle Gate behind them. With the gate open, go to the back and grab the fossil fuel. And fall down the trap floor set under the fuel.

There's good news, and good news. The good news is that you didn't lose the fossil fuel in the fall. The other good news is that your Skylander landed in a room filled with gold coins! The doorway leads to the halted caravan in Frozen Fossil Lane. Hand over the fuel and get ready for a new job.

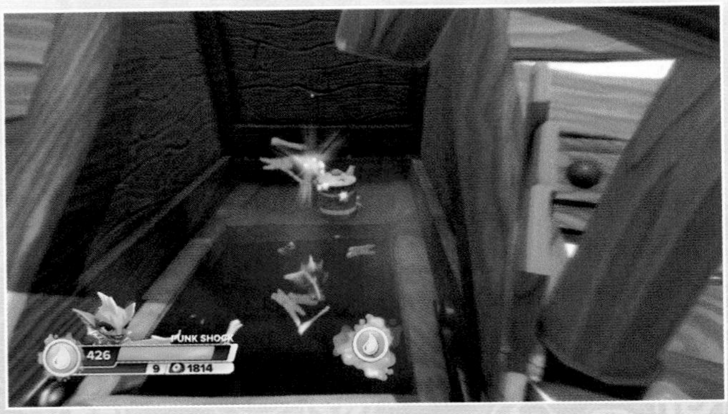

AIR IS STRONGER IN THIS AREA

TRIASSIC TURNS & PALEO PASS

You are put in charge of the defense turrets at the front of the caravan. You must blast the enemies and other hazards blocking the caravan's route to its next destination. Shoot the crates floating under balloons to get extra gold and food, but worry more about things that can damage the caravan! The ride comes to an abrupt end near a Power Pod, but the force tosses your Skylander some distance away, next to a SWAP Zone Challenge.

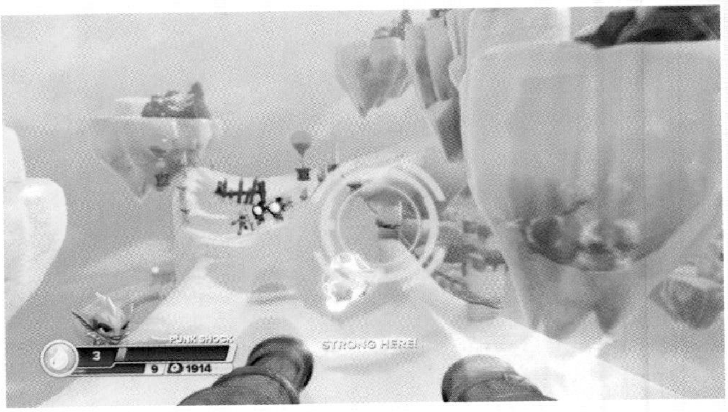

SWAP Zone

Amber Ice Climb

CLIMB TO THE TOP!

Turn to page 269 for tips on how to clear this SWAP Zone Challenge. Your reward for completing this challenge is the **Royal Gems Bonus Mission Map**.

Two paths lead past the SWAP Zone. The icy path is short, but has piles of gold on it. The stone path is dangerous, but it's the way you must go to rejoin the caravan. Dance around the red circles as they appear on the path to avoid taking damage from falling objects.

A new enemy, the Loose Cannon, debuts just beyond where the circles stop appearing. These large trolls employ missiles and shields in combat. They fire off a string of three missiles before applying shields and then reloading. There's a small window to strike them immediately after they fire their missiles and before their shields go up.

Take out the two Loose Cannons and assorted Chompies to open the Battle Gate near the Magic Gate. Before you go through either gate, look to the right for an icy ledge with snowy platforms floating nearby. Jump up to the platforms and grab the **Museum Souvenir**.

Back in the area where you fought the Fire Geargolems, push the orange sliding block into the hole in the ground near the large fossil in the ice. Ride the block up to the apex of its ascent and hop off near the Dig SWAP Zone.

AURORA WAY

The Aurora Way is free of enemies, but filled with one long-range laser puzzle. For the first puzzle, push the emitter to the rising platform. Hop up to the next ledge, which has orange blocks and more crystals. Slide the blocks out of the path of the light, then push the crystal on the left into the beam of light. Turn the valve until the beam hits another crystal in the distance. Cross the bridge and turn the next valve to continue the beam in a straight line. Push the crystal in the next, lower area to the rising platform. Push the final orange block out of the way to open the gate. When you're done, your reward is the **Fishbone Hat.**

A group of enemies, including a pair of Fire Geargolems, guard the area past the Battle Gate and appear in two waves. With the enemies out of the way, smash through the wooden crates on the right side and avoid the hazards (and Cyclops Snowblaster) on the way to a **Treasure Chest**.

SWAP Zone
Ice Hollows

FIND YOUR WAY THROUGH THE DARK! DIG UP THE BLUE CRYSTALS BEFORE TIME RUNS OUT.

Turn to page 271 for tips on how to clear this SWAP Zone Challenge. Your reward for completing this challenge is the **Triassic Tooth** Legendary Treasure.

Push the block on the left over the edge. Follow it down and push it to the stone steps near a shark-like fossil in ice with a Soul Gem Floating over it. Jump up to the orange block, then on top of the frozen fossil to claim Dune Bug's **Soul Gem (Buggy Buddy)**.

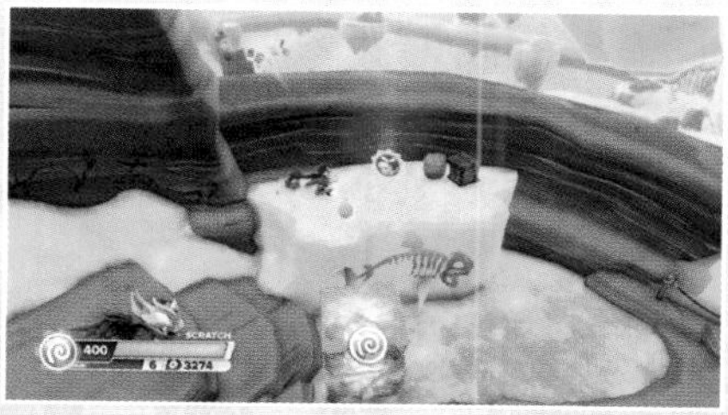

AIR IS STRONGER IN THIS AREA

TICKET TAKER & SECURITY HUTCH

Return to the higher area and push the final orange block into the hole in front of it. Ride the orange block up and walk through the doorway to Ticket Taker. Use the switch on the left to raise the crystal on the platform near the doorway. Push the orange block down to the lower floor. Turn the valve until the emitter crystal hits the crystal on the platform and opens the gate at the back of the room, which leads to a new area in Paleo Pass.

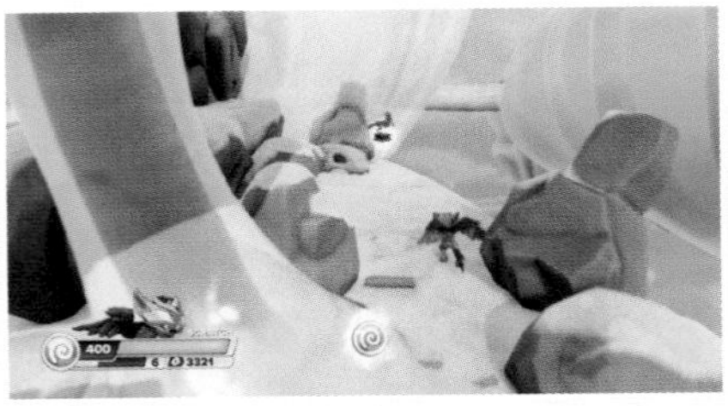

Take out the Cyclops Gazermage, but ignore the orange blocks until you snag the **Museum Souvenir** down the short path on the right. Use the orange sliding blocks to climb up to where more enemies are spoiling for a fight. Before you take them on, jump to the right and pick up the piles of gold. After the action starts, watch for a group of enemies emerging from a doorway across a wooden bridge. When you've defeated every enemy, cross the bridge and enter that door. There's a **Story Scroll** inside the building, but you must take out the enemies inside the building in one minute or less to claim it.

Return outside and go through the other doorway in the area to reach the Security Hutch. Push the emitter crystal across the room, then down to the lower floor. Push the other crystal down to the floor to redirect the beam and open the gate. The checkpoint and caravan are on the other side of the doorway.

There's a **Giant Treasure Chest** near the Power Pod and a SWAP Zone on the other side of the caravan. When you're ready to move on, use the guns on the caravan's front car.

SWAP Zone
Ice Cold Flying

ROCKET TO THE FINISH!

Turn to page 272 for tips on how to clear this SWAP Zone Challenge. Your reward for completing this challenge is the **Bearskin Cap.**

TECH IS STRONGER IN THIS AREA

AMBER ALLEY, GLACIAL GALLERY & FOSSIL FROSTWAY

Expect light enemy resistance on the other side of the gate, but watch out for falling ice! Push the orange blocks into the holes in the ice to create a complete surface for the caravan to cross.

Jump up to the wooden platform with the Loose Cannon. There's a **Treasure Chest** on the end opposite the large troll.

To fill the last gap in the roadway, push the orange block into the path of the final orange block to keep it from sliding too far. With everything in place, the caravan blasts open the gate to Glacial Galley.

If you're playing on the Wii console, this Treasure Chest is on the floating platforms to the left of the second set of rotating platforms in the Glacial Gallery area.

The caravan needs more fuel for its final push. There are two triple-locked gates on either side of a large area dominated by dinosaur fossils emitting beams blocking the path ahead. Head to the far left for a **Museum Souvenir** and an Earth Gate. Head away from the gate, along the wooden platform, to reach the souvenir.

GRANITE WING

Both valves (the one near the entrance and the one on the central platform) spin the central platform. The large gate opposite the entrance is locked twice. One key is on each side platform behind a Battle Gate. Use the valves to move the central platform to reach the side areas and claim the keys. With both keys in hand, open the large gate and claim the **Winged Sapphire**. If you fall down to the lower level, grab the coins there and run back to the entrance.

If you're playing on the Wii console, the Winged Sapphire is the reward for completing the Light Crystal Puzzle inside a house to the left of the triple locked door in Glacial Gallery.

Jump on the revolving platforms under the fossils and grab all three keys (there's one key per platform) and ride a platform around to the back. Unlock the gate, but don't move past it until you go into the small building. Push the orange blocks onto the rising platforms to get them out of the way (this step isn't necessary, but it will make things easier). Push the crystal on the right to the left, and the crystal on the left to the right. Open the **Treasure Chest** after the gate opens.

Take on the enemies beyond the previously triple-locked gate and grab the fossil fuel canister. Repeat the collecting of three keys from the floating platforms to get back to the caravan and deliver the fuel.

You are put back in control of the turrets for the last stage of the escape. Take out the dinosaur fossils so the caravan can get moving. Focus on taking down enemies and hazards before you worry about targeting any bonus crates. The defenses get heavier toward the end, but the caravan hits the airdocks and the elves make their escape.

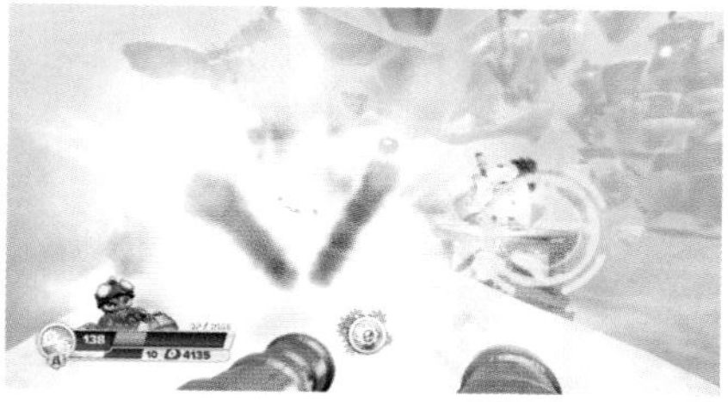

Back in Woodburrow

Avril hands over the Mystic Snowglobe, which shows the location of the Ancient Frosthound. The Chieftess suggests taking some time to rest and train before speaking with Sharpfin at The Airdocks to start the search for the Ancient Frosthound.

WINTER KEEP

OBJECTIVES

Story Goals

- ◯ Clear Out the South Wall
- ◯ Thaw the Furnace
- ◯ Defend the North Wall
- 3 Destroy the Blizzard Ballers
- ◯ Take Back the Tower

Dares

- 4 Lost Mittens
- 50 Enemy Goal
- 0 No Skylanders Defeated

Collections

- 16 Areas Discovered
- 4 Treasure Chests
- 1 Giant Treasure Chest
- 2 Soul Gems
- 2 Legendary Treasures
- 2 Hats
- 1 Bonus Mission Map
- 1 Winged Sapphire
- 1 Story Scroll

New Enemies

Cyclops Sleetthrower

Twistpick Cyclops

Evilized Snowroller

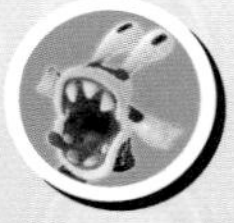

Chompy Blitzbloom

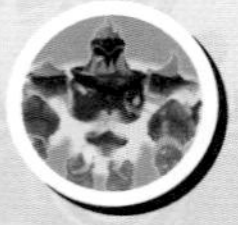

Ice Geargolem

TECH IS STRONGER IN THIS AREA

THE BLIZZARD BRIDGES

After speaking with Duff, run across the bridge and avoid the red circles that appear on the ground. A trio of Cyclops Sleetthrowers guards the end of the bridge. These parka-wearing troublemakers scoop up a shovelful of snow and lob it. A red circle indicates their target location, and their reload time is considerable. Avoid the snowball and get on them before they can reload and fire again.

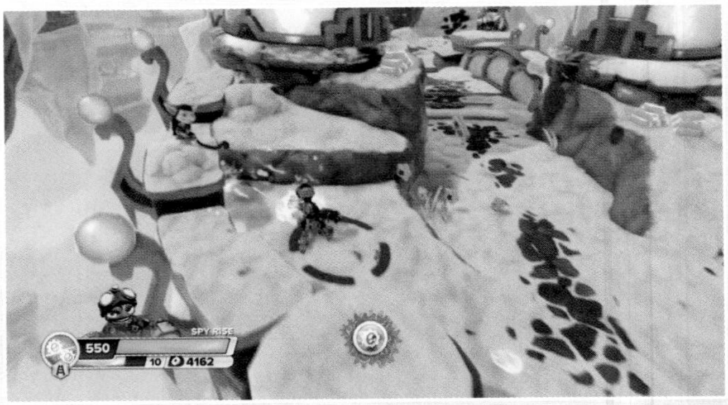

The path beyond the Cyclops Sleetthrowers winds uphill and ends at a lightly defended Battle Gate with a SWAP Zone not too far away. Head toward the SWAP Zone and look for destructible boxes just off the path to the left. Destroy the boxes and pick up the **Story Scroll, Whirwind's Gift** from the small alcove.

Search the area near the SWAP Gate for a large horn mounted on the walls. Interact with the horn to blow it, and cause a shower of coins. You can use it a few times and still get coins. There are horns like this found in a few locations around Winter Keep.

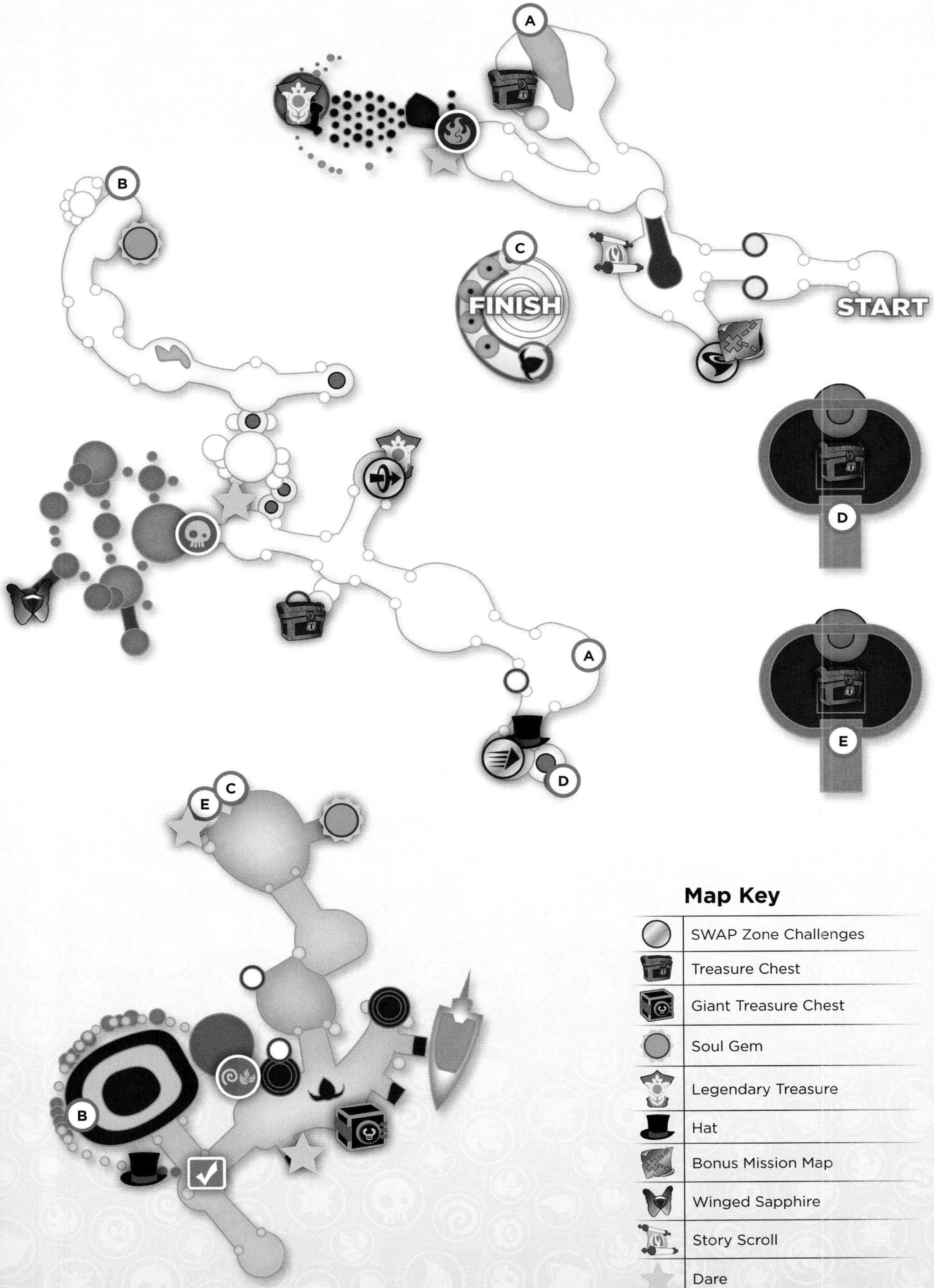

Map Key

	SWAP Zone Challenges
	Treasure Chest
	Giant Treasure Chest
	Soul Gem
	Legendary Treasure
	Hat
	Bonus Mission Map
	Winged Sapphire
	Story Scroll
	Dare
	Checkpoint

SWAP Zone
Frozen Top

DESTROY THE KAOS STATUE

Turn to page 277 for tips on how to clear this SWAP Zone Challenge. Your reward for completing this challenge is the **Ghost Traps Bonus Mission Map**.

THE BLUE ICE BATTLEMENTS

There is a second Battle Gate blocking further progress not far from the first one. Another new enemy, Twistpick Cyclops, is among the defenders of the gate. Twistpick Cyclops are invulnerable while spinning, but they also telegraph their movements. Watch for a red arrow on the ground at their feet as they start spinning. Move your Skylander out of the path indicated by the red arrow, then attack the dizzy Cyclops after its spin ends. Twistpick Cyclops will sometimes change directions after a short spinning dash.

After the Battle Gate opens, go up the snowy path to its left first. The first **Lost Mittens** float above the ground not far from a Fire Gate.

THE FLAME STEPPES

Use the valves to bring a series of magma platforms that span the chasm keeping your Skylander from reaching the locked gate at the other end, and the three keys floating partway between. You must begin moving toward the keys as soon as the platforms appear. Each row starts to fall away a few seconds after it appears. The reward for opening the gate is the **Expensive Souvenir** Legendary Treasure.

Go through the opened Battle Gate and dodge the incoming ice balls while traveling to the nearby village. Bounce on the larger yeti on the left near the entrance to reach the rooftops. Hop over to the **Treasure Chest** on the far roof and open it.

Speak with Duff to learn how to use the catapults to drive off the trolls' Blizzard Ballers. Hold and release Attack 1 to fire the catapult. The longer your hold down the button, the higher your catapult shot flies. Hit the ship three times to blow it out of the sky. Duff directs you to the glowing ring in the back of the village. Use it to begin a trip on the Aurora Rails.

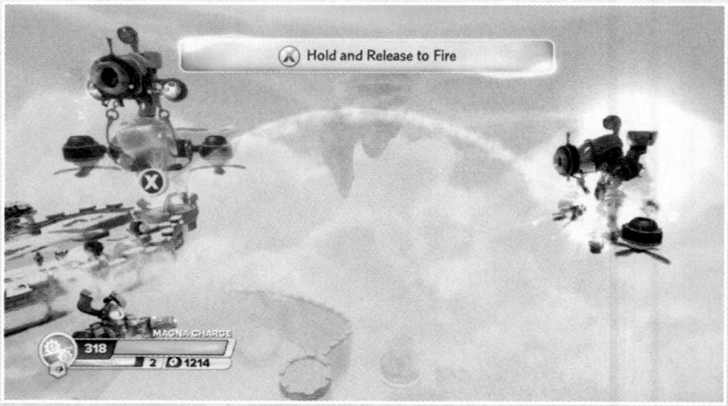

AURORA RAILS, THE SNOW SHOVEL IN THE STONE & HIDDEN VAULT

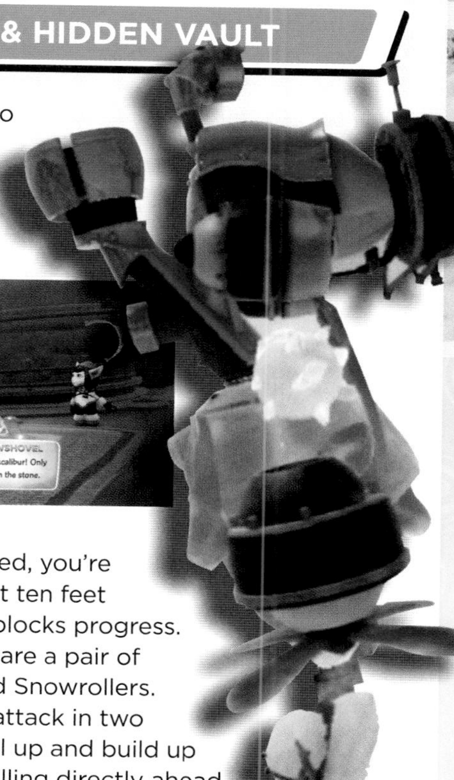

The start of the trip is quiet, but things pick up when the snowman jumps onto the rails with your Skylander. Jump between rails to pick up coins and avoid hazards. When the ship comes into sight, watch the snowman for a button prompt. When prompted, hit the button to fire the snowman at the ship. Hit the ship three times to take it down.

The elf at the end of the ride explains that the key to the gate is buried under the snow. Go into the nearby building and pull the shovel from the stone. Return outside and use the shovel to dig up the piles of snow until you find the key. The snow piles nearest the entrance to The Snow Shovel in the Stone block a path that leads to a SWAP Zone.

SWAP Zone
Wind Whipped

RACE TO THE FINISH!
Turn to page 275 for tips on how to clear this SWAP Zone Challenge. Your reward for completing this challenge is the **Crown of Frost** hat.

Drop down from the left side of the platform with the SWAP Zone. There is an aptly named area called the Hidden Vault and it has a Spark Locked **Treasure Chest** in it.

SPARK LOCK
Choose Your Path

Move Shock to the left and send him down the ice path. The conveyor belts drop him off on his lightning bolt. While he's sliding around, move Bolt to the right and slide him up that ice path, where he ends up with his lightning bolt. Move Bolt to the right and the conveyor belts take him to the top row. Move him to the left and down to the center column of the area. Switch to Shock and move him to the left where he ends up on the bottom row. Bounce over to the right, then up to the center to join up with Bolt.

With the gate unlocked, you're free to proceed about ten feet where a Battle Gate blocks progress. The gate's guardians are a pair of new enemies, Evilized Snowrollers. Evilized Snowrollers attack in two stages. First, they curl up and build up momentum before rolling directly ahead. While they are curled up and rolling, their thick hides protect them from most damage. At the end of the roll, they launch crystallized darkness shards into the air, which come down at the spot marked in red on the ground. They are momentarily vulnerable while on their backs after the shard attack, but spin in place before righting themselves.

WATER IS STRONGER IN THIS AREA

THE FROZEN CURTAIN & THE SECRET KEEP

The first area beyond the Battle Gate has three directions to go, but one is blocked by a Locked Gate. Push the block out of the laser's path, then turn the emitter crystal to thaw the key from the block of ice. Push the sliding block along the path and use it to jump up to the purple doorway.

Grab the **Treasure Chest** inside the Secret Keep. Return to the crossroad and explore the area past the key. There is a SWAP Zone Challenge at the end and a horn to blow for coins.

SWAP Zone
Flash Frost

COLLECT THE MAGIC RUNES TO SEAL THE DIMENSIONAL RIFT!

Turn to page 278 for tips on how to clear this SWAP Zone Challenge. Your reward for completing this challenge is the **Elven Arrow** Legendary Treasure.

Unlock the gate and follow the path ahead. It leads to another crossroads, with the hub guarded by a handful of Cyclopes. The path off to the left ends at an Undead Gate.

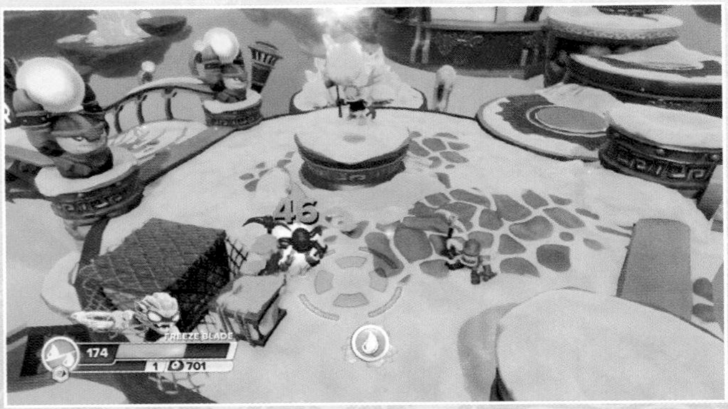

AWESTRUCK ORBITS

The Frost Elf inside the gate needs help uncovering snowrollers caught under piles of snow. Use the shovel to clear away snow piles and open up new platforms to reach different areas. Some piles of snow hide enemies or coins and your ultimate destination is the platform farthest from the gate, but you need to uncover the other snowrollers before you can reach it. After every snowroller has been freed, your reward is a **Winged Sapphire**.

Clear out the enemies and follow the large, circular steps on the right that lead up. Turn the emitter crystal until it melts the ice coating the shovel to the right. Take the shovel back down the steps and uncover the snowroller under the mittens. Bounce off the snowroller's belly to get the **Lost Mittens**.

Back at the top of the steps, turn the emitter to clear out the rest of the ice. Use the shovel to remove the snow pile in front of the gate. Push the block along the path in the snow and dig up the key from on top of the building. Unlock the gate and go uphill at the next intersection.

Dig up all the piles of snow. Use the Seeker Scope to uncover the hidden treasure to pick up later. The downhill slope ends at a Battle Gate guarded by a new type of Chompy, Chompy Blitzbloom.

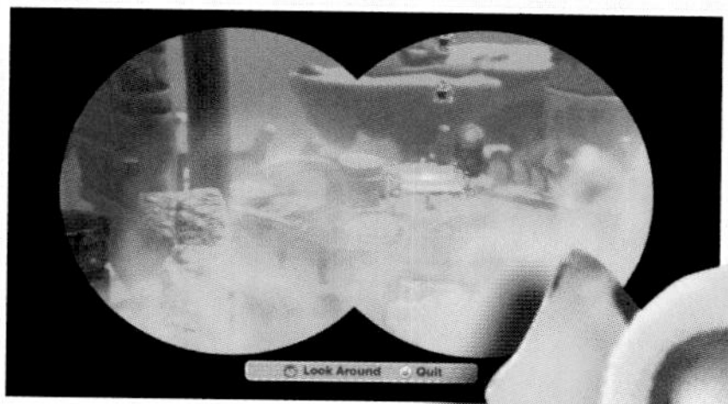

The path beyond the Battle Gate has additional defenders but nothing too worrisome. The path ends near a pair of towers and a lump of ice. Climb the tower to the left and push the emitter crystal over the edge. Step in the gap in the fence along the edge of the tower and drop down to a valve. Turn the valve to bring up six floating pedestals. Jump across the pedestals to get Stink Bomb's **Soul Gem (Tri-Star Technique/ One with the Stink)** from the other tower. Use the glowing circle in the middle of the central tower to take a ride on the Northern Light Rail.

NORTHERN LIGHT RAIL & FROST FURNACE

There are three rails to jump between while collecting coins and avoiding hazards. The ride ends at the Frost Furnace where you face off against your first Ice Geargolem.

The Ice Geargolem fires ice shards from its fists after charging up the attack. Once energy appears on its fists, the Ice Geargolem won't change its position. The ice shards fire out in a spread pattern, so the safest spot to be is directly behind the Ice Geargolem. Attack the Ice Geargolem immediately after it fires, but get away before it fires again. Once the Ice Geargolem falls, a swarm of Blitzbloom Chompies appears to provide some extra XP bubbles for your Skylander.

Look for the Seeker Scope treasures in the furnace core, near where the Ice Geargolem began the fight. When all the enemies and treasures are out of the way, bounce on the bellows in the center of the room. Each bounce stokes the furnace and after enough bounces, it roars back to life and removes the ice.

Duff appears again and asks for help collecting ammunition to use against the Blizzard Ballers. You must send two snowmen to the catapult's location. Fortunately, there are two at the end of the ramp, near the Power Pod.

Load them into the catapult and take aim at the Blizzard Baller. The catapult here works identically to the one you used previously. Hit the ship three times to blast it out of the sky and get the key you need to open the nearby locked gate.

HIBERNAL HARBOR

Cyclopes, Chompies, and Gear Golems attack in force when you first enter Hibernal Harbor. They appear in a few waves, so it may take you a few minutes to clear them out entirely.

With the enemies out of the way, collect the **Lost Mittens** from the short platform to the right. There's a **Giant Treasure Chest** further up the path from them, and a dual elemental gate across from them.

SKY MEADOWS

Sky Meadows is an exercise in patience and coin collecting. There are no enemies to worry about, so take your time and grab the coins in the area. You won't have a hard time finding them. They're everywhere! The large mushrooms give a big boost when your Skylander lands on top of them. Use them to get back on the floating balloons and platforms. If the gold wasn't enough, when you reach the center of the zone, you also get the **Ski Cap**.

Look for Duff at the other end of the docks. He's always near trouble, so be ready to take down a few enemies before speaking with him. The elves need someone to get two snowmen from a nearby boat. They're guarded by a trio of Twistpick Cyclopes waiting in ambush.

Send the snowmen to the catapults and load them up. You must shoot down two Blizzard Ballers this time, but two targets just means it's easier to hit one of them, right? Take the key and unlock the nearby gate to continue.

DIAMOND DOCKS & KALEIDOSCOPIC KILN

Slide the block and emitter crystal until all three pedestals are de-iced. To thaw the center pedestal, push the crystal down, or the block up, so they're in the same row as each other, then push the crystal into the block.

The pedestals end at a Battle Gate with Cyclopes Sleetthrowers and Evilized Snowrollers. A second wave of Blitzbloom Chompies, Coldspear Cyclopes, and Twistpick Cyclopes attack. Take them out and head down the path beyond the gate where you need to pick up another pair of snowmen.

The snowmen are encased in ice near a sliding block and laser puzzle. The emitter crystal needs to be on the circular platform in the middle of the puzzle so it can turn. Push the crystal to the left and slide the block next to it down. Slide the other block down and push the first block against it. Push the emitter crystal onto the platform and melt all the ice in the area (you need to move the blocks to get all the ice).

The path to the left leads to the final pair of **Lost Mittens** and the Kaleidoscopic Kiln. You must light one flame of six different rainbow lamps in the Kaleidoscopic Kiln for a **Treasure Chest**. Bounce twice on each bellows to get the three primary colors (the first bounce lights the color, the second snuffs it). Bounce once on two different bellows to make a new color.

Go past the snowman on the right's initial location and wait for a spinning platform to appear. Follow the string of platforms to reach Rubble Rouser's **Soul Gem (Obsidian Skin/Pop Rock)**.

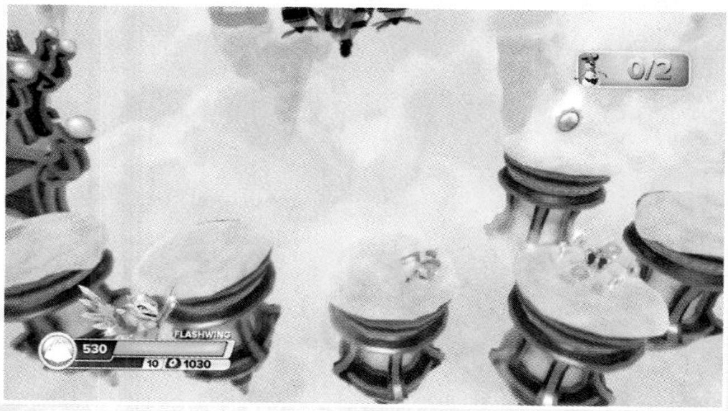

Return to Diamond Docks and step up to the catapult. There are three Blizzard Ballers to shoot down this time. Take down this final trio of ships and Duff sends you to use the glowing platform to ride the rainbow rails again. Cyclopes captured the main tower and you need to clear them out.

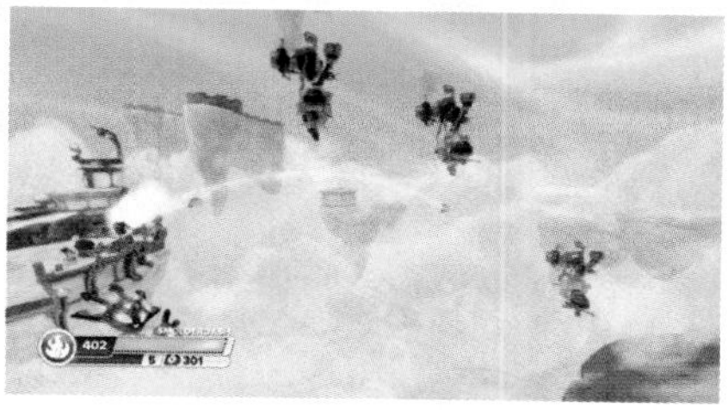

The rail first goes past a line of snowmen that hop on the rails behind your Skylander. When the cyclopes are in range, watch for a prompt from the snowmen. Hit that button to take out the cyclopes on the tower walls.

EARTH IS STRONGER IN THIS AREA

PRISM TOWER

The rainbow rail ends near the top of the Prism Tower. Go to the top area to start a fight against a few waves of enemies. Each group bursts through one of the four double doors. The first wave consists of three cyclopes. The second group includes Chompy Blitzblooms and an Evilized Snowroller. There are four cyclopes and several chompies in the third wave. The final wave includes an Ice Geargolem. When the last enemy of the final wave falls, the elves begin the celebration!

Back in Woodburrow

Rufus, the Chieftess, and Tessa provide an update on the search for the Ancient Frosthound. They send you to speak with Sharpfin at The Airdocks, but before you do, break through the crates near him and open the gift-wrapped box behind him. The Sweet **Blizzard Bonus Mission Map** is inside.

FROSTFEST MOUNTAINS

OBJECTIVES

Story Goals

- ○ Follow the Illuminator

Dares

- **5** Balloon Animals
- **50** Enemy Goal
- **0** No Skylanders Defeated

New Enemies

Cyclops Brawlbuckler

Evilized Chillydog

Collections

- **18** Areas Discovered
- **7** Treasure Chests
- **1** Giant Treasure Chest
- **2** Soul Gems
- **2** Legendary Treasures
- **2** Hats
- **1** Bonus Mission Map
- **1** Winged Sapphire
- **1** Story Scroll

IT'S A SNOWSTORM!

Before you head off to meet up with Fizzy, turn around and look for a ramp that tilts slightly downward. It leads to a series of floating platforms. The last platform in the row has a **Balloon Animal** on it.

Return to Flynn and Sharpfin. Follow the light (and trail of coins) to the frozen river's bank. Jump across the floating platforms quickly to reach the other side. Each platform slowly breaks under the weight of a Skylander on it, so you can't stay on any one of them for long.

★ *If you're playing on the Wii console, there's a Treasure Chest directly behind your Skylander at the start of the level.*

Unfortunately, it's not a yeti greeting you on the other side of the river, but a new, and quite large, enemy, the Cyclops Brawlbuckler. Cyclops Brawlbucklers are shielded before they strike. They telegraph their attack by swinging their mace over their head, where it crackles with energy. They slam the mace into the ground with an overhead smash attack. Striking them when they are extended and vulnerable knocks them back and they drop their mace and shield. Keep attacking them until they drop. Continue through the open gate to reach Typhoon Trail.

FROSTFEST MOUNTAINS

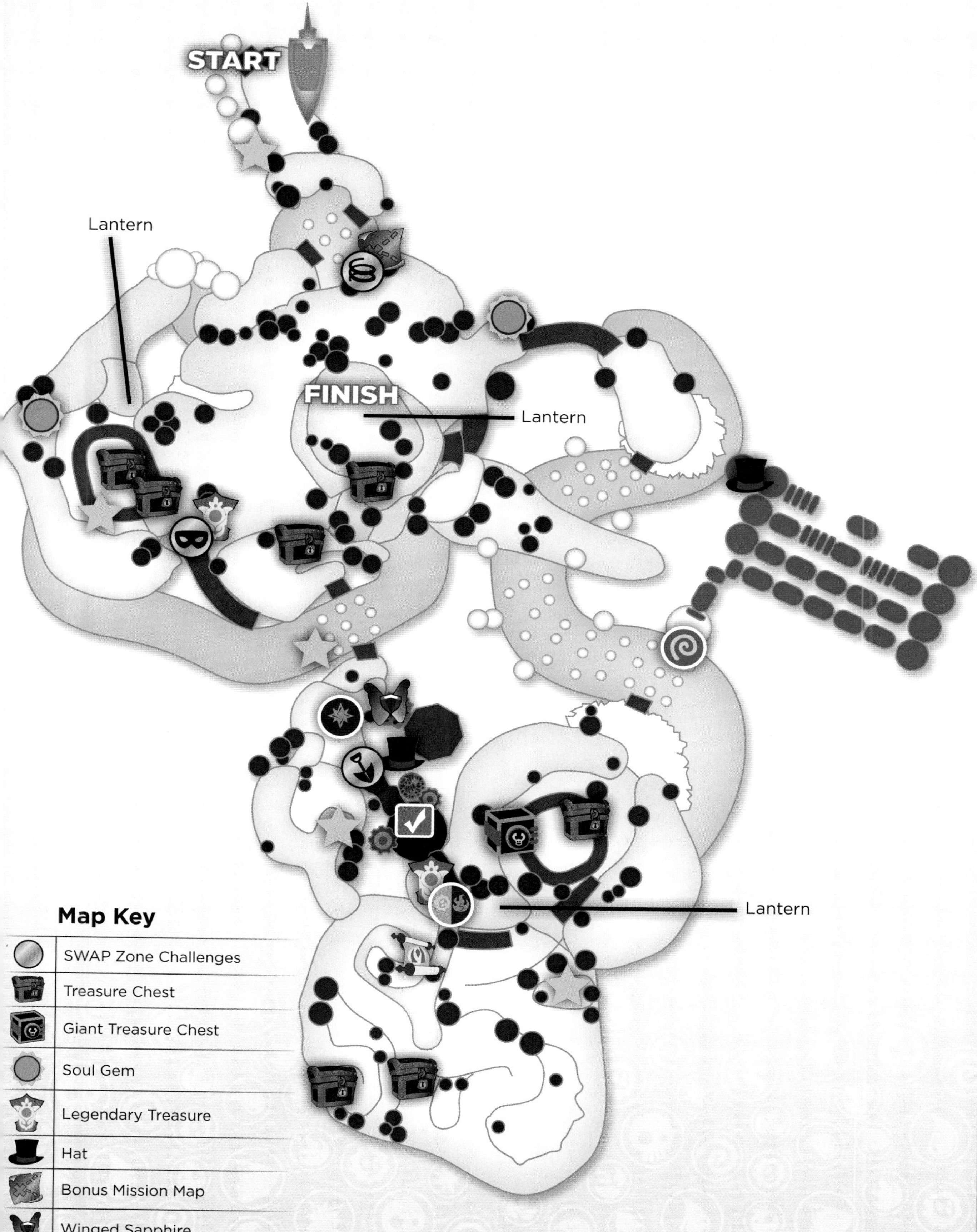

Map Key

- SWAP Zone Challenges
- Treasure Chest
- Giant Treasure Chest
- Soul Gem
- Legendary Treasure
- Hat
- Bonus Mission Map
- Winged Sapphire
- Story Scroll
- Dare
- Checkpoint

EARTH IS STRONGER IN THIS AREA

TYPHOON TRAIL

Watch out for the wind gusts blowing across the screen. They don't inflict damage, but they can push your Skylander into something that does harm, such as the cyclops planning an ambush along the trail. Drop off the side of the trail where the frozen river cuts through the gate. There's a hidden, unnamed area there. Defeat the Cyclops Gazermages lurking in the area and snag Fryno's **Soul Gem (Madness Maxed)** from just beyond them. Continue on the path to return to the frozen river's bank.

Where the path splits, and the lower fork ends at a closed gate, go up the other fork to meet Fizzy at the giant lantern. Follow the on-screen prompt to re-light the lantern and open the way to Hooplaberg.

HOOPLABERG & NUM NUM HALL

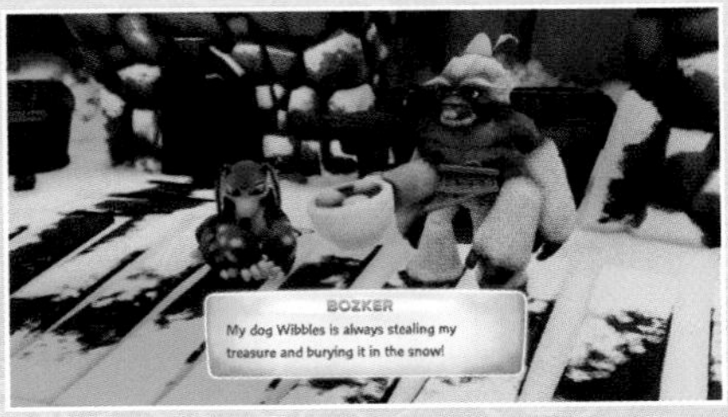

Go through the now-open gate and enter the village. Yurt invites you to explore the village, and you should start by talking with Bozker, standing with his chillydog, Wibbles, behind Yurt. Bozker challenges you to win three chew toys for his dog, and offers a reward when you complete the task.

Before you start on earning the chew toys, grab the **Balloon Animal** floating over the table in the back of the village's common area. Next, go into the doorway across the village from Bozker. It's the entrance to Num Num Hall, where you can get food to restore any lost health from the journey to the village and tackle a Spark Lock **Treasure Chest**.

SPARK LOCK

Fan-Dango

Immediately change to Bolt and hop on the green button to change the active fans. Change the fans again after Shock passes the first pair of fans and he should end up on the orange button. Send Bolt to the lowered orange column and hit the orange button again. Move Bolt to the elevated platform, and have Shock hit the button one more time and grab the blue lightning bolt with Shock. Move Bolt to the orange button, but hit it twice so it remains lowered for Shock. Repeat the fan switch as Bolt slides to the green lightning bolt and again when he returns to the other side. Move Shock past the orange column before Bolt hits the orange button and bring the two together to open the lock.

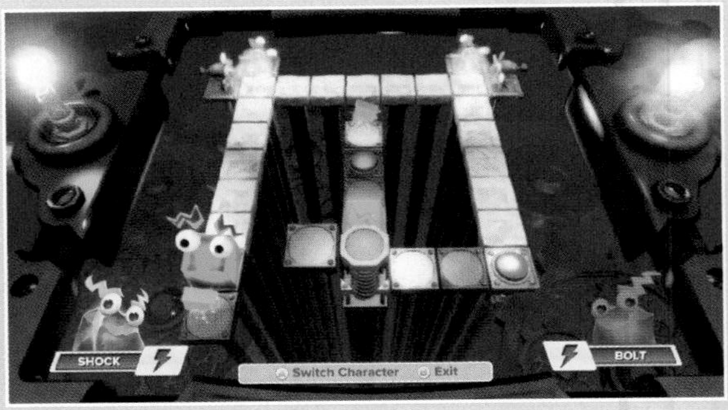

If you're playing on the Wii console, this Treasure Chest is not in your game.

FILBOP'S FETE, NIKNAK'S HOBNOB & BRIKABRACK'S BASH

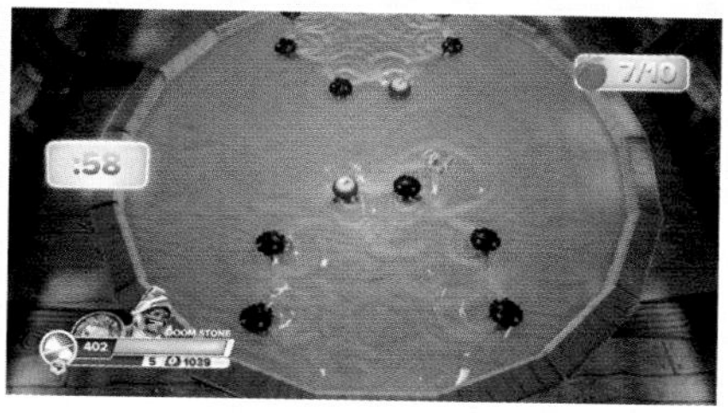

There are three doors behind Bozker, each the entrance to a home with a game that rewards a Chew Toy. The door closest to Bozker is Filbop's Fete. Bobble's challenge is to collect 10 apples, starting with a one minute timer. The apples and mines appear in waves, and each wave moves in a slightly different way. The number of apples and mines changes as well. Touching an apple adds it to your score, puts a few additional seconds on the clock, restores health, and usually removes the mines that spawned with it.

The door closest to Wibbles is NikNak's Hobnob. Puzzles challenges your memory with his game. He displays a series of colored shapes and asks you to repeat the pattern on the machines in the middle of the room. Interact with each machine to change the symbols on them. When the symbols they display match what Puzzles showed to begin the challenge, he hands over a Chew Toy.

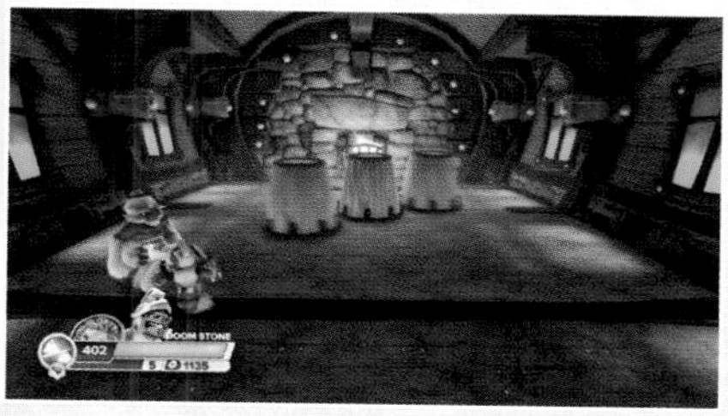

The door closest to the Balloon Animal's location is Brikabrack's Bash. Shuffles the Yeti hides the Chew Toy under one of three buckets and shuffles them around. You must choose the correct bucket, the one with the Chew Toy under it, to win his challenge.

After completing a challenge, the doorway to the home is closed, and Wibbles uncovers gold and other items while burying his new Chew Toy. When he gets the third Chew Toy, he unearths a **Treasure Chest**. When you're ready to continue the search for the Ancient Frosthound, go to the Spark Locked gate at the back of the village.

SPARK LOCK

Near Miss!

The trick to this Spark Lock is timing. You must time sending Shock and Bolt through the center to their lightning bolt being in their path. If getting all three lightning bolts is your goal, don't switch guys until the first one has his lightning bolt. When that's done, start Bolt down his path first and try to intercept him during the return leg of his sliding trip with Shock.

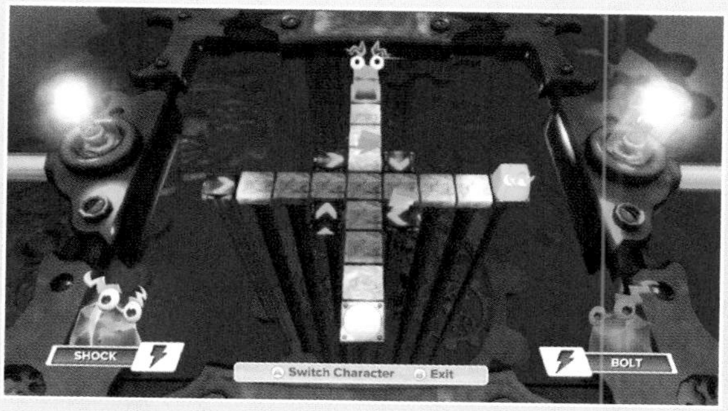

THE GLACIER HILLS & THE TEMPEST MAZE

The area beyond Hooplaberg's gate is known as The Glacier Hills, and the blowing snow is back, reducing your visibility. There's a SWAP Zone Challenge outside the village, and an ambush not far beyond that. Defeat the ambushers and destroy the boxes blocking a short path going uphill off the main path. There is a **Treasure Chest** with Cyclops Gazermages guarding it at the top of this path.

If you're playing on the Wii console, the Treasure Chest isn't here. It's near the end of the chapter, to the right of the area with the spinning axe in IceBreak Atolls, after the river with the floating ice platforms.

SWAP Zone
Nerves of Ice

SNEAK IN AND DESTROY THE FORTRESS! DON'T GET CAUGHT BY SPOTLIGHTS.
Turn to page 274 for tips on how to clear this SWAP Zone Challenge. Your reward for completing this challenge is the **Yeti Teddy** Legendary Treasure.

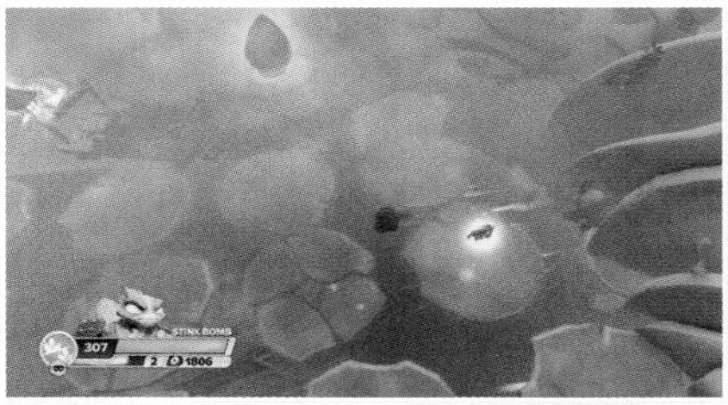

The river ahead hasn't quite frozen over, but large pieces of ice float on top, moving with the current. The bridge over the river is out, so you must cross it by jumping from one piece of ice to the next. The ice isn't thick, and it cracks under the weight of a Skylander landing on it. While you're crossing the river, work against the current and grab the **Balloon Animal** hovering above the water and ice.

Mysterious hands appear next to a Power Pod and drop off a new type of hazard—a dangerous, spinning blade. Before you reach the spinning blade's location, look for both a Magic Gate and a SWAP Zone on the ridge above the Power Pod.

ENCHANTED BIVY

Yuks has a high score in a turret game and challenges you to beat it. You must shoot 50 balloons without hitting a mine to best him. Balloons come in many colors, but mines are always black with red lights. Crates may also fly across the screen, and they're worth extra gold when you hit them. After you successfully shoot 50 balloons, Yuks hands over a **Winged Sapphire**.

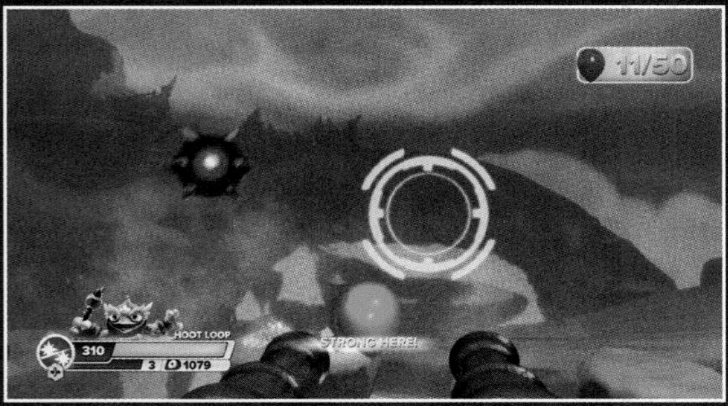

If you're playing on the Wii console, the Winged Sapphire is on a platform on the left o the river with ice platforms in IceBreak Atolls.

SWAP Zone
Glacial Descent

FIND YOUR WAY IN THE DARK! DIG UP THE BLUE CRYSTALS BEFORE TIME RUNS OUT!
Turn to page 271 for tips on how to clear this SWAP Zone Challenge. Your reward for completing this challenge is the **Four Winds Hat**.

The paths beyond the checkpoint have more gusts of wind blowing across them and a Battle Gate guarded by a new enemy, the Evilized Chillydog. Evilized Chillydogs dig up large crystals and throw them at a location on the ground indicated by a large circle. They also flip away before digging up a new crystal.

Don't go through the Battle Gate until you pick up the nearby **Balloon Animal** within the reach of a spinning blade. It's slightly downhill, away from the Battle Gate. When your Skylander passes through the Battle Gate, it closes.

The giant hands appear again and drop off a new hazard that looks like a toy, but is actually a proximity mine. When your Skylander draws close to the mine, it activates. Move out of its blast zone quickly to avoid taking damage. Drop down to the next area past the mine.

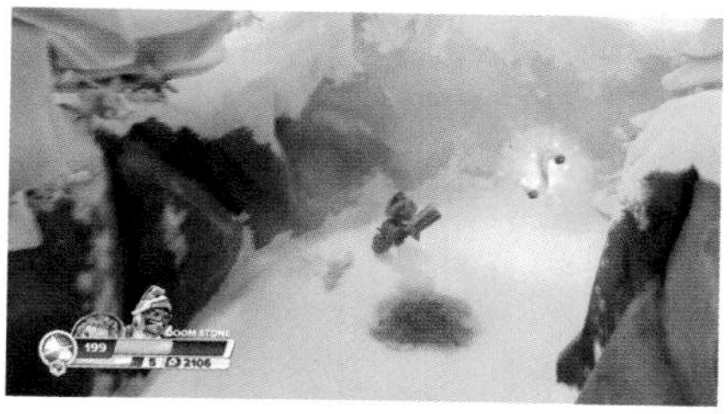

The path splits here. The left side is the gusty and proximity mine-filled Tempest Maze. Once you clear out the mines, there is a **Story Scroll, Party on the Mountains**, floating in an alcove.

Return to where the path split and follow the trail of coins. The path splits again at a lamppost. The path on the right is short but has at least one of every hazard (and some enemies!) encountered so far. However, the **Treasure Chest** at the end makes the struggle worth it.

Return to the main path but don't expect to get far. A Battle Gate blocks the road ahead and you must clear out a few waves of enemies to knock it down.

The path beyond the gate winds around and downward. There's another split in the path at a lamppost. Both paths are filled with hazards and enemy encounters. If you see a Balloon Animal just out of reach, then you are on the path to Slushville. You need to backtrack a bit and get the Treasure Chest from the other path off the split. If you see a Battle Gate-locked **Treasure Chest**, grab it and head back the other way to get to your next destination.

The gate to Slushville is closed. Drop off the ledge near the pine treetop to get the **Balloon Animal** you saw earlier. Walk up the wooden pathway with the guardrail. The lantern you need to light in order to open the gates of Slushville is at the top, as is a dual elemental gate.

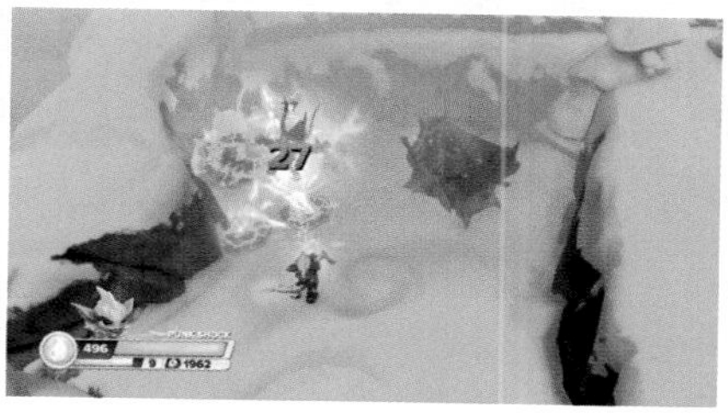

FIEND FURNACE

Get ready for a big fight! To claim the **Endless Cocoa Cup** Legendary Treasure, you must defeat three Cyclops Gazermages and three Cyclops Brawlbucklers while fiery rocks fall from above. Try to focus your damage on one enemy until it falls. The sooner you can cut the numbers advantage your enemies have, the easier the fight gets!

SLUSHVILLE & GRATIS GELD HAUS

Griznik welcomes you to Slushville and mentions the Volcano Games. He also points out the Spark Locked gate that leads to the lands beyond their village. Enter the open door to the right for Gratis Geld Haus. It doesn't have much inside, but it does have a **Giant Treasure Chest**.

Head back outside and speak with the juvenile yeti, Klizzy, near the table stacked with yeti teddy bears. He isn't satisfied with his collection and asks you to win him three more yeti teddy bears.

GRIZNIK'S GALA, SHORTY'S SHINDIG & HOWZIT'S HOOTENANNY

The door farthest from Klizzy is Griznik's Gala. Bobble offers the familiar apple bob game. He ups the difficulty by throwing in more apples and mines, and also asks for twenty apples before he hands over a yeti teddy bear.

The building closest to Klizzy is Howzit's Hootinanny, where you play Memory Eruption Blast with Puzzles. This time, there are four symbols to match with the machines in the room. Interact with the machines to change the symbols. When they match the pattern, Puzzles hands over the next yeti teddy bear.

The building behind Klizzy's table is Shorty's Shindig. Shuffles the Yeti hides the yeti teddy bear under one of the buckets. After he shuffles them around (and he's fast!) pick the correct barrel and he awards the yeti teddy bear to you.

After you deliver the first two yeti teddy bears, Klizzy tosses treasures on top of his table. Deliver the third yeti teddy bear and he reveals a **Treasure Chest**. When you're ready to move on, head to the back of the village and open the Spark Lock gate.

If you're playing on the Wii console, this Treasure Chest isn't in your game.

SPARK LOCK

Circuit Breaker

Shock can't really go anywhere until Bolt reaches the orange button, but you must time his slide to get past the cycling fan. Hit the orange button, which lowers the orange column and activates the fan near Shock. Grab the green lightning bolt and move Bolt to the top row, but don't move past the blue lightning bolt. Slide Shock around his half of the level, hop through the blue lightning bolt and join up with Bolt.

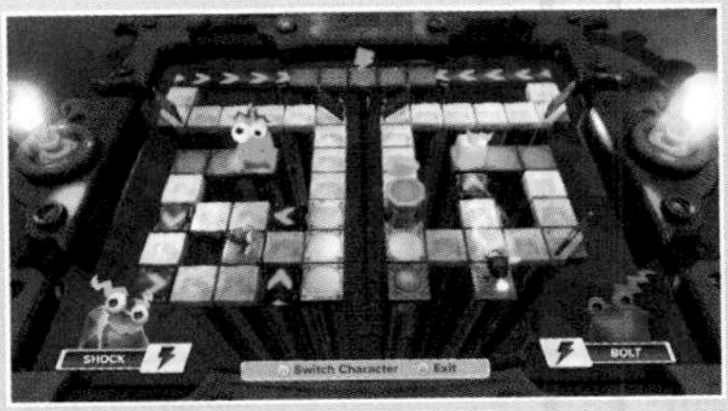

WATER IS STRONGER IN THIS AREA

ICEBREAK ATOLLS

Don't relax! A group including Cyclops Brawlbucklers springs an ambush immediately outside the gate. The river beyond the ambush is like the one you crossed earlier, with bits of breakable ice floating on the water. There's an Air Gate directly across from where your Skylander begins the crossing.

There are extra hazards on this river, in the form of Cyclops Gazermages. The ride ends at a pier, but the path beyond that is blocked by a Battle Gate and a spinning blade hazard.

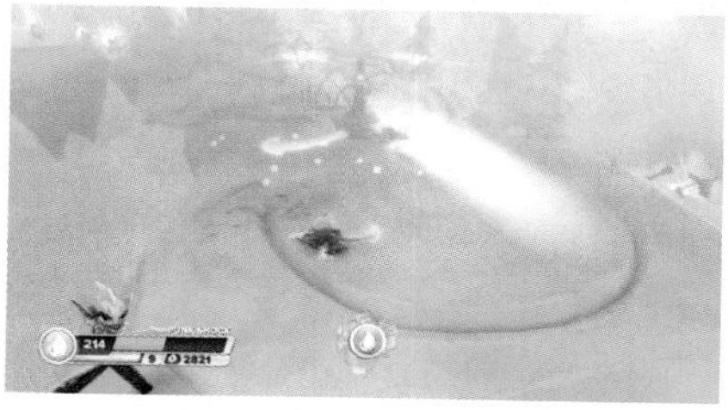

Enemies, blades, and mines all guard the path in waves. Gusts of wind are thrown in for good measure. There's a SWAP Zone behind the proximity mines, but it's not easy to reach.

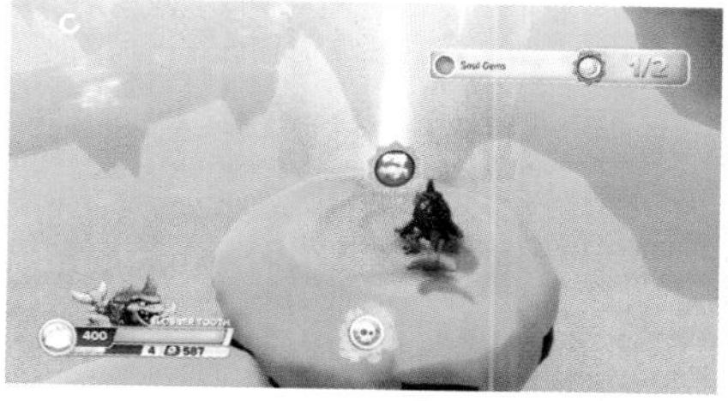

GUSTY GAUNTLET

The main resistance in this area is air resistance. Wind machines are placed around the level, set at different heights. Some machines blow against your Skylander, making coin collection difficult. Others push your Skylander in a blur through rows of coins. There are no enemies to worry about, just wind machines, moving platforms, and tempting coins in sometimes dangerous places. Get to the end of the windy maze and get the **Beacon Hat** before taking the shortcut back to the gate.

If you're playing on the Wii console, the Beacon Hat comes from a gift box to the left in the Tempest Maze area.

UNDEAD IS STRONGER IN THIS AREA

PERILOUS PRECIPICE

Look for a gap in the trees on the right side of the path. You know you're going the right way when the way ahead fills with proximity mines. Carefully get through the mines to get Trap Shadow's **Soul Gem (Shadow Striker/Living Shadow)** before turning back to the main path.

SWAP Zone
Frosty Frolicking

POP THE KAOS BALLOONS!
Turn to page 268 for tips on how to clear this SWAP Zone Challenge. Your reward for completing this challenge is the **Frigid Fright Bonus Mission Map**.

The path continues uphill, and the resistance intensifies with each step. Watch the left side of the path for a spot to step down on a snowy stone. There's a **Treasure Chest** in this area, not far from the uphill path.

The final lantern is at the top of the mountain, and access to it is blocked by a Battle Gate. Cyclops Gazermages and Cyclops Brawlbucklers defend the gate at first, and reinforcements arrive after you take down each wave. Expect to tackle every type of enemy encountered previously in Frostfest Mountains before the lantern opens.

Light the final lantern and the Ancient Frosthound appears, but the good feeling is short-lived. Now you must take on the owner of the giant hands that plagued you throughout your trip through the yeti homelands!

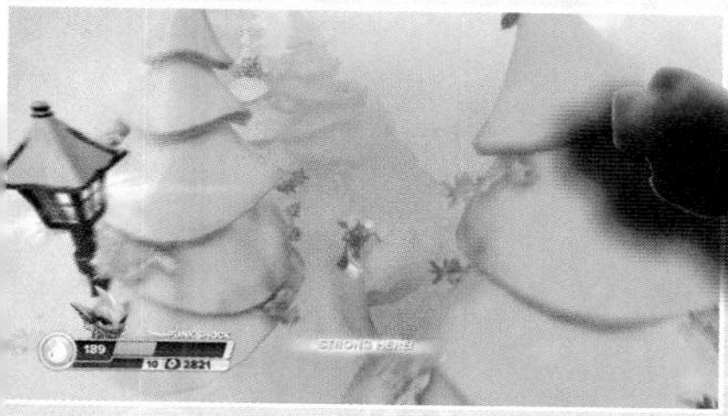

MESMERALDA'S SHOW

OBJECTIVES

Story Goals

- ◯ Defeat Mesmeralda
- ◯ No Skylanders Defeated
- ◯ No Damage Taken

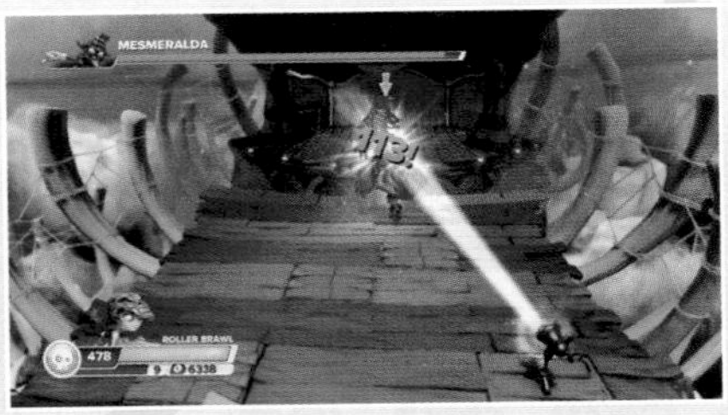

DEFEAT MESMERALDA

Mesmeralda employs three types of puppets during this fight. You encountered two in the previous Story Level, and the new addition, dancing puppets, are the first hazard you must avoid. They project ghostly pink lines across the stage. Stand clear of the lines before the white puppets dash along them. They travel left to right, right to left, and front to back.

After you avoid a few waves of the puppets, two stage lights appear. Each light hits one of the openings in the building on the stage. Look for Mesmeralda's pink eyes to appear in the openings and hit them with the stage light to blind her. She is vulnerable while blinded, which is your opportunity to get in a few shots and reduce her health.

After she recovers, she flies back to the stage and resets the scenery on it, but the building in the set has an extra opening. That is the pattern for each round of this fight. Avoid her minions, blind her with a stage light, then attack her until she recovers and resets the stage.

For the second round, Mesmeralda drops proximity mines during the dancing puppets attack, and continues to drop them when the stage lights appear. There are three lights for three windows this time, so keep watching for her eyes to appear and be ready to attack as soon as she's blinded.

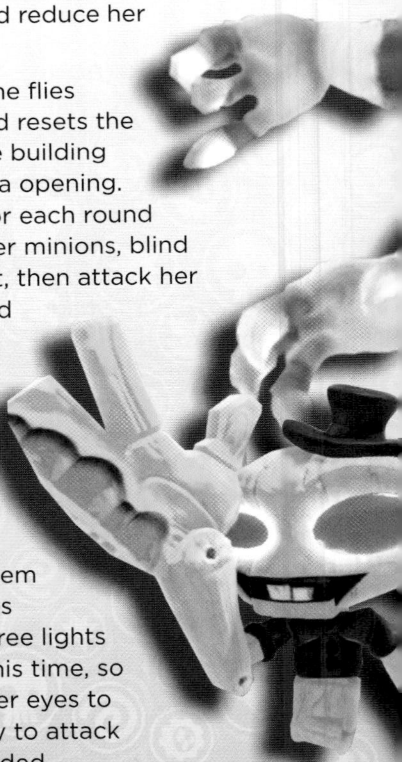

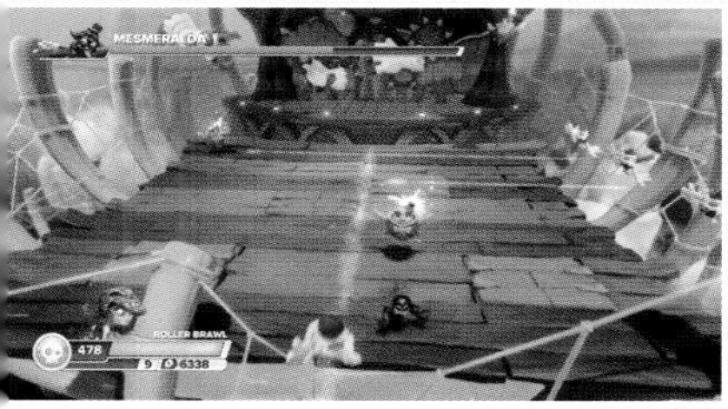

The third round's addition is dancing puppets appearing from two perpendicular directions at closer intervals. The dashing lines for the next batch start to appear before the first batch has faded. She also deploys more proximity mines at a time. There are three stage lights on the stage at the end of this round.

Giant spinning blades make their debut in the fourth round, and the dancing puppets appear in greater numbers. At least the proximity mines are understudies, and off the stage, for this round. There are four stage lights to choose from at the end of this round, and the spinning blade continues to chase your Skylander while you pick a light and attack Mesmeralda.

Mesmeralda adds a second spinning blade to the initial waves of dancing puppets, but she doesn't add any additional stage lights to the end. She also keeps the proximity mines away.

One last round to go! The grand finale begins with a stage filled with dancing puppets and a spinning blade. Mesmeralda gradually adds proximity mines as well. Avoid all the hazards on stage and hit her with one last stage light. When she appears, she drops another spinning blade and a few proximity mines. As each mine explodes, more are added around the stage. When she complains about outside food in the theatre, look around for food in the area if your Skylander is low on health. She's almost down, so don't worry about the food if your Skylander's health is fine. Once you've finished with her it's time to head back to Woodburrow with the Ancient Frosthound.

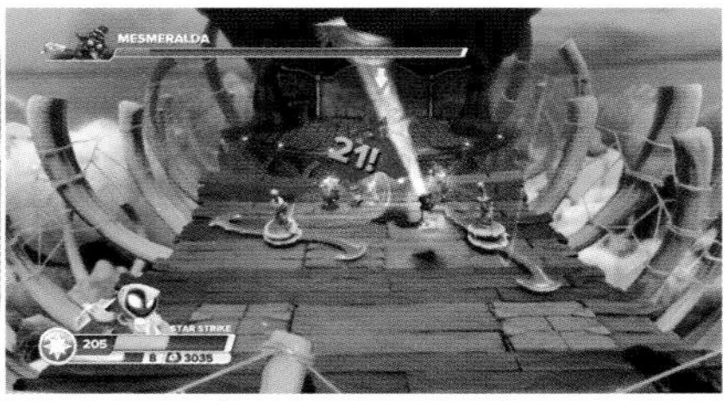

Back in Woodburrow

Rufus and the Chieftess are overjoyed at the return of the Ancient Frosthound, but Tessa's news tempers the celebration. Speak with Sharpfin when you're ready to travel to Fantasm Forest to learn more.

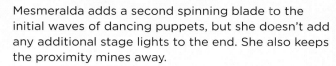

TESSA
urgent message! Kaos has been spotted near
the Fantasm Forest! He's going

FANTASM FOREST

OBJECTIVES

Story Goals

- ◯ Put Out the Evilized Fires
- ◯ Save the Ancient Tree Spirit

Dares

- 6 Wooden Dalmatians
- 50 Enemy Goal
- 0 No Skylanders Defeated

Collections

- 16 Areas Discovered
- 4 Treasure Chests
- 1 Giant Treasure Chest
- 3 Soul Gems
- 2 Legendary Treasures
- 2 Hats
- 1 Bonus Mission Map
- 1 Winged Sapphire
- 1 Story Scroll

New Enemies

Chompy Boomblossom

Undead Spell Punk

Missile Mauler

Evilized Screecher

Tech Geargolem

MAGIC IS STRONGER IN THIS AREA

VERDANT LANDS & TROLL TOLL BRIDGE

Most locked gates throughout Fantasm Forest don't require keys to pass. Instead, you must find a way to extinguish the evilized fires burning in front of them. There are two symbols that appear on these gates and you become familiar with them quickly. The first looks like a bomb inside a circle. The image actually portrays a water balloon. When you see this symbol, such as on the first fiery gate you encounter, there is a fire truck nearby. The other symbol is a fire hydrant, and it means you should find one not too far away that douses the fire in a spray of water when its valve is opened.

Move past the burning gate to meet up with Sprucie. He has a fire truck, but its hoses are dry. He asks you to restore water by following the hose and fixing the problem. A new enemy blocks your way to reaching the hydrant, Chompy Boomblossoms. They take the self-destructive streak shared by Chompies to the next level. When they draw close enough to a Skylander, they glow orange and detonate, inflicting a considerable amount of damage to anything too close. Take them out before they're able to explode or your Skylander will pay the price.

SPRUCIE
Use the pump to fill water balloons to put out these despicable flames!

Turn the valve on top of the hydrant to start the water flowing again. Hurry back to the fire truck and pick up a water balloon. When a fire is in range, throw the balloon to extinguish it.

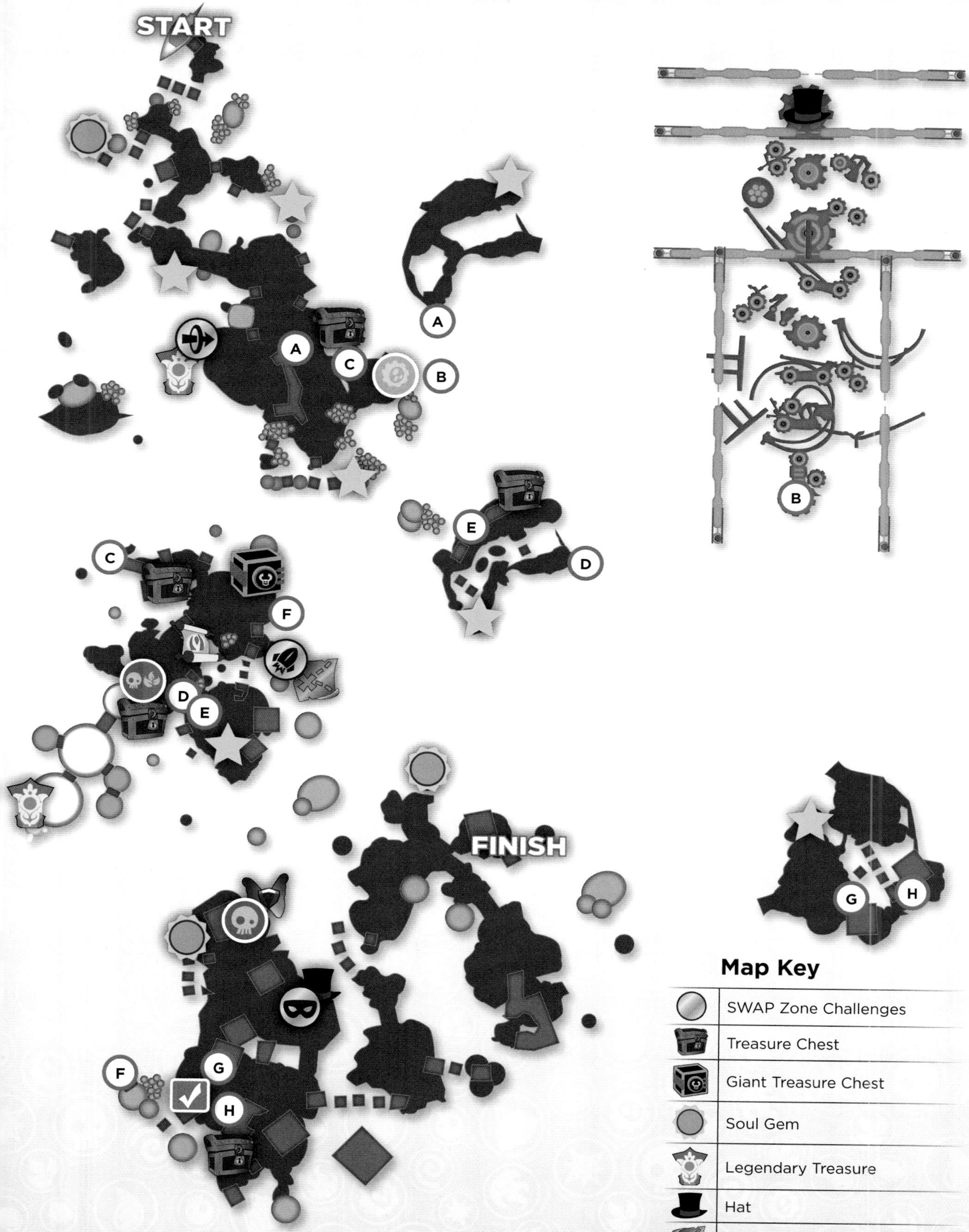

Map Key

	SWAP Zone Challenges
	Treasure Chest
	Giant Treasure Chest
	Soul Gem
	Legendary Treasure
	Hat
	Bonus Mission Map
	Winged Sapphire
	Story Scroll
	Dare
	Checkpoint

Don't forget the burning gate nearest the starting point. The balloons are on timers, so if you're struggling to get back to the gate before the balloon expires, use a Skylander with a dashing ability, a Skylander who can fly, or someone like Roller Brawl, to get there faster.

Wait for a floating platform to appear at the end of the wooden deck. After a few more quick jumps, your Skylander is in position to collect Blast Zone's **Soul Gem (Bomb Party/Hot Feet)**.

There is another nearby fire to extinguish, but it's not a gate. Put out the fire on the pier just behind the fire truck to expose a fishing pole. Catch all the fish for a big gold reward. Clear the burning gate nearest the fire truck and carry another balloon across the bridge to put out the fire at the other end of the bridge.

The bridge has a few holes in it, and there are a number of trolls that appear to try to stop your progress. There's one more burning gate to pass after the bridge ends, and it's the type that requires a hydrant to pass.

Speak with Nolan to learn more about Kaos' plans. Drop down one ledge and look to the left for a floating platform past a small gap. Jump a few times to the left and grab the **Wooden Dalmatian**. Return to the ledge below Nolan and continue down to the area under the bridge.

A group of Cadet Crushers appears and defends their turf. Smash through the wooden fence past the fiery gate to open the way to Fantasm Beach.

LIFE IS STRONGER IN THIS AREA

FANTASM BEACH & STONEYARD CAVE

Keep moving toward the hose ahead. There is a SWAP Zone Challenge to the right and a fire truck around the bend. The fire truck and the gillmen boat both need a good supply of water to help battle the flames. Their supply hose runs down into Stoneyard Cave.

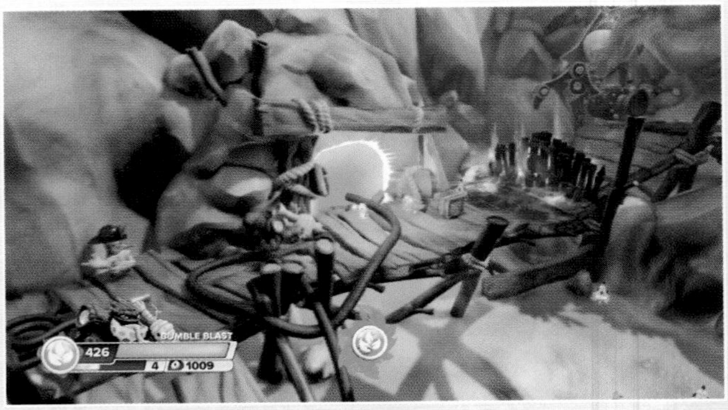

SWAP Zone
Ethereal Transfer

COLLECT THE MAGIC RUNES TO SEAL THE DIMENSIONAL RIFT!

Turn to page 278 for tips on how to clear this SWAP Zone Challenge. Your reward for completing this challenge is the **Topiary of Doom** Legendary Treasure.

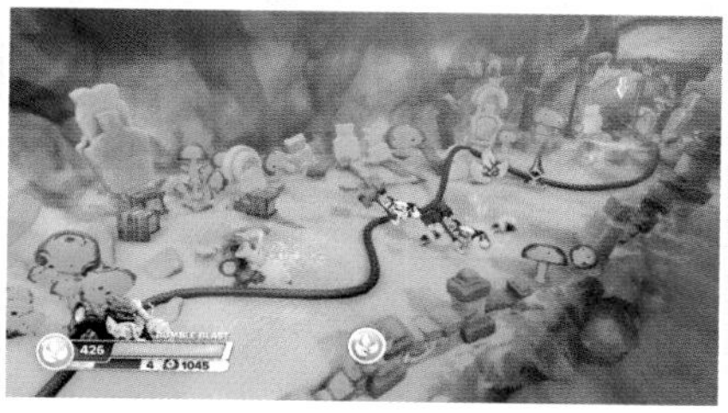

The cave is peaceful at first, but a new enemy, the Undead Spell Punk, makes its debut before your Skylander can touch the hydrant. Undead Spell Punks summon skeletal Cadet Crushers that act much like their fleshy selves. Undead Spell Punks don't attack directly; they let their minions do the dirty work.

Open the valve on the hydrant behind the Undead Spell Punk to restore pressure outside. More enemies appear in the cave, intent on keeping your Skylander from getting back outside to help with the fires. Grab a water balloon and head back to the Troll Toll Bridge. Put out the fire between the large stone columns to reveal a **Wooden Dalmatian**.

Return to the fire truck and take another water balloon to douse the flaming gate nearby. The opened path angles upward as it leaves the beach. As you're hopping between wooden platforms and grassy areas, watch for a jump to the right that goes to a platform with a **Wooden Dalmatian**.

To avoid taking damage from the short-range flamethrowers along the path, watch for the bladders on top of them to fill. When they're fully inflated, the flamethrower is about to spew evilized fire from its nozzle. Move past them while the bladder re-inflates to avoid taking damage.

Where the disconnected platforms give way to solid ground again, look for another burning gate and a Tech Gate. The path to these gates includes a new troll type, the Missile Mauler. These ranged trolls fire a single missile with some tracking capability, but require a long time to reload before they can fire again. Attack them between their missile launches and they should go down quickly. Use the extinguisher near the burning gate to blast it down.

HAMMERHEAD FACTORY

Birchblock's teleporter is meant to help their fire brigade, but they need help testing it. Grab the teleporter ball and throw it to a platform ahead. Your Skylander appears where the ball lands. In some instances, you must wait to throw the ball until the current platform has risen to its highest point to reach the next platform.

The area is almost devoid of enemies. There is one fight against a Tech Geargolem, an enemy that gets his formal introduction a bit later in Fantasm Forest. Use the large teleporting sphere not far beyond the Tech Geargolem to complete the test and get your reward, the **Flower Garland**.

If you're playing on the Wii console, the Flower Garland is in a gift box on the left at the end of the Jet Fire Pass area, beside the door leading to WaterWay Retreat.

LIFE IS STRONGER IN THIS AREA

JET FIRE PASS

As you did before, carefully move past the flamethrowers. A small group of trolls and an Undead Spell Punk pop up just beyond the flamethrowers. When they're defeated, turn around and look for a short path that ends at a **Treasure Chest**. Continue back up the hill to meet Fire Chief Willowbark.

The Fire Chief asks for help with the Fireflooder. You assume control of the Fireflooder's watercannon. It works the same as the turrets you've used previously, except that the cannons fire water (it's an endless supply, so don't worry about conserving water) to put out fires and take out enemy forces. You must save a series of airships from evilized fire to continue.

FIRE IS STRONGER IN THIS AREA

WILDFIRE WILDS & WATERWAY RETREAT

After disembarking the Fireflooder, take the short right fork of the path and open the **Treasure Chest** locked with a Spark Lock before tackling the hazardous path with the rolling barrels.

SPARK LOCK

Help Me Help You!

Press the green button with Bolt. Move Shock to the left, across the conveyor belt and hit the orange button. Send Bolt over the orange sliding pad and use the conveyor belts to hit the purple button. Change to Shock and reset the orange sliding pad, then ride it across to the blue lightning bolt. Move Bolt to the lowered purple platform. Send Shock around the conveyor belts (grab the green lightning bolt with Bolt after Shock raises the purple platform) and join him with Bolt.

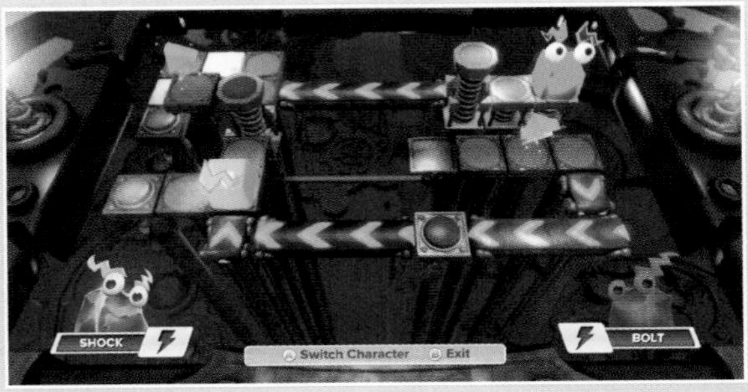

If you're playing on the Wii console, this Spark Lock does not appear in your game.

The barrels rolling down the path are dangerous, so avoid touching them. They can be destroyed, but there are so many it's not worth destroying them individually. Look for a little path to the left of the wooden platform just beyond the second barrel roller. Grab the **Story Scroll, Dangerous Profession**, from the end of a series of floating platforms. Get it before you drop off the wooden walkway and into the next Battle Gate area. You can't get back up to the path afterward.

The Evilized Screecher is the first foe you face at the Battle Gate. After a shrill cry, Evilized Screechers fly just above the ground with a line of evilized fire stretching out from its wings. When the Screechers draw close, jump over them (or the evilized fire) to avoid taking damage. When the Screecher runs into a wall, it becomes stunned. Attack it while it's dazed before it can climb back into the air to begin another attack run.

The longer path, the one that includes a bridge covered by flamethrowers, is the entrance to the 'Notso Lost' Lost Cavern. The short, safe path ends at a dual elemental gate. Destroy the boxes near the elemental gate to reveal a **Treasure Chest**.

GUSTER'S GRAVE

Elder Root's friend is trapped behind a double-locked gate. Each of the side platforms has a Key, and both are guarded by skeletal trolls. Grab the Key from the left platform (it's not heavily guarded) first. The Key on the right is behind a Battle Gate. Its undead protectors are supported by living trolls.

When you unlock the gate, Elder Root supplies one last bit of information. The final fight includes a Life Spell Punk and an Undead Spell Punk. Clear out all the enemies and claim **The Brass Tap** Legendary Treasure from behind the locked gate.

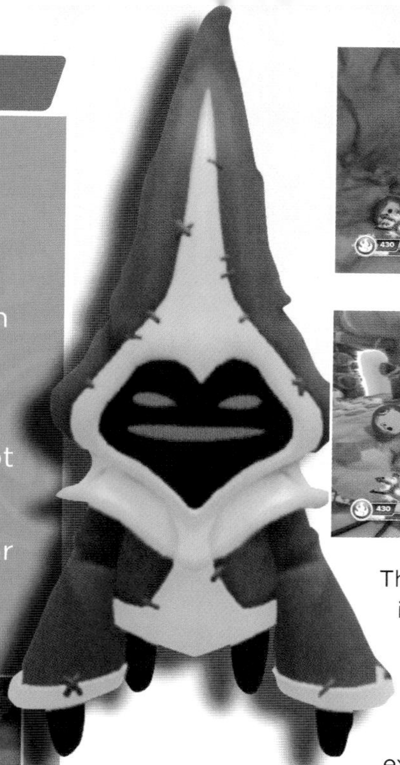

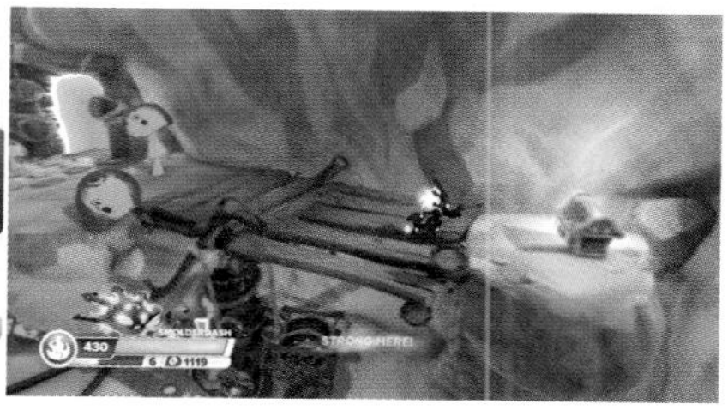

The exit isn't hard to spot; it's blue and glowing. Don't leave just yet! Walk past the exit and claim the **Treasure Chest** on the other side of a wooden walkway. The exit leads to Fantasm Village.

'NOTSO LOST' LOST CAVERN

Take out the Undead Spell Punk and Missile Mauler near the fire truck. Turn on the hydrant to supply water to the fire truck. Use water balloons to douse the fire gate and the fire burning just behind it to reveal a **Wooden Dalmatian**.

There are a few jumps between platforms ahead, and one of them includes running through a flamethrower. Start your jump as soon as the flamethrower's fire stops. Hurry across and make the jump to the next platform as quickly as possible.

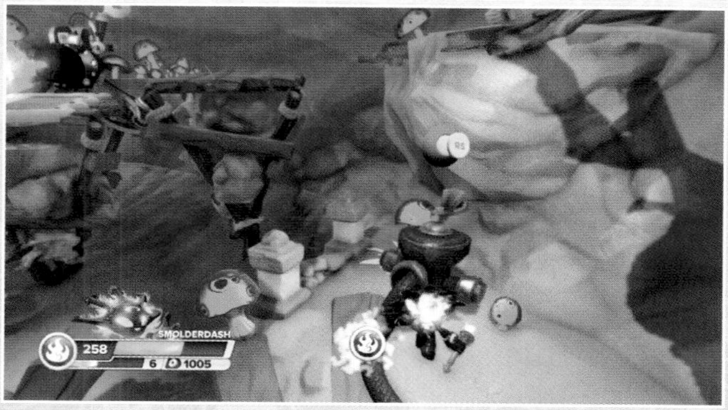

LIFE IS STRONGER IN THIS AREA

FANTASM VILLAGE

The initial hazards in Fantasm Village are burning barrels rolling down the path. You can still avoid them, but this batch of barrels is spaced out more. If you want to be destructive and you're using a Skylander with a ranged attack, commence with the explosions!

At the top of the hill, look for a blue hydrant near the barrel rolling machine. Turn the valve to knock down a nearby gate. With the gate out of the way, you're free to claim the **Wooden Dalmatian** behind it.

The stone fenced area ahead is a Battle Gate with a new type of enemy, the Tech Geargolem. Tech Geargolems fill the area with gears fired at high velocity. Watch for the Tech Geargolem to shrink (its upper body covers its legs) to know when it is preparing to fire. A wave of trolls and Chompy Boomblossoms joins in the fun as well. The area beyond the Battle Gate has a SWAP Zone on one side and Fire Chief Willowbark waiting just beyond it.

SWAP Zone

Fire Flighter

ROCKET TO THE FINISH!

Turn to page 272 for tips on how to clear this SWAP Zone Challenge. Your reward for completing this challenge is the **Chompy Sauce Bonus Mission Map.**

Don't speak with the Fire Chief until after you open the nearby **Giant Treasure Chest**, to the right of the house. Willowbark wants you to take control of the Fireflood's turrets to save Foreverspring Village. Use the water to extinguish fires, take out enemies, and protect the Fireflood from incoming missile attacks.

UNDEAD IS STRONGER IN THIS AREA

BIRCHBERG & BIRCHBERG RESERVOIR

Willowbark drops off your Skylander at Birchberg, near a Power Pod. Follow the hose away from the glowing cellar door to find the fire truck. There's a **Treasure Chest** on the ledge just below it.

Follow the hose back to the cellar door. The Birchberg Reservoir is on the other side, and that's where you must restore the water to the fire truck. A Tech Geargolem guards the area just inside the entrance. Hop across the wooden platforms and turn on the hydrant.

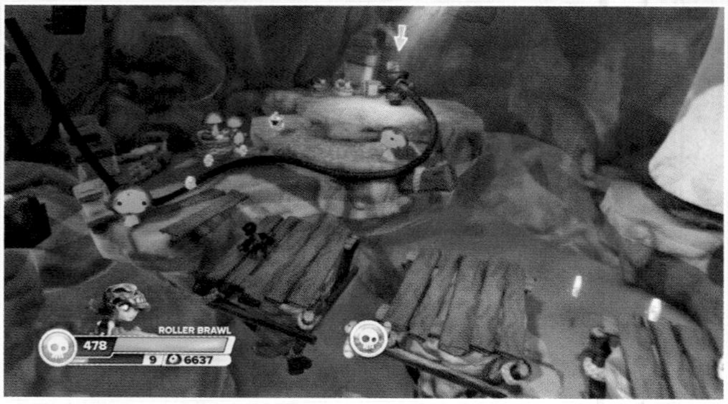

Grab a water balloon from the fire truck and use the closer entrance to the Reservoir to reach the burning gate at the back of the area. Extinguish the flames and grab the **Wooden Dalmatian**. A group of Chompy Boomblossoms appears in Birchberg on the way back to the Fire Truck.

If you're playing on the Wii console, this Wooden Dalmation is not in your game.

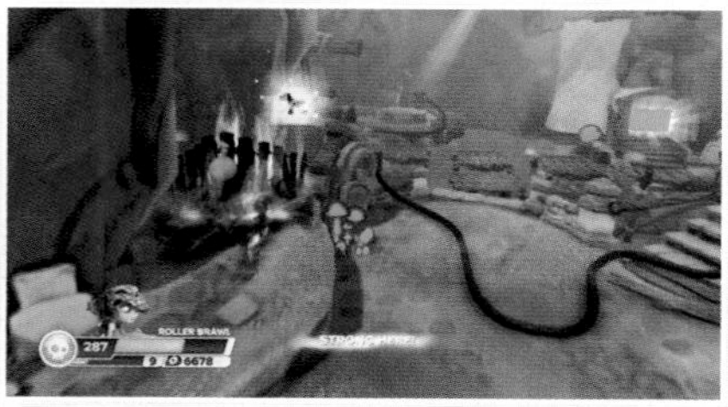

Grab another balloon from the fire truck and douse the fire at the gate. The area on the other side of the bridge turns into a Battle Gate, guarded by Evilized Screechers and trolls. Use the hydrant to open the wooden gate on the other side of the Undead Gate.

SHADOW PATH

The Shadow Path is another sidescrolling area where you must successfully navigate uneven terrain, enemies, and various sharp hazards to earn a **Winged Sapphire**. There aren't any hidden paths, so just keep running ahead and take out the enemies you encounter in this shadowy area.

The stone wall behind the hydrant ends at a series of wooden platforms. Use the platforms (avoid the flamethrower on the top one) to reach a higher area with Freeze Blade's **Soul Gem (Winter Chakram/ Iceberg Endurance)**.

The path beyond the Battle Gate includes an uphill climb made more difficult by the presence of burning barrels. At the top of the hill, the path splits. The short path to the left ends at a SWAP Zone Challenge. The longer path winds through a number of flamethrowers.

SWAP Zone
Fire Fortress

SNEAK IN AND DESTROY THE FORTRESS! DON'T GET CAUGHT BY SPOTLIGHTS.

Turn to page 274 for tips on how to clear this SWAP Zone Challenge. Your reward for completing this challenge is the **Glowy Mushroom Legendary Treasure**.

The landing beyond the flamethrowers is heavily defended. Clear out Kaos' forces and turn on the water supply at the hydrant. Carry a water balloon to the gate to open the way to the Forest Path.

WATER IS STRONGER IN THIS AREA

FOREST PATH & ANCIENT DIG SITE

Forest Path begins with a little bit of everything. Floating platforms, a Missile Mauler, rolling barrels, and flamethrowers! There's no need to rush through the area, so take each step at your own pace.

When you see a flamethrower firing in the same direction as the barrels are rolling, run through the flamethrower's path when it's off. The path just beyond that is made up entirely of flamethrower channels. They are timed to fire together, so dash across to Scratch's **Soul Gem (Gem Affinity)** on the other side, and dash back again after you get it.

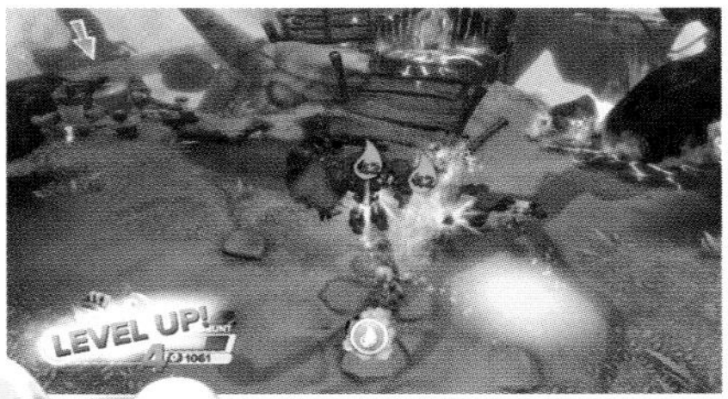

There's one more hydrant ahead, but it is guarded by two Tech Geargolems, trolls, and Chompy Boomblossoms. When the enemies are gone, use the hydrant to open the gate. Speak with Fire Chief Willowbark to begin another mission aboard the Fire Flooder.

Extinguish the fires surrounding the Ancient Treespirit, and take out the trolls standing guard. When Kaos appears, take down the missiles he launches at the Fire Flooder. Kaos sends minion-piloted vessels next. Shoot down as many as you can, but always take down incoming missiles first.

When Kaos's ship turns away, spray his thrusters with water. There's one large thruster and two smaller ones. When a thruster is extinguished, switch to another one. Each time Kaos appears, he first fires missiles, then turns away. When Kaos's ship runs out of health, it crashes, and the Ancient Treespirit is saved!

Back at Woodburrow

What began as a celebration quickly ends in shock and horror. Rufus asks you to speak with Flynn and Sharpfin to begin the rescue operation.

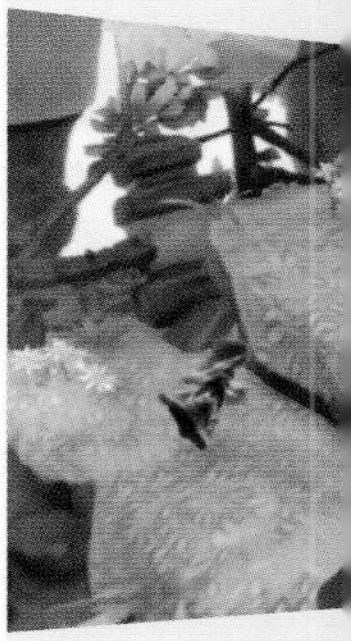

KAOS' FORTRESS

OBJECTIVES

Story Goals

- Destroy the Sheepshooters

Dares

- **4** Wool Sweater
- **50** Enemy Goal
- **0** No Skylanders Defeated

New Enemies

Chompy Pastepetal

Mr. Chompy

K-Bot Gloopgunner

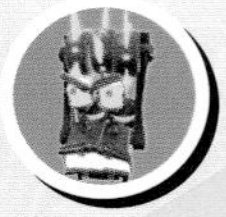

K-Bot Splodeshard

K-Bot Mineminer

Magic Spell Punk

Collections

- **20** Areas Discovered
- **6** Treasure Chests
- **1** Giant Treasure Chest
- **2** Soul Gems
- **2** Legendary Treasures
- **1** Hat
- **2** Bonus Mission Map
- **1** Winged Sapphire
- **1** Story Scroll

LIFE IS STRONGER IN THIS AREA

LIQUID GOO LAB, CONTRAPTION LAB & TOP SECRET STORAGE

The first ring of defense around Kaos' Fortress includes a few oddities. There are destructible bombs that you can knock down and use against enemies. Damaging goo rises and falls to expose and cover up staircases and treasures. The oddest thing you encounter is your contact: Special Agent 321, Designation Softpaw. Softpaw pops up throughout the chapter, offering bits of advice and S.H.E.E.P. disguises as both are needed.

SOFTPAW
PSST! Skylander- Don't look directly at me. They're always watching. ACT CASUAL!

Map Key

	SWAP Zone Challenges
	Treasure Chest
	Giant Treasure Chest
	Soul Gem
	Legendary Treasure
	Hat
	Bonus Mission Map
	Winged Sapphire
	Story Scroll
	Dare
	Checkpoint

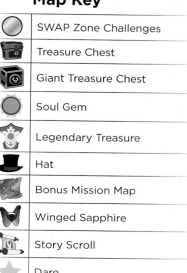

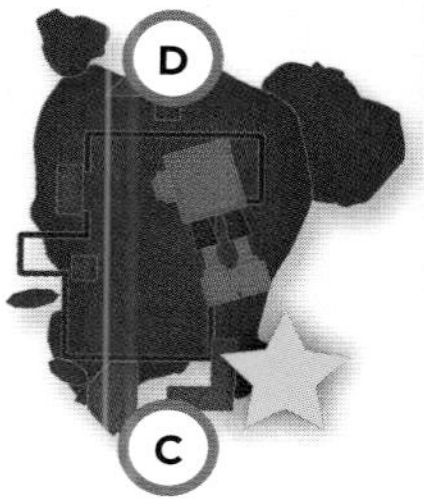

Your Skylander lands in the Liquid Goo Lab, where most of the ground is covered by a yellow liquid that damages anything that touches it. Use the metal surfaces floating on the goo to cross areas safely.

Not far into the lab, you encounter a creepy new Chompy type, the Chompy Pastepetal. The first attack on these bright yellow creatures splits them into two halves. The two halves continue to attack until you take them out.

Softpaw appears when a locked gate blocks further progress. He points out where to find the key you need to unlock the gate. A new enemy, the K-Bot Gloopgunner, appears on the way to the key. These automated defense systems fling a glob of gloop from the top of their heads. Avoid the green glob and attack the machine before it can reload and fire.

Search the left side of the platform below where the K-Bot Gloopgunner appeared. Smash the boxes to reveal a **Treasure Chest**. Grab the key from the middle of the spinning blades and unlock the gate.

There are more K-Bot Gloopgunners and Pastepetal Chompies on the other side of the gate. Take them out and go up the staircase beyond the goo tank. There is a SWAP Zone on the right, near the top of the stairs. Head away from the SWAP Zone to meet another new automated defense enemy, the K-Bot Mineminer.

SWAP Zone: Greenlight Raceway

RACE TO THE FINISH!

Turn to page 275 for tips on how to clear this SWAP Zone Challenge. Your reward for completing this challenge is the **Masterful Disguise** Legendary Treasure.

K-Bot Mineminers fire three explosive spheres at a time from their heads. Watch for the electrical charge build up around the sockets where these mines appear for an idea of when they will be fired. K-Bot Mineminers have two more annoying tricks up their sleeve. First, they extend an electrical charge in two directions from their base and spin it around in a painful circle. Jump over the electricity when it's near. Their final ability is the most annoying. They teleport! Just when you think you have them right where you want them, they'll vanish and appear nearby.

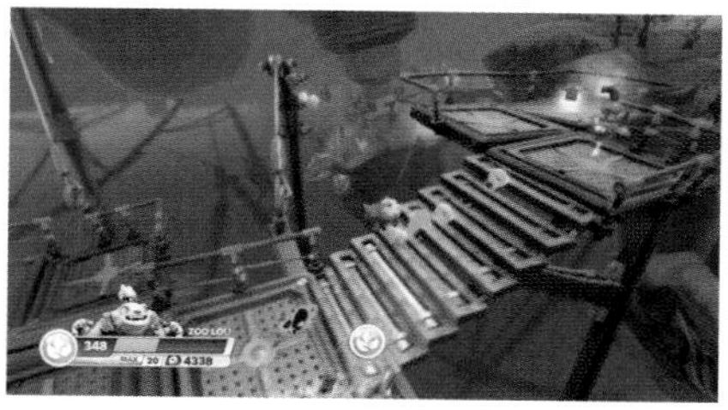

When the Mineminer falls, Softpaw appears again with another way to bypass fortress security. Don't leave the area until after you use the square platforms in the yellow liquid to jump over to a **Treasure Chest**.

Next, hop across the other pool of liquid near the high-speed transport, where a square platform appears briefly in it. The area on the other side is Top Secret Storage. Destroy the objects in the lower area to reveal Pastepetal Chompies. Go up the stairs on the right for a **Wool Sweater** guarded by a K-Bot Gloopgunner. With both items in your possession, use the transport to reach the Sheep Inspection area.

LIFE IS STRONGER IN THIS AREA

SHEEP INSPECTION, EXPERIMENTAL STORAGE & SHEEP TOWER

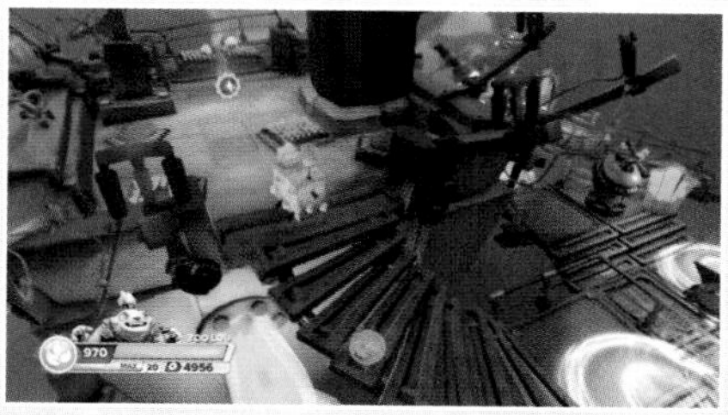

Take a few steps back from the landing spot to open the **Treasure Chest** that was visible just before your Skylander touched down. Softpaw pops up again to warn you about the security in the area. Run across the floor, avoiding the lights, to Softpaw's position. He hands over an upgraded sheep disguise that allows your Skylander to pass through the eye in the sky bots unharmed.

The stairway lined with coins leads to the high-speed transport to the next area. The stairs opposite that path go up to Experimental Storage and Punk Shock's **Soul Gem (Eelectrocute)**. Return to the coin-filled path and zip off to the Sheep Tower.

Destroy the pile of boxes near the landing spot in Sheep Tower to open up a path to a **Wool Sweater**. Don't stand close to the barrels blocking the path ahead. They explode, damaging anything nearby. The platform just ahead is blocked at one end by a Battle Gate. Take out the Pastepetal Chompies and K-Bot units to move past it.

The area beyond the Battle Gate is filled with treasure and includes another appearance from Softpaw. He set up a Spark Lock to destroy the Sheepshooter when solved. After completing the Spark Lock, your Skylander is fired off to Glob Lobber Gangway.

SPARK LOCK

Blowing in the Wind

Slide Shock past the fan when it's off to hit the green button, lowering the column in the middle of the puzzle, and switch which green fan is active. Time Bolt's slide so both fans push him to the spot just under the green column. Move him to the other side of the green column. Move Shock in front of the red fan when it's active so it blows him down to the conveyor belt, past the inactive green fan. As he's sliding across the ice, move Bolt to Shock's starting point. Move Bolt below the green column and send Bolt over to get the green lightning bolt. You can only get the lightning bolt if the green fan at the top of the puzzle is off. After collecting the green lightning bolt, switch the green fans (the lower one must be off) so Shock can reach the blue lightning bolt. With the green column lowered, have the two meet up on it.

AIR IS STRONGER IN THIS AREA

GLOB LOBBER GANGWAY & BELLY FLOP PEAK

This area gets its name from the globs of yellow goo lobbed into the air in various spots. The goo damages your Skylanders if they should come into contact with it.

Go left at the first pool of goo. Look for the Power Pod on a landing atop a row of stairs. Upgrade your Skylanders if necessary, then continue past the Power Pod and get the **Giant Treasure Chest** under the next set of stairs.

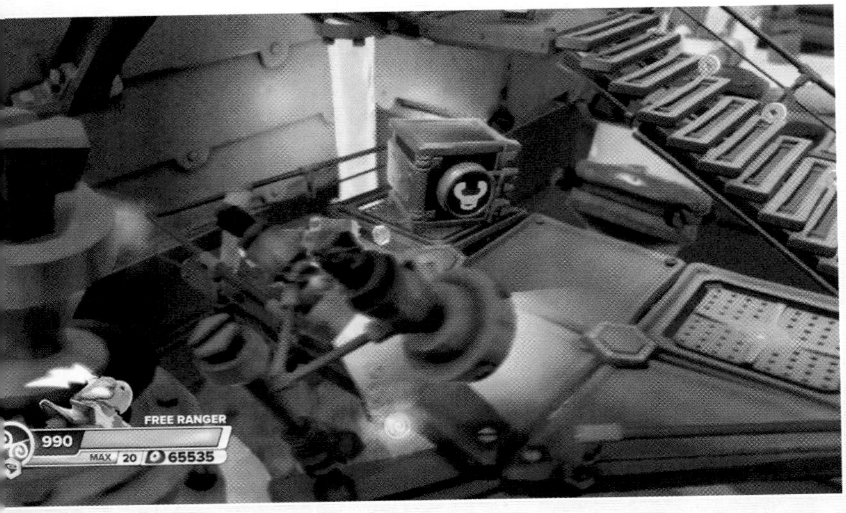

If you're playing on the Wii console, the Giant Treasure Chest is to the left after destroying the first Sheep Shooter.

Belly Flop Peak is farther up the stairs, and beyond a series of disconnected platforms. Doom Stone's **Soul Gem (Stoney Stare/Spin the Tables)** hovers over the end of a metal plank (hop up to reach it) beyond a goo-filled pool guarded by a pair of glob lobbers. Leap from the edge of the plank for a quick trip back down to the main floor.

A new enemy appears on the other side of the yellow goo pool. The K-Bot Splodeshards use a wicked front wheel to pull themselves forward and grind up anything in front of them. Dodge the attack and blast them while they recover. The area just beyond the encounter with the K-Bot Splodeshards is Chompie Churners.

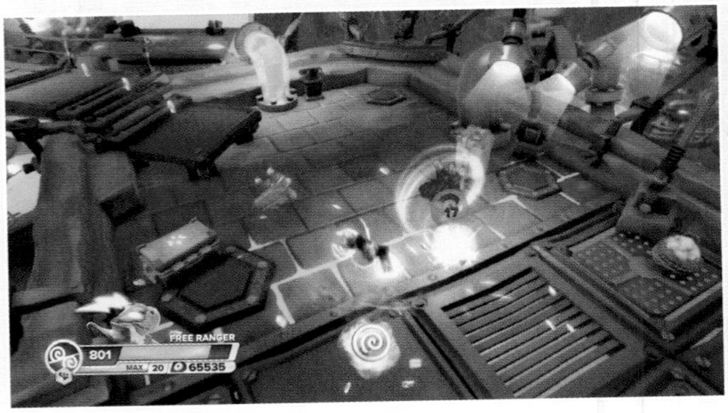

AIR IS STRONGER IN THIS AREA

CHOMPIE CHURNERS & SECRET TESTING GROUNDS

Run up the stairs off the side of the first mixing pool (where the giant fans spin slowly through the goo) and destroy the boxes. Open the **Treasure Chest** located near the back of the platform, past those boxes.

At the second mixing tank, follow the broken platforms to the left to reach the Secret Testing Grounds. It's on the side opposite the SWAP Zone Challenge. The Secret Testing Grounds is a Battle Gate with K-Bot forces guarding a **Wool Sweater**.

SWAP Zone
Kaotic Spring

POP THE CHAOS BALLOONS!
Turn to page 268 for tips on how to clear this SWAP Zone Challenge. Your reward for completing this challenge is the **Cursed Statues Bonus Mission Map.**

Return to Chompie Churners and jump to the goo pool with three small discs in it and take out the enemies on the platform just beyond it. Go left (away from the stairs heading upward) for another mixing pool. There's a **Story Scroll, Kaos' Laboratory**, on one side of the pool, and an Earth Gate not too far from it.

If you're playing on the Wii console, the Story Scroll is on the right just after entering the second part of the level, up the stairs.

DUMPING GROUNDS

Fliplip is working on a less-mean Geargolem (while making it look like a K-Bot Mineminer it seems) but needs a few more parts to finish the job. Run around the area and destroy the piles of boxes to reveal gold, enemies, or Geargolem parts. The three blue boxes have the parts, but enemies usually hide in the other boxes in front of them. After you collect all three parts, return to Fliplip, who then hands over a **Winged Sapphire**.

Return to the Chompie Churners area and go up the winding stairs. The Magic Spell Punk makes its debut on the next landing. Like some other Spell Punks, they don't attack Skylanders directly but instead aid the other enemy units in the area. In this case, Magic Spell Punks turn other enemies invisible. There isn't much to follow when trying to figure out where enemies are (no shadow, no rippling effect, or anything like that). The best thing to do is focus on the Spell Punk. When it is defeated, its spells stop working.

With the enemies cleared out, cross the broken metal walkway to the left. There is a larger mixing tank on the other end. The pool is so deep that each of the mixing arms' three spokes has three blades. The blades rise and sink into the pool as they spin. The walkway on the other side of the tank ends at a broken staircase, which leads to the Sludge Security area (it's a one-way trip down the stairs).

TECH IS STRONGER IN THIS AREA

SLUDGE SECURITY & FLOODED CONTAINMENTS

Sludge Security begins with a tricky Battle Gate. The enemies stick to the three-level mixing blades, so you must fight them there. Security bots patrol the area on the other side of the Battle Gate. Any non-sheep detected in the area are transported to a nearby platform.

Head straight across the pool to Softpaw's location (look for the arrow). He hands over another sheep disguise and sends you to the high-speed transport on another platform.

The goo in Flooded Containments rises and falls often, so you need to stay on the move. Pick up the piles of gold when the goo drops low enough to expose their positions on the stairs. When the main path goes to the left, keep walking straight ahead to bump into a Water Gate.

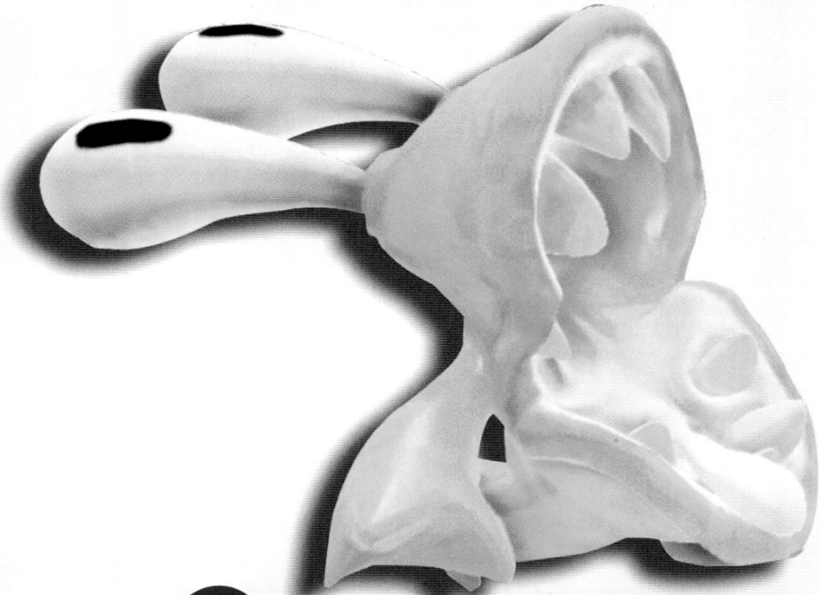

MYSTICAL FOUNTAINS

Trickster found a magical pool, but Mr. Chompy, a giant Chompy Pastepetal, also claimed it. Mr. Chompy splits into smaller and smaller Chompy Pastepetals as he is struck. Try to focus on one piece at a time. Keep one half as large as possible while taking down the smaller and smaller Chompies spawned by the second half. If you aren't worried about being overwhelmed by numbers, then just keep hammering whatever pieces of Mr. Chompy are in range. After you finish off the last little fragment of Mr. Chompy, Trickster gives you the **Asteroid Hat**.

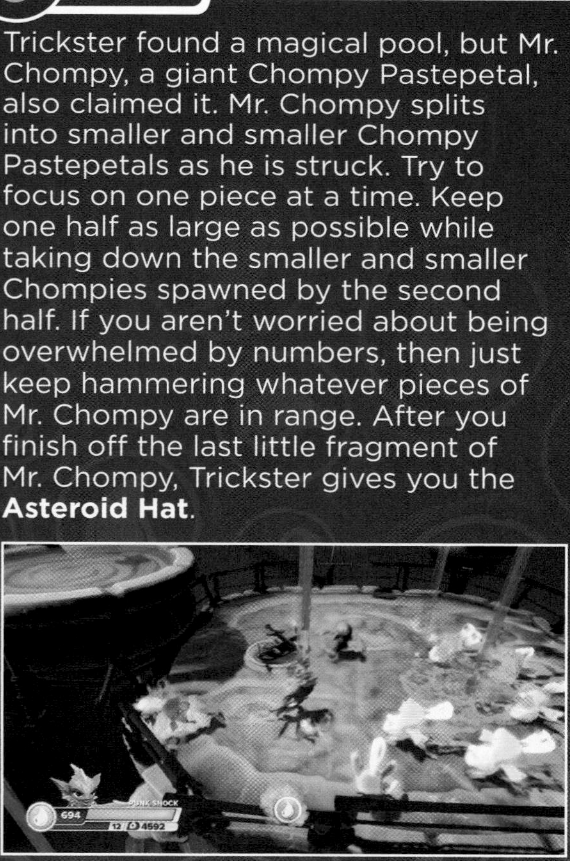

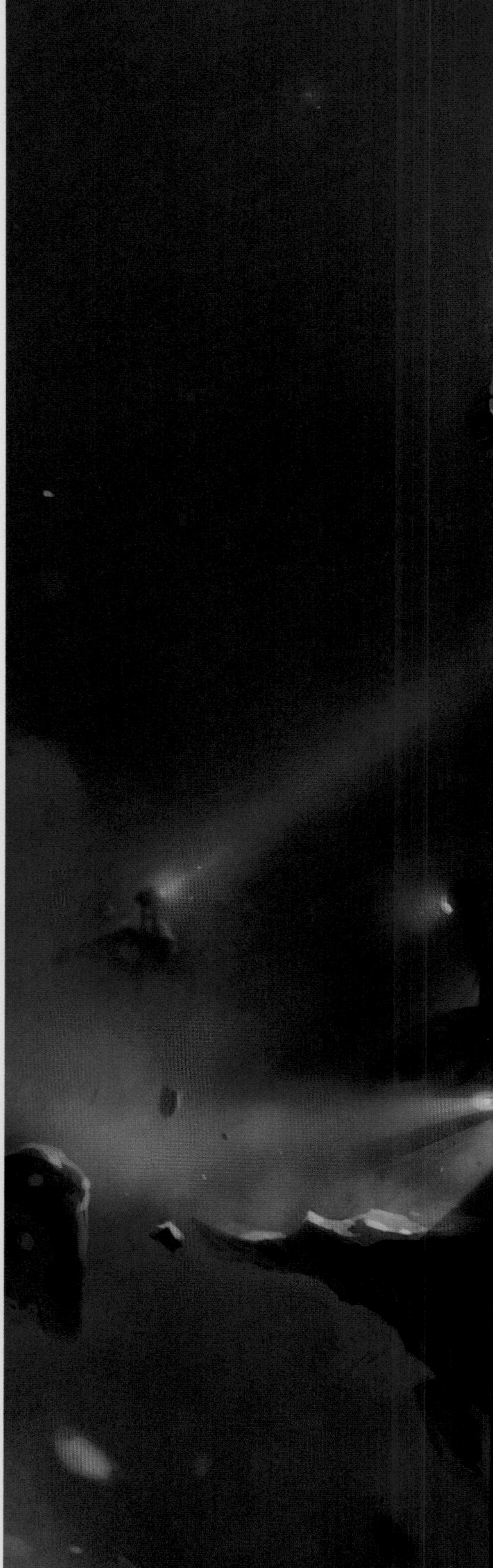

Stepping through the next doorway triggers a Battle Gate sequence. The door your Skylander entered through spins closed and the goo on the floor begins to rise. Take down the K-Bot Gloopgunners on the corner platforms while avoiding the goo. When the Battle Gate drops away, your next task is to solve a Spark Lock to take out the next Sheepshooter.

SPARK LOCK

Icebreaker

Send Bolt down the ice and back to pick up the green lightning bolt. He should end up back near his starting point. Shock needs to cross the ice and trigger the purple button, which powers up the fan near Bolt. Slide Bolt in front of the purple fan, which sends him across the ice to the blue button. Hit the purple button again to power down the purple fan. Slide Shock down the ice in front of the blowing blue fan. Move him up to the conveyor belt under the purple fan, which sends him across the ice just under Bolt. Slide Bolt across the ice (he should stop against the purple fan). Move Shock up to the blue button, then send him through the blue lightning bolt and into Bolt to complete the Spark Lock.

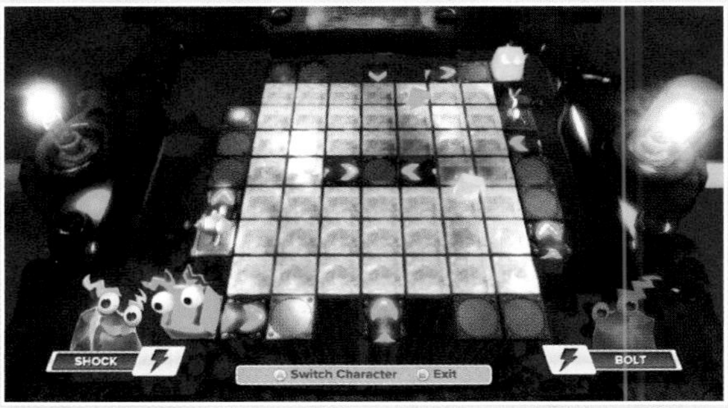

The high-speed transport lands not far from a SWAP Zone Challenge. Take an immediate left and walk through the valves, which spawn Pastepetal Chompies, and open the **Treasure Chest**. Take out the Chompies and head toward the SWAP Zone.

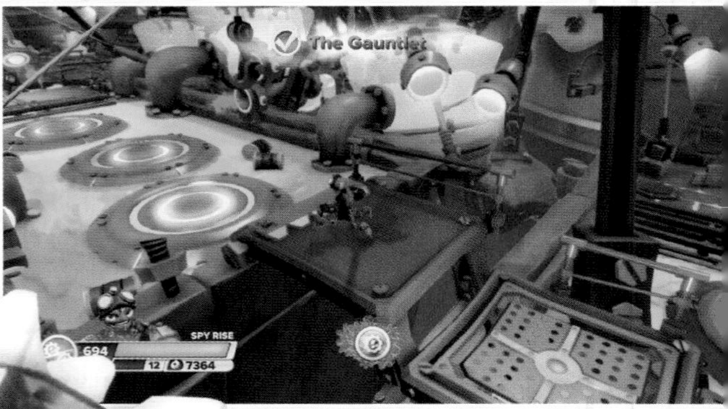

SWAP Zone
Tower of Falling Goo

CLIMB TO THE TOP!
Turn to page 269 for tips on how to clear this SWAP Zone Challenge. Your reward for completing this challenge is the **Undercover Greebles Bonus Mission Map**.

TECH IS STRONGER IN THIS AREA

THE GAUNTLET & GOO PIT OF DOOM

The Gauntlet begins just past the SWAP Zone, in the goo pool with three round platforms. Globlobbers are common at first. Avoid the bouncing balls that come from every direction.

There's a large goo tank part of the way through The Gauntlet called the Goo Pit of Doom. The yellow goo in the pool rises and falls quickly, so you must act fast to grab all the gold coins and the **Wool Sweater** near the bottom. Return to the Gauntlet and head up the staircase.

TECH IS STRONGER IN THIS AREA

SHEEPLIGHT CHECKPOINT & SUPER DUPER GUARDPOST

Take out the small enemy force at the top of the stairs. The next flight of stairs upward leads to a dual elemental gate. The staircase to the left continues toward the last Sheepshooter inside Super Duper Guardpost.

GOO POND

Influenced by wild tales he heard, Mildmaw wants someone to catch a fish in the Goo Pond since he hasn't been able to do it himself. It's a tricky fish to reel in with nearly ten eels in the pool. Hook the fish, reel it in carefully, and Mildmaw hands over the **Skylander Scope** Legendary Treasure. After a moment, he seems pleased with the exchange!

A Battle Gate slams shut just before a goo pool and you must deal with K-Bot units to open it. The goo in the next room rises and falls, and security bots scan the area for non-sheep entities.

The gate at the opposite end is locked. The key needed to unlock the gate is on a nearby platform to the right. Get the key, unlock the gate and report to Softpaw on the other side.

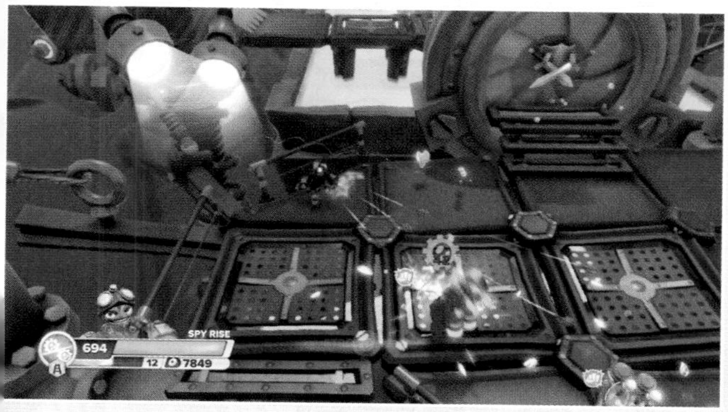

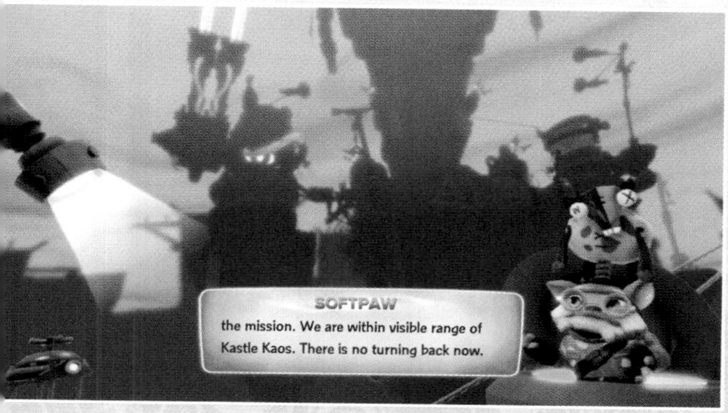

SOFTPAW
the mission. We are within visible range of Kastle Kaos. There is no turning back now.

Super Duper Guardpost is an accurate description of the area where your Skylander touches down. A Battle Gate slams shut immediately. There are glob lobbers in one corner, and there is no shortage of enemies appearing in large groups. When the Battle Gate drops, head through to the other side and solve the Spark Lock to take down the last Sheepshooter. There's no trip to Woodburrow afterward. Instead, you take on Kaos' Mom!

SPARK LOCK

Ping-Pong

Switch to Bolt and hit the orange button. The orange button raises platforms and turns on the orange fan. Hit the blue button with Shock and Bolt should end up against the purple column. Hit the purple button with Shock, move Bolt onto the purple column, and hit the purple button again to raise up Bolt. Move Shock up one space, then slide Bolt across on the orange platform. Move Bolt down to the green lightning bolt and carefully move Bolt onto the orange platform. Slide across and grab the blue lightning bolt, then slide back across to meet up with Bolt.

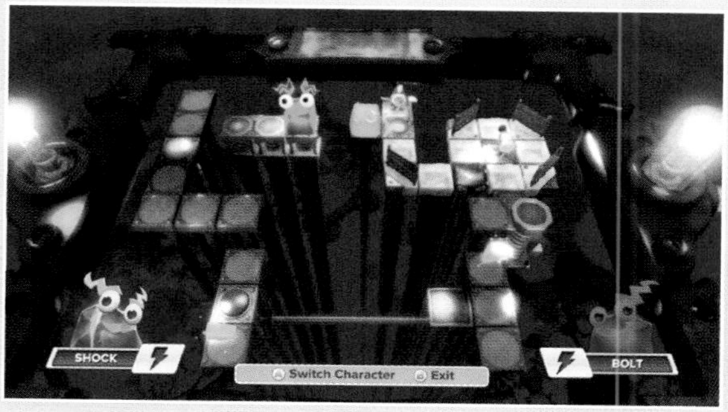

MOTHERLY MAYHEM

OBJECTIVES

Story Goals

- ◯ Defeat Kaos' Mom
- ◯ No Skylanders Defeated
- ◯ No Damage Taken

New Enemies

Bubba Greebs

DEFEAT KAOS' MOM

As if to show that the rotten apple didn't fall from the gnarled old tree, Kaos' Mom floats safely above the floor, keeping her hands clean while you face her minions. She first sends out evilized creatures to deal with you. These creatures are identical to the ones you faced throughout the Story Mode.

When she runs out of minions, Kaos' Mom vanishes! She is trying to hide within her *Portal of Power*. To reveal her location, remove any Skylanders on your *Portal of Power*. She wasn't expecting you to find her, so she flees back to Kaos' Fortress.

Kaos' Mom returns to her position, floating above the floor. However, two large, green crystals appeared on the floor while everyone was in the *Portal of Power*. Kaos' Mom fires a beam at the floor and directs it toward your Skylander. Run behind one of the green crystals so the beam hits it. The crystal absorbs the beam and fires it back at Kaos' Mom, who then flies away to another room.

The next room includes bench seating for an audience, though some of the creatures in the seats join the fight. This round of the fight begins like the last, with evilized enemies attacking in groups while Kaos' Mom stays above the fight on her *Portal of Power*. Watch out for any Life Spell Punks. When one appears, make it your number one target.

After you defeat all the evilized creatures, Kaos' Mom vanishes from her *Portal of Power*. Remove your Skylander from the *Portal of Power* to chase her back into Kaos' Fortress.

When your Skylander is back in the game, Kaos' Mom blasts the ground with her beam attack. Run behind either one of the crystals to deflect it back at her. She flies off again after the beam hits her.

Follow the red carpet, but watch out for glob lobbers on either side. There are a few destructible objects on either side of the hallway at various points along the way.

The red carpet leads from the hallway into the throne room. Kaos' Mom sends out Bubba Greebs, an incredibly large Greeble, to deal with you this time. Bubba Greebs throws various types of Greebles from the balcony. He also throws explosives. You must avoid the red circles on the ground, but watch for a bundle of dynamite to appear on the ground nearby.

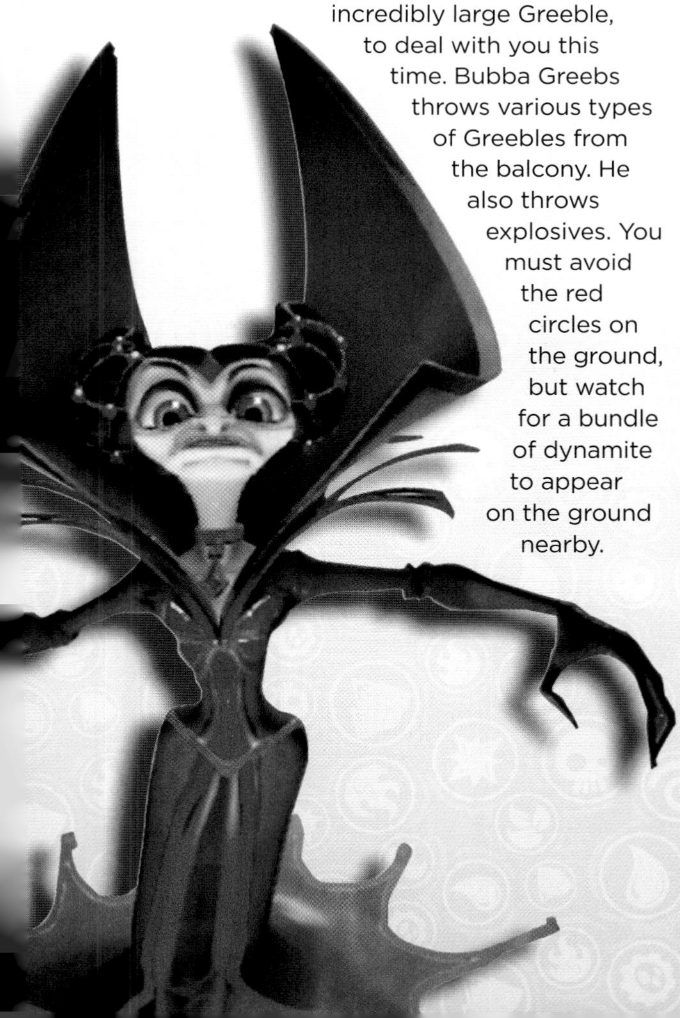

Pick up the dynamite and throw it at Bubba Greebs to knock him down to the floor. He sends out a shockwave where he lands, so jump over it and attack him quickly. The Greebles on the floor don't vanish when Bubba Greebs hits the ground, and they won't sit and watch while you attack their large friend. Bubba Greebs continues to throw dynamite until you knock him down, so don't worry about missing an opportunity if a bundle of dynamite goes unused.

After taking some damage, Bubba Greebs recovers and jumps back up to his spot on the balcony. He resumes throwing Greebles and explosives into the lower area, though the types of Greeble change each time you knock him down and damage him.

Once Bubba Greebs runs out of health, Kaos' Mom reappears just long enough to retreat into her *Portal of Power*. Take your Skylander off your *Portal of Power* to return her to the fight.

When everyone is back in the throne room, she fires her beam attack again, but this time there are no crystals! Run away from the beam until Tessa intervenes. Run onto the mirror's surface when it appears and finally defeat Kaos' Mom!

Back in Woodburrow

Rufus and the Chieftess provide an update on Kaos' plans. Speak with Tessa to begin the final fight to save the Skylands from an age of darkness.

CLOUDBREAK CORE

OBJECTIVES

Story Goals

- ◯ Defeat Super Evil Kaos
- ◯ No Skylanders Defeated
- ◯ No Damage Taken

DEFEAT SUPER EVIL KAOS

The first stage of the fight takes place at the feet of Super Evil Kaos. Avoid the shockwaves after he stomps the ground with the Thundersteps of Doom, and attack the crystallized darkness on his toenails. He attacks with both feet, so you must clear the crystals from both.

After half the crystals on his toes have been destroyed, Kaos stomps on the ground twice before letting his foot rest long enough to be attacked. Keep moving from toe to toe when one is depleted of crystals.

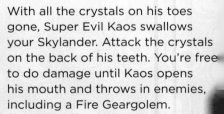

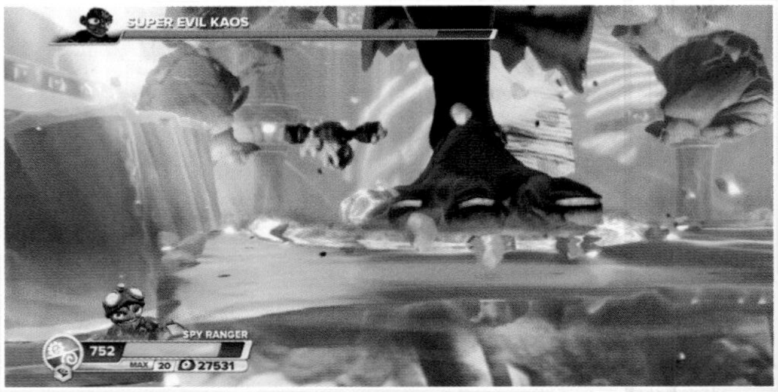

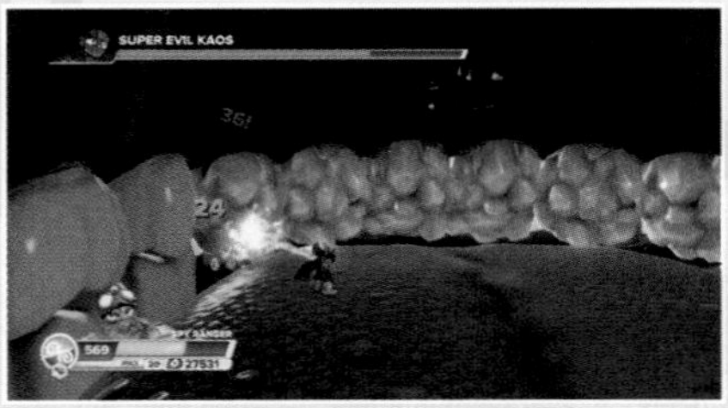

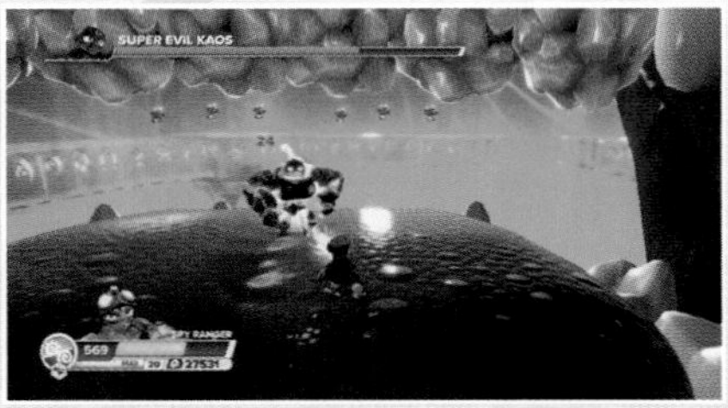

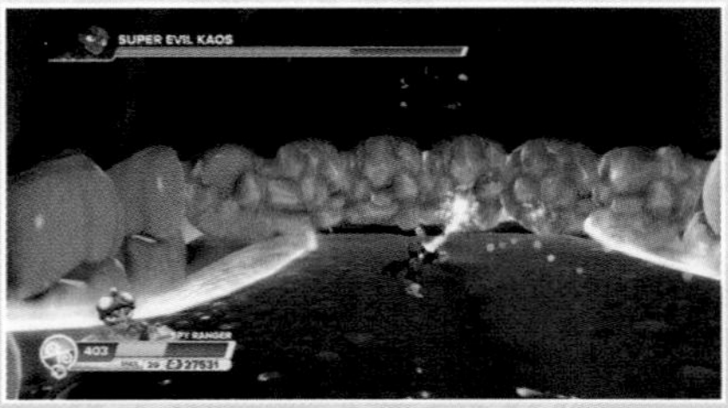

With all the crystals on his toes gone, Super Evil Kaos swallows your Skylander. Attack the crystals on the back of his teeth. You're free to do damage until Kaos opens his mouth and throws in enemies, including a Fire Geargolem.

When you've defeated the enemies, Kaos slams his mouth shut and two shockwaves form from his molars. Jump over both shockwaves and get back to attacking his teeth. Kaos does another bite down, which sends more shockwaves through his mouth.

Kaos throws in another batch of enemies including Ice Geargolem, The group after that has a Tech Geargolem. The next wave of enemies includes both a Tech Geargolem and an Air Geargolem. Keep attacking the teeth and avoiding shockwaves between enemy group appearances. After the final crystal on his teeth is destroyed, your Skylander moves to Kaos' ear canal and into his brain.

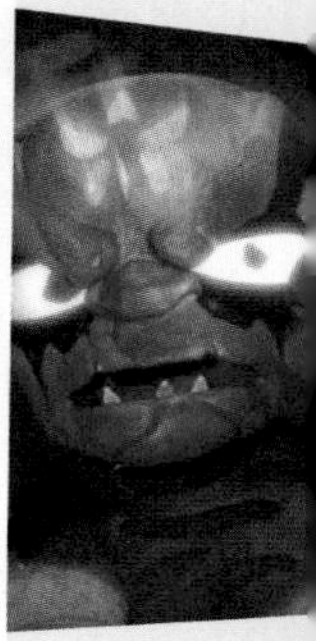

Kaos sends minions to defend himself. First up is Glumshanks in his vehicle. It is invulnerable to damage, so just avoid it until it falls off the edge. Up next are enemies you can damage, so take them down as they appear. Grumblebum Thrashers are up first, along with a Boom Boss.

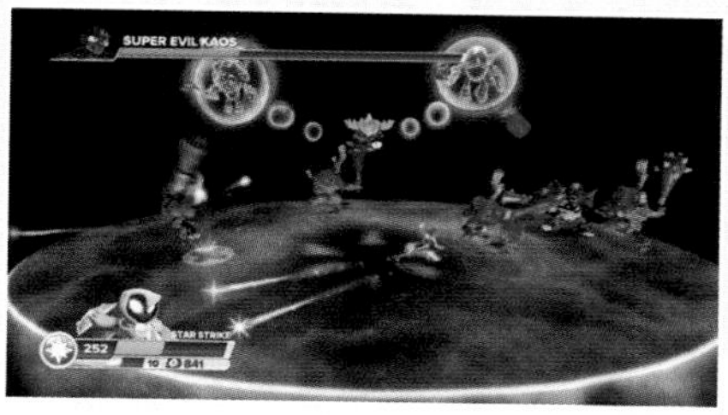

With those enemies out of the way, three shards of crystallized darkness are embedded in the ground. Attack the shards to destroy them, but watch out for the missiles falling from above.

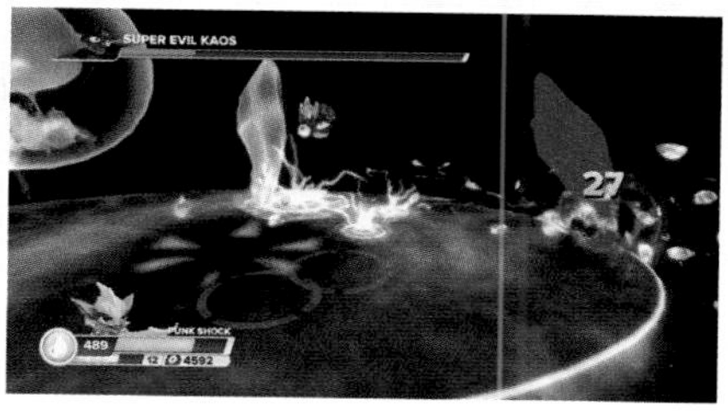

The next wave of enemies is made up of Arkeyan Rip-rotors and Cyclops Gazermages. When you defeat them, three more crystal shards appear. Avoid the incoming missiles and destroy the shards.

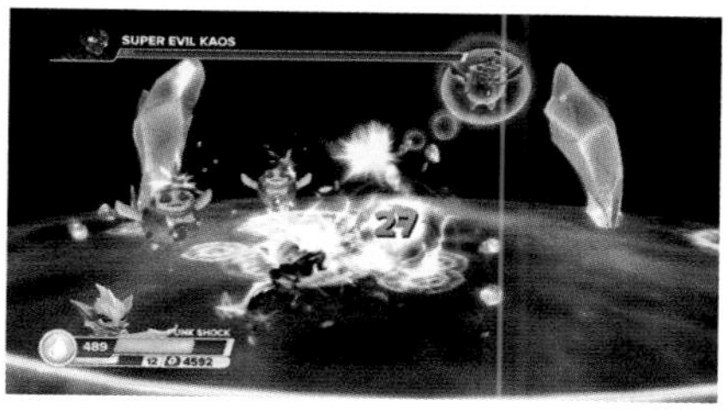

The next wave of enemies is a swarm of Kaos sheep. They don't have any range abilities, so keep on the move so they don't overwhelm you with their numbers. Kaos doesn't bother with missiles this time. Instead he sends out Mesmeralda's proximity mine puppets!

Destroying the final three crystals induces a sneeze from Kaos that sends your Skylander out of his head. There's a nearby weapon that's ready to be used against Kaos, but he makes the sprint there as hard as possible.

Every few seconds, Kaos fires a giant purple beam from his hands that destroys everything in its path. He sweeps the beam back down the path toward your Skylander. When it draws near, jump over the beam and hurry ahead.

When your Skylander reaches the cannon, charge it up quickly and end Kaos' latest threat to the Skylands!

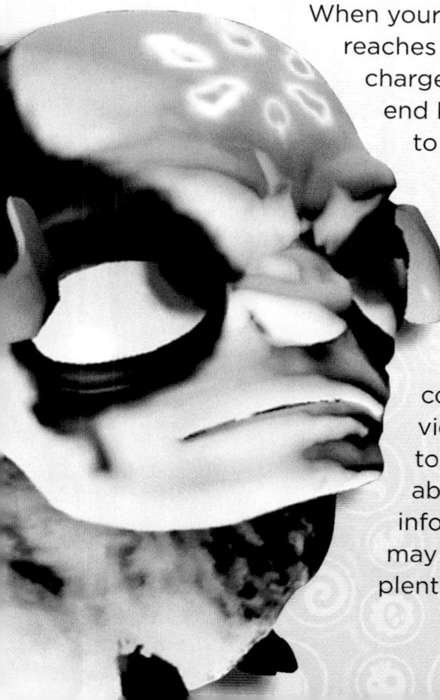

Back at Woodburrow

Rufus, Tessa, and Flynn congratulate you on your amazing victory over Kaos. Rufus urges you to visit with Wheellock to learn about Score Mode, and Avril for more information about Timed Attack. You may have defeated Kaos, but there's still plenty more to do!

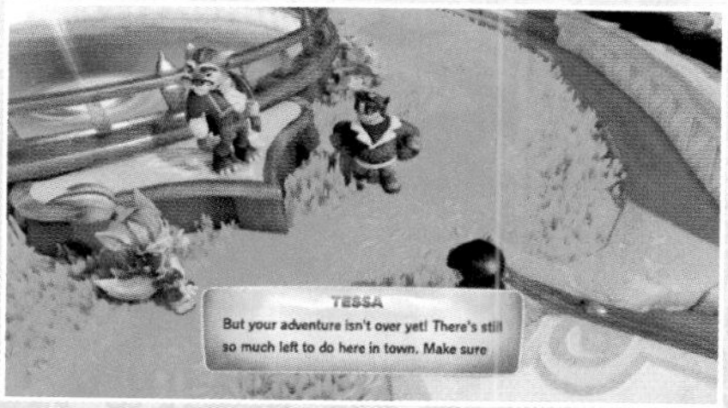

SHEEP WRECK ISLANDS

OBJECTIVES

Story Goals

- ◯ Destroy the Sheep Mage's staff

Dares

- **3** Golden Sheep
- **50** Enemy Goal
- **0** No Skylanders Defeated

New Enemies

Vortex Geargolem

Cyclops Coldspear

Cyclops Brawlbuckler

Cyclops Sleetthrower

Collections

- **16** Areas Discovered
- **3** Treasure Chests
- **1** Giant Treasure Chest
- **0** Soul Gems
- **3** Legendary Treasures
- **3** Hats
- **1** Bonus Mission Map
- **2** Winged Sapphire
- **1** Story Scroll

SHEEPY SHORES

Where the path splits near Sheepy Flynn, follow the trail of coins to the right. The path doesn't go far but it does introduce giant clams, a unique feature of Sheep Wreck Islands. Interact with the giant clams wherever you see them to pry open their shells and pick up a bit of loot.

Follow the other trail of coins near Sheepy Flynn to get a demonstration of another unique feature of Sheep Wreck Islands, a golden vortex. Anything that touches a vortex is sent to a nearby dark hole floating above the ground. These vortices are common on Sheep Wreck Islands, so keep your eyes open for them. They're not always directly in your path.

Follow the sheep's example and zip over to the next area via the vortex. Your first enemies for the level pop up out of the sand here. They look different, but most enemies on Sheep Wreck Islands are Coldspear and other cyclopes dressed for warmer weather. If you aren't convinced yet, just watch their attacks. They all look familiar.

Look for a **Treasure Chest** beyond the second golden vortex. It's on the ground, just past the sheep-themed sliding block. Push the block along the path and use it to reach the vortex. Step into the vortex to reach the next ledge.

A
G
F
D
START
C
A
B
C
B
Map Key
SWAP Zone Challenges
Treasure Chest
Giant Treasure Chest
Soul Gem
Legendary Treasure
Hat
Bonus Mission Map
Winged Sapphire
Story Scroll
Dare
Checkpoint
Vortex
E
D
FINISH
E
F
G

UNDEAD IS STRONGER IN THIS AREA

BLIND BEARD'S SHIP & ANCIENT RUINS

Push the sliding block under the vortex destination point, then step through the vortex. Walk around the ship's deck to grab a few extra coins and a **Story Scroll, The Platinum Sheep**.

The area down the gangplank is the Ancient Ruins, where a triple-locked gate blocks your progress. The Sheep Mage is there as well, and he turns into a giant sheep that sucks in and blows out air. The keys for the gate are caught in this shifting windstorm. Grab the keys as quickly as you can, but avoid the orange spiny creatures on the beach. Their spines hurt and the Sheep Mage tries his best to push your Skylander into them. The houses in the area are sturdy enough to shelter you from the wind when you need it.

The golden vortex beyond the locked gate sends your Skylander to a small, floating island nearby. There's a SWAP Zone to the left and a few cyclopes waiting not far from it.

SWAP Zone
Sheep Strafing

ROCKET TO THE FINISH!

Turn to page 272 for tips on how to clear this SWAP Zone Challenge. Your reward for completing this Challenge is a **Winged Sapphire**.

The next vortex leads to a long, narrow island a short distance ahead, with giant columns which rise and dip. Walk toward them, but when you see a sliding block on a raised ledge, push it into the vortex in front of it. After the block settles in, send your Skylander through the vortex.

Jump on the first column then wait for it to descend. Jump to the right and grab the **Golden Sheep**. Ride the column back up and move across the remaining columns. The Sheep Mage pops up again at the end of the columns, but he's only there to boast this time.

UNDEAD IS STRONGER IN THIS AREA

CYCLOPS' SHIP

The Battle Gate at the opposite end of the deck blocks access to a Bounce Pad. You must clear out a small army of various cyclopes to clear the Battle Gate from the Bounce Pad. The glowing doorway leads to the Temple Islands. Before you step through the doorway, step to the left for an Undead Gate.

SKULL FIELDS

Spinning arms of flaming skulls are everywhere in this zone. Treat them like other, similar hazards: carefully walk behind the arms when you can and jump over the skulls when they're coming at your Skylander.

There's a quick fight against a few cyclopes, including a Bucklebrawler, but there aren't enough of them to be a real threat. Open the gift box just beyond the cyclops encounter for a new hat, the **Tree Branch**.

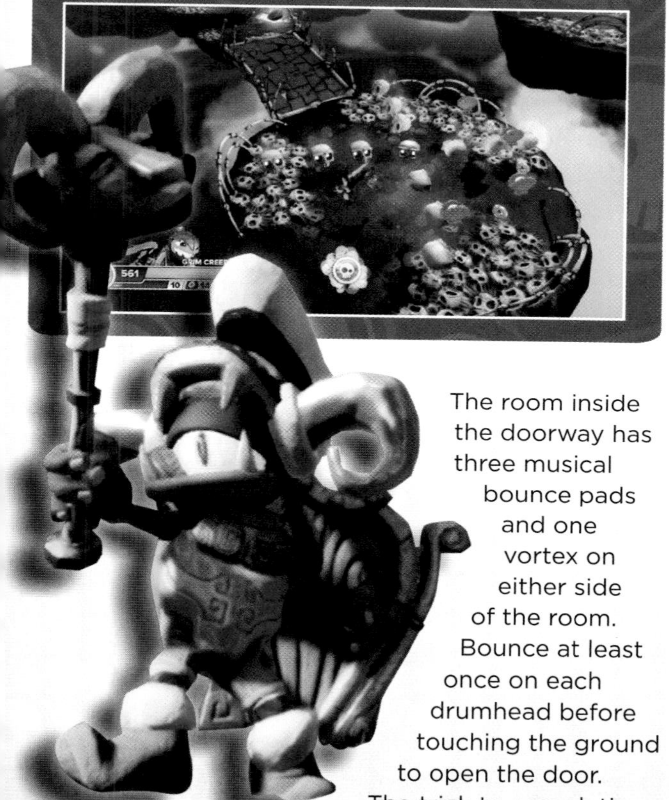

The room inside the doorway has three musical bounce pads and one vortex on either side of the room. Bounce at least once on each drumhead before touching the ground to open the door. The trick to completing this puzzle is that you must start with the drumhead nearest the entrance, and then bounce from there into either vortex. From the second drumhead, bounce into the vortex on the same side when it is in range.

TEMPLE ISLANDS, TEMPLE OF WOOL & ARR-SHEEP-ELAGOS

A vortex hops your Skylander across a few small floating islands, though the trip is interrupted by a new enemy, the Vortex Geargolem. Vortex Geargolems employ a variety of tricks. First, they spawn enemies from the vortex in their chest that gives them their name. Second, they shoot out golden vortices that pull whatever they touch directly in front of the Vortex Geargolem. Finally, they have a ground slam attack that sends a shockwave over a small area.

When the Vortex Geargolem falls, it drops the missing piece to the door it was defending. Carry it to the doorway to get it to open, speak with Blind Beard, then head inside the Temple of Wool.

The gift box visible near the entrance of the Temple is too high to reach with a jump. Push the block on the lowest floor into the vortex in front of it. Get on top of that block (either use the vortex as well, or jump up to it from the floor) to reach the next higher floor. Push the nearby block over the edge and into the same vortex.

When the block appears on top of the block you moved earlier, push it across the raised platform to create a bridge to the ledge with the gift box. Open the box and claim your hard-earned **Winged Sapphire**.

Go back up one level and pull the lever to raise a platform in the waterway. Jump into the nearby vortex and try to avoid the mine circling it. Use the rising column to reach the next door. Use the vortex on the left to move inside the sliding block puzzle area.

Push the block into the vortex, and follow it in. Slide the next two blocks to create a clear path. The first block ends up in front of the vortex again and it's fine there for now. Push the second block over the edge and follow it down. Grab the **Thief on the Run Bonus Mission Map** from behind the water.

Head back up to the sliding puzzle area and push sliding blocks out of the way to make a clear path. The exit is just ahead, but don't leave until you grab the **Giant Treasure Chest** near the exit. Step into the moving vortex flanked on both sides by mines to reach the higher area. There's a quick fight against a Cyclops Brawlbuckler before you can claim the treasure.

The bridges linking the floating islands that make up Arr-sheep-elagos end at a tricky jump where a vortex spins with a pair of mines. The next vortex hop drops your Skylander into the middle of a group of cyclopes. Take them down, open the nearby giant clam, and use the vortex to hop to the next island.

There are two vortices nearby. One is on the island, not far away. Go through that vortex first, claim the **Treasure Chest** on that island, and use the vortex there to jump back to the island with two vortices. The second vortex, the one that is floating off the platform, leads to a Checkpoint, and there's no return trip back from it.

ITCHY CAVES & RAM GALLEY

✓ The area past the Power Pod is the Itchy Caves, and it starts off with a Battle Gate. The defenders are primarily cyclopes, but a Vortex Geargolem shows up as well.

There are more cyclops defenders ahead, and they like to attack when mines are in the area, so be careful. Watch to the right, off the side of the path, for a vortex. It leads to a small island with a SWAP Zone Challenge.

SWAP Zone
Wool Over Their Eyes

SNEAK IN AND DESTROY THE FORTRESS! DON'T GET CAUGHT BY SPOTLIGHTS.

Turn to page 274 for tips on how to clear this SWAP Zone Challenge. Your reward for completing this challenge is the **Aviator's Cap**.

The Ram Galley kicks off with another puzzle that involves sliding blocks and vortices. Push all the blocks into position on the ground before jumping into the first vortex. One block starts on top of an immobile box and must be pushed through the vortex in front of it to be positioned correctly. The final block in the puzzle must be slid under the vortex drop off point directly in front of the glowing yellow entrance on the ledge above.

Don't immediately go through the doorway when you reach the higher ledge. Walk around to the side and pick up the **Golden Sheep**. Now you're free to continue.

The next room is another musical bounce pad puzzle. There are four drumheads to bounce off of before touching the ground this time. The first jump must be between the two drumheads nearest the entrance of the area. When they're both lit, jump into a vortex for the third drumhead, and finally into the other vortex to hit the last drumhead.

Go through the opened door and move toward the bottom of the screen. The vortex a short jump away leads up to the top of the ship. There is a **Treasure Chest** behind a mine up there. Drop off the side of the higher deck and run across the floating round platforms ahead.

EARTH IS STRONGER IN THIS AREA

WOOLY CAVES

A Cyclops Brawlbuckler and Cyclops Sleethrowers appear and block your path. Use the vortex floating in the air off to the right to reach the Sleetthrowers and the dual elemental gate behind them.

VOLCANO RIDE

The glowing skull hazards are back, but this time, they are stationary while your Skylander is the one riding a moving platform! Look for gaps in the lines of skulls and jump over them when you can't find a gap.

During the second round of dealing with the skulls, they move from side to side, making passage even trickier. After a few jumps through a vortex or two, you end up at a gift box containing the **Creepy Helm**.

The Sheep Mage makes an amusing appearance at a Battle Gate, but the Vortex Geargolem and cyclopes left behind mean business. Take them down, but don't go through the opened Battle Gate yet.

Flip the switch on the right and go up the staircase formed by the columns. Hop into the vortex to land on a boat with a **Golden Sheep**. Use the nearby vortex to return to the Battle Gate area. The switch on the left side creates a path to a ship filled with piles of gold.

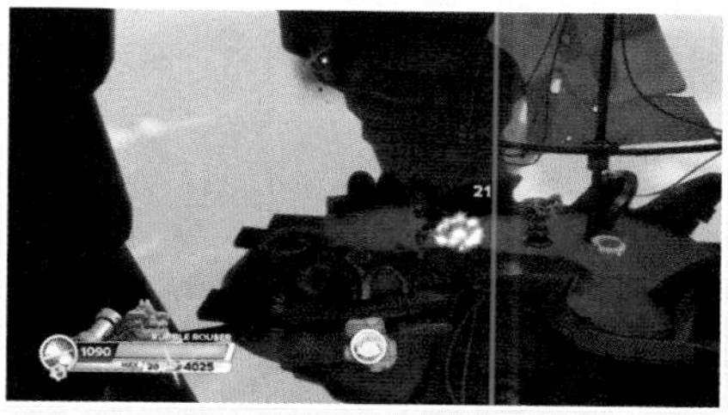

Go through the blue doorway to enter an area filled with rising and falling columns. The path splits near another blue doorway. The path away from the door ends at a few piles of gold. After you collect them, head for the exit.

LIFE IS STRONGER IN THIS AREA

OLD SHEEP CLIFF

The way ahead is blocked by another door with a large medallion missing from its center. Take out the enemies guarding the door, but none of them have the missing part. Go to the right, past the rising and falling columns, and pick up the **Deputee Badge** Legendary Treasure from a gift box.

The vortex between the rising and falling columns and the nearby ledge is the only way to get the piles of gold on that ledge. Return to the broken doorway area by dropping off the edge to the left and landing on the larger island area.

The area to the left of the broken doorway is another encounter with the Sheep Mage's breathing. Duck behind shelter when the Sheep Mage breathes in or out and move quickly across the area while his mouth is shut.

There's a SWAP Zone and a blue doorway just past the Sheep Mage. The blue doorway leads to a small cave and the missing piece to the door. Grab the medallion by jumping into the vortex, then stop for a quick chat with Blind Beard. Return to the door and fix it, then step inside the Temple of Baaaaa.

SWAP Zone

Beached Blinkout

COLLECT THE MAGIC RUNES TO SEAL THE DIMENSIONAL RIFT!

Turn to page 278 for tips on how to clear this SWAP Zone Challenge. Your reward for completing this challenge is the Legendary Treasure, **Urban Art**.

TEMPLE OF BAAAAA

There's an Air Gate all the way across from the entrance on the lowest level. You need to clear out a few boxes to reach it. Push the sheep-themed block not far from the Air Gate across the room into the vortex near the entrance.

LAMBALLOON

The first half of the area requires patience if you want to collect all the coins. A few balloons pass lazily through lines of coins, and there's nothing you can do to speed them up. The next area has tents that continually pop up your Skylanders as they land on them.

Outside of a fight against a Vortex Geargolem and lines of mines scattered around, the challenge to crossing this area is timing your jumps to land in the right spot at the right time instead of falling a long way before reappearing on a nearby platform. When you finally reach the end, the gift box waiting there has the **Amber Treasure** Legendary Treasure

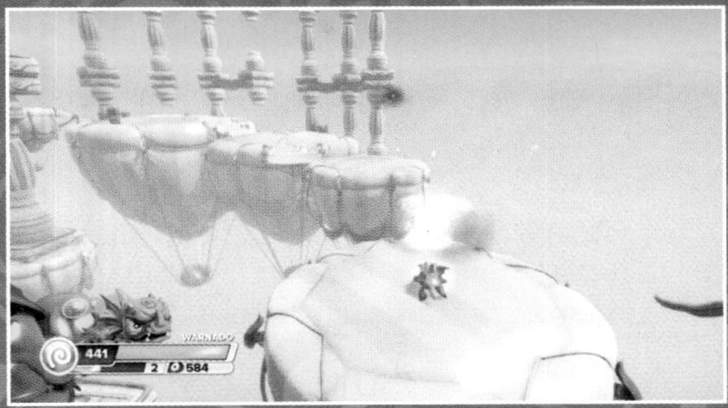

Before you can leave the Temple, you must clear the Battle Gate blocking the exit. Clear out the cyclopes and a Vortex Geargolem to remove the gate, then head outside for the final confrontation with the Sheep Mage.

Use the vortex nearest the Air Gate to reach a ledge above the entrance. Push the sliding block off the ledge, jump to the next ledge and repeat the process. Drop down to the floor, slide the block against the broken staircase, then use it to reach the next floor.

Mines and the Sheep Mage's breath complicate the trip across the upper floor. Fortunately, the statues lining the hallway block the breathing. Use the vortex at the end of the hall to reach the uppermost level of the Temple.

ALTAR OF WORSHEEP

The Sheep Mage changes into his giant sheep form and spends most of his time sucking in and blowing out air, pushing and pulling your Skylander and the Sheep Mage's own cyclops minions, around the Altar of Worsheep.

Stay as far from the giant sheep as possible. The spiny orange creatures that appeared throughout Sheep Wreck Islands line the area directly in front of the Sheep Mage. Try to take down any cyclopes when the opportunity presents itself, but staying away from the spiny orange creatures is your number one priority.

When Blind Beard appears, he tosses a timed bomb that you must retrieve and throw at the Sheep Mage. When the Mage falls to the ground and drops the Magic Staff, a few mines spawn and circle the area. Avoid the mines and attack the Magic Staff. After a short while, the Sheep Mage recovers and returns to his position outside the battle area. The mines are destroyed and more cyclopes spawn.

The types of cyclopes spawning are slightly tougher than the first group you faced. Repeat your tactics from the first stage. Stay clear of the area directly in front of the Sheep Mage and take down the cyclopes when you can. When you use the timed bomb on the Sheep Mage the second time, far more mines spawn, and getting past them is trickier. Watch for the ones that move and run through the gaps that appear. Attack the Magic Staff until the Sheep Mage recovers and resets the area.

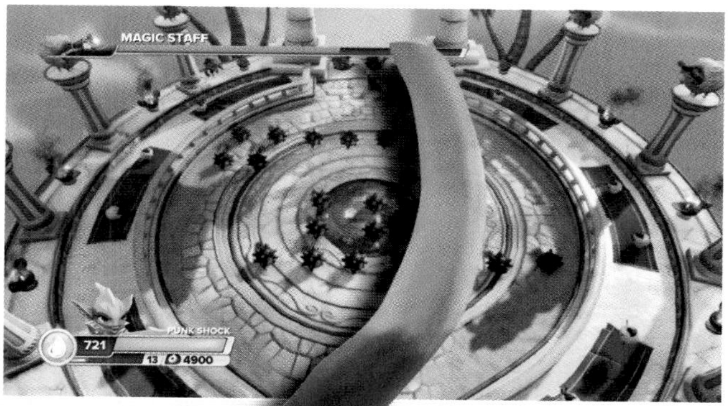

The next wave of minions includes a Vortex Geargolem. Don't relax after you take down the first one. Two more spawn immediately! Focus on one enemy at a time until it's down, then switch to the other one. When Blind Beard appears with the third bomb, the mines that appear around the Magic Staff are set up similar to the first set, but are more numerous and move around the area faster. Attack the Magic Staff again and destroy it. It's a happy ending for everyone, especially Flynn.

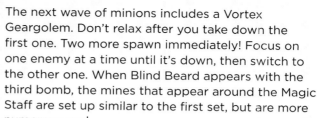

TOWER OF TIME

OBJECTIVES

Story Goals

- Place the missing gears in the town center
- Find the gear in the Steam Works
- Find the gear in the Wind Works
- Find the gear in the Water Works
- Enter the Tower and defeat Cluck

Dares

- 3 Tool Box
- 50 Enemy Goal
- 0 No Skylanders Defeated

Collections

- 9 Areas Discovered
- 3 Treasure Chests
- 1 Giant Treasure Chest
- 0 Soul Gems
- 3 Legendary Treasure
- 2 Hats
- 1 Bonus Mission Map
- 2 Winged Sapphire
- 1 Story Scroll

New Enemies

Time Spell Punk

Clock Geargolem

Boom Boss

Cadet Crusher

Loose Cannon

TIMES CIRCLE

The Tower of Time introduces two new objects that are a big part of playing through this Adventure Pack, and the first one comes up immediately. Time-Freeze switches stop time for everything except your Skylander and a type of Spell Punk who shows up soon and, yes, you'll loathe them immediately.

Use the Time-Freeze switch when the bridge behind the Timekeeper is in place. The Time-Freeze effect doesn't last long, but it's enough time to get past the bridge. Listen for the sound in the background to speed up for a clue when the effect is about to end. The background flickers and the area's normal colors slowly return.

The trolls in Times Circle are time-themed versions of more familiar trolls encountered earlier in the Story Mode (in this case, Cadet Crushers). They might be a bit tougher, but their attacks are the same.

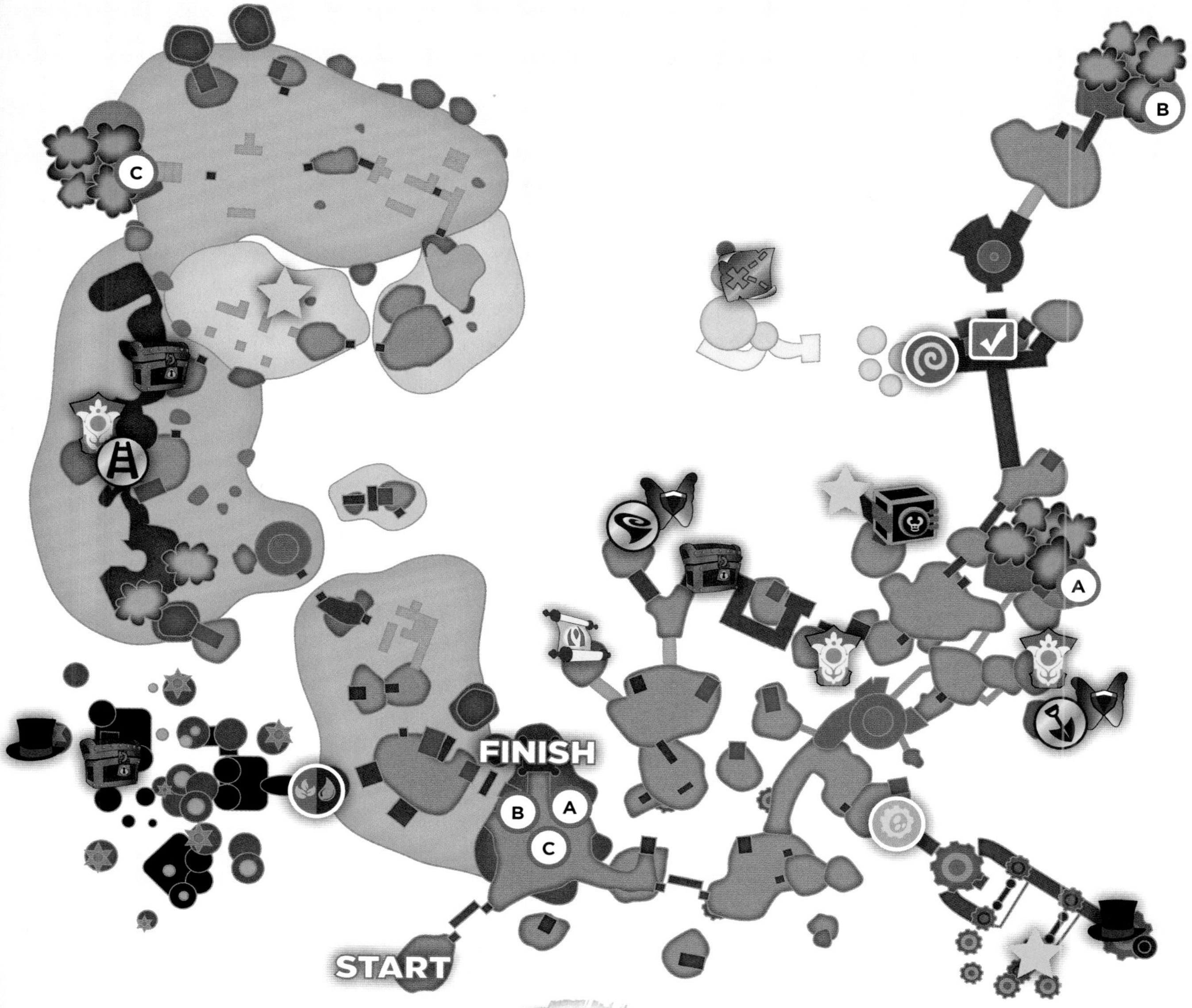

Map Key

	SWAP Zone Challenges
	Treasure Chest
	Giant Treasure Chest
	Soul Gem
	Legendary Treasure
	Hat
	Bonus Mission Map
	Winged Sapphire
	Story Scroll
	Dare
	Checkpoint

Use the Time-Freeze switch to your advantage whenever you can. It's not like you earn bonus points for taking down active enemies instead of time frozen ones.

With the trolls out of the way, the Timekeeper points out the way to pick up one of the gears needed to open the Tower of Time. Head through the gate and use the Time-Freeze switch to cross the bridge.

When you run into the Timekeeper again, he introduces the other new feature of the Tower of Time, a control valve. In this case, it's a steam control valve but later valves control water. There are pipes running in two directions from the valve, usually with a platform at the end of both pipes. The arrow above the valve shows the direction of the steam pressure.

The platform at the end with the steam pressure is pushed above the pipe just a bit higher than Skylanders can jump. Interact with the switch to change the pressure to the other direction. Move Skylanders to the lowered platform before the steam reaches it and they'll be lifted into the air on a cushion of steam. The pitch of the steam changes as it moves through pipes, and provides an idea of how close it is to reaching the lowered platform. For this first use of steam power, switch the steam pressure and ride the platform up to grab the key needed to open the Locked Gate ahead and enter the Steam Works.

STEAM WORKS

Not far from a Tech Gate, there are both a Time-Freeze Switch and a steam valve control. Whenever you see a Time-Freeze switch near a control valve, the steam moves too quickly to reach the platforms before the steam pushes it into the air.

RICKARD'S GEAR

The first things to greet you inside Rickard's Gear are both a Time-Freeze switch and a steam valve control. To make things more interesting, the only way to use the steam valve control is to freeze time so the bridge under the steam valve control is up. Hit the Time-Freeze switch and switch the steam direction, but don't worry about getting on top of the lowered steam platform. There is a **Tool Box** on the right side to pick up first. When the left platform is up, freeze time again, switch the steam direction, and hop up on the platform to the right to pick up the **Tool Box.**

Use the Time-Freeze switch and steam valve controls again and ride the platform on the left up to the top. There's another pair of controls beyond the first. Use the controls together to earn some extra gold from the right platform and the **Leprechaun Hat** from the left.

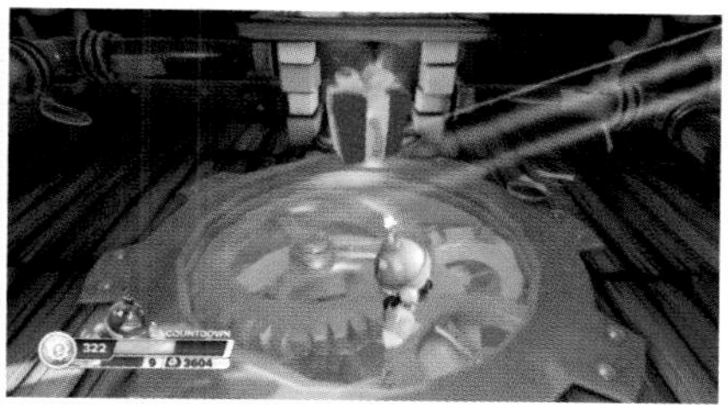

Use the steam valve control along with the Time-Freeze switch to get the key from the right side and use it to unlock the gate on the left. The next gate is a Battle Gate and you must take down a few trolls before it opens. Use the Time-Freeze switch in the middle of the battle area to make the fight easier.

In the area beyond the Battle Gate, the right side platform leads up to a little house and a SWAP Zone. Go inside the house, which has the **Waterfall Decanter** Legendary Treasure is inside.

If you're playing on the Wii console, the Waterfall Decanter is in front of the house to the left of the Dig Swap Zone.

SWAP Zone
Tick Tock Tunneling

FIND YOUR WAY THROUGH THE DARK! DIG UP THE BLUE CRYSTALS BEFORE TIME RUNS OUT!

Turn to page 271 for tips on how to clear this SWAP Zone Challenge. Your reward for completing this challenge is a **Winged Sapphire**.

Head back down to the Time-Freeze switch. Ride the steam platform on the left up to the higher ledge. Use the Time-Freeze switch on the higher ledge to lock the bridge ahead in place. It's a long run, so if your Skylander has a dash ability, put it to use here.

Head up the path beyond the bridge, which bends around a corner and ends at a nest. Pick up the gear floating over the middle of the nest and wait for your ride to appear.

Flynn drops off your Skylander back in Times Circle. The Timekeeper congratulates your progress, but Cluck interrupts him by sending in his clockwork troll minions. They're supported by a new enemy, the Time Spell Punk. Time Spell Punks have the ability to negate the effects of Time-Freeze switches. They also project fireballs for a long-range attack, and ignite a blast of fire directly in front of themselves to ward off melee attacks. Whenever you see them, attack them first. That won't be hard to remember since they will frustrate you to no end when they're around.

Even though the effect won't last long, hit the Time-Freeze switch to give yourself a second or two to get to the Time Spell Punk. When the Time Spell Punk falls, take down the rest of the attackers while freezing time as often as possible. With the enemies defeated, the Timekeeper points out another open doorway that leads to the Wind Works.

AIR IS STRONGER IN THIS AREA

WIND WORKS

Use the Time-Freeze switch to halt the fan and slide the block between the platforms in front of the fan. Hop across before time resumes and the fan blows the block back to its starting point.

The guards for the Battle Gate at the end of the next area include trolls and a Time Spell Punk. Put the Time-Freeze switch to use, take down the Time Spell Punk, then work on the trolls. Before you move through the opened Battle Gate, walk down the short path to the left of the battle area and pick up the **Story Scroll, The Clock Tower** there.

There is a SWAP Zone just off the path beyond the Battle Gate, across from the first of a few giant elevators in Wind Works. Ride one of the platforms on the first elevator to the top.

You need to take out a few trolls before you can reach the **Treasure Chest** visible from the landing. A red and yellow Boom Boss fires from a higher platform, near the second elevator.

SWAP Zone
Spinning Cogs

DESTROY THE KAOS STATUE!
Turn to page 277 for tips on how to clear this SWAP Zone Challenge. Your reward for completing this challenge is a **Winged Sapphire**.

Step up to the second elevator and ride one of the platforms all the way down to its lowest point. Jump over to the ledge with the gift box, which contains the **Volcano Party Pass** Legendary Treasure.

Jump back on the next platform and ride it up and around to the higher platform on the elevator's path. There is another puzzle that involves fans and a Time-Freeze switch ahead, but first visit the house to the left. Go inside the house and open the **Giant Treasure Chest**, then go up the stairs in the back and out the window to reach the **Tool Box** that was visible from the elevator earlier.

If you're playing on the Wii console, the Giant Treasure Chest is in front of the small house to the left of the push block puzzle. The Tool Box is on the push block puzzle after the wind elevator.

At the Time-Freeze switch and fan puzzle, the push block will do a complete circuit around the track after it is pushed. It hesitates for a second at each corner before moving, but not for long.

Use the Time-Freeze switch to stop the block in front of the platform with the key first. After you have the key, stop the block in front of the path that leads to the Locked gate.

Use the Time-Freeze switch to keep the bridge ahead clear of the long windmill arms spinning through it. It's another long run, so reach the other side of the bridge as quickly as possible, where you hit Tower of Time's Checkpoint.

There is an Air Gate to the left, and the Power Pod is on the right. The path directly ahead leads to a Battle Gate. Visit the Power Pod if your Skylander has any upgrades available.

WINDIANAPOLIS

Activate the Time-Freeze switch and push the sliding block twice. Jump on top of the block, which flies across a short gap. Jump from the block to the rectangular canvas when they're close together. The block is about to drop and you don't want your Skylander on it when that happens.

At the next puzzle area, push the block twice and freeze time. Run up the stairs behind the fans on the left side and hop on the block. Jump off quickly when the block is near the platform with the gift box. Open the box for the **Serpent Attack Bonus Mission Map**.

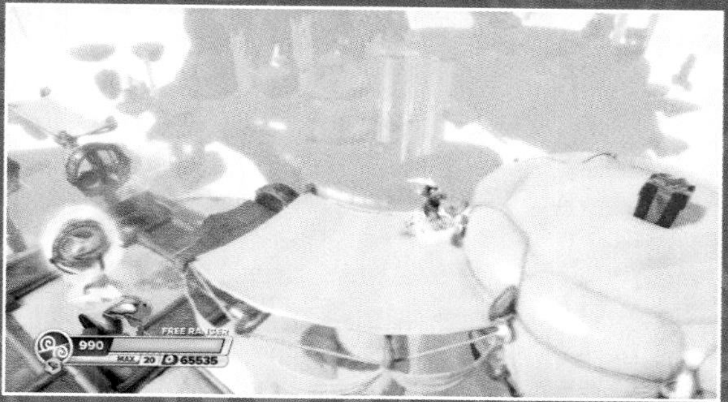

There's a new enemy waiting in the Battle Gate area, and it's nasty. The Clock Geargolem spins constantly and its arms deflect every sort of attack thrown at it. To make matters worse, the Clock Geargolem isn't alone. A few trolls join the fight to make it a bit tougher.

Keep away from the Clock Geargolem and get up to the Time-Freeze switch atop the platforms. While keeping time frozen, take out the trolls first. They're not as big of a threat, but they're also easier to lose track of during the fight. When they're out of the way, hammer away at the Clock Geargolem and always keep time stopped.

When the Battle Gate vanishes, head through to the next area. The sliding block and fan puzzle gets an added twist here, a Time Spell Punk. The first time you use the Time-Freeze switch, a Time Spell Punk appears on the platform next to the place you're trying to reach.

Push the block so the fans start to move it around the track and hop on the platform in the center. Stop time when the block is in front of the platform where the Spell Punk spawns. Jump over to his platform and take him out. The next time you move the block, stop it in the top right corner and use the stairs on the right to get on top of it. Head up the path and grab the gear from the nest. Flynn appears again in the balloon to provide a lift back to Times Circle.

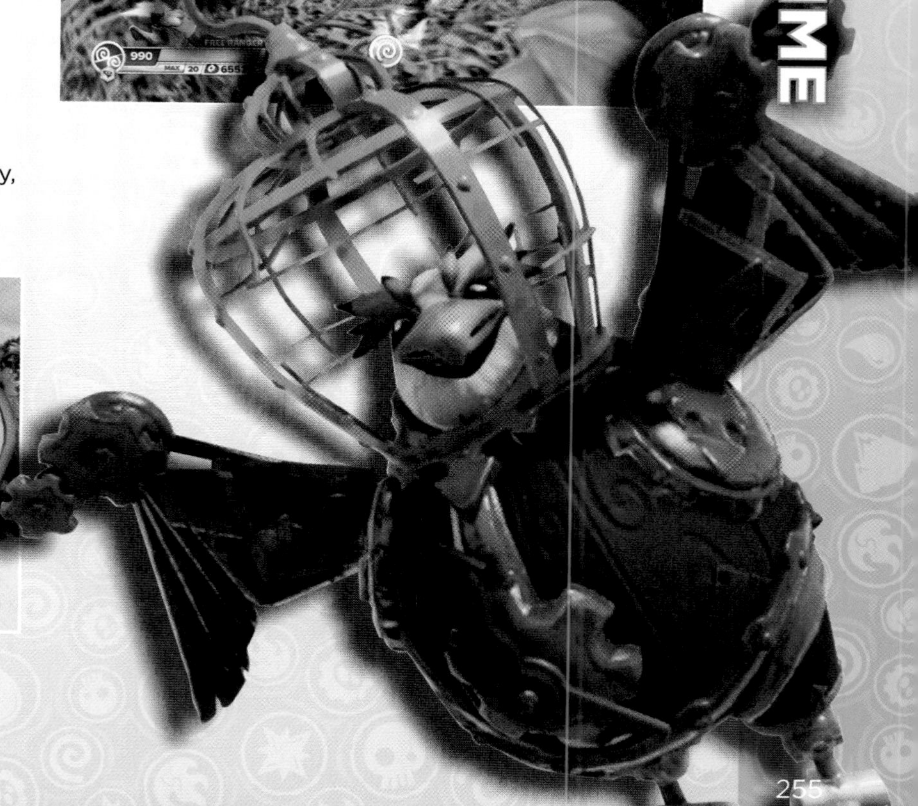

With the second gear in place, Cluck decides to take a more active role in trying to keep everyone out of the Tower of Time. He drops heavily onto the ground, sending out a shockwave that deals damage. Jump over the shockwave, hit the Time-Freeze switch, and attack Cluck while he's on the ground. Cluck calls for troll reinforcements while he recovers from being attacked, though he does shoot energy spheres into the area. Watch for glowing circles on the ground and keep away from them when they appear.

When you've eliminated the trolls, Cluck returns to fight. This time he hits the ground multiple times before he stays down. Use the Time-Freeze switch any time he's on the ground to lock him in place and attack. Just keep track of the shockwaves on the ground. If your Skylander is near one when time flows again, there could be some pain in store. When Cluck is down to about one-quarter health, he decides to tuck tail and run. After the fight, the Timekeeper points out another opened gate that leads to the Water Works.

WATER IS STRONGER IN THIS AREA

WATER WORKS

The Water Works uses water boosters to send Skylanders across long distances. They're on the ground, like standard Bounce Pads, but they always have a spray of white water over them. The water booster just inside the entrance to Water Works leads to a dual elemental gate.

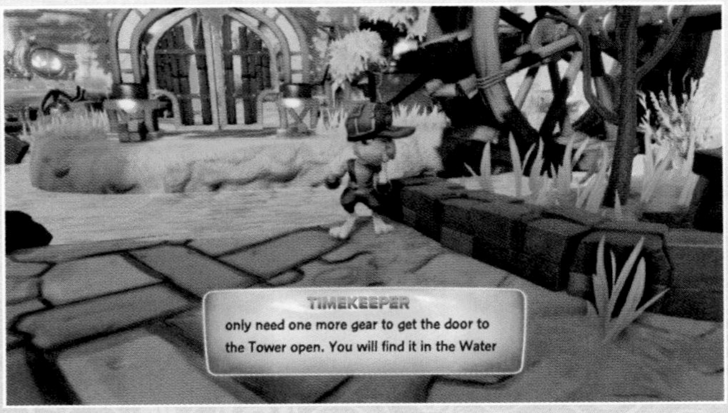

CLOCK SPRINGS

Use the water boosters to grab gold and head toward the back of Clock Springs. There's a fight against a group of trolls near a **Treasure Chest** and a Battle Gate blocks the booster needed to reach the end of the area, and the gift box containing a **Beanie** hat.

Use the water booster ahead to reach a puzzle that involves using water pressure to push a floating hut between two pipes. Use the Time-Freeze switch, turn the water control valve and jump on the hut when it's on the left. When time returns, ride it over to the right side. Hop over to the platform with the key and pick it up.

Hit the water control valve again and hurry over to the Time-Freeze switch. Stop the hut when it's lined up between the area where your Skylander has been running around and the platform in front of the locked gate. Use the key and walk through the gate.

Use the water booster on the other side of the gate to reach a platform with a Time-Freeze switch. A group of trolls appears and attacks. Freeze time as often as possible to keep the fight simple. When the lily pads appear at the back of the platform, jump across them to reach a water booster that flings your Skylander up to the entrance of Mount Clockmore.

MOUNT CLOCKMORE

There's a group of trolls waiting to welcome your Skylander to the area. Look off to the left of where they attacked for a path that ends at a SWAP Zone. When the trolls are out of the way, use the water booster behind them to move up to higher areas.

SWAP Zone

Windy Tower

CLIMB TO THE TOP!

Turn to page 269 for tips on how to clear this SWAP Zone Challenge. Your reward for completing this challenge is the **Epic Soap of Froth** Legendary Treasure.

Jump up another level where there is an entrance to a small house on the left. Step inside the house briefly and open the unguarded **Treasure Chest** within.

If you're playing on the Wii console, this Treasure Chest is in front of the small house in Mount Clockmore.

The water booster just past the house sends your Skylander to a new water and Time-Freeze switch puzzle. There's also a **Tool Box** on the platform next to the key needed to unlock the gate.

The hut closer to the Time-Freeze switch moves back and forth on its own. The water valve controls the hut that begins near the Tool Box.

To get the key, stop time when the nearest hut is where your Skylander can reach it with a jump and it's on a return trip to the platform with the key.

Use the water valve to send the hut across the channel. Move to the Time-Freeze switch and hit it when the nearest hut is in a position that allows your Skylander to jump on it and then to the platform in the middle of the water. Use the water valve again, get to the middle and wait for time to move again. Jump on the hut heading back toward the Tool Box, then up to the Tool Box. (If you're adept at diagonal jumps, it's possible to reach the Tool Box with both huts to the far left.) The water booster sends your Skylander back to the platform, where you should be able to reach the platform with the locked gate.

The water booster beyond the locked gate sends your Skylander to an area blocked by a Battle Gate guarded by a dangerous pair, a Clock Geargolem and a Time Spell Punk.

The Time Spell Punk must go down first, otherwise you'll never be able to stop the Clock Geargolem long enough to damage it. Hit the Time-Freeze switch and track down the Spell Punk. If he stays on the higher ledge, use the water booster near the Battle Gate to get up to him, or the troll who spawns once the Time Spell Punk goes down. When the Battle Gate drops, use the water boosters beyond it to reach another water puzzle.

You only have one hut to work with this time, but that doesn't make for an easier solution. The water valve controls two pipes at a time. The two on the side with the key are linked, as are the two pipes on the same side of the puzzle as the valve.

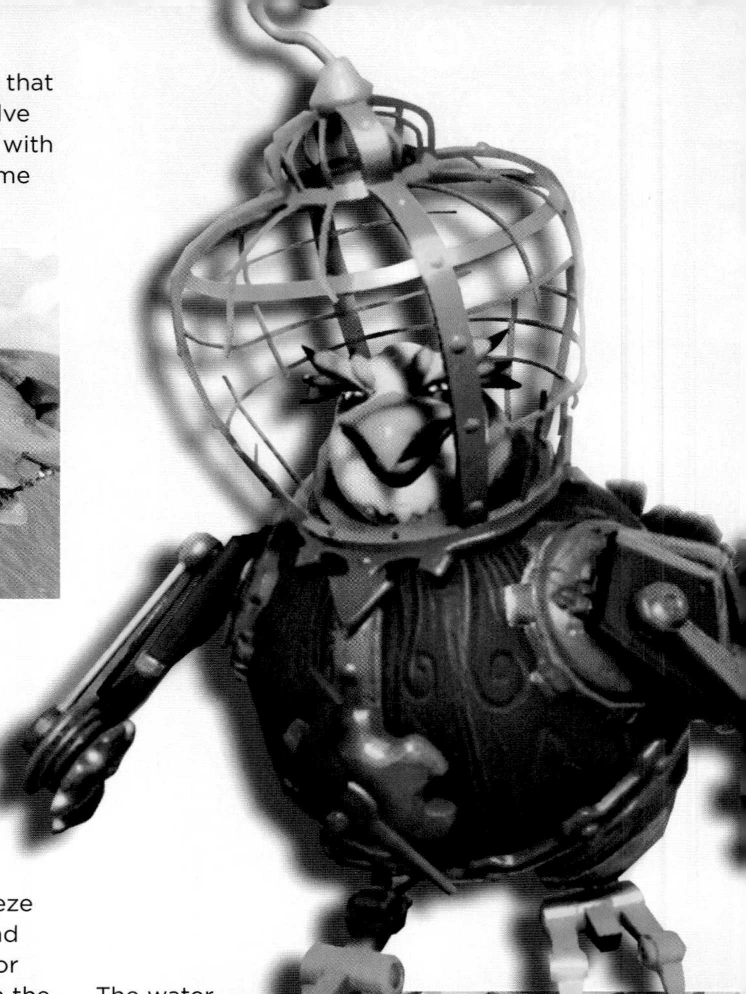

Use the valve once to move the hut into position in front of the pipe nearest the valve. Use the Time-Freeze switch and quickly jump up to the platform with the gold. The first use of the Time-Freeze switch spawns a Time Spell Punk. The sooner you get him out of the way, the easier this puzzle becomes.

Return the hut back around to the pipe nearest the valve. Turn the valve again. Use the Time-Freeze switch to stop the hut in line with the platform and the Locked Gate. Jump up to the hut, then wait for time to flow again and ride it to the platform with the key. Grab the key and use the water booster at the other end of the platform to return to the water valve. Repeat the process again, but this time use the key to open the gate.

The water booster beyond the Locked Gate flings your Skylander into another round Battle Gate area, where a group of trolls appears and attacks. The trolls are on their own at first, though a Clock Geargolem shows up when the trolls are all down. He's supported by a Time Spell Punk on the left platform. Use the water boosters on the lower level to reach enemies set up on the higher ledges. With this last Battle Gate clear, the path up to the final gear is open.

MAGIC IS STRONGER IN THIS AREA

TOWER OF TIME

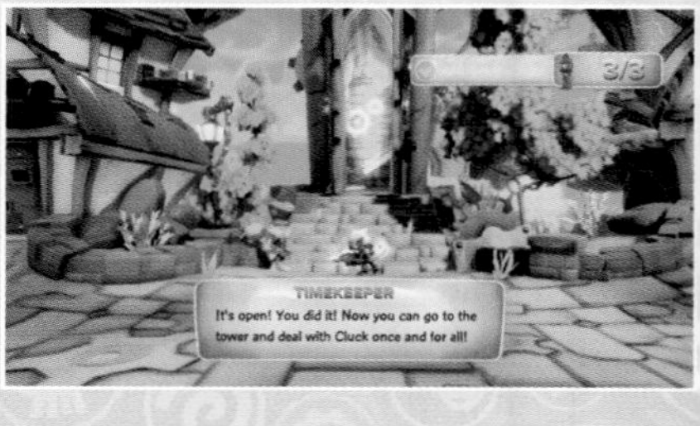

After another trip to Times Circle courtesy of Flynn, the way to the Tower of Time (and a final battle with Cluck) is clear.

The first portion of the Tower of Time involves riding a spinning wooden platform from the lowest level to the top.

Unfortunately, the platform is not a non-stop trip. There's one stop during the ascent where you must fend off waves of attackers. In addition to trolls, there are multiple Time Spell Punks and a Clock Geargolem. The Time-Freeze switch is outside the platform. Use it as much as possible, despite the distance to it. With the last line of defense out of the way, it's time to head up and face Cluck.

The final fight against Cluck is similar to the previous fight against him, but this time you must stop time to get through his energy shield. Cluck continues to jump and land and send out shockwaves until you freeze time.

When Cluck is down to about one-third of his total health, he summons Time Spell Punks and discharges a laser blast across the room. When he resumes dropping down from above, he pauses every few jumps and spits energy balls into the air. Orange rings on the ground mark their destination. Take out the Time Spell Punks as soon as they spawn and use the Time-Freeze switch to destroy Cluck's battle suit. Don't worry, he's still able to leave with his dignity intact.

WOODBURROW

Woodburrow is the village you save shortly after Tessa first introduces herself to Flynn. It also becomes your central hub after your first visit. As you progress through the game, you gain access to additional areas of Woodburrow.

In all, there are nine areas in Woodburrow for you to discover, and you earn an Accolade after discovering them all.

THE AIRDOCKS

The Airdocks are where most Story Levels begin. You often speak with Flynn, Tessa, or Sharpfin for transport to your next mission.

The area between the Central Plaza and the Airdocks includes Tuk's Emporium and Snagglescale's tent, where he runs the Arena Challenges. He begins with just four, but you can unlock 20 Arena Challenges in all.

Shortly after the events in Winter Keep, the **Sweet Blizzard Bonus Mission Map** appears wrapped in a box not far from Sharpfin's location.

When you unlock Sheep Wreck Islands, the entrance to the Adventure Pack Area is at the end of the docks opposite where you summon Master Eon after completing Mudwater Hollow.

WOODBURROW

Map Key

	Treasure Chest
	Giant Treasure Chest
	Soul Gem
	Legendary Treasure
	Legendary Item Pedestals
	Hat
	Bonus Mission Map
	Winged Sapphire
	Story Scroll
	Dare
	Checkpoint

CENTRAL PLAZA

The Central Plaza is the heart of Woodburrow, with Rufus standing at its center. Rufus should be a familiar figure by now! After you complete the Story Mode, Avril sets up her Time Attack Challenges in the Central Plaza, near the stairs to the Airdocks.

MUSHROOM STAIRWAY

The Chieftess opens up this area of Woodburrow while summoning Master Eon. The Mushroom Stairway leads up to Treetrunk Peak, but don't miss out on Hoot Loop's **Soul Gem (Wand of Dreams/ Infinite Loops)** on your way to the top.

THE GREAT HOLLOW

You first visit the Great Hollow after the events in Cascade Glade. You should visit the Great Hollow after every completed Story Mode level, or each time you begin playing your game on a new day. There will be a different Treasure Chest and Spark Lock puzzle available there for you.

TOWN GATES

The Town Gates are available at the end of the first Story Level. There isn't much going on at the Town Gates, except for the **Puma Hat** found there.

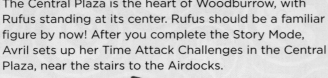

TREETRUNK PEAK

There's a **Winged Sapphire**, boxes of fireworks, and an Epic Launch Pad in this area at the end of the Mushroom Stairway. Use a fire-based attack on the fireworks to set them off. Using the Epic Launch Pad sends your Skylander to a hidden area filled with coins and the gift-wrapped **Turkey Hat**.

THE TROPHY ROOM

The Trophy Room is Tibbet's corner of Woodburrow. He unlocks the Treasure Pedestals in Woodburrow and explains how to use them. Legendary Treasure Pedestals appear all over Woodburrow, though you must increase your Portal Master Rank to gain access to them all.

The Pedestal locations are the Trophy Room, in the tree above the Trophy Room, in the Yard near the training dummies, two at the base of the stairs leading to the Great Hollow from Central Plaza, at the Airdocks near the path to Master Eon, and one final one in the Under Hollow.

Tessa and Wheellock set up a turret mini-game after you defeat the Fire Viper. There are a few instances where you must use turrets through the adventure, so having a practice range comes in handy.

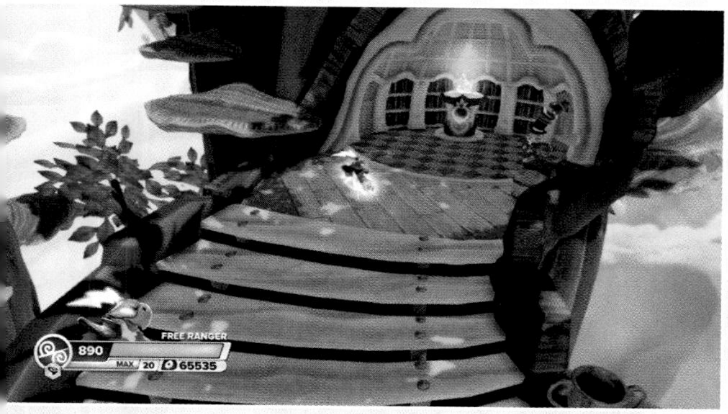

UNDER HOLLOW

Wheellock decides to leave Motleyville at the end of Story Level 7, and takes up residence in Woodburrow. When he does, he opens a door to the Under Hollow, where he sets up a fishing pole. More importantly, you also find Smolderdash's **Soul Gem (Smolder Dash)** and a **Story Scroll, The Great Hollow**, down there as well. After you complete the main adventure, Wheellock sets up his Score Mode Challenges at the doorway heading down into the Under Hollow.

YARD

The Yard is available shortly after your first talk with Rufus. The Yard features a group of training dummies where you can try out the new abilities purchased nearby at Gorm's Power Pod. The Epic Jump Pad near Gorm is a quick way to reach the Airdocks.

The Rainbow Bridge also appears at the yard. Every day between 3pm and 6pm (based on your console's time), a bridge appears in the yard and leads to a platform with a **Story Scroll, Enchanted Pool**, and a **Treasure Chest**. The Tower of Time entrance appears in the Yard, once you have unlocked it.

SPARK LOCKS

After you complete Cascade Glade, the Gillman Councilor in the Great Hollow offers you the chance to practice your Spark Lock skills. There are eight different Spark Lock chests, one of which appears randomly each day. Solve the Spark Lock puzzles to collect your rewards!

SPARK LOCK
All in the Timing

The fans are on a timed cycle. Time Shock and Bolt to pass in front of the fans nearest them when they are off.

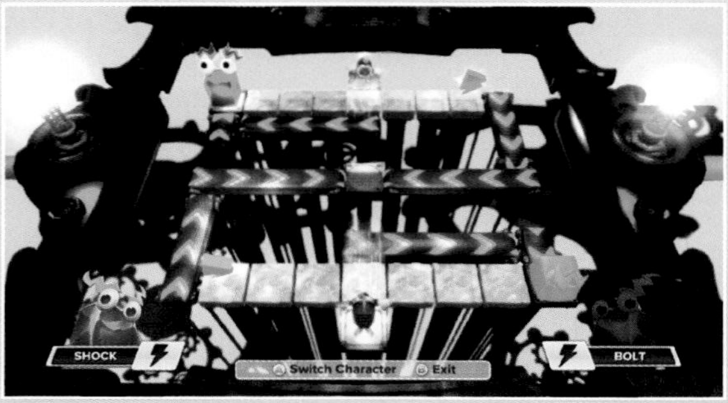

SPARK LOCK
Up and Over

Move Bolt over the orange button, then push Shock on top of the orange column. Raise the column and send Shock to get his lightning bolt. Pick up Bolt's lightning bolt, then run him back around the track to meet up with Shock.

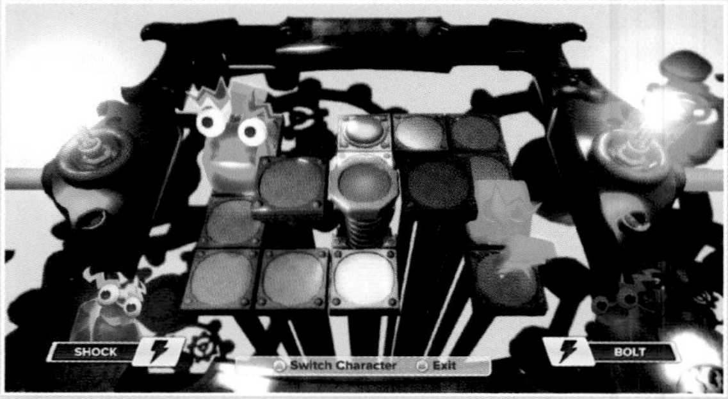

SPARK LOCK
Gatekeeper

Move both Shock and Bolt to the buttons in the middle to lower the platforms. Move either one of them back to their starting point, then the other to pick up his lightning bolt. Reverse the process (remember to hit the center buttons enough times to leave the path open for both Shock and Bolt) and bring the two together after the second lightning bolt is collected.

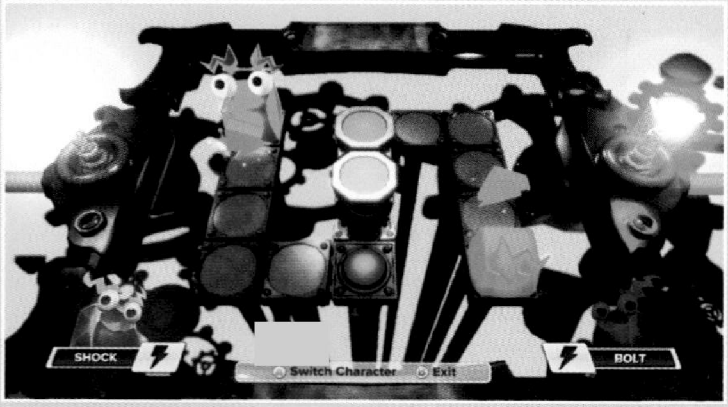

SPARK LOCK
Sliding into Home

Push Shock to the right. When he stops on the one non-ice block, slide him down and immediately switch to Bolt and move him left. Slide Bolt in front of the fan while it's on to get his lightning bolt. After Shock gets the blue lightning bolt, bring the two together somewhere in the middle.

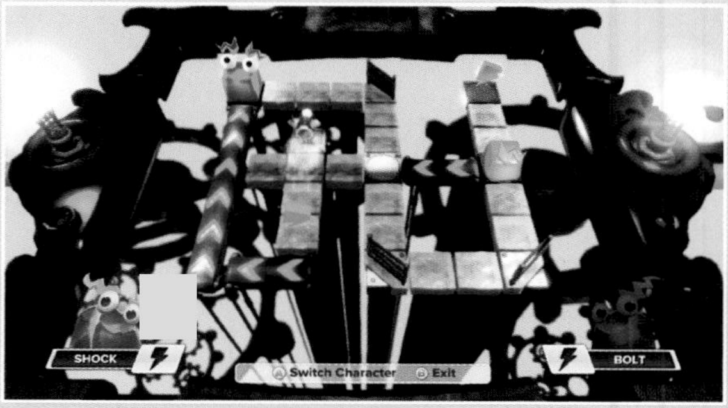

SPARK LOCK

Brought Together

Move Bolt on top of any of the green columns, then hit the green button with Shock. Move Shock to the space with the green lightning bolt, then move Bolt on top of the purple button. Send Shock across on the purple slider, then avoid Bolt while going up to get the blue lightning bolt. Move Shock back to the other side of the orange columns, then get the green lightning bolt with Bolt. Send Bolt back on the purple slider and join the two together.

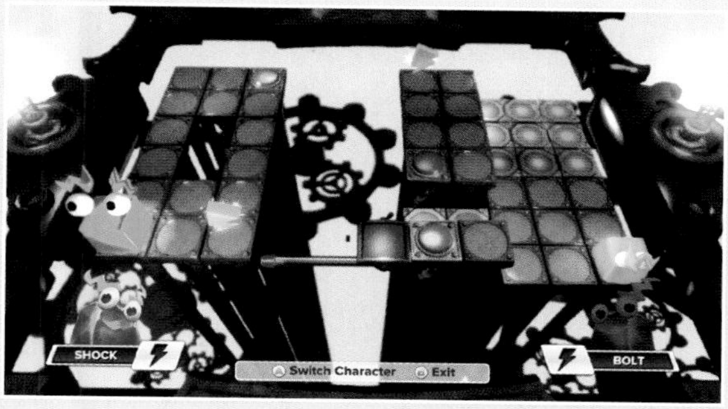

SPARK LOCK

Amping Joules

Hit the green button with Bolt. Switch to Shock and turn off the purple fan with the purple button. Continue around the ice with Bolt to the orange button. With both platforms lowered, move Bolt up to Shock's original starting point. Restart the fan with Shock, then send him around to pick up his lightning bolt. Turn the fan off and start around the ice, but don't hit the green button until Bolt is on top of the green pedestal. Get the lightning bolt and bring the two together.

SPARK LOCK

See the Problem from My Side

Move Bolt on top of the orange button to clear Shock's path down to the green button via the orange slider. After Shock steps on the green button, move Bolt to the center green column. Hit the green button again and move Bolt to the square with the blue lightning bolt. Drop the columns down and move Shock past Bolt's location. Send Bolt to the green button, but do not press it until Shock is on top of a green column.

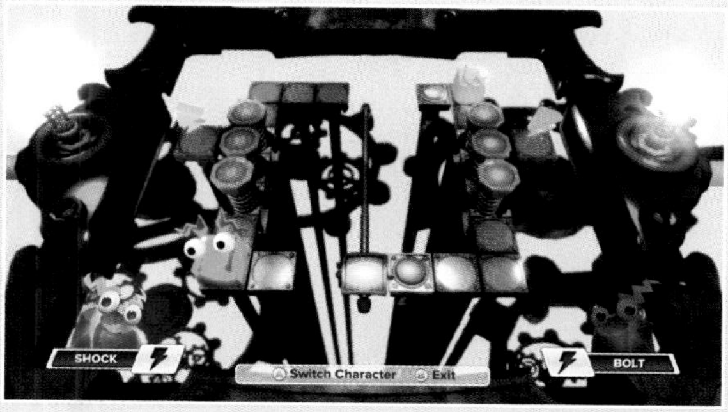

SPARK LOCK

Ready or not Here I Come!

Hit the purple button with Shock, then move him directly behind the orange column. Once Bolt hits the orange button, switch back to Shock immediately and move him past the conveyor belt before Bolt finishes his trip up to the top area. Send both Shock and Bolt to their respective lightning bolts, then have them meet back in the middle.

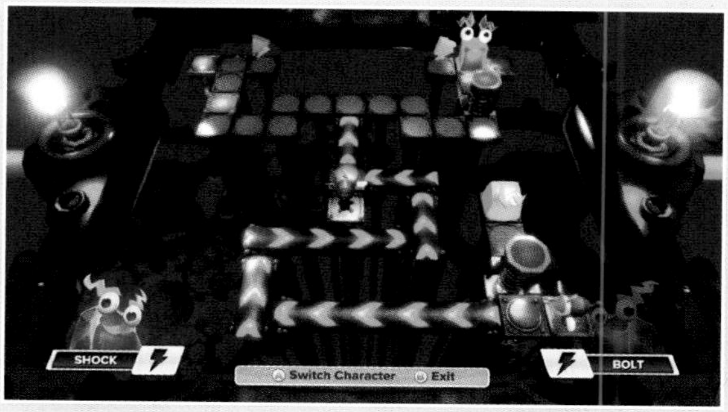

SWAP ZONE CHALLENGES

SWAP Zone Challenges appear throughout the Story Mode, and you must successfully complete them during a Story Level to make them available from the Portal Master screen of the Pause Menu.

Only *SWAP Force* Skylanders with the matching base ability can access SWAP Zone Challenges. Which figure is used for the top half of the *SWAP Force* Skylander doesn't matter when you're trying out SWAP Zone challenges; you must select legs with the correct ability.

Each SWAP Zone challenge has an objective you must complete to clear it. Each type of challenge has its own objective; no two are the same. Each SWAP Zone also requires a special ability activated with the Attack 2 button. The objectives and special abilities are covered in greater detail on the following pages.

Story Level versus Going for Stars versus Score Mode

The zones are identical whether you run them from within a Story Level, in Score Mode, or if you are going for Stars (choose them from the Pause Menu), with minor differences based on what you're looking for in each mode.

During the Story Mode, the coins you collect are added to the total for the current Skylander. Coins do not add to your Score Mode total, and they do nothing for you while going for Stars.

There are three gems that appear in each SWAP Zone Challenge. These gems always appear in the same locations across all three modes. In the Story Mode and SWAP Mode, these gems are red. Gems collected while in Story Mode and Score Mode burst into smaller red gems that you can pick up for extra gold. In Score Mode, the red gems that drop after running a SWAP Zone Challenge are the only items that count toward your score. Always get all three gems in Score Mode!

While you're going for Stars, they are yellow. Picking up all the gems is the second challenge Star for all SWAP Zone Challenges.

GET HELP FROM A FRIEND

A second Skylander on the *Portal of Power* provides a special power to help out with these challenges. The second Skylander can be any playable character. You don't need two *SWAP Force* Skylanders with the same ability.

The second Skylander's portrait appears in the bottom corner of the screen, next to a button and a meter that refills over time. Press the indicated button to activate a special ability. The meter empties and must refill before the ability can be used again. Each SWAP Zone type offers one different ability, which are covered in more detail in the SWAP Zone Challenge sections on the following pages.

Swap Zone Challenges by Type

The following table breaks down the forty-two challenges into the eight base abilities.

Type	Skylanders with Ability	Name of Challenges
	Fire Kraken, Rattle Shake	Sunny Heights, Lonely Springs, Parched Heights, Frosty Frolicking, Kaotic Spring
	Spy Rise, Wash Buckler	Tree Top Jaunt, Robot Ramparts, Junkside Climb, Amber Ice Climb, Tower of Falling Goo, Windy Tower
	Grilla Drilla, Rubble Rouser	Spiky Pit, Submerged Sands, Ice Hollows, Glacial Descent, Tick Tock Tunneling
	Blast Zone, Boom Jet	Forest Flyby, Tree Scraping, Storm of Sands, Ice Cold Flying, Fire Flighter, Sheep Strafing
	Stink Bomb, Trap Shadow	Area Fifty Tree, Sunken Sand Base, Nerves of Ice, Fire Fortress, Wool Over Their Eyes
	Freeze Blade, Magna Charge	Woodlands Speedstacle, Frenetic Fog, Drag Stripped, Wind Whipped, Greenlight Raceway
	Doom Stone, Free Ranger	Marbled Gardens, Twisted Towers, Warped Sands, Frozen Top, Spinning Cogs
	Hoot Loop, Night Shift	Going Whoosh, Hourglass Blink, Flash Frost, Ethereal Transfer, Beached Blinkout

Swap Zone Challenges by Story Level

This table shows which SWAP Zone Challenges are available from each Story Level.

Story Level		SWAP Zone Challenge
Mount Cloudbreak		Tree Top Jaunt
		Forest Flyby
		Spiky Pit
Cascade Glade		Sunny Heights
		Area Fifty Tree
		Woodlands Speedstacle
Mudwater Hollow		Tree Scraping
		Marbled Gardens
		Going Whoosh
Rampant Ruins		Robot Ramparts
		Frenetic Fog
		Lonely Springs
Iron Jaw Gulch		Hourglass Blink
		Submerged Sands
		Storm of Sands
Motleyville		Twisted Towers
		Junkside Climb
		Drag Stripped
Twisty Tunnels		Parched Heights
		Sunken Sand Base
		Warped Sands

Story Level		SWAP Zone Challenge
Boney Islands		Ice Hollows
		Amber Ice Climb
		Ice Cold Flying
Winter Keep		Flash Frost
		Wind Whipped
		Frozen Top
Frostfest Mountains		Nerves of Ice
		Frosty Frolicking
		Glacial Descent
Fantasm Forest		Ethereal Transfer
		Fire Flighter
		Fire Fortress
Kaos' Fortress		Kaotic Spring
		Tower of Falling Goo
		Greenlight Raceway
Sheep Wreck Islands		Sheep Strafing
		Beached Blinkout
		Wool Over Their Eyes
Tower of Time		Windy Tower
		Spinning Cogs
		Tick Tock Tunneling

BOUNCE CHALLENGES

During Bounce Challenges, you must pop a Kaos Balloon by landing on it. Your Skylander begins at one end of an area and must bounce between disconnected platforms and other floating objects to reach the Kaos balloon in the same area. Pop three Kaos balloons to complete the challenge. There is always one SWAP Zone Medal on the way to each of the Kaos Balloons.

The most important thing to keep track of during Bounce Challenges is your Skylander's shadow as it appears on each platform. Trust the shadow for your Skylander's location more than how they appear in mid-air.

After a bounce off an object, you can press the Attack 2 button for an extra mid-air bounce. Use your extra bounce wisely. Save it for the highest point in a jump to reach a far away platform and always remember when you still have it should you misjudge a bounce and need a quick save.

To earn the third Star in Bounce Challenges, you must bounce at least one time on every platform. There's no time limit, so be patient while you try to hit all the platforms. There are many levels with platforms that crumble after one use, which means you must carefully plan your route to ensure you have a place to land after each jump.

With a second Skylander active, you get the Triple Jump ability. The second player creates a platform directly under your Skylander, which acts exactly like any other bounce platform, including allowing your Skylander to jump again. Keep this ability available for last-second saves whenever possible. There's never a time when an extra platform is a requirement to reach a platform from any other platform unless you've knocked out a crumbling one.

SUNNY HEIGHTS

Bounce over to this great tourist attraction.

Unlocked: Chapter 2: Cascade Glade

Hazards: Moving platforms

Star Requirements

★	Complete the SWAP Zone
★★	Collect all the SWAP Zone Medals
★★★	Bounce On Every Island

SWAP Zone Medal Locations

1st	Highest platform nearest the Kaos Balloon
2nd	High platform, left side, about halfway to the Kaos Balloon
3rd	High platform, left side, about halfway to the Kaos Balloon

LONELY SPRINGS

Bounce around the Robot Graveyard.

Unlocked: Chapter 4: Rampant Ruins

Hazards: Crumbling platforms

Star Requirements

★	Complete the SWAP Zone
★★	Collect all the SWAP Zone Medals
★★★	Bounce On Every Island

SWAP Zone Medal Locations

1st	Low platform on right, halfway to Kaos Balloon
2nd	High platform on left, use second bounce to reach it, halfway to Kaos Balloon
3rd	High platform on left, close to Kaos Balloon

PARCHED HEIGHTS

Springing around on the squid.

Unlocked: Chapter 7: Twisty Tunnels

Hazards: Moving platforms, crumbling platforms, fire geysers (deals damage but allows jumps after touching, not required for third Star)

Star Requirements

★	Complete the SWAP Zone
★★	Collect all the SWAP Zone Medals
★★★	Bounce On Every Island

SWAP Zone Medal Locations

1st	Highest platform on left side, near Kaos Balloon
2nd	Platform just to the right of Kaos Balloon
3rd	On the right, halfway to the Kaos Balloon

FROSTY FROLICKING

Spring up the mountains and don't slip!

Unlocked: Chapter 12: Frostfest Mountains

Hazards: Air columns (narrow target), crumbling platforms (vanish after one bounce)

Star Requirements

★	Complete the SWAP Zone
★★	Collect all the SWAP Zone Medals
★★★	Bounce On Every Island

SWAP Zone Medal Locations

1st	On the left about halfway from the start to the first air column
2nd	On the right near the second air column
3rd	First air column

KAOTIC SPRING

Don't bounce too high. I think I see the atmosphere.

Unlocked: Chapter 15: Kaos' Fortress

Hazards: Moving platforms, moving goo clouds (coats Skylander and makes them heavier)

Star Requirements

★	Complete the SWAP Zone
★★	Collect all the SWAP Zone Medals
★★★	Bounce On Every Island

SWAP Zone Medal Locations

1st	On the left, halfway to the Kaos Balloon
2nd	On the left, halfway to the Kaos Balloon
3rd	On the right, almost to the Kaos Balloon

CLIMB CHALLENGES

It doesn't get much more basic than Climb Challenges. Start at the bottom of a structure and climb to the top. There are two checkpoints along the way, and each offers extra gold and some food to restore any health lost to falling objects or other hazards.

There are two types of items to watch during your ascent. There are other hazards, but these appear on every level. First, there are the stationary objects. Some are helpful platforms you can use for shielding from the falling objects (more on those next). Others seem helpful, but they also have hazards attached to them, such as spikes. The second type of item is the aforementioned falling objects. Falling objects match the theme of the level (such as acorns when climbing a tree) and they come in three varieties.

The first kind hurt Skylanders, but are blocked by stationary objects. The second type are the harmless fragments of the first type that appear when they are smashed against a stationary object. Until you learn how to identify the first two objects, assume everything that falls will cause damage!

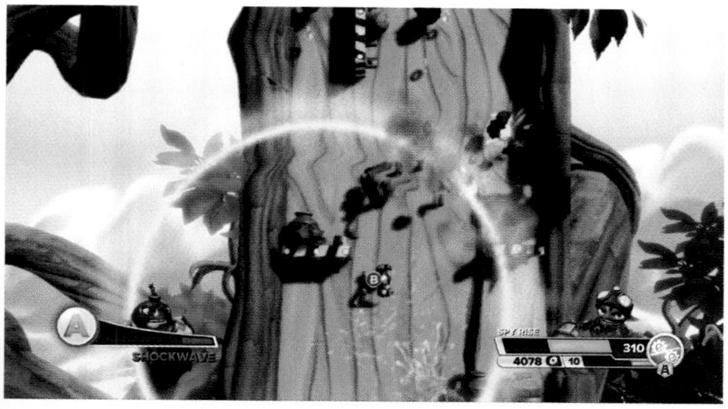

Some levels also include environmental effects that obscure your vision (clouds, or ships buzzing the level and leaving behind smoke). The final type of falling object are the very large, very heavy items that destroy the platforms you planned on using for shelter. Not every level has them, but they're doubly bad. They harm your Skylander on contact and remove your resting spots.

Wall Dash is an ability that should be saved for lateral or downward movement. Going upward quickly, unless you're trying to reach safety before something hits you, generally leads to trouble.

To get the third star in Climb Challenges, you must avoid taking damage. The best way to earn this star is to become familiar with the level. The pattern of items falling is the same each time through a level. Be patient and be careful. Being reckless is for clearing these levels quickly in Story Mode or trying to grab all three SWAP Zone medals!

The second player Skylander ability is Shockwave. Shockwave spreads out from the Skylander doing the climbing and clears off every destructible object and hazard on the screen.

TREE TOP JAUNT

Get climbing above the trees!

Unlocked: Chapter 1: Mount Cloudbreak

Hazards: Tree nuts, jets obscure vision

Star Requirements

★	Complete the SWAP Zone
★★	Collect all the SWAP Zone Medals
★★★	No Damage Taken

SWAP Zone Medal Locations

1st	Left side before first check point
2nd	Right side before second check point
3rd	Middle before the finish

ROBOT RAMPARTS

Scale to the tippety top of the robot wall.

Unlocked: Chapter 4: Rampant Ruins

Hazards: Falling boxes, moving platforms, missiles, clouds obscure vision

Star Requirements

★	Complete the SWAP Zone
★★	Collect all the SWAP Zone Medals
★★★	No Damage Taken

SWAP Zone Medal Locations

1st	Left side before first checkpoint
2nd	Right side before second checkpoint
3rd	Left side before the finish

JUNKSIDE CLIMB

Ascend to the highest heights of the heap!

Unlocked: Chapter 7: Motleyville

Hazards: Falling barrels, spinning and moving saw blades, falling mine carts (destroys platforms)

Star Requirements

★	Complete the SWAP Zone
★★	Collect all the SWAP Zone Medals
★★★	No Damage Taken

SWAP Zone Medal Locations

1st	Right side before first checkpoint
2nd	Middle before second checkpoint
3rd	Left side before the finish

AMBER ICE CLIMB

Careful the air gets thin up there.

Unlocked: Chapter 10: Boney Islands

Hazards: Ice shards, fossils (destroys platforms), missiles

Star Requirements

★	Complete the SWAP Zone
★★	Collect all the SWAP Zone Medals
★★★	No Damage Taken

SWAP Zone Medal Locations

1st	Right side before first check point
2nd	Middle before second check point
3rd	Left side before the finish

TOWER OF FALLING GOO

No wall can hold you back!

Unlocked: Chapter 15: Kaos' Fortress

Hazards: Falling goo, flamethrowers

Star Requirements

★	Complete the SWAP Zone
★★	Collect all the SWAP Zone Medals
★★★	No Damage Taken

SWAP Zone Medal Locations

1st	Left side before first checkpoint
2nd	Right side before second checkpoint
3rd	Middle before the finish

WINDY TOWER

Make the trip in the nick of time.

Unlocked: Tower of Time Adventure Pack Level

Hazards: Tree nuts, fan blowing across course, spinning saw blades, clouds obscure vision

Star Requirements

★	Complete the SWAP Zone
★★	Collect all the SWAP Zone Medals
★★★	No Damage Taken

SWAP Zone Medal Locations

1st	Left side before first checkpoint
2nd	Right side before second checkpoint
3rd	Left side before the finish

DIG CHALLENGES

In Dig Challenges, you move through dark areas where you must jump over gaps, avoid hazards, and get to gems. More than any other challenge, Dig Challenges require learning a pattern through a level to earn all the stars. Digging up the first and second crystals adds 30 seconds to the countdown clock. There's no extra ability in Dig. Digging is your ability!

To get the third Star in Dig challenges, learn the shortest path between crystal locations, and ignore everything else. Don't try to get the second and third stars in the same run. Even with a second player helping, it's incredibly tough to pull off. To buy yourself an extra second or two, don't wait for your Skylander to come into view when a level begins. Start moving forward as soon as the level loads.

The Second player ability is Time Stop. When active, it stops the countdown clock briefly and freezes everything on the screen. To get the most out of each application (it has a considerable recharge time) only use it when the path ahead is clear. That means having no mining carts in the way, and seeing that all spikes are retracted and not blocking the path.

SPIKY PIT

Tunnel down into the Cascade Caves

Unlocked: Chapter 1: Mount Cloudbreak

Hazards: Spike traps

Star Requirements

★	Complete the SWAP Zone
★★	Collect all the SWAP Zone Medals
★★★	Over 53 Seconds Left

SWAP Zone Medal Locations

1st	To the left of the starting point
2nd	To the right of rightmost blue crystal
3rd	To the right (over gaps)of leftmost blue crystal

SUBMERGED SANDS

Everyone likes to play in the sand.

Unlocked: Chapter 6: Iron Jaw Gulch

Hazards: Mining carts

Star Requirements

★	Complete the SWAP Zone
★★	Collect all the SWAP Zone Medals
★★★	Over 53 Seconds Left

SWAP Zone Medal Locations

1st	On the left side, past blue gem closest to start point
2nd	To the right of blue gem in the center of the map
3rd	From the blue gem in the center of the map, move to the back and go left, then climb steps back to the right

ICE HOLLOWS

It's where they keep the fossils.

Unlocked: Chapter 10: Boney Islands

Hazards: Mining carts

Star Requirements

★	Complete the SWAP Zone
★★	Collect all the SWAP Zone Medals
★★★	Over 58 Seconds Left

SWAP Zone Medal Locations

1st	Follow tracks to the right of the starting point (or fall down the gap between first and second blue gems)
2nd	To the left of blue gem in middle of map
3rd	From blue gem at the back of the map, go to the right over gaps

GLACIAL DESCENT

Tunneling through solid ice is not easy. Good thing you're awesome.

Unlocked: Chapter 12: Frostfest Mountains

Hazards: Spiky wall traps

Star Requirements

★	Complete the SWAP Zone
★★	Collect all the SWAP Zone Medals
★★	Over 58 Seconds Left

SWAP Zone Medal Locations

1st	Go left from the start, all the way back
2nd	From leftmost blue crystal, move toward front then jump left over gap
3rd	All the way in the back, near middle, on the highest row of platforms

TICK TOCK TUNNELING

Can you dig far enough to reach yesterday? That's deep.

Unlocked: Tower of Time Adventure Pack Level

Hazards: Burning rocks,

Star Requirements

★	Complete the SWAP Zone
★★	Collect all the SWAP Zone Medals
★★★	Over 48 Seconds Left

SWAP Zone Medal Locations

1st	Directly ahead at start
2nd	Just past (behind) leftmost blue crystal
3rd	From second Medal, go to the right

ROCKET CHALLENGES

In Rocket challenges, you guide your Skylander through a designated course marked by rings within an allotted time. You can steer to the left or right by tapping or holding the control stick to the left or right. Pull down on the control stick to spin around and backtrack on the rocket path. Passing through the rings is not mandatory, but they do add five seconds to the timer. That means if you miss a ring and you would lose more than five seconds trying to get back through it, skip it! The final ring on the course does not add any time to the clock.

Your Skylander's extra ability is Boost. Press the Attack 2 button to activate it. Unlike most other abilities, there is no limit on using Boost. It stays active as long as you hold down the button.

To earn the third Star in Rocket Challenges, your Skylander must pass through the course without taking damage. The hazards in Rocket challenges are usually floating mines, so avoid hitting them to get the third Star. Skip trying to get all the Medals on the same run as one where you want to get No Damage Taken. There's always one medal in a dangerous location.

The second player ability is Super Ring. Super Ring briefly causes the rings marking the course to grow to an enormous size. The ability is available often, so don't be shy about putting it to use. It's most helpful when mines surround the ring. The ring pushes the mines as it grows.

FOREST FLYBY

High velocity forest flying!

Unlocked: Chapter 1: Mount Cloudbreak

Hazards: Floating rocks, stationary metal discs, sliding rows of rocks

Star Requirements

★	Complete the SWAP Zone
★★	Collect all the SWAP Zone Medals
★★★	No Damage Taken

SWAP Zone Medal Locations

1st	Moving around rock after fourth ring
2nd	Between second and third ring past first checkpoint
3rd	Left side, near finish ring

TREE SCRAPING

Flutterfly through the Flashfin Cove!

Unlocked: Chapter 3: Mudwater Hollow

Hazards: Connected and electrified balls, stationary metal discs

Star Requirements

★	Complete the SWAP Zone
★★	Collect all the SWAP Zone Medals
★★★	No Damage Taken

SWAP Zone Medal Locations

1st	After fourth ring
2nd	Second ring after second checkpoint, on the right
3rd	Just before finish ring, floating across the course

STORM OF SANDS

Time to do a little bit of refacing.

Unlocked: Chapter 6: Iron Jaw Gulch

Hazards: Stationary mines, moving mines

Star Requirements

★	Complete the SWAP Zone
★ ★	Collect all the SWAP Zone Medals
★ ★ ★	No Damage Taken

SWAP Zone Medal Locations

1st	After third ring, on left
2nd	Past third ring after first check point
3rd	Just before finish ring in mines on the right

ICE COLD FLYING

Not many people get to rocket around in a museum. Don't break anything.

Unlocked: Chapter 10: Boney Islands

Hazards: Frozen mines, spinning rings

Star Requirements

★	Complete the SWAP Zone
★ ★	Collect all the SWAP Zone Medals
★ ★ ★	No Damage Taken

SWAP Zone Medal Locations

1st	In large minefield on left just before first checkpoint
2nd	Between fifth and sixth rings after first checkpoint
3rd	Near the last ring before the finish ring

FIRE FLIGHTER

This is the way to take in the scenery.

Unlocked: Chapter 13: Fantasm Forest

Hazards: Mines, evilized fire

Star Requirements

★	Complete the SWAP Zone
★ ★	Collect all the SWAP Zone Medals
★ ★ ★	No Damage Taken

SWAP Zone Medal Locations

1st	Circling large island clockwise near start
2nd	Spinning around island just past first checkpoint
3rd	After second gate past second checkpoint

SHEEP STRAFING

Off you go into the wild wooly yonder.

Unlocked: Sheep Wreck Islands Adventure Pack Level

Hazards: Stationary metal discs, stationary mines, moving mines

Star Requirements

★	Complete the SWAP Zone
★ ★	Collect all the SWAP Zone Medals
★ ★ ★	No Damage Taken

SWAP Zone Medal Locations

1st	Just before third ring
2nd	Between first and second gates beyond first checkpoint
3rd	Immediately after second gate beyond second checkpoint

SNEAK CHALLENGES

Sneak Challenges technically have two objectives. The first is to activate switches that open up the next area. The final objective is to reach a big red button to destroy the base you infiltrated. Your Skylander is limited to two actions between activating switches and pressing buttons: walking and using stealth. There's no jumping, no dashing, and no attacks of any sort. There are two common hazards while attempting to sneak to the base-destruct button: search lights and laser panels.

Search lights are always red. They sometimes sweep areas, while other times they are stationary and the floor moves through it. If your unstealthed Skylander is spotted by a search light, you must act quickly or fail the challenge (more on this in the next paragraph). Laser panels appear on floors, ceilings, and walls. They fire a short-range laser that damages anything it strikes.

Stealth is your Skylander's secondary ability. Stealth is effective only against the search lights covering areas of each base. Skylanders cannot move while using the Stealth ability in a Sneak Zone. Laser panels don't care about stealth. Their beams harm your Skylander whenever it hits them. Stealthed Skylanders are undetectable by search lights. They pass over your Skylander so long as Stealth is active. Even if your Skylander is detected, going into Stealth quickly enough prevents the search light from ejecting you from the base. You just need to be patient until the threat level has dropped.

To earn the third Star in a Stealth challenge, you must avoid detection. That means never drawing the interest of a search light. If you must use Stealth because a search light grazed your Skylander's toe, it's too late. Being hit by a laser, on the other hand, does not affect your third Star eligibility. It is only the search light that counts.

The second player ability is Lights Out. Lights Out shuts down search lights for a few seconds, but it does nothing for laser panels. Lights Out makes earning a third Star much easier, so invite a friend to help you if you're struggling with it. Save Lights Out for areas near the end of a search light's scanning area. The last thing you want to do is use it in the middle of its path only to have it respawn on top of your Skylander who is an inch from that next platform!

AREA FIFTY TREE

Tiptoe through the tulips. And other foliage.

Unlocked: Chapter 2: Cascade Glade

Hazards: No extra hazards

Star Requirements

★	Complete the SWAP Zone
★★	Collect all the SWAP Zone Medals
★★★	Never Got Spotted

SWAP Zone Medal Locations

1st	To the left of the first security light
2nd	To the right just past first security gate
3rd	To the left just past second security gate

SUNKEN SAND BASE

Don't get caught with sand in your eyes.

Unlocked: Chapter 8: Twisty Tunnels

Hazards: Elevator platforms

Star Requirements

★	Complete the SWAP Zone
★★	Collect all the SWAP Zone Medals
★★★	Never Got Spotted

SWAP Zone Medal Locations

1st	Past first elevator platform
2nd	Ride second elevator platform to highest point, then backtrack
3rd	After second security gate, fall to the right (keep pushing right) between two sets of double lasers to land on a platform

NERVES OF ICE

Don't get spotted. There's weird stuff out there.

Unlocked: Chapter 12: Frostfest Mountains

Hazards: Sliding platforms

Star Requirements

★	Complete the SWAP Zone
★★	Collect all the SWAP Zone Medals
★★★	Never Got Spotted

SWAP Zone Medal Locations

1st	Ride first sliding platform all the way left
2nd	Past first security gate, take sliding platform to the right
3rd	Past second security gate, take sliding platform to the right

FIRE FORTRESS

Stay focused and don't get distracted by...LOOK AT THE PRETTY FLOWERS!

Unlocked: Chapter 13: Fantasm Forest

Hazards: Delayed path formation

Star Requirements

★	Complete the SWAP Zone
★ ★	Collect all the SWAP Zone Medals
★ ★ ★	Never Got Spotted

SWAP Zone Medal Locations

1st	To the right at the start
2nd	To the right of second security switch
3rd	Follow path in front of base destruct switch to the left

WOOL OVER THEIR EYES

Sheep are always up to something. Be wary.

Unlocked: Sheep Wreck Islands Adventure Pack Level

Hazards: Top down view

Star Requirements

★	Complete the SWAP Zone
★ ★	Collect all the SWAP Zone Medals
★ ★ ★	Never Got Spotted

SWAP Zone Medal Locations

1st	After second elevator, go left
2nd	After first security gate, go right
3rd	After second security gate, go straight ahead

SPEED CHALLENGES

Speed challenges require you to guide your Skylander through hazard-filled courses within a certain time limit. Your only control options are pushing the control stick left and right to steer your Skylander in those directions. Pushing forward and back has no effect on your Skylander's speed.

The secondary ability for Speed challenges is Boost. Boost gives your Skylander a quick burst of speed. It only lasts about one second, but it recharges quickly.

The third Star in Speed challenges requires the timer to have a minimum amount of time left after completing the course. To earn the third Star, get into the habit of using Boost as soon as it is available. You can delay it a second if it helps you avoid hitting anything that slows down your Skylander.

The second player ability is Sonic Blast. Sonic Blast emits a destructive wave, clearing most hazards from the path ahead. Some hazards are immune to it, but most stationary hazards are destroyed by Sonic Blast. To get the most out of Sonic Blast, use it at the same time as Boost. Sonic Blast does not have much reach, but it is extended quite a bit when used with a Boost.

WOODLANDS SPEEDSTACLE

Speed through the jungle but watch out for low branches.

Unlocked: Chapter 2: Cascade Glade

Hazards: Stationary hazards, jump ramps

Star Requirements

★	Complete the SWAP Zone
★ ★	Collect all the SWAP Zone Medals
★ ★ ★	Over 10 Seconds Left

SWAP Zone Medal Locations

1st	Sliding across the track halfway to first checkpoint
2nd	After first check point, center of track, jump to reach it
3rd	After second check point, second jump of a double jump, angle to the right

FRENETIC FOG

Cut through the mist at super-duper speeds!

Unlocked: Chapter 4: Rampant Ruins

Hazards: Fog, stationary hazards

Star Requirements

★	Complete the SWAP Zone
★ ★	Collect all the SWAP Zone Medals
★ ★ ★	Over 10 Seconds Left

SWAP Zone Medal Locations

1st	In the food during the jump after the first check point, left side
2nd	In the food during the jump after the second check point, in the middle
3rd	On the right side before shorter hazards

DRAG STRIPPED

Outrun, outlast and race past!

Unlocked: Chapter 7: Motleyville

Hazards: Stationary hazards, moving mines, jump ramps

Star Requirements

★	Complete the SWAP Zone
★ ★	Collect all the SWAP Zone Medals
★ ★ ★	Over 10 Seconds Left

SWAP Zone Medal Locations

1st	On the left behind a barrel
2nd	After first checkpoint, moving back and forth between moving mines
3rd	Above the track after back to back jump ramp rows

WIND WHIPPED

Fleet feet through the icy sleet.

Unlocked: Chapter 11: Winter Keep

Hazards: Stationary hazards, rolling ice boulders

Star Requirements

★	Complete the SWAP Zone
★ ★	Collect all the SWAP Zone Medals
★ ★ ★	Over 15 Seconds Left

SWAP Zone Medal Locations

1st	On the uphill slope, to the right
2nd	After the first checkpoint, sliding across track in the middle of multiple ice boulders
3rd	After the second checkpoint, Sliding across track after multiple ice boulders, on an uphill slant

GREENLIGHT RACEWAY

Currently traveling at six times the speed of awesome.

Unlocked: Chapter 15: Kaos' Fortress

Hazards: Stationary hazards, moving and bouncing green goo balls, jump ramps

Star Requirements

★	Complete the SWAP Zone
★ ★	Collect all the SWAP Zone Medals
★ ★ ★	Over 14 Seconds Left

SWAP Zone Medal Locations

1st	On the right, between two tall hazards
2nd	On the right, almost to second checkpoint
3rd	Floating over the track on the left after a three-wide jump ramp

SPIN CHALLENGES

The goal of spin challenges is to destroy a statue of Kaos. Before you reach the platform with the statue of Kaos, however, your Skylander must reach the center of two other platforms. Each platform has a single SWAP Zone medal.

There are a few things complicating this journey. First, Skylanders are harder to control when they start bouncing around, but you can influence their course. Second, your Skylander must remain on the platforms, or the challenge ends immediately. Finally, you must break through layers of bumpers while avoiding hazards tucked in the middle of the layers to reach the center areas.

There are three bumper varieties. The first type are dark gray. These bumpers are the weakest and break down quickly. The yellow bumpers are sturdier and require multiple hits before they break. The bumpers with red and white tops are the sturdiest bumpers. They don't break often, and only after considerable effort on your part.

Super Spin is your Skylander's extra ability. It briefly increases your Skylander's spinning velocity. Be careful about using it. Spinning Skylanders are already challenging to control, and Super Spin magnifies that challenge. One quick burst and your Skylander may end up flying off the edge of the platform!

The third Star for Spin challenges is deceptively easy: don't use Super Spin. Earning this third Star requires a bit more patience than what the other challenges require. They generally ask you to complete things quickly. With no Super Spin, it takes more time!

The second player ability is Multiball. The Multiball acts like a second Skylander, but one you can't control at all. It crashes into objects and caroms around the platform. Save Multiball for clearing explosive hazards, like mines. Just be careful that your eyes stay on your Skylander and not the Multiball when it's active.

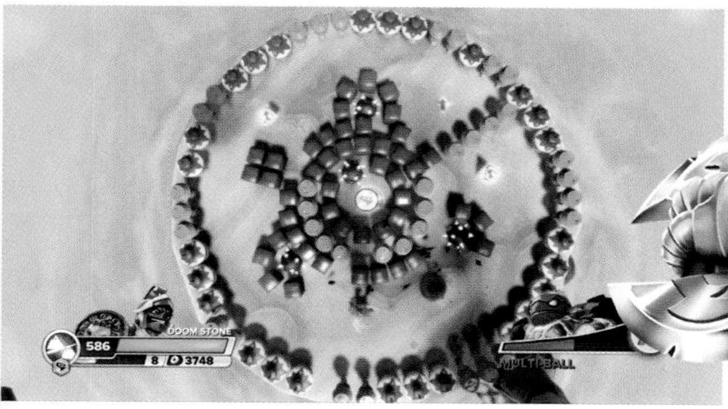

MARBLED GARDENS

Take a spin down the river!

Unlocked: Chapter 3: Mudwater Hollow

Hazards: No additional hazards

Star Requirements

★	Complete the SWAP Zone
★★	Collect all the SWAP Zone Medals
★★★	Never Used Super Spin

SWAP Zone Medal Locations

1st	Just to the right of the center
2nd	Right side of platform
3rd	Lower right of platform

TWISTED TOWERS

It's a whirly ride of junk. In a good way.

Unlocked: Chapter 7: Motleyville

Hazards: Mines

Star Requirements

★	Complete the SWAP Zone
★★	Collect all the SWAP Zone Medals
★★★	Never Used Super Spin

SWAP Zone Medal Locations

1st	Top of the platform, just right of center
2nd	Top of the platform, just right of center
3rd	Right side, just above center

WARPED SANDS

Spinning in the Twisty Tunnels might seem redundant but it sure is fun.

Unlocked: Chapter 8: Twisty Tunnels

Hazards: Fan blowing across platforms

Star Requirements

★	Complete the SWAP Zone
★★	Collect all the SWAP Zone Medals
★★★	Never Used Super Spin

SWAP Zone Medal Locations

1st	Right side center, behind rows of bumpers
2nd	Inside the circles of bumpers in the lower right
3rd	Top of platform, left of center, behind rows of bumpers

FROZEN TOP

Take a turn through the frosty parapets!

Unlocked: Chapter 11: Winter Keep

Hazards: No additional hazards

Star Requirements

★	Complete the SWAP Zone
★ ★	Collect all the SWAP Zone Medals
★ ★ ★	Never Used Super Spin

SWAP Zone Medal Locations

1st	Top left of platform
2nd	Top of platform, slightly left of center
3rd	Top center of platform

SPINNING COGS

Whirling around the clock.

Unlocked: Tower of Time Adventure Pack Level

Hazards: No additional hazards

Star Requirements

★	Complete the SWAP Zone
★ ★	Collect all the SWAP Zone Medals
★ ★ ★	Never Used Super Spin

SWAP Zone Medal Locations

1st	Slightly left of center, in the middle of many rows of bumpers
2nd	To the left of the starting point
3rd	Far right center of platform, behind many rows of bumpers

TELEPORT CHALLENGES

Teleport challenges are the least consistent type of challenge. Not because of what is asked of you. You collect three Rune Stones on three different maps to complete each challenge. However, the random nature of the platforms that make up each map keeps each visit to the same Teleport zone a little different.

The general layout of the maps is always the same, but the individual platforms that make up the maps are a little different each time you visit a map. In addition, platforms fall away and are replaced at regular intervals during each map. The change isn't instantaneous (although, after each set of three Rune Stones are collected, you get a bonus round and a fresh set of platforms). A white glow grows around the platform. When it completely surrounds the platform, the platform falls away. If your Skylander is on the platform when it falls, the challenge is over.

Teleport is the only ability your Skylander has for these challenges. It is always available, so you can keep Attack 2 pressed while tapping the control stick in different directions to move between platforms.

To earn the No Damage Taken third Star, learn to recognize hazard platforms and how they work. With some experience, you will know when it is safe to be on certain platforms, when they're about to be dangerous, and when you need to avoid them entirely.

The second player ability is Clean Slate. Clean Slate locks the platform the Skylander is currently standing on, even if it is about to drop away, and causes every other platform to vanish, and be replaced with random new platforms. Save this ability for the times when the platform under the Skylander is about to fall away and has no escape route.

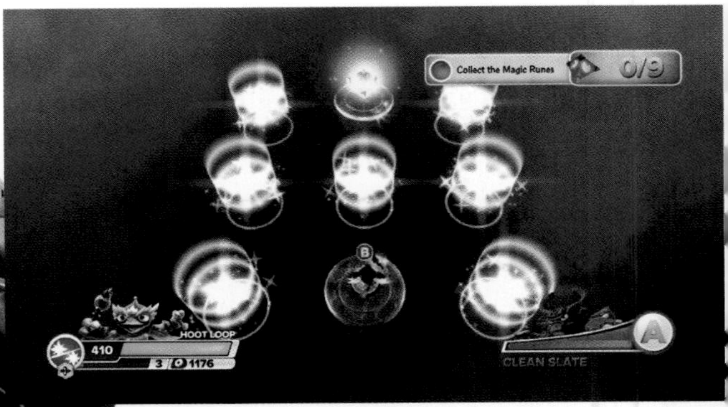

GOING WHOOSH

Bug Eyed Blinking around the Bayou!

Unlocked: Chapter 3: Mudwater Hollow

Hazards: Damaging platform, square platform

Star Requirements

★	Complete the SWAP Zone
★★	Collect all the SWAP Zone Medals
★★★	No Damage Taken

SWAP Zone Medal Locations

1st	Appears from lower center
2nd	Appears from top right
3rd	Appears from top right

HOURGLASS BLINK

Home of the great big glass hat.

Unlocked: Chapter 6: Iron Jaw Gulch

Hazards: Damaging platform, square platform, energy blasters

Star Requirements

★	Complete the SWAP Zone
★★	Collect all the SWAP Zone Medals
★★★	No Damage Taken

SWAP Zone Medal Locations

1st	Appears from lower center
2nd	Appears from top right
3rd	Appears from lower right

FLASH FROST

Unlock the secrets of the Winter Keep!

Unlocked: Chapter 11: Winter Keep

Hazards: Damaging platforms

Star Requirements

★	Complete the SWAP Zone
★★	Collect all the SWAP Zone Medals
★★★	No Damage Taken

SWAP Zone Medal Locations

1st	Appears from lower left
2nd	Appears from top right
3rd	Appears from top center

ETHEREAL TRANSFER

Pop in and see the poppies.

Unlocked: Chapter 12: Fantasm Forest

Hazards: Damaging platform, square platform

Star Requirements

★	Complete the SWAP Zone
★★	Collect all the SWAP Zone Medals
★★★	No Damage Taken

SWAP Zone Medal Locations

1st	Appears from center right
2nd	Appears from lower right
3rd	Appears from top left

BEACHED BLINKOUT

It will take sharp-sheared skill to navigate this one.

Unlocked: Sheep Wreck Islands Adventure Pack Level

Hazards: Damaging platform, square platform (can't jump to it), energy blasters (fires from outside active area)

Star Requirements

★	Complete the SWAP Zone
★★	Collect all the SWAP Zone Medals
★★★	No Damage Taken

SWAP Zone Medal Locations

1st	Appears from top center
2nd	Appears from top left
3rd	Appears from center right

BONUS MISSIONS

Bonus Missions are another way for you to earn Stars as a Portal Master. These are quick missions in a confined area. You are sent by Master Eon to help different groups who are dealing with an invasion by Kaos' Forces.

Bonus Mission Maps are found throughout Story Mode and Adventure Pack levels, with a few also for sale from Tuk's Emporium. Completing a challenge rewards you with a Charm.

Many of these missions are challenging, and should be attempted only after your Skylanders are high level and you have purchased most of their upgrades.

You earn Stars based on your total score, and scoring works the same way as other modes that keep track of scoring. You earn points and build your multiplier meter by attacking enemies. The number that appears in the circle near your score is your multiplier, which shows how much more valuable each enemy you defeat, and coin you collect, is than when the meter is at one. Playing Missions at higher difficulties awards more points. Also, when playing on a higher difficulty, the time limit is longer. You receive extra points for the seconds left on the timer.

TREBLE THEFT

Map Acquired: Tuk's Emporium for 1000 gold. Requires Portal Master Rank 15.

Reward: Body Armor Charm

Mission: Bring 5 instruments to the music group

TIME

Easy & Medium: 6:00

Hard: 8:05

Nightmare: 15:00

Score Requirements

★	Earn Over 0 Points
★ ★	Earn over 150,000 Points
★ ★ ★	Earn over 200,000 Points

Each musical instrument is suspended above the ground not far from the musician who plays it. There are Battle Gates blocking access to the instruments and you must defeat a variety of trolls to remove the Battle Gate. There is also a gate locked by a musical note near each musician. When you hand over the instrument to the musician, the gate is blown away by the music.

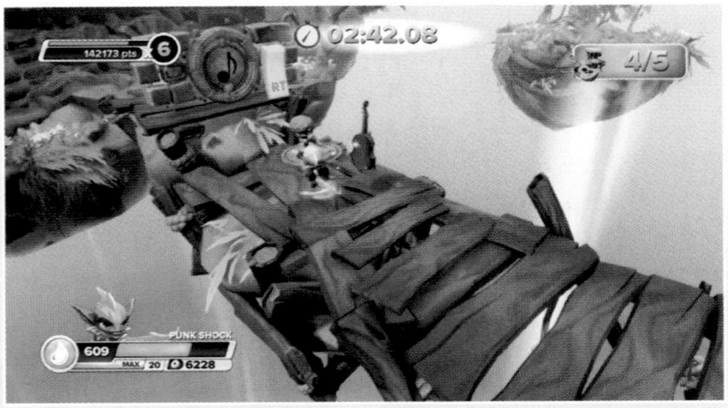

CHOMPY CHALLENGE

Map Acquired: After completing Mudwater Hollow.

Reward: Elemental Shield Charm

Mission: Beat 95 Chompies

TIME

Easy & Medium: 4:00

Hard: 5:10

Nightmare: 9:35

Score Requirements

★	Earn Over 0 Points
★ ★	Earn over 175,000 Points
★ ★ ★	Earn over 250,000 Points

There are many kinds of Chompies to tackle here, and you must take down 95 of them to complete the challenge. The number of Chompies and Chompy Pods in a given area is limited, and defeating them all opens teleporters. The first area has a single teleporter, but the next three areas each have two. When you choose the correct teleporter, you are sent to an area with more Chompies. If you choose the wrong teleporter, you end up fighting a group of Greebles that you must defeat before the teleporter pad in that area is available for use. The correct teleporters to use are (in order): right, top, and right.

UNDERCOVER GREEBLES

Map Acquired: Chapter 15: Kaos' Fortress
Reward: Elemental Fortune Charm
Mission: Eliminate 10 Greebles disguised as Sheep.

TIME
Easy & Medium: 4:20
Hard: 5:50
Nightmare: 10:50

Score Requirements

★	Earn Over 0 Points
★ ★	Earn over 175,000 points
★ ★ ★	Earn over 250,000 points

Greebles are disguising themselves as sheep to steal items from the archaeologists. There are sheep all over the area, but the imposters are easy to spot when they get up and run on two legs. Move close to them to get them to reveal themselves. You generally face the Greebles one on one, but they sometimes appear in pairs, or supported by other allies, such as Spellpunks. Battle Gates block your progress, which also serve to let you know when a Greeble is nearby.

CURSED STATUES

Map Acquired: Chapter 15: Kaos' Fortress
Reward: Air Freshener Charm
Mission: Defeat the Greeble Corruptors and destroy 8 statues.

TIME
Easy & Medium: 5:00
Hard: 6:45
Nightmare: 12:30

Score Requirements

★	Earn Over 0 Points
★ ★	Earn Over 175,000 Points
★ ★ ★	Earn Over 250,000 Points

There are cursed statues being defended by Greeble Corruptors. You must defeat the Greeble Corruptors and destroy eight statues. Before you can attack a statue, you must take down the Greeble Corruptors. Some statues have more than one Corruptor guarding it. Because time is limited, you should defeat each statue as you come to it and not go looking for another one that is more lightly defended. Some statues have other defenders helping the Greebles as well.

CHOMPY SAUCE

Map Acquired: Chapter 14: Fantasm Forest
Reward: Greeble Be Gone Charm
Mission: Mission Shut down 6 valves to stop the spilling Chompy sauce.

TIME
Easy & Medium: 5:05
Hard: 6:52
Nightmare: 12:43

Score Requirements

★	Earn Over 0 Points
★ ★	Earn Over 150,000 Points
★ ★ ★	Earn Over 200,000 Points

Greebles are fouling the area inhabited by the elder fish with the Chompy sauce and you must shut down the valves the Greebles are using to pump the sauce into the water. The valves are blocked by Battle Gates, so you must take down the Greeble chefs and other defenders before you can get to it. Life Spellpunks are among the enemies supporting the Greebles, and they should always be your first targets. Opening two valves also causes keys to drop, which are needed to unlock nearby gates. They appear near waterfalls, so watch for them after the announcement that a key has appeared.

FISHY FISHING

Map Acquired: Chapter 4: Rampant Ruins
Reward: Rabbit's Foot Charm
Mission: Destroy 5 giant harpoons with bombs.

TIME
Easy & Medium: 4:30
Hard: 6:05
Nightmare: 11:15

Score Requirements

★	Earn Over 0 Points
★ ★	Earn Over 150,000 Points
★ ★ ★	Earn Over 230,000 Points

Greebles in the area are using giant harpoons at the Elder Fish sanctuary, and it's harming the local ecosystem. You must find giant bombs and use them to destroy the harpoons. Unfortunately, the bombs you need are blocked by Battle Gates, so you must defeat a number of enemies at each to unlock them. The defenders of the Battle Gates aren't always just Greebles. You must also take on more powerful enemies, like Tech Geargolems. The other problem you face is that you need to cross rolling bridges while carrying some bombs to reach the harpoons. If you're having trouble crossing the bridges while carrying the bombs, try this challenge with one of the flying Skylanders, such as Spyro.

MASTER CHEF

Map Acquired: Chapter 3: Mudwater Hollow
Reward: Major Meal Charm
Mission: Fight your way to get to the boss.

TIME	
Easy & Medium:	3:50
Hard:	5:10
Nightmare:	9:35

Score Requirements

★	Earn Over 0 Points
★ ★	Earn Over 200,000 Points
★ ★ ★	Earn Over 350,000 Points

There are a few different types of locked gates to pass through in order to reach the Head Chef in the middle of the map, so be ready for fights at Battle Gates and a search for the key needed for a Locked Gate (sometimes keys are hidden behind Battle Gates!). When the game warns you about a Pumpkin Attack, avoid the red circles on the ground, which indicate where a pumpkin is about to land. Watch for Life Spellpunks during the battle against the Head Chef.

PLANTS VS CAKES

Map Acquired: Chapter 2: Cascade Glade
Reward: Four Leaf Clover Charm
Mission: Push 6 cakes to feed the Gobble Pods.

TIME	
Easy & Medium:	5:00
Hard:	6:45
Nightmare:	12:30

Score Requirements

★	Earn Over 0 Points
★ ★	Earn Over 75,000 Points
★ ★ ★	Earn Over 125,000 Points

For this mission, cakes become part of sliding stone puzzles. To feed a cake to a Gobble Pod, you must push the cake on top of the white square directly in front of the Gobble Pod. The only enemies you face during this mission are Greebles, which should not be much of a threat. Enjoy ruining their party!

FRUIT FIGHT

Map Acquired: Chapter 1: Mount Cloudbreak
Reward: Tasty Food Charm
Mission: Collect 95 fruits.

TIME	
Easy & Medium:	5:50
Hard:	7:53
Nightmare:	14:35

Score Requirements

★	Earn Over 0 Points
★ ★	Earn Over 100,000 Points
★ ★ ★	Earn Over 230,000 Points

Grabbing individual fruits floating around is the slow way to complete this mission. Look for food boxes (they're marked with an 'X') and wait for the outside attacker (who has been lobbing explosives from the start) to mark your Skylander's location with a red circle. When the explosive hits the food box, all the fruits inside are scattered around, ready to be picked up. When all the fruit in an area has been collected, look for a Battle Gate on a cannon. Defeat the Greebles in the area and use the cannon to travel to another area.

SERPENT ATTACK

Map Acquired: Tower of Time Adventure Pack Level
Reward: Elemental Fist Charm
Mission: Find the flute to hypnotize the Sand Monster and hit its three heads.

TIME	
Easy & Medium:	3:40
Hard:	4:55
Nightmare:	9:10

Score Requirements

★	Earn Over 0 Points
★ ★	Earn Over 50,000 Points
★ ★ ★	Earn Over 75,000 Points

When you find a crate with notes coming out of it, break it open to reveal the flute. Play the flute to put the serpent's head to sleep, and then attack it to knock it out. Move on to the next area and repeat the process. The last area is a bit trickier. There are more crates and enemies appear in larger numbers. The task remains the same, however. Reveal the flute, put the Sand Monster's head to sleep, and attack it until its life is depleted. If you're feeling overwhelmed, don't attack the Sand Moster's head while it is asleep. Focus on the enemies to thin their numbers before attacking the Sand Monster.

THIEF ON THE RUN

Map Acquired: Sheep Wreck Islands Adventure Pack Level

Reward: Charmed Actions Charm

Mission: Retrieve 75 packages.

TIME

Easy & Medium: 3:30

Hard: 4:45

Nightmare: 8:45

Score Requirements

★	Earn Over 0 Points
★ ★	Earn Over 150,000 Points
★ ★ ★	Earn Over 230,000 Points

There are two different ways to acquire packages during this mission. The first way is to collect the individual packages that are on the ground. These packages also serve to guide you to the locations of the other source of packages, a Package Thief. The bright red bag slung over their shoulder makes them stand out among the other Greebles who try to stop you during this level. Take out each Package Thief you find to pick up around ten packages at once.

FROZEN DELIGHTS

Map Acquired: Tuk's Emporium for 1000 gold. Requires Portal Master Rank 25.

Reward: Vitamin Supplements Charm

Mission: Melt 5 ice creams with the crystal lasers.

TIME

Easy & Medium: 3:50

Hard: 5:10

Nightmare: 9:35

Score Requirements

★	Earn Over 0 Points
★ ★	Earn Over 250,000 Points
★ ★ ★	Earn Over 300,000 Points

This mission is a series of laser crystal puzzles. You must direct the laser to strike the large mounds of ice cream that hold Yeti Elders, and block your path. The enemies on this level are different cyclops types, along with Air Spellpunks. You rarely need to stick around to fight enemies.

SWEET BLIZZARD

Map Acquired: Behind Sharpfin at Woodburrow's Airdocks, after completing Chapter 11: Winter Keep

Reward: Eye Poker Charm

Mission: Turn off 5 Ice Cream Machines.

TIME

Easy & Medium: 4:00

Hard: 5:25

Nightmare: 10:00

Score Requirements

★	Earn Over 0 Points
★ ★	Earn Over 100,000 Points
★ ★ ★	Earn Over 250,000 Points

To turn off each Ice Cream Machine, simply interact with it. That's the easy part. The harder part is that many Ice Cream Machines are blocked by Battle Gates, and the enemies and hazards in this Bonus Mission are a step above many others encountered so far. Mesmeralda's proximity mines make an appearance, as do Air Geargolems. Skip the fights that you can, and save your energy for Battle Gates.

FRIGID FIGHT

Map Acquired: Chapter 12: Frostfest Mountains
Reward: Unbridled Energy Charm
Mission: Bring 12 ghosts to the appropriate gate.

TIME
Easy & Medium: 4:00
Hard: 5:25
Nightmare: 10:00

Score Requirements

★	Earn Over 0 Points
★ ★	Earn Over 100,000 Points
★ ★ ★	Earn Over 150,000 Points

Guiding ghosts to the appropriate gate is not difficult. The trick is collecting more than one ghost of the same color and avoiding a ghost of a different color. As soon as you touch a ghost with a different color from the ones you already have, you lose all the previous ghosts to pick up the new one. And it's better to collect more than one ghost per trip to the gates because of the time you save. Drop off ghosts at the gates with the matching color to get credit for them. One bit of good news for this Bonus mission: taking damage has no effect on ghosts being carried.

ROYAL GEMS

Map Acquired: Chapter 10: Boney Islands
Reward: Wizard Repellant Charm
Mission: Defeat 9 armored cyclopes to retrieve the gems.

TIME
Easy & Medium: 5:00
Hard: 6:45
Nightmare: 12:30

Score Requirements

★	Earn Over 0 Points
★ ★	Earn Over 175,000 Points
★ ★ ★	Earn Over 250,000 Points

Each armored cyclops (they're all Brawlbucklers) has at least one helper Spellpunk. The further you get into the Mission, the more Cyclops Brawlbucklers and Spellpunks you face at once. Take down the Spellpunks first. They're generally the greater threat, and the Brawlbucklers are fairly slow. Lead them away from their support, then go after the Spellpunk when the Brawlbuckler misses an attack.

GHOST TRAPS

Map Acquired: Chapter 11: Winter Keep
Reward: Might of the Ancients Charm
Mission: Destroy the ghost traps with bombs.

TIME
Easy & Medium: 4:20
Hard: 5:50
Nightmare: 10:50

Score Requirements

★	Earn Over 0 Points
★ ★	Earn Over 150,000 Points
★ ★ ★	Earn Over 240,000 Points

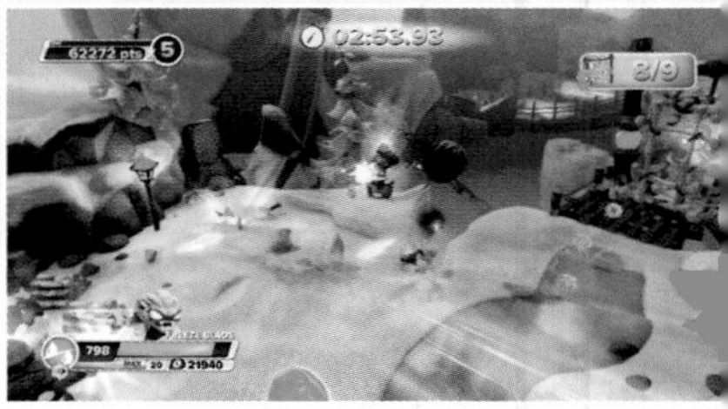

There are nine ghost cages you must destroy with bombs during this Bonus Mission. The bombs are on a timer, so if you are having problems reaching the gates before the bomb explodes, try this mission with a Skylander who has a dashing ability. There are Battle Gates all over the place as well. Most block your progress, but one blocks the bomb you need to destroy the final cage.

MAGIC CELLS

Map Acquired: Chapter 8: Twisty Tunnels
Reward: Electro Magnet Charm
Mission: Collect 95 Blue Energy Cells. Avoid the red cells.

TIME
Easy & Medium: 3:50
Hard: 5:10
Nightmare: 9:35

Score Requirements

★	Earn Over 0 Points
★ ★	Earn Over 50,000 Points
★ ★ ★	Earn Over 75,000 Points

The good news for this Bonus Mission is that there are few enemy encounters. The bad news is that there wasn't any room for many enemies because there are hazards everywhere! In addition to familiar hazards, you must watch out for the red cells. They don't hurt much, but they briefly lock any Skylander that touches them into place. The larger red hazards that look like pinball bumpers act like them too, throwing Skylanders around, usually into the red cells you were warned to avoid. There are also laser hazards that can only be avoided by jumping over them.

SLEEPY TURTLES

Map Acquired: Chapter 7: Motleyville
Reward: Small Shield Charm
Mission: Bring 6 turtles back to their nests.

TIME
Easy & Medium: 6:00
Hard: 8:05
Nightmare: 15:00

Score Requirements

★	Earn Over 0 Points
★ ★	Earn Over 175,000 Points
★ ★ ★	Earn Over 250,000 Points

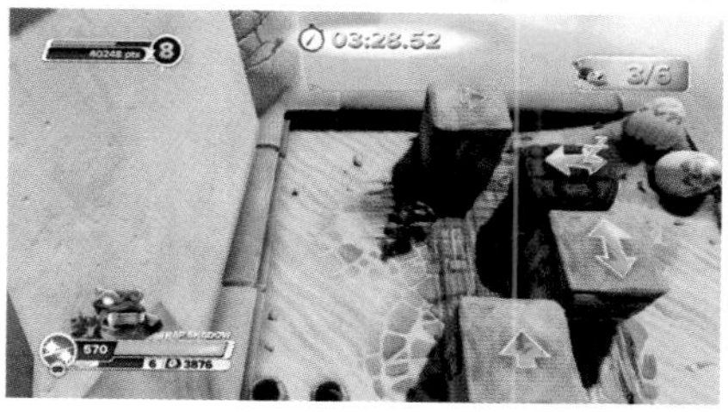

Harkening back to early sliding block puzzles, you must push turtles along a path. For this Bonus Mission, you need to move turtles closer to their nests. Move the stone blocks to create a clear path for the turtle first. If there are any Chompies or Chompy Pods in the way, don't worry about destroying them first. Just crush them with the stone blocks.

EGG ROYALE

Map Acquired: Chapter 6: Iron Jaw Gulch
Reward: Elemental Outlet Charm
Mission: Bring 6 eggs to the royal nest.

TIME
Easy & Medium: 5:00
Hard: 6:45
Nightmare: 12:30

Score Requirements

★	Earn Over 0 Points
★ ★	Earn Over 175,000 Points
★ ★ ★	Earn Over 250,000 Points

The eggs ou need are cattered round the level, nd it's possible o carry more han one at a ime. You need o be careful if ou try to gather too many eggs at once. If you get it by anything while carrying an egg, every egg you ave is returned back to where you picked it up. To omplicate things, some enemies appear on your way o an egg's location, and others wait until after you ick up the egg and are returning it to the nest before hey pop up and attack. The path back is never as lear as it seems.

GOLEM INVASION

Map Acquired: Tuk's Emporium for 1000 gold. Requires Portal Master Rank 35.
Reward: Element Deflect Charm
Mission: Destroy 12 Golems to free the turtles.

TIME
Easy & Medium: 5:30
Hard: 7:25
Nightmare: 13:45

Score Requirements

★	Earn Over 0 Points
★ ★	Earn Over 150,000 Points
★ ★ ★	Earn Over 200,000 Points

This Bonus Mission helpfully blocks your path when you're near a turtle to free. You face almost every type of Geargolem at some point during this battle, and there are a few fights that pit your Skylander against two Geargolems at the same time. Spellpunks sometimes stick their unwanted noses into fights, so keep an eye open for them to be aiding the Geargolems while hiding behind barriers. Greebles pop up from time to time, but only between Geargolem fights and only to be annoying. You can run past them if you want.

ARENA MODE

There are five total Arena Modes. Two of the modes, Solo Survival and Team Survival, award Stars based on how well you perform on your own and with a partner. The final three modes, Rival Survival, Battle Arena, and Ring Out, pit two players against each other in different styles of player versus player combat.

Completing an Arena Survival challenge for the first time, whether it's Solo or Team, awards a Charm.

SURVIVAL MODE

Survival Mode pits Skylanders under your control against large groups of enemies on small maps. Each challenge is divided into three stages, with a Bonus Stage after the first and second stages. During the Bonus Stage, the Food Thief appears and tries to escape from the arena. He isn't heading for an exit; he appears for a certain time before vanishing. If you take him down, your rewards include food and gold, and plenty of both!

UNLOCKING MAPS

All three Survival modes use the same set of maps, which are made available in groups of four. You must complete the first map in each group to open the second, then the second to open the third, and finally the third map to open the fourth. The first map, Super Hungry Gobble Pods, is available at the conclusion of Chapter 5: Jungle Rumble. Three groups of Survival maps are unlocked by continuing through the Story Mode. To open the final eight Survival maps, you must place the Arkeyan Crossbow figure and the Sheep Wreck Islands figure on your Portal of Power. These maps are opened in the same manner as the maps from Story Mode.

SCORING

To earn points and build your multiplier meter, attack enemies and objects. Destroying objects does not award points, but it does help build your meter. Collecting gold items awards points, but does not increase your multiplier meter.

The number that appears in the circle near your score is your multiplier, which shows how much more valuable each enemy you defeat, and coin you collect, is than when the meter is at one. The maximum value of your multiplier is 10. When playing Team Survival, both Skylanders contribute to the multiplier meter, and damage taken by either one lowers the multiplier number. In Rival Survival, each Skylander's progress is tracked individually, with the player with the higher score being declared the winner.

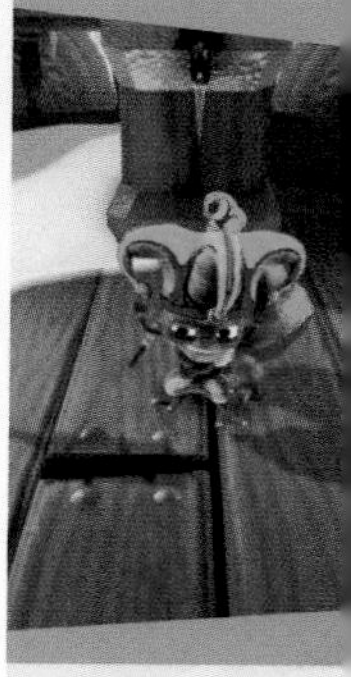

SUPER HUNGRY GOBBLE PODS

Unlocked: Complete Chapter 5: Jungle Rumble.

Reward: Elemental Noms Charm

Enemies

Stage 1	Chompy, Evilized Greeble, Greeble Ironclad
Stage 2	Chompy, Chompy Powerhouse, Greeble Ironclad, Life Spell Punk, Greeble Blunderbuss
Stage 3	Chompy, Chompy Powerhouse, Evilized Greeble, Air Spell Punk, Greeble Ironclad, Life Spell Punk

Score Requirements

★	Earn Over 5000 Points
★ ★	Earn Over 30,000 Points
★ ★ ★	Earn Over 65,000 Points

Super Hungry Gobble Pods is a straightforward brawl against waves of enemies with the added twist of potential allies in the form of the four Gobble Pods in cages around the arena. When a Gobble Pod is free of its cage, it eats nearby enemies, which still count toward your score. The Gobble Pods are returned to their cages, so you may need to free them multiple times. They are indestructible.

POKEY POKEY SPIKES

Unlocked: Complete the Super Hungry Gobble Pods arena.

Reward: Pointy Spear Charm

Enemies

Stage 1	Evilized Greeble, Greeble Heaver, Life Spell Punk, Greeble Slamspin
Stage 2	Evilized Greeble, Greeble Blunderbuss, Greeble Slamspin, Chompy, Earth Geargolem
Stage 3	Evilized Greeble, Greeble Heaver, Earth Geargolem, Chompy Powerhouse, Life Spell Punk

Score Requirements

★	Earn Over 7500 Points
★ ★	Earn Over 50,000 Points
★ ★ ★	Earn Over 80,000 Points

Skylanders are Cursed for Pokey Pokey Spikes, and rain clouds fly over their heads as a reminder. Cursed Skylanders suffer periodic damage, but the good news is that enemies are more likely to drop food when defeated. Spear traps serve as an extra hazard for this arena. During the first two stages, only half the spears are active. However, for the final round all spears are in play.

ANGRY ANGRY PLANTS

Unlocked: Complete the Pokey Pokey Spikes Pods arena.

Reward: Sword Breaker Charm

Enemies

Stage 1	Chompy, Chompy Pastepetal, Chompy Pod, Evilized Greeble, Greeble Heaver, Greeble Slamspin
Stage 2	Evilized Greeble, Chompy Pod, Chompy Powerhouse, Chompy, Greeble Slamspin, Arkeyan Slamshock
Stage 3	Chompy Pod, Chompy, Evilized Greeble, Greeble Heaver, Greeble Slamspin, Chompy Pastepetal, Chompy Powerhouse, Arkeyan Slamshock

Score Requirements

★	Earn Over 5000 Points
★ ★	Earn Over 40,000 Points
★ ★ ★	Earn Over 65,000 Points

Chompy Pods appear at the start of every stage, but they're not the only source of Chompies on this map. Enemies are dropped in from above, climb up from under the ground, and down the tunnels on the sides of the arena.

ARENA MODE

CHOMP CHOMP CHOMPIES

Unlocked: Complete the Angry Angry Plants arena.

Reward: Delicious Food Charm

Enemies

Stage 1	Chompy, Grumblebum Rocketshooter, Grumblebum Thrasher
Stage 2	Chompy Rustbud, Grumblebum Rocketshooter, Grumblebum Thrasher
Stage 3	Chompy Powerhouse, Grumblebum Rocketshooter, Grumblebum Thrasher

Score Requirements

★	Earn Over 7500 Points
★ ★	Earn Over 50,000 Points
★ ★ ★	Earn Over 80,000 Points

Your goal in this mission is to keep the pile of fruit in the middle of the arena from being destroyed by the attacking Chompies and Grumblebums. The hardest part of the mission begins when Grumblebum Rocketshooters start to appear. You can't move or shoot through the fruit, which complicates dealing with the ranged attacks of the Rocketshooters. Melee Skylanders, especially slow melee Skylanders, will have a though time here.

SAND-PIT-FALL

Unlocked: Complete Chapter 9: Serpent's Peak.

Reward: Power Blend Charm

Enemies

Stage 1	Evilized Greeble, Greeble Blunderbuss
Stage 2	Greeble Slamspin, Greeble Blunderbuss, Greeble Ironclad, Fire Geargolem
Stage 3	Fire Geargolem, Greeble Slamspin, Life Spell Punk, Greeble Ironclad

Score Requirements

★	Earn Over 7500 Points
★ ★	Earn Over 50,000 Points
★ ★ ★	Earn Over 80,000 Points

The sinkhole in the middle of the stage spells the end for enemies, but your Skylander takes a hit of damage and is returned to the arena floor. Forcing enemies into the pit still earns points for you, but XP bubbles are likely out of your reach.

SHELLSHOCK'S CURSE

Unlocked: Complete the Sand-Pit-Fall arena.

Reward: Greeble Grapplers Charm

Enemies

Stage 1	Arkeyan Barrelbot, Evilized Greeble, Arkeyan Slamshock
Stage 2	Greeble Heaver, Fire Geargolem, Arkeyan Rip-Rotor, Chompy Rustbud, Evilized Greeble
Stage 3	Arkeyan Barrelbot, Life Spell Punk, Chompy Rustbud, Arkeyan Knuckleduster

Score Requirements

★	Earn Over 10,000 Points
★ ★	Earn Over 60,000 Points
★ ★ ★	Earn Over 90,000 Points

The Cursed status is back, as is the sinkhole in the middle of the arena floor. Arkeyan Rip-rotors are surprisingly easy to lure into flying over the top of the sinkhole, which still pulls them in at the height of the spin. During the last round, keep on the Life Spell Punks when they spawn. They hug the edges of the arena and heal from the fringes as much as they can.

BEWARE OF THE BIRD

Unlocked: Complete the Shellshock's Curse arena.

Reward: Eight Leaf Clover Charm

Enemies

Stage 1	Arkeyan Knuckleduster, Chompy Rustbud, Arkeyan Rip-Rotor, Arkeyan Barrelbot, Arkeyan Slamshock
Stage 2	Arkeyan Knuckleduster, Chompy Rustbud, Arkeyan Rip-Rotor, Tech Geargolem
Stage 3	Chompy Rustbud, Arkeyan Rip-Rotor, Tech Geargolem, Arkeyan Knuckleduster, Arkeyan Slamshock

Score Requirements

★	Earn Over 10,000 Points
★★	Earn Over 60,000 Points
★★★	Earn Over 90,000 Points

The sinkhole is covered with wood planks for this battle. The Bird flies down and gets its head stuck (after one or two attacks) at the end of each round. Jump in and attack while it is vulnerable. At the end of the second round, it flies to the roof and fires into the arena floor between jumping attacks. During the third round, it pulls its head out of the ground and fires a laser beam from its mouth.

SNAKE IN THE HOLE

Unlocked: Complete the Beware of the Bird arena.

Reward: Health Extender Charm

Enemies

Stage 1	Evilized Greeble, Greeble Blunderbuss
Stage 2	Greeble Slamspin, Greeble Blunderbuss, Greeble Ironclad
Stage 3	Evilized Greeble, Life Spell Punk, Greeble Slamspin

Score Requirements

★	Earn Over 10,000 Points
★★	Earn Over 60,000 Points
★★★	Earn Over 90,000 Points

The sinkhole remains covered for this challenge. A giant snake watches over the arena and spits spiky balls on to the floor (watch out for the red circles) while you're fighting the waves of Greebles. When a horn appears on the arena floor, try to take out as many Greebles as you can and then use the horn to charm the snake. When the snake is charmed, attack it quickly. Repeat this process for all three rounds, until the snake's health bar is depleted.

BOARDING PARTY

Unlocked: Complete Chapter 13: Mesmeralda's Show

Reward: Gourmet Meal Charm

Enemies

Stage 1	Coldspear Cyclops, Twistpick Cyclops, Missile Mauler
Stage 2	Coldspear Cyclops, Cyclops Gazermage, Cyclops Bucklebrawler
Stage 3	Magic Spell Punk, Missile Mauler, Twistpick Cyclops

Score Requirements

★	Earn Over 15,000 Points
★★	Earn Over 60,000 Points
★★★	Earn Over 100,000 Points

Boarding Party is a basic brawler in an arena with no hazards and no obstructions. It takes place on a boat, so enemies appear by climbing over the sides. You can knock them back off the boat at those same spots with a well-timed attack.

ICICLE BOMBING

Unlocked: Complete the Boarding Party arena.

Reward: Ultimate Defense Charm

Enemies

Stage 1	Coldspear Cyclops, Twistpick Cyclops, Magic Spell Punk, Cyclops Gazermage
Stage 2	Coldspear Cyclops, Twistpick Cyclops, Cyclops Gazermage
Stage 3	Ice Geargolem, Coldspear Cyclops, Twistpick Cyclops, Cyclops Gazermage

Score Requirements

★	Earn Over 15000 Points
★ ★	Earn Over 90,000 Points
★ ★ ★	Earn Over 150,000 Points

There's quite a bit going on in this map. Your Skylander is Cursed, which always makes things more interesting. The bottom half of the map is covered by snow. Finally, a ship flies in the background and it's covered with Cyclops Snowblasters. The Snowblasters fire a stream of ice pellets into the arena as they pass by.

EXPLODING SNOWMEN

Unlocked: Complete the Icicle Bombing arena.

Reward: Kaos Kruncher Charm

Enemies

Stage 1	Coldspear Cyclops, Twistpick Cyclops, Missile Mauler,
Stage 2	Coldspear Cyclops, Cyclops Gazermage, Cyclops Bucklebrawler
Stage 3	Cyclops Brawlbuckler, Chompy Frostflower, Magic Spell Punk, Twistpick Cyclops

Score Requirements

★	Earn Over 10,000 Points
★ ★	Earn Over 60,000 Points
★ ★ ★	Earn Over 100,000 Points

Each stage is fairly standard until you hit the point where the Food Thief normally makes his appearance. He still appears, but you must first survive a wave of the proximity mines used by Mesmeralda, though they're called ice bombs here. Avoiding the ice bombs becomes increasingly more difficult in each stage. They move across the arena in unison, and you need to keep your Skylander on the move to avoid being blown up.

PERFECT CAPTAIN

Unlocked: Complete the Exploding Snowmen arena.

Reward: Instant Experience Charm

Enemies

Stage 1	Coldspear Cyclops, Twistpick Cyclops, Cyclops Gazermage
Stage 2	Chompy Frostflower, Cyclops Brawlbuckler, Cyclops Gazermage
Stage 3	Chompy Frostflower, Cyclops Brawlbuckler, Twistpick Cyclops, Magic Spell Punk

Score Requirements

★	Earn Over 15,000 Points
★ ★	Earn Over 25,000 Points
★ ★ ★	Earn Over 45,000 Points

Perfect Captain refers to the fact that your Skylander has only 1 HP for this arena! You must avoid being hit by the enemies on the ship, and you must also avoid the Cyclops Snowblasters firing on the ship as well. The cold hinders your movement if you are hit. Hide behind the higher walls on either end of the ship, and stay on the move. One hit and it's over! Not that you will miss him with only 1 HP, but the Food Thief does not make an appearance in this challenge.

VORTEX BANQUET

Unlocked: Place the Sheep Wreck Islands figure on your Portal of Power.

Reward: Mountain's Resolve Charm

Enemies

Stage 1	Coldspear Cyclops, Cyclops Gazermage, Twistpick Cyclops, Vortex Geargolem
Stage 2	Coldspear Cyclops, Cyclops Gazermage, Twistpick Cyclops, Vortex Geargolem
Stage 3	Coldspear Cyclops, Cyclops Gazermage, Twistpick Cyclops, Cyclops Sleetthrower, Vortex Geargolem

Score Requirements

★	Earn Over 25,000 Points
★ ★	Earn Over 120,000 Points
★ ★ ★	Earn Over 200,000 Points

The cyclops units carry over their visual theme from Sheep Wreck Islands, but they're the same cyclops you're used to. When a vortex appears in a set of columns in the back of the arena, look for a Vortex Geargolem. You must keep the Vortex Geargolems away from the Vortex when they appear. They don't attack, so you are free to take it down quickly without worrying about defense. If Vortex Geargolems reach three vortices, you fail the challenge.

CYCLOPS MAKEOVER

Unlocked: Complete the Vortex Banquet arena.

Reward: Good Luck Charm

Enemies

Stage 1	Coldspear Cyclops, Cyclops Sleetthrower, Twistpick Cyclops, Cyclops Brawlbuckler
Stage 2	Coldspear Cyclops, Cyclops Sleetthrower, Twistpick Cyclops, Magic Spell Punk, Cyclops Brawlbuckler
Stage 3	Twistpick Cyclops, Chompy, Coldspear Cyclops, Cyclops Sleetthrower, Chompy Boomblossom, Cyclops Brawlbuckler

Score Requirements

★	Earn Over 20,000 Points
★ ★	Earn Over 115,000 Points
★ ★ ★	Earn Over 190,000 Points

Your Skylander is Cursed for this challenge. When a vortex appears, be on the lookout for a Coldspear Cyclops (they stand out because they're the original green skinned version, and they're larger than the other cyclopes in the area). If the Coldspear Cyclops reaches the vortex, it is upgraded to a Cyclops Brawlbuckler.

SHEEP MAGE RAGE

Unlocked: Complete the Cyclops Makeover arena.

Reward: Mage Masher Charm

Enemies

Stage 1	Coldspear Cyclops, Cyclops Gazermage, Vortex Geargolem, Twistpick Cyclops, Small and Giant Blitzbloom Chompy
Stage 2	Coldspear Cyclops, Cyclops Sleetthrower, Vortex Geargolem, Cyclops Brawlbuckler, Chompy Boomblossom, Cyclops Gazermage
Stage 3	Coldspear Cyclops, Vortex Geargolem, Cyclops Brawlbuckler, Cyclops Sleetthrower

Score Requirements

★	Earn Over 20,000 Points
★ ★	Earn Over 115,000 Points
★ ★ ★	Earn Over 190,000 Points

Vortex Geargolems spawn at the vortices only, so watch the vortices for trouble. Toward the end of the first round, the Sheep Mage gets involved by spewing thorny objects into the area, and then sucking in and blowing out air. Avoid the thorny objects during the wind storm as best you can. There is no cover, which makes things tougher. After the second round, Chompy Boomblossoms are added to the already dangerous mix, so take them out before they can get close enough to deal damage.

CHUNKY CHOMPIES

Unlocked: Complete the Sheep Mage Rage arena.

Reward: Power Clover Charm

Enemies

Stage 1	Chompy, Coldspear Cyclops, Vortex Geargolem
Stage 2	Coldspear Cyclops, Chompy Powerhouse, Cyclops Gazermage, Twistpick Cyclops
Stage 3	Coldspear Cyclops, Chompy Blitzbloom, Cyclops Sleetthrower, Chompy Boomblossom

Score Requirements

★	Earn Over 15,000 Points
★ ★	Earn Over 75,000 Points
★ ★ ★	Earn Over 125,000 Points

This is a battle primarily against large waves of Chompies followed up by a wave of large Chompies. The Chompies that spawn from the vortices are much larger than other Chompies you fought before. They're much tougher and won't go down easily. The type of Chompy changes with each level, and the big guys always match the little ones.

SAND CASTLE

Unlocked: Place the Arkeyan Crossbow figure on your Portal of Power.

Reward: Cyclops Swatter Charm

Enemies

Stage 1	Chompy, Cadet Crasher, Loose Cannon, Boom Boss, Missile Mauler
Stage 2	Chompy, Giant Chompy, Cadet Crasher, Loose Cannon, Boom Boss, Missile Mauler
Stage 3	Chompy Boomblossom, Cadet Crasher, Loose Cannon, Boom Boss, Missile Mauler

Score Requirements

★	Earn Over 15,000 Points
★ ★	Earn Over 50,000 Points
★ ★ ★	Earn Over 100,000 Points

You must protect the Sand Tower from swarms of tropically themed trolls. The Loose Cannons are the trolls assigned to ignore everything and go after the Sand Tower, so they should be your main targets. Activate the water cannons atop sand castles by sliding them to the front, where they fire water balloons for a bit before they slide back.

BEACH BREACH

Unlocked: Complete the Sand Castle arena.

Reward: Big Pants Charm

Enemies

Stage 1	Chompy, Cadet Crasher, Missile Mauler
Stage 2	Chompy, Giant Chompy, Cadet Crasher, Air Geargolem
Stage 3	Chompy, Giant Chompy, Chompy Boomblossom, Cadet Crasher, Missile Mauler

Score Requirements

★	Earn Over 5000 Points
★ ★	Earn Over 25,000 Points
★ ★ ★	Earn Over 50,000 Points

Your Skylander is Cursed for this challenge. You are back defending the Sand Tower from trolls and Chompies. The trolls are more concerned with attacking your Skylander but the Chompies appear to be devoted to attacking the Sand Tower. Some Chompies that spawn from the surf are a bit larger and tougher than standard Chompies.

TROLL BEACH ATTACK

Unlocked: Complete the Beach Breach arena.

Reward: Impervious Charm

Enemies

Stage 1	Chompy, Cadet Crusher, Missile Mauler
Stage 2	Chompy Boomblossom, Giant Chompy Boomblossom, Cadet Crusher, Missile Mauler, Air Geargolem
Stage 3	Loose Cannon, Giant Chompy, Cadet Crusher, Missile Mauler, Air Geargolem

Score Requirements

★	Earn Over 15,000 Points
★ ★	Earn Over 50,000 Points
★ ★ ★	Earn Over 100,000 Points

Troll Beach Attack is a return to traditional challenges. You must survive three stages of troll and Chompy attacks. No need to defend anything here. The one twist to this level is that the cannons that you were using to help on defense are now trained on your Skylander! Watch out for red circles appearing on the beach and stay clear to avoid taking damage. At the end of each stage, even the final stage, the cannons blanket the beach with cannonballs. Stay on the move, otherwise your Skylander won't last long.

CHOMPY TSUNAMI

Unlocked: Complete the Troll Beach Attack arena.

Reward: Luck of the Mabu Charm

Enemies

Stage 1	Chompy, Cadet Crusher, Missile Mauler
Stage 2	Chompy, Chompy Powerhouse, Cadet Crusher, Missile Mauler, Loose Cannon, Boom Boss
Stage 3	Chompy, Chompy Boomblossom, Cadet Crusher, Missile Mauler, Loose Cannon, Air Geargolem

Score Requirements

★	Earn Over 10,000 Points
★ ★	Earn Over 50,000 Points
★ ★ ★	Earn Over 85,000 Points

The Chompy Castles that appear in the sand spawn Chompies until they are destroyed. When the castles appear, destroy them quickly or the beach will be overrun with Chompies before you know it.

BATTLE ARENA & RING OUT

Battle Arena and Ring Out share two maps (Rampart Ruins and Fiery Forge) but otherwise have maps unique to them. Both modes have three maps available immediately, even before you start playing the Story Mode. Place the Arkeyan Crossbow figure on your *Portal of Power* to unlock the Treacherous Beach Battle arena. The Tower of Time figure adds the Ring Out arena, Tic Toc Terrace. The Fiery Forge figure opens an arena of the same name that is available in both modes.

BATTLE ARENA

In Battle Arena, the goal is to reduce the other Skylander's health to zero before the same happens to your Skylander. Power-ups and food appear at random times at different locations on the map, so long as they are turned on for the fight. The other options allow you to change the number of lives each Skylander has (the number of lives left appears near their names), and whether to make two Skylanders of different levels more equal in the arena.

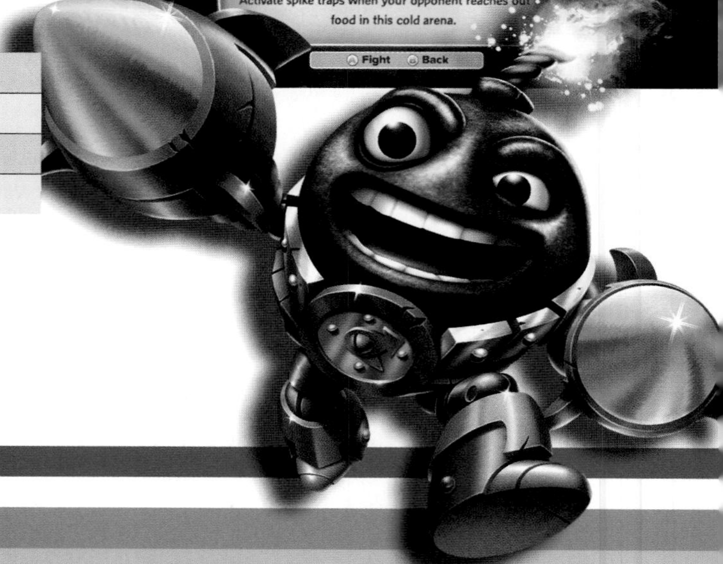

Battle Arena Settings

Power-Ups	On/Off
Food	On/Off
Lives	1, 3, 5, 7, 9
Fair Fight	On/Off

BATTLE ARENA MAPS

RAMPART RUINS

Unlocked: Available with purchase of game

Rampart Ruins is a compact map that resembles the tops of two castle towers connected by a wooden ramp. Stepping on the teleporters sends your Skylander to the highest point of the opposite tower. The mines blocking the wooden ramp respawn quickly should they be destroyed.

QUICKSAND QUARRY

Unlocked: Available with purchase of game

Quicksand Quarry gets its name from the areas of flowing sand around the map. Skylanders caught in the moving sand are pulled down into it slightly, and suffer reduced movement speed. Skylanders can fall through the hole in the middle of the map (on the quicksand side only) and fall over the edge of the map that isn't protected by a fence. Falling off the map does not count against your life total.

FROZEN OUTPOST

Unlocked: Available with purchase of game

The large spear trap in the center of Frozen Outpost's lower floor is activated by any of the three green pads around it. Once it is triggered, there is a short cooldown before it's ready to use again. The two teleporters on the topmost level send Skylanders to the same spot in the center of the spear trap. The teleporters on the lower level lead to the same spot in the middle of the upper area.

FIERY FORGE

Unlocked: Place the Fiery Forge figure on your Portal of Power

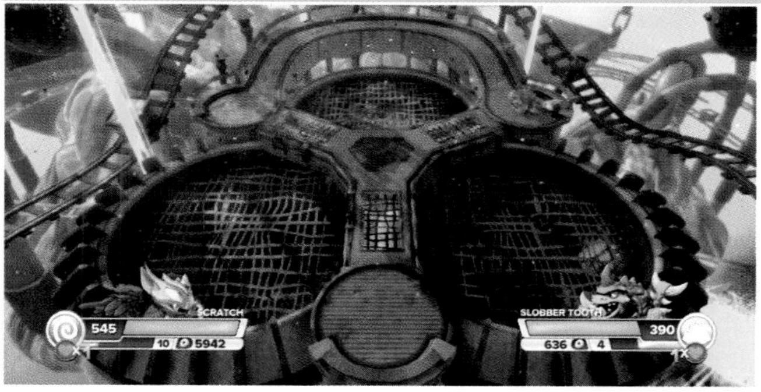

All the action in Fiery Forge takes place either on the narrow walkway looping around the three lava pits, or in the lava pits themselves. Lava appears in the pits often, and either comes up from under a pit, or pours into a pit from above. The lava briefly fills one of the three pits, then drains away.

TREACHEROUS BEACH

Unlocked: Place the Arkeyan Crossbow figure on your Portal of Power

Despite its dangerous-sounding name, Treacherous Beach is relatively quiet for a place where two Skylanders try to knock each other out. The map extends from the tops of both sand castles to the fence in the surf below. Beyond Power-ups and two bounce pads that send Skylanders to the top of the sand castles, there aren't any other environmental items to worry about.

RING OUT

In Ring Out, the goal is to knock the opposing Skylander over the side of the map with a power hit. Each successful attack on your opponent builds a Super Punch meter that appears near your Skylander's name (Skylanders do not have health bars in Ring Out). When the meter is full, the next press of Attack 1 is a Super Punch attack that knocks your opponent's Skylander over the edge if they're close enough.

Power-ups appear at random times at different locations on the map, so long as they are turned on for the fight. The other options allow you to change the number of times each Skylander can be knocked out (the number of lives left appears near their names) before one is declared the winner, and whether to make two Skylanders of different levels more equal in the arena.

Ring-Out Settings

Power-Ups	On/Off
Lives	1, 3, 5, 7, 9
Fair Fight	On/Off

RING OUT MAPS

RAMPART RUINS

Unlocked: Available with purchase of game

The two castle tops that make up Rampart Ruins appear to be either in the process of being built or being dismantled. There are barely any standing walls, which makes fighting near any edge dangerous. The lack of walls makes Bounce Pads on the level dangerous to use. Try to avoid using them, save as a last resort to escape a Super Punch.

QUICK DRAW CORRAL

Unlocked: Available with purchase of game

Quick Draw Corral is one of the safer arenas in terms of not defeating yourself by falling over the edge unaided. A low wall outlines the outer edge of the walkway around the arena, and it keeps Skylanders contained unless they jump over it or get knocked over it by a Super Punch.

BLOSSOM ISLANDS

Unlocked: Available with purchase of game

The wooden walkway connecting the three Blossom Islands is the dangerous way to move between the islands. There are six total teleporter locations, with two on each island. However, at most there are only five teleporters active at the same time. The teleporters send Skylanders to the island closest to its location, meaning two islands have two teleporters while the third island has only one. For example, the teleporters on the left and right islands nearer to the top island send Skylanders to the center of the top island.

TIC TOC TERRACE

Unlocked: Place the Tower of Time figure on your Portal of Power

The outer ring and gears of Tic Toc Terrace are perpetually moving. Be careful when moving to the outer ring. The spinning gears and large gaps between the gears make movement between the platforms tricky. The teleporters on the outer ring send Skylanders back to the clock face that makes up the central platform.

FIERY FORGE

Unlocked: Place the Fiery Forge figure on your Portal of Power

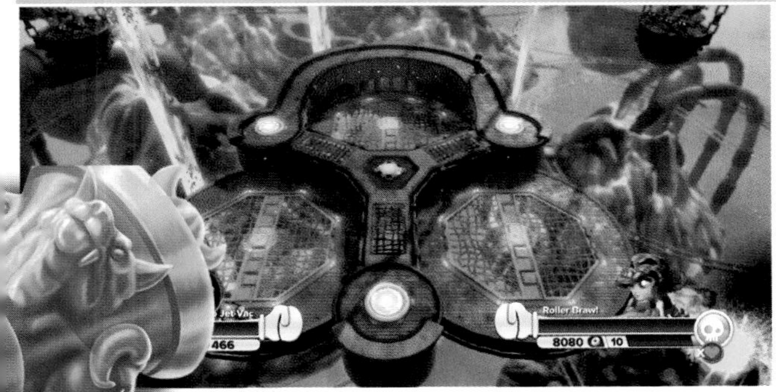

The hazard switch in the center of the map drops the floor out from under the three circular bowls that make up the lowest part of this arena. If the green hazard circle is lit, avoid using the teleporters. They send Skylanders to the center of the areas that lose their floors. The lowest teleporter sends Skylanders to the top bowl. The teleporter on the left sends Skylanders to the right bowl, and the right teleporter goes to the bowl on the left.

TIME ATTACK MODE

In Time Attack Mode, you earn Stars by completing Story Mode and Adventure Pack levels in under a certain time limit. Each level has its own time requirements for earning Stars, and that information is included on the following pages. Playing on your own and playing with a friend both have the same time requirements.

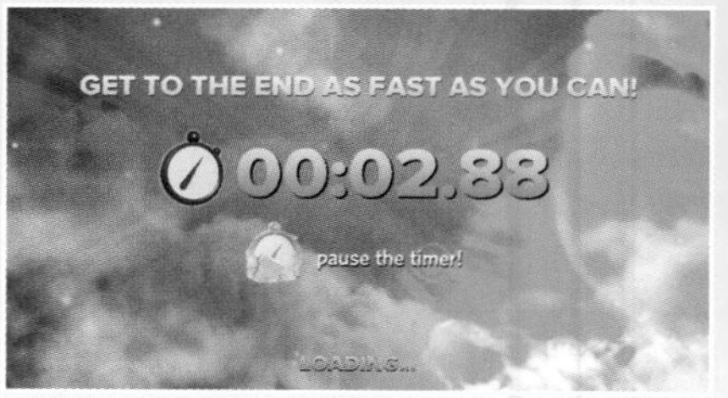

CHANGES IN TIME ATTACK MODE VERSUS STORY MODE

The collectible items on each map (Soul Gems, Legendary Treasures, Hats, and other similar objects) change into objects that freeze the clock for 20-25 seconds. They appear as a blue oval with a clock icon inside. The amount of time the clock is frozen appears in a light blue icon to the left of your timer.

These time-stopping clock icons also appear randomly from destroyed objects and defeated enemies, though these items stop the clock for a much shorter time, about six seconds. Picking up a blue oval item while another one is active adds additional time to the light blue timer.

In-game events, such as Spark Locks, cinematics, or conversations with other characters, pause the clock until the event ends. In all other areas, your timer continues its countdown. That means you should skip every non-essential pick up, SWAP Zone Challenge, and Elemental Gate.

QUICK TIPS FOR MAXIMIZING YOUR SCORE

SKIP EVERYTHING YOU CAN

There is no scoring. There's no bonus for completeness. The only thing that matters is getting to the end. Avoid fights unless defeating enemies is faster than letting them nip at your heels.

USE SKYLANDERS WITH A DASH ABILITY

There are a handful of Skylanders who have an ability that allows them to move through areas faster than others. Get them to level 20, buy all their abilities, and put them to use in Time Attack Mode!

FAMILIARITY IS YOUR GREATEST ASSET

Get to know the levels and what you must do and what you can skip. Learn which clock-stopping pick ups are worth the detour to get, and which ones are just too far away to bother with.

MAGIC ITEMS ARE GREAT

Everything helps when you're trying to get through places quickly. Not just the Winged Boots, but also the Adventure Pack pieces that make Battle Gate encounters go much faster.

TIME REQUIREMENTS FOR EARNING STARS

Mount Cloudbreak

★	Set a Personal Best Time
★★	Cleared in Under: 6:30
★★★	Cleared in Under: 5:30

Mudwater Hollow

★	Set a Personal Best Time
★★	Cleared in Under: 15:00
★★★	Cleared in Under: 12:00

Jungle Rumble

★	Set a Personal Best Time
★★	Cleared in Under: 3:00
★★★	Cleared in Under: 1:45

Motleyville

★	Set a Personal Best Time
★★	Cleared in Under: 12:30
★★★	Cleared in Under: 11:00

Serpent's Peak

★	Set a Personal Best Time
★★	Cleared in Under: 3:00
★★★	Cleared in Under: 2:30

Winter Keep

★	Set a Personal Best Time
★★	Cleared in Under: 16:00
★★★	Cleared in Under: 14:00

Mesmeralda's Show

★	Set a Personal Best Time
★★	Cleared in Under: 4:40
★★★	Cleared in Under: 4:00

Kaos' Fortress

★	Set a Personal Best Time
★★	Cleared in Under: 9:30
★★★	Cleared in Under: 8:30

Cloudbreak Core

★	Set a Personal Best Time
★★	Cleared in Under: 9:30
★★★	Cleared in Under: 8:20

Tower of Time

★	Set a Personal Best Time
★★	Cleared in Under: 22:00
★★★	Cleared in Under: 20:00

Cascade Glade

★	Set a Personal Best Time
★★	Cleared in Under: 6:30
★★★	Cleared in Under: 4:50

Rampant Ruins

★	Set a Personal Best Time
★★	Cleared in Under: 8:00
★★★	Cleared in Under: 6:00

Iron Jaw Gulch

★	Set a Personal Best Time
★★	Cleared in Under: 7:30
★★★	Cleared in Under: 5:50

Twisty Tunnels

★	Set a Personal Best Time
★★	Cleared in Under: 11:30
★★★	Cleared in Under: 10:00

Boney Islands

★	Set a Personal Best Time
★★	Cleared in Under: 14:30
★★★	Cleared in Under: 11:40

Frostfest Mountains

★	Set a Personal Best Time
★★	Cleared in Under: 8:30
★★★	Cleared in Under: 6:30

Fantasm Forest

★	Set a Personal Best Time
★★	Cleared in Under: 25:00
★★★	Cleared in Under: 20:00

Motherly Mayhem

★	Set a Personal Best Time
★★	Cleared in Under: 8:30
★★★	Cleared in Under: 7:45

Sheep Wreck Islands

★	Set a Personal Best Time
★★	Cleared in Under: 18:00
★★★	Cleared in Under: 16:00

SCORE MODE

In Score Mode, you earn Stars by completing Story Mode and Adventure Pack levels and hitting certain scores. Each level has its own minimum scores for earning Stars, and that information is included on the following pages. Playing on your own and playing with a friend both have the same score requirements.

To earn points and build your multiplier meter, attack enemies and objects. Destroying objects does not award points, but it does help build your meter. Collecting gold items awards points, but does not increase your multiplier meter.

The number that appears in the circle near your score is your multiplier, which shows how much more valuable each enemy you defeat, and coin you collect, is than when the meter is at one. The maximum value of your multiplier is 30. Changing Skylanders during a Score Mode level does not affect your scoring or multiplier. When playing with a friend, both Skylanders contribute to the multiplier meter, and damage taken by either one lowers the multiplier number.

CHANGES IN SCORE MODE VERSUS STORY MODE

The collectible items on each map (Soul Gems, Legendary Treasures, Hats, and other similar objects) change into bonus multipliers. They appear as a blue 1X object. These multipliers also appear randomly from destroyed objects and defeated enemies. A shield power up also appears from time to time. The shield protects your Skylander from losing a multiplier for one hit.

Coins collected during SWAP Zone Challenges do not add to your score. Only the SWAP Zone Medals collected while running a challenge matter. When the medals turn into gems to gather up and the SWAP Zone has been completed, you get a 1X multiplier (it replaces the collectible from completing the challenge) and the gold from gathering the gems.

Spark Locks, whether they're blocking chests or gates, award a big multiplier bonus when you complete the lock with all three bolts.

QUICK TIPS FOR MAXIMIZING YOUR SCORE

TAKE YOUR TIME

There is no time limit in Score Mode, so it's more important to be thorough than it is to be fast. Solve every Spark Lock with three bolts. Complete every SWAP Zone with three gems. Don't skip Elemental gates.

...UNLESS THERE'S A CHANCE TO LOSE THE MULTIPLIER

If you're worried about passing through a hazard- or enemy-filled area unharmed, grab everything before you start a fight or run through a dangerous spot.

SAVE THE GOLD FOR LAST...

If your multiplier is not maxed out and you run into an area with enemies or objects to destroy, or a bonus multiplier is nearby, don't pick up any gold until after you eliminate everything and build up your multiplier as high as it can be.

PLAY IN NIGHTMARE DIFFICULTY

If you're an experienced Portal Master, you can maximize your score by playing in Nightmare Difficulty. Though more challenging, you earn more points.

SCORE REQUIREMENTS FOR EARNING STARS

Mount Cloudbreak

★	Set a Personal Best Score
★ ★	Earn over 100,000 Points
★ ★ ★	Earn over 150000 Points

Cascade Glade

★	Set a Personal Best Score
★ ★	Earn over 40,000 Points
★ ★ ★	Earn over 65,000 Points

Mudwater Hollow

★	Set a Personal Best Score
★ ★	Earn over 100,000 Points
★ ★ ★	Earn over 140,000 Points

Rampant Ruins

★	Set a Personal Best Score
★ ★	Earn over 150,000 Points
★ ★ ★	Earn over 200,000 Points

Jungle Rumble

★	Set a Personal Best Score
★ ★	Earn over 10,000 Points
★ ★ ★	Earn over 19,000 Points

Iron Jaw Gulch

★	Set a Personal Best Score
★ ★	Earn over 120,000 Points
★ ★ ★	Earn over 170,000 Points

Motleyville

★	Set a Personal Best Score
★ ★	Earn over 350,000 Points
★ ★ ★	Earn over 450,000 Points

Twisty Tunnels

★	Set a Personal Best Score
★ ★	Earn over 250,000 Points
★ ★ ★	Earn over 400,000 Points

Serpent's Peak

★	Set a Personal Best Score
★ ★	Earn over 9000 Points
★ ★ ★	Earn over 15,000 Points

Boney Islands

★	Set a Personal Best Score
★ ★	Earn over 250,000 Points
★ ★ ★	Earn over 350,000 Points

Winter Keep

★	Set a Personal Best Score
★ ★	Earn over 200,000 Points
★ ★ ★	Earn over 250,000 Points

Frostfest Mountains

★	Set a Personal Best Score
★ ★	Earn over 150,000 Points
★ ★ ★	Earn over 200,000 Points

Mesmeralda's Show

★	Set a Personal Best Score
★ ★	Earn over 6500 Points
★ ★ ★	Earn over 8500 Points

Fantasm Forest

★	Set a Personal Best Score
★ ★	Earn over 200,000 Points
★ ★ ★	Earn over 400,000 Points

Kaos' Fortress

★	Set a Personal Best Score
★ ★	Earn over 100,000 Points
★ ★ ★	Earn over 150,000 Points

Motherly Mayhem

★	Set a Personal Best Score
★ ★	Earn over 25,000 Points
★ ★ ★	Earn over 40,000 Points

Cloudbreak Core

★	Set a Personal Best Score
★ ★	Earn over 60,000 Points
★ ★ ★	Earn over 90,000 Points

Sheep Wreck Islands

★	Set a Personal Best Score
★ ★	Earn over 300,000 Points
★ ★ ★	Earn over 400,000 Points

Tower of Time

★	Set a Personal Best Score
★ ★	Earn over 350,000 Points
★ ★ ★	Earn over 450,000 Points

COLLECTIBLES

In previous installments of the series, collecting everything was a source of pride that conveyed a feeling of accomplishment. After all, not everyone cared to collect every hat when a few had stats that weren't as good as ones they'd already obtained. However, in *Skylanders SWAP Force* being a completionist is vital to increasing your Portal Master rank and creating the most powerful Skylanders possible.

There are five types of collectibles: Hats, Legendary Treasures, Charms, Bonus Mission Maps, and Story Scrolls. The following pages provide more information on each, including how to acquire them all.

Hats

There are 147 hats to collect. Every hat is either found in one of the Story Levels, or purchased at Tuk's Emporium in Woodburrow. You must complete Chapter 2: Cascade Glade and meet certain requirements to purchase some hats.

Each Skylander can wear one hat at a time. Hats convey positive statistical effects while they're worn. To change the hat worn by a Skylander, select the Hats option from the Skylanders Stats screen.

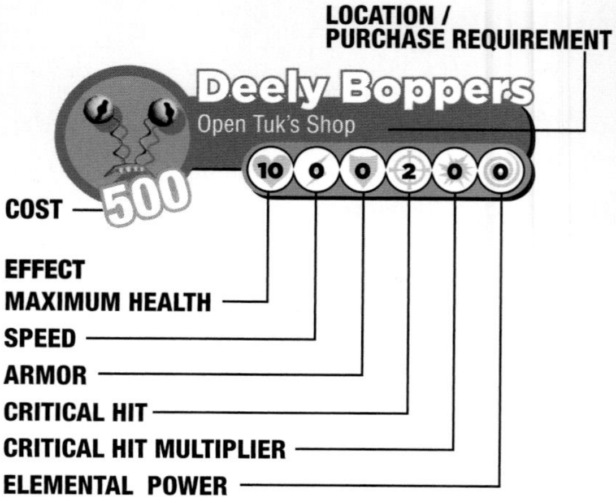

HATS FROM STORY MODE

Hat	Location	Maximum Health	Speed	Armor	Critical Hit	Critical Hit Multiplier	Elemental Power
Asteroid Hat	Kaos' Fortress	60	0	0	0	0	0
Aviator's Cap	Sheep Wreck Islands	0	0	0	0	0	30
Beacon Hat	Frostfest Mountains	30	0	0	0	0	15
Beanie	Tower of Time	0	5	0	0	0	20
Bearskin Cap	Boney Islands	10	0	0	5	0	10
Boater Hat	Mudwater Hollow	20	3	0	0	0	0
Boonie Hat	Rampant Ruins	10	0	0	0	0	10
Capuchon	Motleyville	10	0	20	0	0	0
Creepy Helm	Sheep Wreck Islands	0	0	15	9	0	0
Crown of Frost	Winter Keep	0	0	30	0	0	0
Fishbone Hat	Boney Islands	0	9	0	7	0	0
Flower Garland	Fantasm Forest	0	0	0	10	0	0
Four Winds Hat	Frostfest Mountains	0	15	0	0	0	0
Gaucho Hat	Iron Jaw Gulch	10	0	10	0	0	10
Glittering Tiara	Cascade Glade	10	6	0	2	0	0

Greeble Hat	Mount Cloudbreak	20	0	0	0	0	0
Leprechaun Hat	Tower of Time	10	0	5	2	0	0
Life Preserver Hat	Mount Cloudbreak	30	0	0	0	0	0
Peacock Hat	Twisty Tunnels	10	0	10	0	0	10
Puma Hat	Woodburrow	0	0	10	2	0	10
Rain Hat	Cascade Glade	0	0	7	2	0	0
Roundlet	Motleyville	20	0	5	0	0	5
Sawblade Hat	Rampant Ruins	0	0	0	7	0	5
Ski Cap	Winter Keep	30	6	0	0	0	0
Stone Hat	Mudwater Hollow	0	0	5	7	0	0
Stovepipe Hat	Mount Cloudbreak	0	0	5	2	0	5
The Outsider	Cascade Glade	8	0	0	0	0	7
Tree Branch	Sheep Wreck Islands	30	0	0	7	0	0
Tricorn Hat	Twisty Tunnels	0	0	15	2	0	0
Turkey Hat	Woodburrow	50	0	0	0	0	0
UFO Hat	Place the UFO Hat Magic Item on the Portal of Power	40	9	0	0	0	15
Volcano Hat	Complete Story Mode on Nightmare difficulty!	50	15	25	0	0	0
Zombeanie	Iron Jaw Gulch	40	0	0	0	0	0

HATS FROM TUK'S EMPORIUM

Deely Boppers	Open Tuk's Shop	500	10	0	0	2	0	0
Purple Fedora	Open Tuk's Shop	200	0	1	2	0	0	0
Jester Hat	Summon Eon	200	0	1	0	0	0	2
Happy Birthday!	Summon Eon	200	0	0	2	2	0	0
Flower Hat	Summon Eon	200	0	0	2	2	0	0
Straw Hat	Summon Eon	200	0	0	2	2	0	0
Cowboy Hat	Summon Eon	200	0	0	2	2	0	0
Anvil Hat	Portal Master Rank 4	200	0	0	5	0	0	0
Plunger Head	Portal Master Rank 4	200	0	0	0	2	0	2
Kufi Hat	Portal Master Rank 4	200	0	0	0	0	2	2
Balloon Hat	Portal Master Rank 4	200	0	0	2	2	0	0
Pan Hat	Portal Master Rank 4	200	0	0	2	0	0	2
Fancy Ribbon	Portal Master Rank 5	400	20	0	0	0	0	0
Elf Hat	Portal Master Rank 6	250	0	2	0	0	0	2
Viking Helmet	Portal Master Rank 6	250	0	0	0	3	0	0
Fancy Hat	Portal Master Rank 6	250	0	1	2	0	0	0
Lampshade Hat	Portal Master Rank 6	250	0	0	0	0	0	5
Bowler Hat	Portal Master Rank 6	250	0	0	2	2	0	0

Birthday Hat
Portal Master Rank 8
0 1 0 2 0 0
300

Atom Hat
Portal Master Rank 8
0 0 0 4 0 0
300

Pilgrim Hat
Portal Master Rank 8
0 1 2 0 0 0
300

Turban
Portal Master Rank 8
0 0 5 0 0 0
350

Flower Fairy Hat
Portal Master Rank 10
0 2 0 0 0 0
350

Fast Food Hat
Portal Master Rank 10
0 0 2 2 0 0
300

Police Siren Hat
Portal Master Rank 10
0 0 4 0 0 0
300

Fez
Portal Master Rank 10
0 0 0 0 0 5
320

Beret
Portal Master Rank 12
0 0 0 6 0 0
500

Spy Gear
Portal Master Rank 12
0 2 0 2 0 0
500

Biter Hat
Portal Master Rank 12
0 0 0 0 5 0
400

Propeller Cap
Portal Master Rank 12
0 3 0 0 0 0
400

Tropical Turban
Portal Master Rank 14
0 2 0 0 0 5
550

Bone Head
Portal Master Rank 14
0 3 0 0 0 7
550

Fishing Hat
Portal Master Rank 14
0 0 5 0 0 5
500

Toy Solider Hat
Portal Master Rank 14
0 2 0 5 0 0
500

Coonskin Hat
Portal Master Rank 16
0 0 0 7 0 0
600

Rocker Hair
Portal Master Rank 16
0 0 0 3 0 3
600

Safari Hat
Portal Master Rank 16
0 2 5 0 0 0
600

Miner Hat
Portal Master Rank 16
0 0 7 0 0 7
550

Obsidian Helm
Portal Master Rank 17
0 9 10 7 0 0
3500

Eye Hat
Portal Master Rank 18
0 0 0 5 0 5
700

Top Hat
Portal Master Rank 18
0 0 5 5 0 0
700

Sombrero
Portal Master Rank 18
0 0 5 0 3 0
650

Lilypad Hat
Portal Master Rank 18
0 9 0 7 0 10
3500

Carrot Hat
Portal Master Rank 18
0 0 0 0 0 10
750

Pumpkin Hat
Portal Master Rank 20
0 0 10 0 0 0
750

Cossack Hat
Portal Master Rank 20
0 0 0 0 0 10
750

Officer Cap
Portal Master Rank 20
0 3 7 0 0 0
750

Trojan Helmet
Portal Master Rank 20
0 0 10 0 0 0
750

Pirate Doo Rag
Portal Master Rank 22
0 4 0 0 0 0
750

Tiki Hat
Portal Master Rank 22
0 0 0 0 0 10
800

Moose Hat
Portal Master Rank 22
0 2 5 0 0 0
850

Mariachi Hat
Portal Master Rank 22
0 0 10 0 0 0
750

Pirate Hat
Portal Master Rank 24
0 0 0 8 0 0
900

Princess Hat
Portal Master Rank 24
0 3 0 0 0 7
1000

Hat	Portal Master Rank	Stats	Cost
Battle Helmet	Portal Master Rank 24	0 0 7 0 7 0	1000
Funnel Hat	Portal Master Rank 24	0 0 7 0 0 7	900
Dancer Hat	Portal Master Rank 24	0 6 0 0 0 0	900
Chef Hat	Portal Master Rank 26	0 0 0 3 0 10	1000
Combat Hat	Portal Master Rank 26	0 0 0 0 0 15	1000
Rasta Hat	Portal Master Rank 26	0 0 0 3 0 7	1000
Napoleon Hat	Portal Master Rank 26	0 0 5 0 0 5	1000
Royal Crown	Portal Master Rank 28	0 0 0 10 0 0	1100
Bowling Pin Hat	Portal Master Rank 28	0 0 10 0 10 0	1100
Firefighter Helmet	Portal Master Rank 28	0 0 0 20 0 0	1000
Spiked Hat	Portal Master Rank 28	0 0 7 3 0 0	1000
Rocket Hat	Portal Master Rank 28	0 6 0 0 0 0	1100
Archer Hat	Portal Master Rank 30	0 0 0 10 0 0	900
Bacon Bandana	Portal Master Rank 30	10 9 0 0 0 0	1900
Space Helmet	Portal Master Rank 30	30 0 15 0 0 0	2000
Wabbit Ears	Portal Master Rank 32	0 5 12 0 0 0	1200
General's Hat	Portal Master Rank 32	0 0 0 7 0 7	1100
Crown of Light	Portal Master Rank 32	0 0 15 0 0 0	1200
Bottle Cap Hat	Portal Master Rank 32	0 0 15 0 0 0	1200
Bronze Top Hat	Portal Master Rank 34	0 2 5 5 0 0	1500
Dangling Carrot	Portal Master Rank 34	0 4 0 0 0 10	1300
Graduation Hat	Portal Master Rank 34	0 0 0 0 0 15	1300
Traffic Cone Hat	Portal Master Rank 34	0 0 0 11 0 0	1200
Shark Hat	Portal Master Rank 36	3 0 5 2 0 0	1200
Eyefro	Portal Master Rank 36	30 0 20 0 0 0	2500
Silver Top Hat	Portal Master Rank 38	3 0 7 5 0 0	1500
Scrumshanks Hat	Portal Master Rank 38	0 4 0 3 0 0	1500
Sailor Hat	Portal Master Rank 38	0 4 10 0 0 0	1500
Nefertiti Hat	Portal Master Rank 38	0 0 0 3 0 10	1500
Baseball Cap	Portal Master Rank 38	0 8 0 0 0 0	1500
Santa Hat	Portal Master Rank 40	0 0 20 0 0 0	1600
Lil Devil	Portal Master Rank 40	0 9 0 0 0 0	1800
Caesar Hat	Portal Master Rank 40	0 0 0 0 0 25	1800
Wizard Hat	Portal Master Rank 40	0 0 0 0 0 25	2000
Umbrella Hat	Portal Master Rank 40	0 0 20 0 0 0	1600
Trucker Hat	Portal Master Rank 40	0 0 25 0 0 0	2100

Future Hat
Portal Master Rank 40
0 | 10 | 0 | 0 | 0 | 0
2000

Gold Top Hat
Portal Master Rank 42
0 | 4 | 10 | 10 | 0 | 0
2200

Card Shark Hat
Portal Master Rank 42
0 | 0 | 25 | 5 | 0 | 0
2800

Pants Hat
Portal Master Rank 42
0 | 6 | 0 | 4 | 0 | 0
2200

Gloop Hat
Portal Master Rank 42
30 | 9 | 0 | 0 | 0 | 0
3000

Winged Hat
Portal Master Rank 44
0 | 12 | 0 | 0 | 0 | 0
2500

Elephant Hat
Portal Master Rank 46
0 | 0 | 10 | 0 | 0 | 25
3000

Tiger Skin Cap
Portal Master Rank 47
0 | 6 | 10 | 0 | 0 | 15
3200

Awesome Hat
Portal Master Rank 48
0 | 12 | 10 | 2 | 0 | 0
3500

Showtime Hat
Portal Master Rank 50
0 | 0 | 0 | 0 | 0 | 25
2500

Crown of Flames
Portal Master Rank 50
30 | 9 | 0 | 0 | 0 | 10
3500

Crystal Hat
Portal Master Rank 55
0 | 6 | 0 | 0 | 0 | 25
3500

Runic Headband
Portal Master Rank 55
50 | 9 | 0 | 0 | 0 | 0
4500

Skullhelm
Portal Master Rank 56
0 | 9 | 0 | 10 | 0 | 0
3500

Unicorn Hat
Portal Master Rank 60
0 | 0 | 12 | 10 | 0 | 0
2500

Whirlwind Diadem
Portal Master Rank 60
30 | 9 | 10 | 0 | 0 | 0
3500

Knight Helm
Portal Master Rank 65
0 | 6 | 15 | 7 | 0 | 15
4700

Cactus Hat
Portal Master Rank 70
0 | 9 | 25 | 0 | 0 | 0
4000

Clockwork Hat
Portal Master Rank 75
0 | 9 | 0 | 0 | 0 | 25
4000

Teeth Top Hat
Portal Master Rank 75
0 | 0 | 25 | 10 | 0 | 20
6000

Great Helm
Portal Master Rank 80
0 | 15 | 20 | 3 | 0 | 0
9500

Legendary Treasures

There are 48 Legendary Treasures. Every Legendary Treasure is either found in a Story Level, or purchased at Tuk's Emporium in Woodburrow after meeting certain requirements.

After you complete Chapter 6: Iron Jaw Gulch and speak with Tibbet in Woodburrow's Trophy Room, place Legendary Treasures on the Legendary Pedestals scattered around Woodburrow to boost your Skylanders in various ways. For more information about Legendary Treasures, check out the Improving Your Skylanders section of this guide.

LEGENDARY TREASURES FROM STORY MODE

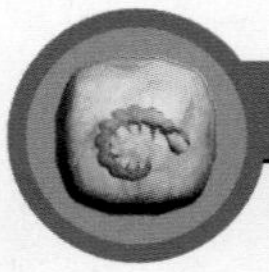

Amber Treasure
Sheep Wreck Islands
+12 Ranged Armor

Bubble Chest
Mudwater Hollow
+5 Gold Boost

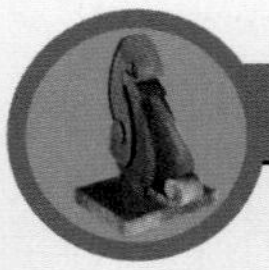

Cascade Bust
Cascade Glade
+5 Elemental Strength Boost

Crooked Currency
Motleyville
+10 Gold Boost

Crystal Fire Hearth
Twisty Tunnels

+5 Elemental Luck Boost

Deputee Badge
Sheep Wreck Islands

+10 Elemental Strength

Elven Arrow
Winter Keep

+3 Critical Hit Multiplier

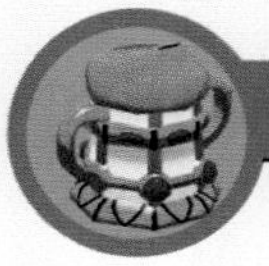

Endless Cocoa Cup
Frostfest Mountains

+12 Armor

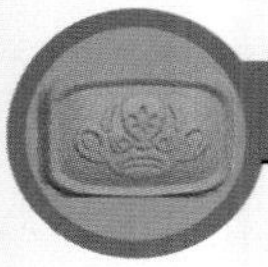

Epic Soap of Froth
Tower of Time

+4 Critical Hit%

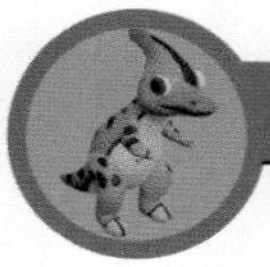

Expensive Souvenir
Winter Keep

+5 Critical Hit Multiplier

Geode Glider
Boney Islands

+12 Melee Armor

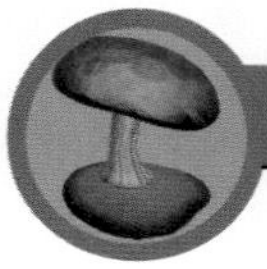

Glowy Mushroom
Fantasm Forest

+15 Pickup Range

Jolly Greeble
Iron Jaw Gulch

+10 Maximum Health

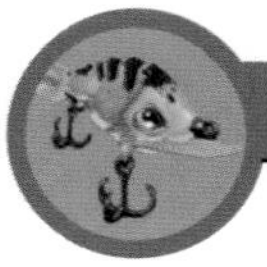

Luminous Lure
Mudwater Hollow

+10 Ranged Armor

Major Award Monkey
Rampant Ruins

+10 Luck

Masterful Disguise
Kaos' Fortress

+15 Elemental Armor Boost

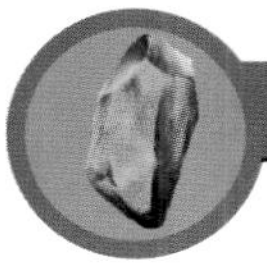

Moltenskin Scale
Twisty Tunnels

+10 Elemental Food Boost

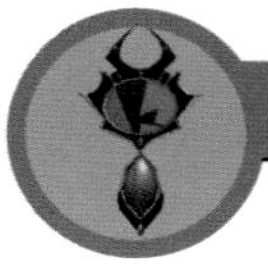

Mostly Magic Mirror
Mount Cloudbreak

+5 Armor

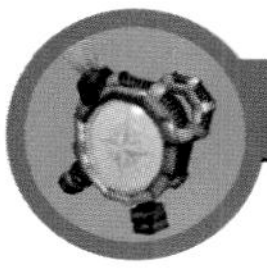

Navigator Compass
Woodburrow

+5 Ranged Armor

Skylander Scope
Kaos' Fortress

+2 Critical Hit Multiplier

The Bling Grille
Motleyville

+5 Elemental Food Boost

The Brass Tap
Fantasm Forest

+5 Gold Boost

The Monkey's Paw
Rampant Ruins

+5 Food Gain

Tik Tok Neck Clock
Iron Jaw Gulch

+10 XP Boost

Topiary of Doom
Fantasm Forest

+15 Elemental Power

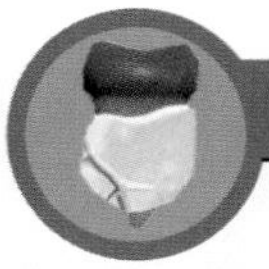

Triassic Tooth
Boney Islands

+2 Speed

Urban Art
Sheep Wreck Islands

+15 XP Boost

Volcano Party Pass
Tower of Time

+10 Melee Armor

Waterfall Decanter
Tower of Time

+5 Armor

Whizzing Whatsit
Complete 36 SWAP Zone Challenges on Nightmare difficulty

+30 Pickup Range

Yeti Teddy
Frostfest Mountains

+5 XP Boost

LEGENDARY TREASURES FROM TUK'S EMPORIUM

Bog Chowder
Portal Master Rank 58

+10 Melee Armor

Cost: 600

Bonnie Bonsai
Portal Master Rank 37

+15 Luck

Cost: 900

Boomboom Box
Portal Master Rank 17

+10 Elemental Armor Boost

Cost: 600

Bottled Warship
Portal Master Rank 23

+3 Critical Hit %

Cost: 600

Buttering Blade
Portal Master Rank 68

+15 Armor

Cost: 900

Chieftess Figure
Portal Master Rank 13

+10 Elemental Power

Cost: 600

Crustaceous Clothes
Portal Master Rank 7

+20 Maximum Health

Cost: 600

Frozenish Flag
Portal Master Rank 78

+15 Ranged Armor

Cost: 900

Golden Crunchy
Unlocks after Chapter 3: Mudwater Hollow

+10 Armor

Cost: 600

Lichen Lantern
Portal Master Rank 9

+5 Melee Armor

Cost: 300

Mabu Carving
Portal Master Rank 33

+5 Speed

Cost: 600

Refurbished Engine
Portal Master Rank 27

+10 Elemental Luck Boost

Cost: 600

Shiniest Stone
Portal Master Rank 7

+10 Ranged Armor

Cost: 600

Singing Puppet
Portal Master Rank 55

+15 Ranged Armor

Cost: 900

Snowboulder +1
Portal Master Rank 45

+15 Melee Armor

Cost: 900

Spyro Duo Balloon
Portal Master Rank 43

+15 Melee Armor

Cost: 900

Sweet Sasparilla
Unlocks after Chapter 3: Mudwater Hollow

+10 Food Gain

Cost: 600

Charms

Charms are the one type of collectible not found in Story Levels. You must earn Charms by completing Bonus Mission Maps and Arena challenges. Tuk's Emporium has four Charms for sale as well.

Each Charm is active as soon as you acquire it. All the effects are cumulative and the bonuses from Charms are active at all times.

CHARMS FROM STORY MODE

Air Freshener
Cursed Statues bonus mission

+5 Corrupt Creature Armor

Big Pants
Beach Breach arena

+10 Maximum Health

Body Armor
Treble Theft bonus mission

+4 Armor

Charmed Actions
Thief on the Run bonus mission

+3 Elemental Luck Shot

Cyclops Swatter
Sand Castle arena

+1 Critial Hit Multiplier

Delicious Food
Chomp Chomp Chompies arena

+5 Food Gain

Eight Leaf Clover
Beware of the Bird arena

+4 Luck

Element Deflect
Golem Invasion bonus mission

+5 Golem Armor

Elemental Fortune
Undercover Greebles bonus mission

+2 Elemental Luck Boost

Elemental Fist
Serpent Attack bonus mission

+2 Elemental Strength Boost

Electro Magnet
Magic Cells bonus mission

+5 Pickup Range

Elemental Noms
Super Hungry Gobble Pods arena

+5 Elemental Food Boost

Elemental Shield
Chompy Challenge bonus mission

+2 Elemental Armor Boost

Elemental Outlet
Egg Royale bonus mission

+2 Elemental Power

Eye Poker
Sweet Blizzard bonus mission

+5 Cyclops Armor

Four Leaf Clover
Plants Vs Cakes bonus mission

+2 Luck

Good Luck Charm
Cyclops Makeover arena

+1 Critical Hit %

Gourmet Meal
Boarding Party arena

+5 Gourmet Meal

Greeble Be Gone
Chompy Sauce bonus mission

+5 Greeble Armor

Greeble Grappler
Shellshock Curse arena

+1 Critical Hit Multiplier

Health Extender
Snake in the Hole arena

+50 Maximum Health

Impervious
Troll Beach Attack arena

+5 Ranged Armor

Instant Experience
Perfect Captain arena

+5 XP Boost

Kaos Kruncher
Exploding Snowmen arena

+1 Critical Hit Multiplier

Luck of the Mabu
Chompy Tsunami arena

+1 Critical Hit %

Mage Masher
Sheep Mage Rage arena

+1 Critical Hit Multiplier

Major Meal
Master Chef bonus mission

+5 Food Gain

Might of the Ancients
Ghost Traps bonus mission

+3 Elemental Strength Boost

Mountain's Resolve
Vortex Banquet arena

+3 Elemental Armor Boost

Pointy Spear
Pokey Pokey Spikes arena

+1 Critical Hit %

Power Blend
Sand-Pit-Fall arena

+1 Critical Hit %

Power Clover
Chunky Chompies arena

+6 Luck

Rabbit's Foot
Fishy Fishing bonus mission

+1 Critical Hit %

Small Shield
Sleepy Turtles bonus mission

+2 Armor

Sword Breaker
Angry Angry Plants arena

+5 Melee Armor

Tasty Food
Fruit Fight bonus mission

+5 Food Gain

Ultimate Defense
Icicle Bombing arena

+6 Armor

Unbridled Energy
Frigid Fight bonus mission

+10 Elemental Power

Vitamin Supplement
Frozen Delight bonus mission

+15 Elemental Food Boost

Wizard Repellant
Royal Gems bonus mission

+5 Spell Punk Armor

CHARMS FROM FROM TUK'S EMPORIUM

Life Elixir
Portal Master Rank 19

750 +100 Maximum Health

Overcharged
Portal Master Rank 39

750 +1 Critical Hit Multiplier

Golden Abacus
Portal Master Rank 30

750 +5 Gold Boost

Rocket Propellant
Portal Master Rank 50

750 +1 Speed

Bonus Mission Maps

There are 16 Bonus Mission Maps hidden in Story Levels (one per level), and 3 additional maps are available for purchase from Tuk's Emporium in Woodburrow, after meeting certain requirements.

Chompy Challenge is available once Master Eon unlocks the Bonus Missions.
For more information about completing these challenging maps, turn to the "Bonus Mission Maps" section of this guide.

BONUS MAPS FROM STORY MODE

Undercover Greebles
Kaos' Fortress

Find the Greebles in sheep's clothing and stop them.

Cursed Statues
Kaos' Fortress

Defeat the Greebles and destroy the evil statues.

Chompy Sauce
Fantasm Forest

Close the valves pumping Chompy sauce into the water.

Fishy Fishing
Rampant Ruins

Destroy the giant harpoons in the Elder Fish Sanctuary.

Master Chef
Mudwater Hollow

Defeat the head chef of the Greebles.

Plants Vs Cakes
Cascade Glade

Push 6 cakes to feed the Gobble Pods.

Fruit Fight
Mount Cloudbreak

Collect fruits for the archeologists' expedition.

Serpent Attack
Tower of Time

Free the airship from the sand monster's grasp.

Thief on the Run
Sheep Wreck Islands

Catch the thieves and retrieve the stolen packages.

Sweet Blizzard
Woodburrow

Turn off the Yetis' ice ceam machines.

Frigid Fight
Frostfest Mountains

Bring the wandering ghosts to the right colored gate.

Ghost Traps
Winter Keep

Free the peaceful ghosts from their cages.

Royal Gems
Boney Islands

Defeat the armored Cyclopes to retrieve the royal gems.

Magic Cells
Twisty Tunnels

Recharge the power plant by collecting blue cells.

Sleepy Turtles
Motleyville

Push the sleeping turtles back into their nest.

Egg Royale
Iron Jaw Gulch

Bring the stolen royal eggs to the Queen of the Turtles!

BONUS MISSION MAPS FROM TUK'S EMPORIUM

REE

Chompy Challenge
Unlocks after Chapter 3: Mudwater Hollow

Take out the Chompies and their Chompy Pods.

1000

Treble Theft
Portal Master Rank 15

Retrieve the Kangarats' musical instruments.

1000

Frozen Delight
Portal Master Rank 25

Free the Yetis stuck in ice cream!

000

Golem Invasion
Portal Master Rank 35

Defeat the Golems and set the turtles free!

Story Scrolls

There are 16 Story Scrolls to collect and each includes an interesting piece of information about the Cloudbreak Isles. Each of the non-boss fight Story Mode Chapters has one Story Scroll hidden in it. Woodburrow has two Story Scrolls that become available as you progress through the Story Mode and uncover new areas within it. Finally, both Adventure Pack levels, Sheep Wreck Islands and Tower of Time, have a Story Scroll.

Kaos' Laboratory
Kaos' Fortress

Dangerous Profession
Fantasm Forest

Frozen Galleries
Boney Islands

The Great Hollow
Woodburrow

The Grave Monkey
Rampant Ruins

Enchanted Pool
Woodburrow

Whirlwind's Gift
Winter Keep

Magical Pyrotechnics
Mount Cloudbreak

Greeble Lands
Cascade Glade

Party on the Mountains
Frostfest Mountains

The Clocktower
Tower of Time

The Platinum Sheep
Sheep Wreck Islands

Motleyville Junk
Motleyville

The Fire Vipers of Doom
Twisty Tunnels

Magic Recycling
Mudwater Hollow

The Glass Hat
Iron Jaw Gulch

ACCOLADES

Accolades measure your progress in completing the game. They track everything from how well you perform in Story Mode Chapters to the size of your Skylanders collection.

Accolades award Stars based on the difficulty in meeting the conditions of a given Accolade. These Stars count toward your Portal Master rank, which in turn unlocks better items and rewards from Tuk's Emporium in Woodburrow.

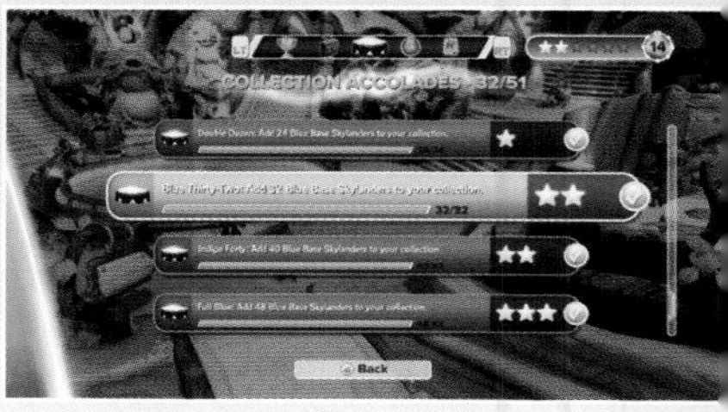

Challenge Accolades

ACCOLADES	DESCRIPTION	STARS
Full Spark	Complete 20 unique Spark Lock puzzles.	★
Charged Up	Earn 2 Bolts in 20 unique Spark Lock Puzzles	★★
Complete Circuit	Earn 3 Bolts in 20 unique Spark Lock Puzzles	★★★
Knock Knock	Open 50 Single Element Gates in Story Mode.	★★
Unhinged	Open 100 Element Gates in Story Mode	★★★
Safe Passage	Open 40 Dual Element Gates in Story Mode	★★
Swap Unlock	Unlock 12 SWAP Zone Challenges.	★
Unswappable	Unlock 24 SWAP Zone Challenges	★★
The Full Swap	Unlock 36 SWAP Zone Challenges	★★★
Big Loot	Open 30 Giant Chests in Story Mode.	★★★
Maxed Out	Level any Skylander to 20.	★★★
Ultrapowered!	Purchase every ability upgrade for any Skylander.	★★★
Buy Now or Bye Now	Purchase every item in Tuk's Emporium	★★★
Repair the Bridge	Build a bridge to the Elemental Platform.	★★★
Summon Eon	Progress through Story Mode and summon Eon.	★★★
Pedestal Pioneer	Unlock all Legendary Treasure Pedestals.	★
Diligent Displayer	Place a Legendary Treasure on every Pedestal	★★★
Unlock Time Attack	Progress through Story Mode to unlock Time Attack.	★
Unlock Score Mode	Progress through Story Mode to unlock Score Mode.	★
Adventurin' Time	Open all Elemental Gates, SWAP Zones, and Giant Chests in Sheep Wreck Islands. (7 Total)	★★

ACCOLADES	DESCRIPTION	STARS
Watching the Clock	Open all Elemental Gates, SWAP Zones, and Giant Chests in the Tower of Time. (7 Total)	★
Dapper Copper	Earn a Bronze Toy Quest Medal for any Skylander.	★
Sliver of Silver	Earn a Silver Toy Quest Medal for any Skylander.	★★
Bold Gold	Earn a Gold Toy Quest Medal for any Skylander.	★★★

Exploration Accolades

ACCOLADES	DESCRIPTION	STARS
Half-A-Dasher	Find 12 Hats hidden in Story Chapters.	★
Haberdasher	Find 24 Hats hidden in Story Chapters.	★ ★
Fasion Ace	Collect 120 Hats.	★ ★ ★
Lucky Find	Open 20 different Treasure Chests in Story Levels.	★
Payday	Open 40 different Treasure Chests in Story Levels.	★ ★
Jackpot	Open 60 different Treasure Chests in Story Levels.	★ ★ ★
Treasure Hunter	Find 12 Legendary Treasures hidden in Story Chapters.	★
Artifact Seeker	Find 23 Legendary Treasures hidden in Story Chapters.	★ ★
Master Collector	Collect 48 Legendary Treasures.	★ ★ ★
Diligent Researcher	Find 6 Story Scrolls in Story Mode.	★
Worldly Scholar	Find 12 Story Scrolls in Story Mode.	★ ★
Literary Master	Find 16 Story Scrolls.	★ ★ ★

ACCOLADES	DESCRIPTION	STARS
Charter Adept	Find 6 Bonus Mission Maps in Story Mode.	★
Cartographer	Find 13 Bonus Mission Maps in Story Mode.	★ ★
Master Georgrapher	Collect 20 Bonus Mission Maps.	★ ★ ★
Power Locator	Find 10 Soul Gems.	★
Soul Gatherer	Find 21 Soul Gems.	★ ★
Spiritual Warden	Find all 32 Soul Gems.	★ ★ ★
Butterfly Catcher	Find 6 Winged Sapphires in Story Mode.	★
Painted Lady Pilferer	Find 12 Winged Sapphires in Story Mode.	★ ★
Monarch Master	Find 18 Winged Sapphires.	★ ★ ★
Charm Bracelet	Collect 22 Charms.	★
Charm Champion	Collect 44 Charms.	★ ★ ★
Woodburrow Wanderer	Discover every area in Woodburrow. (9 Total)	★ ★ ★
Special Specialty	Find every special collectible in Woodburrow. (10 Total)	★ ★ ★

Collection Accolades

ACCOLADES	DESCRIPTION	STARS
Score Four	Add 4 Blue Base Skylanders to your collection.	★
Great Eight	Add 8 Blue Base Skylanders to your collection.	★
Blue Dozen	Add 12 Blue Base Skylanders to your collection.	★
Super Sixteen	Add 16 Blue Base Skylanders to your collection.	★
Double Dozen	Add 24 Blue Base Skylanders to your collection.	★
Blue Thirty-two	Add 32 Blue Base Skylanders to your collection.	★ ★
Indigo Forty	Add 40 Blue Base Skylanders to your collection.	★ ★
Full Blue	Add 48 Blue Base Skylanders to your collection.	★ ★ ★
Mean Green Machine	Add 32 Green Base Skylanders to your collection.	★ ★ ★
Gigantic Hero	Add 8 Giant Skylanders to your collection.	★
Second Wave	Add 30 Orange Base Skylanders to your collection.	★ ★ ★
Supreme Portal Master	Add 80 Skylanders to your collection.	★ ★ ★
Force for Good	Add one SWAP Force Skylander of each SWAP Skill to your collection.	★ ★ ★
Bounce into Action	Add both Bounce SWAP Force Skylanders to your collection.	★
Blast Forward	Add both Rocket SWAP Force Skylanders to your collection.	★
Twist and Turn	Add both Spin SWAP Force Skylanders to your collection.	★
Matched Velocities	Add both Speed SWAP Force Skylanders to your collection.	★
Great Heights	Add both Climb SWAP Force Skylanders to your collection.	★
Tunneling Team	Add both Dig SWAP Force Skylanders to your collection.	★
Shhhhhh!	Add both Sneak SWAP Force Skylanders to your collection.	★
Now You See me	Add both Teleport SWAP Force Skylanders to your collection.	★
Transmutation	Add one SWAP Force Skylander of each elemental type to your collection.	★
Ambassador	Add one Blue Base Skylander of each elemental type to your collection.	★
Abracadabra	Add 4 Blue Base Magic Skylanders to your collection.	★
Mystic Channeler	Add 10 Magic Skylanders to your collection.	★ ★
Drop in the Ocean	Add 4 Blue Base Water Skylanders to your collection.	★
Sea of Power	Add 10 Water Skylanders to your collection.	★ ★
Gizmo Hero	Add 4 Blue Base Tech Skylanders to your collection.	★
Cutting Edge	Add 10 Tech Skylanders to your collection.	★ ★

ACCOLADES	DESCRIPTION	STARS
Dug Freshly	Add 4 Blue Base Earth Skylanders to your collection.	[illegible]
Mountain of Power	Add 10 Earth Skylanders to your collection.	★ ★
Third Degree	Add 4 Blue Base Fire Skylanders to your collection.	★
Blaze of Glory	Add 10 Fire Skylanders to your collection.	★ ★
No Bones About it	Add 4 Blue Base Undead Skylanders to your collection.	[illegible]
Six Feet Deep	Add 10 Undead Skylanders to your collection.	★ ★
Floral Foura	Add 4 Blue Base Life Skylanders to your collection.	★
Go Team Green	Add 10 Life Skylanders to your collection.	★ ★
Cloudbreakers	Add 4 Blue Base Air Skylanders to your collection.	[illegible]
Storming Through	Add 10 Air Skylanders to your collection.	★ ★
Little Chum	Add a Sidekick to your collection.	★ [illegible] ★
Stockpile of Magic	Add 4 Blue Base Magic Items to your collection.	[illegible]
Wild Blue Yonder	Add 2 Blue Base Adventure Pack Location Pieces to your collection.	★ ★ ★
Legacy of Magic	Add 12 Magic Items to your collection.	★ [illegible] ★
Glowing	Add a Lightcore Skylander to your collection.	[illegible]
Blue Lightning	Add 8 Lightcore Skylanders to your collection.	★ ★
Overbright	Add 16 Lightcore Skylanders to your collection.	★ [illegible] ★
Big Footprint	Add 30 Series 2 Skylanders to your collection.	★
Reimagined in Blue	Add 6 Blue Base Series 2 Skylanders to your collection.	[illegible]
New and Blue	Add 5 Series 3 Skylanders to your collection.	[illegible]
Cloubreak Warriors	Add 10 Series 3 Skylanders to your collection.	[illegible]
SWAP Cadet	Play with 4 different SWAP Force combinations	[illegible]
SWAP Officer	Play with 8 different SWAP Force combinations	★
SWAP Detective	Play with 16 different SWAP Force combinations	★
SWAP Sergeant	Play with 32 different SWAP Force combinations	★ ★
SWAP Lieutenant	Play with 64 different SWAP Force combinations	★ ★
SWAP Commander	Play with 128 different SWAP Force combinations	★ ★
SWAP Chief	Play with 256 different SWAP Force combinations	★ ★ ★
Arm Yourself	Add 2 Blue Base Battle Pieces to your collection.	★ ★ ★

Completion Accolades

ACCOLADES	DESCRIPTION	STARS
Mega Awesome Ending	Complete 17 Story Levels on any difficulty.	★
Digging In	Complete 8 Story Levels on Medium difficulty or harder.	★
Meaty Plot	Complete all Story Levels on Medium difficulty or harder	★★
Tough Sample	Complete 6 Story Levels on Hard difficulty or harder.	★
Epic Ballad	Complete 17 Story Levels on Hard difficulty or harder.	★★★
Rise in Action	Complete 12 Story Levels on Hard difficulty or harder.	★★
Fitful Slumber	Complete 4 Story Levels on Nightmare difficulty.	★
Bad Dreams	Complete 8 Story Levels on Nightmare difficulty.	★
Waking Nightmare	Complete 12 Story Levels on Nightmare difficulty.	★★
Night Terrorizer	Complete 17 Story Levels on Nightmare difficulty.	★★★
Twinkle Twinkle	Earn at least 2 Stars on 8 Story Levels	★
Shooting Stars	Earn at least 2 Stars on all Story Levels	★
Meteoric	Earn 3 Stars on 6 Story Levels	★
Superstar	Earn 3 Stars on 12 Story Levels	★
Going Nova	Earn 3 Stars on 17 Story Levels.	★★★
Navigator of Fun	Complete both Adventure Pack levels on any difficulty.	★
Simple Sojourn	Earn at least 2 Stars on both Adventure Pack Levels.	★
Challenging Journey	Complete both Adventure Pack levels on Medium difficulty or harder.	★
Charting Adventure	Complete both Adventure Pack levels on Hard difficulty or harder.	★
Endless Odyssey	Complete both Adventure Pack levels on Nightmare difficulty.	★★★
Perfect Journey	Earn 3 Stars on both Adventure Pack Levels	★★
Scrapper	Complete 10 Solo Survival Levels on any difficulty.	★
No Equal	Earn 3 Stars on 10 Solo Survival Levels.	★★★
Champion	Complete 10 Solo Survival Levels on Medium difficulty or harder.	★
Iron Skylander	Complete 10 Solo Survival Levels on Hard difficulty or harder.	★★
Gladiator of All Worlds	Complete 10 Solo Survival Levels on Nightmare difficulty.	★★★
Star of Swords	Earn at least 2 Stars on 10 Solo Survival Levels.	★★
Skylands Hero	Complete 18 Bonus Missions on any difficulty.	★
People's Champion	Complete 18 Bonus Missions on Medium difficulty or harder.	★
Epic Warrior	Complete 18 Bonus Missions on Hard difficulty or harder.	★★
Immortal Soldier	Complete 18 Bonus Missions on Nightmare difficulty.	★★★
Force for Justice	Earn at least 2 Stars on 18 Bonus Missions.	★★
A Time of Peace	Earn 3 Stars on 18 Bonus Missions.	★★★
Number Cruncher	Complete 17 Score Mode levels on any difficulty.	★
Point Puncher	Complete 17 Score Mode levels on Medium difficulty or harder.	★
Know the Score	Complete 17 Score Mode levels on Hard difficulty or harder.	★★
Exponential Digits	Complete 17 Score Mode levels on Nightmare difficulty.	★★★
Seeing Stars	Earn at least 2 Stars on 17 Score Mode levels.	★
Number Burst	Earn 3 Stars on all Score Mode Levels	★★
Fast Track	Complete 17 Time Attack levels on any difficulty.	★
Speedster	Complete 17 Time Attack levels on Medium difficulty or harder.	★
Dangerous Race	Complete 17 Time Attack levels on Hard difficulty or harder.	★★
High Velocity	Complete 17 Time Attack levels on Nightmare difficulty.	★★★
Silver Medal Run	Earn at least 2 Stars on 17 Time Attack Levels.	★
Go for the Gold	Earn 3 Stars on 17 Time Attack Levels.	★★
Challenge Novice	Complete 36 SWAP Zone Challenges on any difficulty.	★
Expert Swapper	Complete 36 SWAP Zone Challenges on Medium difficulty or harder.	★
Tough Customer	Complete 36 SWAP Zone Challenges on Hard difficulty or harder.	★★
Zone Crusher	Complete 36 SWAP Zone Challenges on Nightmare difficulty.	★★★
Advanced Exchange	Earn at least 2 Stars on 36 SWAP Zone Challenges.	★
Unstoppable	Earn 3 Stars on 36 SWAP Zone Challenges	★★

ACHIEVEMENTS & TROPHIES

Achievements and Trophies are awarded by the console on which you're playing *Skylanders SWAP Force*. Not all consoles award Achievements and Trophies.

Story Mode Achievements

TITLE	DESCRIPTION	XBOX 360 GAMERSCORE	PS3 TROPHY
Welcome To Woodburrow	Complete Mount Cloudbreak on any difficulty	25	Bronze
Chieftess Rescued	Complete Cascade Glade on any difficulty	15	Bronze
Swamp Secured	Complete Mudwater Hollow on any difficulty	15	Bronze
Ruins Romped	Complete Rampant Ruins on any difficulty	15	Bronze
Glumshanks De-Evilized	Complete Jungle Rumble on any difficulty	25	Bronze
Lawman	Complete Iron Jaw Gulch on any difficulty	15	Bronze
New Law in Town	Complete Motleyville on any difficulty	15	Bronze
Squid Squabble	Complete Twisty Tunnels on any difficulty	15	Bronze
Vexed Viper	Complete Serpent's Peak on any difficulty	25	Bronze
Cold Caravan	Complete Boney Islands on any difficulty	15	Bronze
Snowball Fight!	Complete Winter Keep on any difficulty	15	Bronze
Blizzard Bailout	Complete Frostfest Mountains on any difficulty	15	Bronze
Puppet Master Pounded	Complete Mesmeralda's Show on any difficulty	25	Bronze
Woods Wetted	Complete Fantasm Forest on any difficulty	15	Bronze
Kastle Krashed	Complete Kaos' Fortress on any difficulty	15	Bronze
Kalamity Averted	Complete Motherly Mayhem on any difficulty	15	Bronze
Kaos Quashed	Complete Cloudbreak Core on any difficulty	25	Bronze
Champion of Skylands	Complete all main chapters in Story Mode on any difficulty	100	Gold
Times are Hard	Complete main chapters in Story Mode on Hard difficulty	150	Gold
Knight of Nightmares	Complete main chapters in Story Mode on Nightmare difficulty	200	Gold

Miscellaneous Achievements

TITLE	DESCRIPTION	XBOX 360 GAMERSCORE	PS3 TROPHY
Boom!	Light the fireworks in Woodburrow	10	Bronze
Perch Plunge	Dive off the Tree in Woodburrow	10	Bronze
Newsworthy	Use the mailbox in Woodburrow to see the Message of the Day (Online Only)	15	Bronze
Golem Graveyard	Defeat 10 Golems	10	Bronze
NO WAY!!!!!!!!!!!!!!!!!	Obtain all other Trophies	—	Platinum

Portal Master Achievements

TITLE	DESCRIPTION	XBOX 360 GAMERSCORE	PS3 TROPHY
Race to the Finish	Complete your first Time Attack level	10	Bronze
Mad Dash	Earn a 3-star rating in any Time Attack level	10	Bronze
Speed Demon	Earn a 3-star rating in 3 Time Attack levels	15	Bronze
Fastest One Around	Earn a 3-star rating in 17 Time Attack levels	20	Silver
Reach for the Sky	Complete your first Score Mode level	10	Bronze
Racking Up the Points	Earn a 3-star rating in any Score Mode level	10	Bronze
High Roller	Earn a 3-star rating in 3 Score Mode levels	15	Bronze
Winning Streak	Earn a 3-star rating in 17 Score Mode levels	20	Silver
New Challenger	Complete your first Bonus Mission level	10	Bronze
Up and Coming	Earn a 3-star rating in any Bonus Mission level	10	Bronze
Rising Star	Earn a 3-star rating in 3 Bonus Mission levels	15	Bronze
Heroic Champion	Earn a 3-star rating in 5 Bonus Mission levels	20	Silver
Slings and Arrows	Complete your first Team Survival Arena level	10	Bronze
Enduring the Onslaught	Earn a 3-star rating in any Team Survival Arena level	10	Bronze
Coming out Ahead	Earn a 3-star rating in 3 Team Survival Arena levels	15	Bronze

Take Your Game Further with the

OFFICIAL MAP APP

FROM BRADYGAMES

Download the perfect digital companion to *Skylanders SWAP Force*. This handy app allows gamers to track and find all the collectibles in the game.

The *Skylanders SWAP Force* Official Map App provides players with expertly crafted area maps complete with icons indicating the exact location of every cool collectible.

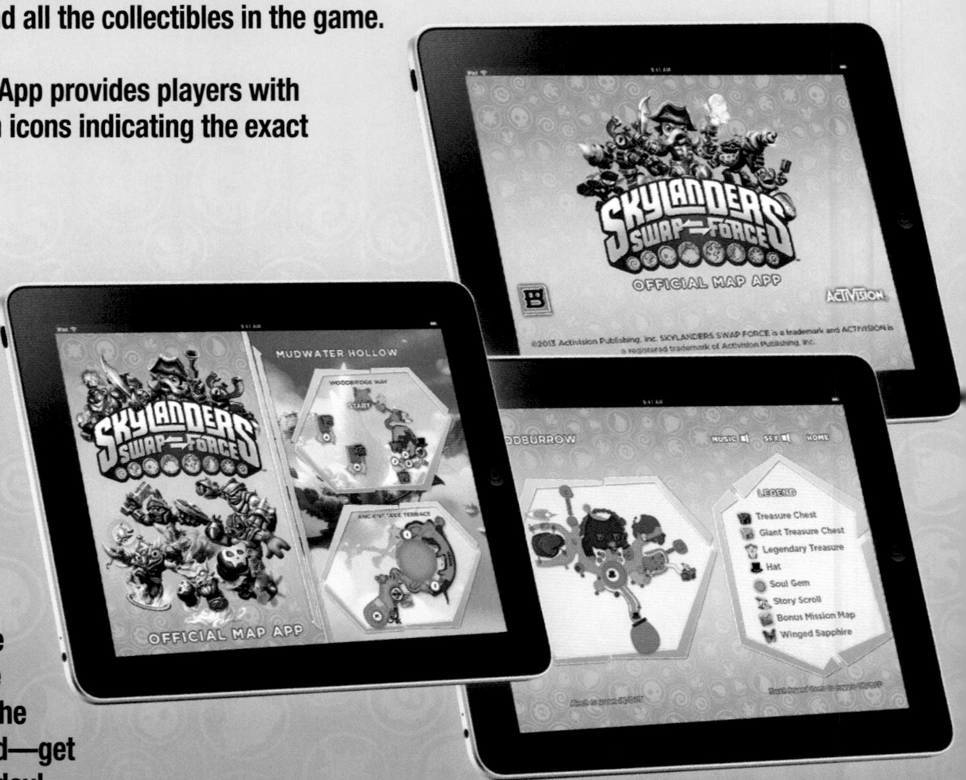

Includes:

- Hats
- Legendary Treasures
- Bonus Mission Maps
- Story Scrolls
- Soul Gems
- Treasure Chests
- Winged Sapphires

Each collectible is precisely placed on the maps, serving as an easy quick reference resource that can be used while playing the game. Don't let any collectible go unfound—get your *Skylanders SWAP Force* Map App today!

ONLY $2.99

AVAILABLE FOR APPLE AND ANDROID DEVICES

BRADYGAMES

www.bradygames.com

ACTIVISION

www.deepsilver.com

FOLLOW US ONLINE!

COLLECTOR'S EDITION STRATEGY GUIDE

Ken Schmidt and V.H. McCarty

DK/BradyGames, a division of Penguin Group (USA).
800 East 96th Street, 3rd Floor
Indianapolis, IN 46240

ISBN: 978-0-7440-1515-7

Printing Code: The rightmost double-digit number is the year of the book's printing; the rightmost single-digit number is the number of the book's printing. For example, 13-1 shows that the first printing of the book occurred in 2013.

16 15 14 13 4 3 2 1

Printed in the USA.

Brady Acknowledgements

BradyGames would like to thank Alex Gomez, Elías Jiménez, Jeffery Lee, Andrew Lee, Jack Joseph, Ryan Magid, Chris Wassum, Justin Wharton, Danielle Godbout, Scott Moore, Barclay "Buck" Chantel, Brent Gibson, Barry Morales, Pierre-Olivier "POP" Paré, Dominic Morin, Martin Tessier, Raphael Readman, Gabriel Lapointe, Charles Kirouac, Janne Richard, Raphael Corbin, Vincent Auger, Sasan "Sauce" Helmi, and the rest of the team at Activision for the help and support on this project.

BradyGAMES Staff

Vice President and Publisher
Mike Degler

Editor-In-Chief
H. Leigh Davis

Licensing Manager
Christian Sumner

Digital Publishing Manager
Tim Cox

Marketing Manager
Katie Hemlock

Operations Manager
Stacey Beheler

Credits

Development Editor
Jennifer Sims

Book Designer
Colin King

Production Designers
Areva
Julie Clark
Jeff Weissenberger